The American Negro Academy

The American Negro Academy

Voice of the Talented Tenth

Alfred A. Moss, Jr.

Louisiana State University Press
Baton Rouge and London

Designer: Patricia Douglas Crowder
Typeface: Linotron 202 Sabon
Typesetter: G & S Typesetters, Inc.
Printer: Thomson-Shore, Inc.
Binder: John Dekker and Sons, Inc.

LIBRARY OF CONGRESS CATALOGING IN PUBLICATION DATA

Moss, Alfred A   1943–
The American Negro Academy.

Bibliography: p.
Includes index.
1. American Negro Academy, Washington, D.C.—History.
2. Afro-Americans—History.   I. Title.
E185.5.A53M67   975.3'00496073   80-18026
ISBN 0-8071-0699-2
ISBN 0-8071-0782-4 (pbk.)

To Alice

Contents

Photographs

The American Negro Academy

Introduction

The American Negro Academy, the first major black American learned society, was founded March 5, 1897, in Washington, D.C. The constitution of the ANA defined it as "an organization of authors, scholars, artists, and those distinguished in other walks of life, men of African descent, for the promotion of Letters, Science, and Art." This same document described the society's purposes as follows: "a. To promote the publication of scholarly work; b. To aid youths of genius in the attainment of the higher culture, at home or abroad; c. To gather into its archives valuable data, and the works of Negro authors; d. To aid, by publications, the dissemination of the truth and the vindication of the Negro race from vicious assaults; e. To publish, if possible, an 'Annual' designed to raise the standard of intellectual endeavor among American Negroes." Although the chief concerns of the men who founded the ANA were to strengthen the intellectual life of their racial community, improve the quality of black leadership, and insure that henceforth arguments advanced by "cultured despisers" of their race were refuted or at the very least challenged, it was equally significant that the organization was established at a time when white Americans were creating hundreds of learned, professional, and ethnic historical societies. The ANA's birth was also an expression of this general movement among educated members of the American middle class.

From its establishment until its demise in 1928, the ANA claimed as members some of the most important leaders in the black American community. Alexander Crummell, the first president, was an Episcopal clergyman who held an A.B. degree from Queen's College, Cambridge University. Other founders included Francis J. Grimké, a Presbyterian clergyman trained at Lincoln University and the Princeton Theological Seminary; W. E. B. Du Bois, professor of economics and history at Atlanta University; William H. Crogman, professor of classics at Clark University in Atlanta; William S. Scarborough, a scholarly classicist who was on the faculty of Wilberforce University; and John W. Cromwell, a lawyer, politician, and former editor of *The People's Advocate*, a black newspaper published in Washington, D.C., from 1878 to 1884. Throughout its existence the ANA attracted a number of the most intellectually creative blacks in the United States. Some of the men associated with the organization who achieved their greatest prominence after the turn of the century were John Hope, president of Morehouse College and later of Atlanta University; Alain L. Locke, writer, critic, and key figure in the Harlem Renaissance; Carter G. Woodson, the historian; and James Weldon Johnson, poet, writer, and civil rights leader.

Relatively speaking though, only a handful of educated blacks were ever members of the ANA. There were several reasons for this: the ANA was a selective organization to which entrance was controlled by the membership; its activities and goals appealed mainly to a small group of blacks who sought to function as intellectuals and who believed that the results of their efforts were crucial to the development and defense of their racial group; it experienced continuous difficulties in realizing its goals; and it never enjoyed the support of Booker T. Washington, the powerful principal of Tuskegee Institute, who, for over half the life of the organization, was the dominant figure in the black community.

Between 1897 and 1924 the ANA published twenty-two occasional papers on subjects related to the culture, history, religion, civil and social rights, and the social institutions of black Americans. While the quality of the papers varied, all of them help to illuminate the many ways in which, during the first quarter of the twentieth century, an important segment of the small community of educated American blacks attempted to intellectually defend their people, justify their own existence, and challenge ideas, habits, attitudes, and legal proscriptions that seemed to be locking their race permanently into an inferior caste.

Throughout its existence the ANA was preoccupied with survival. As a result, its officers and members were forced to put as much energy into keeping the organization alive as they did into conducting its programs. And yet the society survived for thirty-one years, functioning as a setting in which members and friends shared their intellectual and scholarly work with each other and engaged in critical reflection on it. Through annual meetings, occasional papers, exhibits, and the public interest they generated the ANA was able, here and there, to initiate dialogues in both the black and white communities that were important contributions to a growing discussion in the United States, Africa, and Europe about race and the relationships between blacks and whites; to introduce the concerns and opinions of educated blacks into quarters where, previously, they had been ignored or gone unnoticed; and to encourage the growing pride among blacks in their culture and history. For these reasons the story of the American Negro Academy has an important place in the larger history of efforts by educated blacks in the early twentieth century to use their skills and abilities as a means of both leading and protecting their people and as a weapon to secure equality and destroy racism.

At its birth the ANA was hailed by blacks on three continents as a welcome step forward in the efforts of their own race to liberate itself from the crippling legacy of slavery and the problems created by the hostilities of prejudiced whites. Through its work the ANA proved this to be an accurate prediction. It was both a sustainer and perpetuator of the black protest tradition in an age of accommodation and proscription. By functioning as a source of affirmation and encouragement for an important segment of the black intelligentsia and as a setting in which they could seek to understand the meaning of the black American experience, it was a model for other and sometimes more successful black organizations founded after 1897 which engaged in similar work or attempted to realize goals that the ANA had found unattainable. By strengthening and adding to the intellectual autonomy and insight of those blacks associated with it, the ANA helped to prepare them for more honest, informed dialogue with each other, with blacks outside the society and in other parts of the world, and when they would listen, with whites.

I am deeply indebted to Professor John Hope Franklin for encouraging my interest in the American Negro Academy and for invaluable assistance in helping me to gain access to previously unresearched materials on the organization. He has been a vigorous and insightful critic as well as a wise friend and counselor. For both forms of support, I am more grateful than I can ever express.

To Professor Adelaide Cromwell Gulliver I owe special thanks for kindly allowing me to make extensive use of the important and valuable family papers in her possession. Without them, it would have been impossible for me to examine and interpret in depth the history and influence of the American Negro Academy.

I also wish to thank Professors H. Samuel Merrill and Louis R. Harlan, who graciously consented to read the manuscript. Both usefully criticized it and gave me the benefit of their uncommon editorial skills and knowledge of American and black American history.

It would be unthinkable for me not to acknowledge, with gratitude, the support of a marvelous circle of friends who, in some instances, provided practical assistance and, on other occasions, that special kind of emotional encouragement that is so important to a laborer whose reward lies far in the future. In this connection I am especially grateful to Professors Nathan A. Scott, Walter Rundell, Emory Evans, and Eric Anderson, Ms. Olive Petro, The Reverend and Mrs. John W. Pyle, Dr. George Bernstein, and Dr. Steven Hertzberg.

Thanks are also due to the staffs of the Moorland-Spingarn Research Center at Howard University, the Schomburg Collection of the New York Public Library, Widner Library of Harvard University, Mugar Library of Boston University, the Library of Congress' Manuscript Division, and the University of Chicago's Regenstein Library for the many ways in which they helped me.

Throughout the long period in which she shared her life with the American Negro Academy and me, my wife's wells of patience, good humor, critical insight, and support have never run dry. More than all this, however, she has been the steadiest and truest of companions.

I *"Imperative Necessity"*

During the last two decades of the nineteenth century black Americans experienced a relentless attack on their social, political, and economic rights. This resulted in a decline in their status throughout the United States and especially in the South, where slightly less than 90 percent of them lived. Beginning in 1890, measures designed to disfranchise blacks began to be written into the constitutions of southern states; and, by 1910, most blacks had been eliminated as voters. It was in this same period that racial segregation, or Jim Crow ideas, began to be translated into law and steadily extended to all areas of life in the South. Theoretically, facilities for both races were to be equal; in practice this was never so, and blacks were forced to accept inferior services and accommodations or none at all. In 1896, the United States Supreme Court, with its decision in the case of *Plessy v. Ferguson*, legalized segregation, thus giving implicit support to all the theories of racial inferiority that lay behind it, and affirming what was rapidly becoming a national approach to race relations. Consequently, from the late 1890s to World War I, the southern states extended and codified the Jim Crow system. To insure the acquiescence of blacks many white southerners did not hesitate to use extralegal violence as a form of intimidation.[1]

Most blacks were Republicans and, with a profound lack of realism, hoped for some protection from the leaders of "their party." But the northern industrialists who dominated the Republican party were not interested

1. For information on the black population during the last quarter of the nineteenth century see George A. Davis and O. Fred Donaldson, *Blacks in the United States: A Geographic Perspective* (Boston, 1975), 29–94. The following works deal with the situation of blacks during the late nineteenth century: C. Vann Woodward, *Origins of the New South, 1877–1913* (Baton Rouge, 1951); and Rayford W. Logan, *The Betrayal of the Negro* (New York, 1965).

in guaranteeing the social rights, or the political and economic independence of blacks. These men were extending their businesses into the South and viewed the primarily agricultural region as a source of raw materials and cheap labor. They also believed that their interests would be best served by building ties with the white groups that dominated the economic and political life of the former Confederate states. As a result, at a time when Republicans usually controlled both the executive and legislative branches of government, blacks witnessed the gradual but steady elimination of officeholders of their race, and the repeated defeat of congressional bills designed to support or protect them.

Southern black laborers, both the vast majority who were farmers and the small percentage employed in industry, found themselves increasingly at the mercy of a legal system that was structured and manipulated to keep them in "their place." Numerous laws existed whose main purposes were to restrict the movement of black workers, keep their wages low, prevent the improvement of working conditions, and, in the case of farmers, to prevent them from becoming landowners. In practice, however, southern courts were willing to twist the meaning of any statute to achieve these purposes. For black artisans and industrial workers the American labor movement offered no recourse. In almost all cases—this was especially true of the craft unions—blacks were barred from membership or relegated to separate locals. One of the most visible results of this situation was the steady decline of black craftsmen in the South, a region where, in 1865, they had constituted over 80 percent of the artisans.[2]

The situation of northern blacks, which had improved somewhat in the two decades following the Civil War, also began to deteriorate. Though the antebellum North had been a better place for blacks to be than the slave states of the South, the majority of blacks in the North had been required to attend separate schools, were denied the vote, and were often denied public accommodations; in some states, they were forbidden to marry outside their race. In the post–Civil War period many of these restrictions were abolished. Blacks had been given the vote, large numbers of segregated schools were eliminated, and, in some states, civil rights laws and statutes forbidding discrimination in public accommodations had been passed. However, after 1890, in numerous parts of the North, blacks witnessed a resurgence of many earlier attitudes and practices. Two of the most out-

2. Logan, *Betrayal*, 62–104; Woodward, *Origins of the New South*, 205–63.

standing changes were the further reduction of the limited economic opportunities open to blacks, and the tightening of residential patterns, which would eventually result in the restriction of the black community to a racial ghetto. These and other detrimental trends were accelerated by negative changes in many white northerners' perceptions of and attitudes toward blacks.[3]

Throughout these years, the white American intellectual community failed to challenge the increasing political, social, and economic debasement of black Americans and, in numerous instances, reinforced these trends. In the 1890s there was a marked increase in antiblack publications. Many of these books, articles, and essays were the product of southern efforts to strip blacks of political power, both real and potential, and to restrict them to the bottom of the social order. But, as Rayford Logan has accurately observed, "the effort was facilitated by the respectability of racist thought in all sections of the country." Americans had long been acquainted with various strains of what has been termed "scientific racism." This involved use of anthropology, Egyptology, craniology, phrenology, biblical criticism, ethnology, and anatomy to prove the inferiority of blacks and other non-Caucasians. In the post–Civil War period, this body of thought, by appropriating large segments of Charles Darwin's evolutionary theory, "updated" itself intellectually, acquiring a new vigor and persuasiveness.[4]

Social Darwinism became the dynamic force that provided intellectual justification for belief in the inferiority of blacks. Darwin's theories concerning the struggle for existence in the animal kingdom were applied to the human situation and linked with the belief of the Frenchman, Joseph Arthur de Gobineau, that blacks were fixed unalterably on the lowest level in the hierarchy of races. Herbert Spencer, an Englishman and one of the most articulate exponents of Social Darwinism, argued that science provided explicit proof of the survival of the fittest, these being the Caucasian race, and especially those members of it who were Anglo-Saxons. The fact that the 1890s were also years in which the United States became a colonial power made this kind of intellectually grounded racism even more attractive.[5]

3. Gilbert Osofsky, *Harlem: The Making of a Ghetto* (New York, 1963), 3–123; Allan H. Spear, *Black Chicago: The Making of a Negro Ghetto, 1890–1920* (Chicago, 1967), 1–49.

4. Logan, *Betrayal*, 242–74; George M. Frederickson, *The Black Image in the White Mind: The Debate on Afro-American Character and Destiny, 1817–1914* (New York, 1971), 198–319.

5. Logan, *Betrayal*, 171–74.

The white Protestant churches, which in this period dominated America's religious life, provided little assistance or support for black Americans. The churches, like the American intellectual community, were also the inheritors, and in many ways the perpetuators, of a racist tradition; theirs, however, rested on a scattered series of biblical and theological interpretations. Conditioned by its history as a religion whose members were almost all white, and its proclivity for becoming culturally and intellectually identified with a particular nation or group, Protestantism often had little capacity or willingness to include other races within its world view.

In the post–Civil War years, when an almost unparalleled harmony existed between the major Protestant denominations and the prevailing American culture, a number of clergymen began to challenge the orthodox theologies and to question the Protestant churches' comfort with the then current economic and political situation. This was the origin of the Social Gospel movement which attempted to address itself to the problems of social injustice. However, at no time did the social gospellers and their followers seriously turn their attention to the political, social, and economic abuses of black Americans. The proponents of the Social Gospel movement, America's religious liberals, and, on some issues, its religious radicals, when not actually adding their voices to the chorus of racism, said little or nothing about the condition of blacks or the country's treatment of them. As the historian Martin E. Marty has observed,

the American Social Gospel movement . . . was if anything a retarding agency in the matter of foreseeing a full brotherhood in world Protestantism. Its liberal theologians often fused personal observation with Social Darwinian theory to justify a pattern of racial condescension. The white Anglo-Saxon was considered the normative or standard race, against which others were to be measured and graded.

Though they produced a number of creative theological reconceptualizations, and were, at times, perceptive and courageous in tackling some sources of social injustice, these religious liberals were unable to transcend the orthodox racism of the day.[6]

The hostility toward blacks that ran through so much of American life was clearly reflected in the country's secular and religious newspapers and magazines, as well as in the serious literature of the period. Not surprisingly, southern white newspapers were especially blatant in their hos-

---

6. See Martin Marty, *Protestantism* (New York, 1972), 190, 192–94, 200, Martin Marty, *Righteous Empire: The Protestant Experience in America* (New York, 1970), 140–42, 204–209.

tility and condescension toward blacks. "Derogatory, jocular, derisive stories and . . . stereotypes," demeaning and insulting to blacks, regularly appeared in their pages, while editorial support was usually given both to the various devices for disfranchising blacks and to the cause of white supremacy, which often involved implicit approval of lynching. At the same time, the opinion that "the southern white man is the negro's best friend" was repeatedly expressed. Blacks who expected the northern press to be more sensitive to their plight and supportive of their causes were often sorely disappointed. Their articles and feature stories usually differed little from those printed in the South and frequently depicted blacks as violent, criminally inclined, comic, pretentious, and supersensitive. A majority of the northern papers opposed federal aid for black education and congressional bills designed to protect the political rights of blacks. Similarly, little disapproval that was not politically or regionally self-serving was expressed in regard to the violence to which blacks were increasingly subject. A striking example of the northern press's insensitivity to the plight of blacks was the minimal attention given to the decision of the United States Supreme Court in 1896 in the case of *Plessy v. Ferguson*, which sanctioned the South's segregation policies. In their willingness "to sacrifice the Negro on the altar of reconciliation, peace, and prosperity," the northern press was at one with the dominant political and economic forces in the nation.[7]

The black community was not passive in the face of these assaults. Both in the North and South, a small but vocal group of politicians, newspaper editors, teachers, and ministers, through their speeches and writings, protested against the disfranchisement and segregation of their people. For some in the North this took the form of a bitter denunciation and rejection of the Republican party, and influenced by the second Cleveland administration's benign attitude toward black appointments, they urged blacks to vote Democratic, or at least to begin to vote for their "true friends" rather than being predictably faithful to the party which had freed them. The results of their efforts were meager. Most blacks remained Republicans, largely because the Democratic party in the South was committed to their elimination from the political process; while in the North, the small black population seemed to preclude the possibility of bargaining with either party for consideration of their issues. Throughout the 1880s and 1890s,

7. Logan, *Betrayal*, 195–275, 287–306; Seymour L. Gross and John Edward Hardy, *Images of the Negro in American Literature* (Chicago, 1966), 2–5.

blacks, employing a tactic they had used effectively in the antebellum period, met in national and state conventions to express their special "concern over the franchise, civil rights, mob violence, and Republican policy." From time to time these meetings also went on record against the crop-lien system, the lack of educational opportunities for blacks, discrimination in the selection of juries, the convict-lease system, and inequities in public accommodations. Efforts were also made on community, state, and national levels to create organizations that would act to protect the interests of blacks and to champion their rights aggressively. Until the end of the century, however, none of the organizations founded for these purposes enjoyed more than a brief existence.[8]

As the political and social situation continued to worsen, a number of black leaders urged that the race put more effort into its economic and moral development and less stress on political activity. Many, as did Alexander Crummell, Fanny Jackson Coppin, John R. Lynch, William H. Crogman, John Wesley Edward Bowen, Lucy Laney, and others, made it clear that they viewed such an emphasis as temporary, believing that if blacks achieved economic strength and moral respectability, whites would have to restore their political and social rights. There were other leaders, however, who carried this emphasis in a different direction. Linking it with a conciliatory and apologetic stance toward southern whites, they ceased to protest the mistreatment of blacks, and charged the race with being responsible for many, if not all, of its difficulties. Beginning in 1895, Booker T. Washington, principal of the industrial and agricultural institute at Tuskegee, Alabama, was the leading spokesman for this latter point of view.[9]

By the mid-1880s blacks of all classes, in the North as well as the South, were coming to feel that the intense and implacable hostility of whites left them no alternative but to accept a separate existence apart from the larger American community. Many continued to protest and agitate for all their rights as citizens, but the impossibility of halting their exclusion had to be acknowledged. Confronted with this situation black Americans began to pour their energies into the creation of cultural, welfare, religious, educational, economic, and social institutions that would be counterparts to the ones from which whites barred them. In a less self-conscious way, a number

8. August Meier, *Negro Thought in America, 1880–1915* (Ann Arbor, 1968), 26, 39–40, 69–71, 72–73, 74–77, 79–82; Logan *Betrayal*, 237.
9. Meier, *Negro Thought*, 85–113; Louis R. Harlan, *Booker T. Washington: The Making of a Black Leader, 1856–1901* (New York, 1972), 204–28.

of new ideologies that attempted to provide perspectives on their special situation also began to emerge. Older institutions, in particular the black churches, were pressured into making themselves more serviceable, in terms of meeting both religious and social needs. There were blacks who vociferously resisted this shift, seeing it as acquiescence to racism, but fed by the conditions that created it, it continued and grew in strength. As Allen Spear has pointed out, this turning inward of the black community "was not an unalloyed step backward" for the blacks:

Increasingly forced to rely on their own resources, black people began to build self-sufficient communities and to develop strong, independent leadership. The point then, is not that the quality of Afro-American life declined, but that race relations changed, that the attitudes and policies of whites toward blacks became more repressive and contact between the races more distant.[10]

Educated blacks, who constituted less than 3 percent of their racial community, took the lead in efforts to establish new institutions that would meet the needs of their people. During the last two decades of the nineteenth century, they participated in the formation of religious organizations, publications, fraternal groups, mutual aid societies, charitable organizations, and racial defense associations. These same men and women also led in the establishment of cultural, learned, and professional societies— groups that in many ways were a direct expression of their identities and need for affirmation. In 1880, the editors of black religious and secular publications met and formed the Colored Press Association. The following year, Daniel A. Payne, an African Methodist Episcopal bishop with a strong commitment to black education, helped form the Bethel Literary and Historical Association in Washington, D.C. This group, a discussion and debating society, became an important local forum for the exchange of ideas, and was a model for similar groups that sprang up in other cities. In 1890, the Society for the Collection of Negro Folklore was established by a group of black Bostonians. Four years later the National Medical Association, a professional society for black physicians, was organized. The following year the National Federation of Afro-American Women and the National League of Colored Women's Clubs came into being. Though, for a brief time, these two organizations were competitors, by 1896, they had consolidated as the National Association of Colored Women. In 1897, the American Negro

10. Allan H. Spear, "The Origins of the Urban Ghetto, 1870–1915," in Nathan I. Huggins, Martin Kilson, and Daniel M. Fox (eds.), *Key Issues in the Afro-American Experience* (2 vols.; New York, 1974), II, 160.

Historical Society of Philadelphia was organized. All the founders and members were from that city and their stated purpose was the collection of "relics, literature, and facts relative to the negro race [,] illustrating their progress and development in this century." [11]

The basic reason behind the establishment of these and other all-black societies was the forced segregation of educated blacks from their white counterparts. However, the formation of these groups also reflected the influence on blacks of a similar movement among the educated leadership of white ethnic communities, as well as movement toward organization among educated Americans in general.

Beginning in the 1880s a number of American ethnic groups had begun to establish cultural and learned societies. Many of them, despite the fact that their purposes and activities were more far-ranging, were called historical societies, and most—even those that exhibited a serious historical interest—were also group defense and propaganda organizations. Several factors stimulated their establishment.

The primary impetus was the anxiety that "native" Americans were beginning to express about the continuous flow of foreigners into the country. Between 1860 and 1900 fourteen million immigrants entered the United States. The majority of them came from England, Ireland, Germany, and Scandinavia, and were related culturally and historically to the mass of white Americans, whose ancestors had emigrated from the same places. However, beginning around 1880 the peasant and ghetto peoples of southern and eastern Europe—Italians, Jews, Magyars, and Slavs—began to form the predominant part of the human flow coming into this country. Their language and dress, as well as their social, political, and religious customs were strange and unfamiliar to people in the United States. Negative feelings were strengthened by the fact that they came from countries most Americans considered among the most backward, despotic, and un-

11. Meier, *Negro Thought*, 207–47; Emma Lou Thornbrough, *T. Thomas Fortune, Militant Journalist* (Chicago, 1972), 40, 105–16, 119–22, 126–27; John Wesley Cromwell, *History of the Bethel Literary and Historical Association: A Paper Read before the Association on Founders' Day, February 24, 1896* (Washington, D.C., 1896), 1; John Hope Franklin, *From Slavery to Freedom* (New York, 1974), 296–405; Meier, *Negro Thought*, 264; Clement Richardson (ed.), *The National Cyclopedia of the Colored Race* (Montgomery, Ala., 1919), I, 583; Henry L. Phillips, *In Memoriam of the Late Rev. Alexander Crummell, D.D. of Washington, D.C.: An Address Delivered before the American Negro Historical Society of Philadelphia, November, 1898* (Philadelphia, 1899), back cover; H. Harrison Wayman, "The American Negro Historical Society of Philadelphia, and Its Officers," *Colored American Magazine*, VI (February, 1903), 287–94; Gerda Lerner (ed.), *Black Women in White America: A Documentary History* (New York, 1971), 440–41.

enlightened in the world. This new immigration accounted for 18.3 percent of the foreigners who entered the United States between 1881 and 1890, and 52 percent in the decade 1891 to 1900. By the 1890s nativist feelings had become so thoroughly aroused that measures which would have drastically reduced immigration came close to being enacted. Americans of all classes felt and expressed numerous reservations about the number of immigrants entering the country, their worth as persons, and their assimilability. The conspicuous entry of these new peoples into American society came at a time of vast economic and social upheaval in the United States; and much, if not most, of the criticism and hostility they met masked the fears and insecurities of Americans frustrated by the problems of their changing society.[12]

These trends were both disturbing and offensive to Americans of recent immigrant parentage, as well as those connected by ancestry with the groups under attack. Ethnic minorities found the hostile statements of intellectuals such as Francis A. Walker, president of the Massachusetts Institute of Technology and head of the American Economic Association, especially reprehensible. Addressing a group of scholars in 1890, Walker depicted immigrants arriving in the United States as a "race of . . . the very lowest stage of degradation." Nativist themes also began to be expressed in the writing of history, with some historians placing the blame for America's urban and industrial ills on immigrants. Many ethnic groups—this was especially true of the Irish and the Jews—contained significant numbers of people who were both culturally assimilated and economically secure; and some—the Irish and the Germans were outstanding examples—had begun to control important sectors of American politics. Confronted by hostile challenges to their worth and assimilability, an increase in social snobbery and discrimination, and assaults on their religious institutions, many members of ethnic minorities felt the need to answer their attackers and justify their place in the country.

As a result, between 1882 and 1902 at least ten ethnic cultural organizations were founded. These included the Scotch-Irish Society (1882), the American Jewish Historical Society (1892), the Huguenot Society (1883), the Holland Society (1885), the German-American Historical Society (1892), and the American-Irish Historical Association (1897). Many of these organizations expended a great deal of energy—often with mixed re-

12. John Higham, "Origins of Immigration Restriction, 1882–1897: A Social Analysis," *Mississippi Valley Historical Review*, XXXIX (June, 1962), 77–79; John Higham, *Strangers in the Land* (New York, 1963), 35–67, 68–105.

sults—in challenging historians deemed hostile to their people. Their chief activity, however, was gathering information and materials that stressed their ethnic community's contribution to American life, and attempting to exert an influence on issues related to their interests and reputation.[13]

The societies' organizers were almost invariably elite members of the minority group who, out of a combination of self-interest and group pride, felt the need to combat nativist ideas concerning their people. Membership was frequently limited to persons whose education, occupation, or public activities were of great "respectability," thus making the organization a showcase of the group's best people. At the same time, this was a way of proclaiming the difference and distance of these people from members of their minority group who were poor, criminal, or unmistakably foreign in their habits. The founders were also committed to preserving the group's ethnic identity and creating a definition of American nationality that included their people and institutions. Not surprisingly, the effort to be faithful to both of these goals was a frequent source of tension.[14]

The other movement influencing the organizational activity of educated blacks was the widespread proliferation of associations linking people in the same professions and occupational specialties. This movement, which had its greatest impact between 1877 and 1918, involved a significant minority of Americans who attempted to deal with their personal sense of dislocation and the problems created by the new industrial order by using their vocational roles as a means of clarifying their identities and social roles. In the 1870s, groups as widely diverse as the American Forestry Association (1875), the American Library Association (1876), and the American Bar Association (1878) were founded. The 1880s saw the appearance of numerous other societies, some of the more notable being the Academy of Political Science (1880), the Modern Language Association of America (1883), the American Historical Association (1884), the American Economic Association (1885), and the American Academy of Political and Social Science

13. Kenneth James Moynihan, "History as a Weapon for Social Advancement: Group History as Told by Jewish, Irish, and Black Americans, 1892–1950" (Ph.D. dissertation, Clark University, 1973), 7–8, 11, 12, 16, 20; see also John J. Appel, "Immigrant Historical Societies in the United States, 1885–1950" (Ph.D. dissertation, University of Pennsylvania, 1964), 13–17, 46, 135, 204; Francis A. Walker, "The Tide of Economic Thought," *Publications of the American Economic Association*, VI (January–March, 1891), 37; Charles H. Wesley, "Racial Historical Societies and the American Heritage," *Journal of Negro History*, XXXVII (January, 1952), 15–26.

14. Appel, "Immigrant Historical Societies," 383–90; Moynihan, "History as a Weapon," 7–8, 11–15, 16, 18–19, 21.

(1889). The 1890s and the first five years of the new century represented the highpoint of this movement as almost every profession and occupational specialty sought to organize itself.[15]

Such associations were multipurpose: they became the means for demanding societal deference for members and for their work; meetings were forums in which entrance requirements, corporate standards, and corporate goals were shaped and codified; and they provided the membership with a structure and voice whereby they could lobby in the larger society for desired political and social programs. The ticket of admission to the majority of the professional groups, and the more specialized learned societies they generated, was university training and/or active involvement in the specialty or profession. During the closing years of the nineteenth century, as the United States moved with increasing rapidity from its older, small town agricultural orientation, into an urban-industrial system, the demand for specialization in the various fields of knowledge and work accelerated this trend. Organization was the means whereby many Americans, confronted with a society in rapid transition, attempted to link themselves to others who affirmed their professional, occupational, class, and even personal identities. In the company of people with whom they shared numerous perspectives, they devised responses to those issues and problems that touched their lives.[16]

Many blacks were aware of both these movements—the forming of professional and learned organizations, and the founding of ethnic cultural societies. They both occurred during the same years that black Americans were attempting to strengthen the institutional life of their increasingly segregated communities, and were important models.

A small, select group of educated blacks became acquainted with several professional and learned societies through involvement in them as members or as participants in their activities. In 1879, a paper written by Frederick Douglass—at that point in his long career a federal official in Washington, D.C.—was read at the annual meeting of the American Social Science Association. This was also the year Richard T. Greener, dean of Howard University's Law School, addressed the association on the black migration from the gulf states. In 1896, this same organization heard Booker T. Wash-

15. Robert H. Wiebe, *The Search for Order: 1877–1920* (New York, 1967), 111–13; Mary O. Furner, *Advocacy and Objectivity: A Crisis in the Professionalization of American Social Science, 1865–1905* (Lexington, 1975).
16. Wiebe, *Search for Order,* 113, 121.

ington, principal of Tuskegee Institute, and Hugh M. Browne, a teacher in Washington, D.C., speak on issues involving black education. Five black educators—William H. Crogman, Booker T. Washington, Simon G. Atkins, Joseph C. Price, and Richard R. Wright—were invited to address various meetings of the National Education Association between 1880 and 1896. They had been preceded, however, by Alexander Crummell, an Episcopal clergyman, educator, and missionary to Liberia, who, in 1865, presented his thoughts on "Negro Education" to a convention of this body.[17]

Blacks were also involved with a number of other professional and learned societies. Almost from its founding in 1889, blacks were members of the American Academy of Political and Social Science. In 1891 the roster of this organization carried the names of Matthew Anderson, pastor of Berean Presbyterian Church in Philadelphia; William Hooper Councill, principal of the Alabama State Industrial School at Huntsville; John Mercer Langston, a lawyer, educator, and former United States congressman from Virginia; Isaiah T. Montgomery, a plantation owner and businessman who lived in Mound Bayou, Mississippi; and Joseph C. Price, president of Livingstone College in Salisbury, North Carolina. During the next six years other blacks joined the academy, among them Simon G. Atkins, president of the North Carolina State Industrial School at Winston; James Theodore Holly, Anglican bishop of Haiti; Antenor Firmin, a Haitian politician who had earlier served as his country's minister of foreign affairs; Louis Joseph Janvier, a Haitian diplomat assigned to his country's mission in London; and Henry L. Phillips, rector of the Episcopal Church of the Crucifixion in Philadelphia. John Wesley Edward Bowen, who held a Ph.D. degree in theology from Boston University, was a member of the Institute of Sacred Literature, and from 1889 to 1893, served as one of its examiners of new applicants. For many years Bowen was the only black member of the institute

17. Frederick Douglass, "The Negro Exodus from the Gulf States" and Richard T. Greener, "The Emigration of Colored Citizens from the Southern States," both in *Journal of Social Science*, XI (May, 1880), 1–21 and 22–35; "Remarks of Mr. B. T. Washington" and "Remarks of Mr. Hugh M. Browne, of Washington, D.C.," *Journal of Social Science*, XXXIV (November, 1896), 86–88, 89–97; and see also William H. Crogman, "Negro Education" (1884), 48, Booker T. Washington, "Educational Outlook in the South" (1884), 202, and "Influence of the Negroes' Citizenship" (1896), 202, Simon G. Atkins, "Discussion on Normal Schools in the South" (1889), 11, Joseph C. Price, "Education and the Problem of the Negro" (1890), 150, Richard R. Wright, "Education of Negroes" (1894), 210, and Alexander Crummell, "Remarks on Negro Education" (1865), 48, all cited in Martha Furber Nelson (ed.), *Index by Authors, Titles, and Subjects to the Publications of the National Education Association for Its First Fifty Years, 1859–1906* (Winona, Minn., 1907).

and of the American Society of Church History. In 1891, W. E. B. Du Bois, at the time a student in his second year of graduate studies at Harvard University, became the first black to present a paper before the American Historical Association. William Saunders Scarborough, professor of classical languages at Wilberforce University, was a member of the Modern Language Association and the American Philological Society. An extremely active participant in the latter group, Scarborough delivered ten papers before the society between 1884 and 1896.[18]

The idea of establishing a national black cultural organization was first proposed in 1873, when delegates attending the National Equal Rights Convention passed a resolution urging the formation of a black historical society. Their resolution produced no results, though the various literary and debating societies beginning to flourish in the black community heard papers on historical themes, observed the births and deaths of "black heroes and white friends," and in other ways sought to focus for their members the culture and history of their race. In 1883, the black historian George Washington Williams issued another call for the formation of a black historical society. Despite his stature as an intellectual and political figure in the black community, nothing came of his suggestion. Though some black historical societies were founded after 1885, like the American Negro Historical Society of Philadelphia, all of them had small, local memberships, and were more antiquarian societies than intellectually critical, scholarly groups. However, in the early 1890s the increasingly negative assessments by educated whites of blacks and their struggles, coupled with the

18. *Handbook of the American Academy of Political and Social Science: Supplement to the Annals of the American Academy of Political and Social Science* for 1891, pp. 13, 28, 54, 62, 69, and for 1897, pp. 25, 47, 67. For John Wesley Edward Bowen see Frank Lincoln Mather (ed.), *Who's Who of the Colored Race: A General Biographical Dictionary of Men and Women of African Descent* (Chicago, 1915), 32, and *Papers of the American Society of Church History*, VI, 302. On Du Bois see W. E. B. Du Bois, "The Enforcement of the Slave Trade Laws," *Annual Report of the American Historical Association for the Year 1891* (*Senate Miscellaneous Documents*, 52nd Cong., 1st Sess., No. 173). For Scarborough's papers given before the American Philological Association, see the following articles under his name in the *Transactions of the American Philological Association*: "The Theory and Function of the Thematic Vowel in the Greek Verb," XV (1884), vi; "Fatalism in Homer and Vergil," XVI (1885), xxxvi; "Observations of the Fourth Eclogue of Vergil," XIX (1888), xxxvi–xxxviii; "Notes on Androcides," XX (1889), v–vi; "The Negro Element in Fiction," XXI (1890), xlii–xliv; "Bellerophon's Letters," XXII (1891), l–lii; "Hunc Inventum Inveni," XXIV (1893), xiv–xix; "Variable Meanings of Certain Latin and Greek Nouns," XXV (1894), xxiii–xxv; "The Language of Africa," XXVI (1895), xi; and "The Function of Modern Language in Africa," XXVII (1896), xlvi–xlviii.

widespread efforts by blacks to expand the institutional base of their community, caused several black intellectuals to begin discussing the need for a new and different kind of black literary and cultural society.[19]

In the autumn or winter of 1893, Richard R. Wright of Savannah suggested to his friend William H. Crogman of Atlanta that they take the lead in bringing together a group of black scholars and thinkers to establish a national society whose main work would be to formulate strategies for solving the problems of their people and to respond to the attacks of white intellectuals. Wright and Crogman, who were both teachers in small southern black schools, had been classmates at Atlanta University where they received their bachelors' and masters' degrees in the same years (1876 and 1879). Wright had taught in high schools in Georgia after finishing college, and in 1891 accepted appointment as president of the State Industrial College near Savannah. An ambitious man, he was an active figure in his profession as well as in Georgia state politics. Born on the island of St. Martin, British West Indies, the scholarly, puritanic Crogman was professor of Greek and Latin at Clark University, a Northern Methodist college in Atlanta.[20]

Crogman liked the idea and shared it with several persons whom he felt would be both interested and suitable potential members. One of the people he attempted to interest was Francis James Grimké, pastor of the Fifteenth Street Presbyterian Church in Washington, D.C. Similar in temperament to Crogman, Grimké was a disciplined, austere man, who had begun to receive wide recognition for the force and sophistication of his sermons and his qualities as a pastor. The son of a former slave and a wealthy South Carolina planter (whose last name he carried), Grimké was also the publicly acknowledged nephew of the two abolitionist sisters, Angelina and Sarah

19. Wesley, "Racial Historical Societies," 27; New York *Globe*, June 16, 1883; Meier, *Negro Thought*, 260–67.

20. John W. Cromwell, "The American Negro Academy," *Horizon*, V (February, 1910), 11–12; [John W. Cromwell], "American Negro Academy," *African Times and Orient Review*, II (November–December, 1913), 243; [John W. Cromwell], "The Negro Academy," Washington *Record* [*ca.* December, 1902] (clipping in Cromwell's Book of Newspaper Clippings on the American Negro Academy, in John Wesley Cromwell Papers in possession of Dr. Adelaide Cromwell Gulliver, Director of the Afro-American Studies Center, Boston University). This collection, which is private and as yet unprocessed, is hereinafter cited as JWCG/M. For biographical information on Wright see Mather (ed.), *Who's Who*, 293–94. For Crogman see Thomas Yenser (ed.), *Who's Who in Colored America: A Biographical Dictionary of Notable Living Persons of African Descent in America* (New York, 1933), 112; and Carter G. Woodson (ed.), *The Works of Francis J. Grimké* (4 vols.; Washington, D.C., 1942), IV, 34.

Grimké. A graduate of Lincoln University in Pennsylvania and the Princeton Theological Seminary, he had held pastorates in Florida and Washington.[21]

Grimké suggested that Crogman communicate the idea to Alexander Crummell, another Washington, D.C., cleric and a person whose support was deemed essential to the success of the proposed enterprise. Crummell, a man of seventy-four in 1893, was a towering figure in the black community. Born into a distinguished free black family of New York City, he entered the Episcopal ministry in the face of tremendous opposition from white clergymen of that denomination, and was an active figure in the antebellum black convention movement. Eventually, however, the meager return from his efforts to minister to black Episcopal congregations convinced him that it was his calling to find a solution to his people's problems, which he conceived as moral weakness, self-hatred, and industrial primitiveness. He went to England to study and in 1853 received an A.B. degree from Cambridge University. From 1853 to 1873 Crummell lived and worked as a missionary-educator in Liberia. When shifts in Liberian politics led to his removal from his post at Liberia College, he returned to the United States and settled in Washington, D.C., where in 1875 he founded St. Luke's Episcopal Church. Several years later he was the moving force in the formation of the interdenominational Union of Colored Ministers in that city. As the result of Crummell's efforts, in 1883 a national caucus of black Episcopal clergy and laity was organized to fight racism in the Protestant Episcopal Church. And in 1892, as white Washingtonians increasingly divorced themselves from the social concerns of their black fellow citizens, he strongly urged the black clergy of the city to take the lead in establishing charitable institutions for the race.[22]

21. William H. Crogman to Francis J. Grimké, September 24, 1894, in Woodson (ed.), *Works of Francis J. Grimké*, IV, 34–35. Volume I of this work also has an excellent short biography of Francis J. Grimké; see also Joseph J. Boris (ed.), *Who's Who in Colored America: A Biographical Dictionary of Notable Living Persons of Negro Descent in America*, (New York, 1927), I, 82; Gerda Lerner, *The Grimké Sisters from South Carolina: Pioneers for Women's Rights and Abolition* (New York, 1971), 358–66.

22. The following three works contain discussions of various phases of Crummell's life and activities: Monday Benson Akpan, "Alexander Crummell and His African 'Race-Work': An Assessment of His Contributions in Liberia to Africa's 'Redemption,' 1853–1873," *Historical Magazine of the Protestant Episcopal Church*, XLVI (June, 1977), 177–99; Wilson J. Moses, "Civilizing Missionary: A Study of Alexander Crummell," *Journal of Negro History*, LX (April, 1975), 229–51; Otey M. Scruggs, *We the Children of Africa in This Land: Alexander Crummell* (Washington, D.C., 1972). See also Crogman to Grimké, September 4, 1894, in Woodson (ed.), *Works of Francis J. Grimké*, IV, 34–35.

Crummell also had a lengthy history of encouraging learning and scholarship among his people. As early as 1847, addressing the Negro Convention meeting in Troy, New York, he urged the establishment of a national newspaper and a college for blacks. While a missionary in Liberia his most important work had been as a teacher, and the notion of organizing a national black cultural society had been in Crummell's mind almost from the earliest days of his return to America. In 1864, during the Liberian experience, he and his friend Edward Wilmot Blyden, a Liberian intellectual and diplomat, founded the Atheneum Club of Monrovia. Lectures, debates, and discussions were held in order to acquaint the young men who were to be the leaders of that country with the use and exchange of ideas. In 1877, in company with a group of black Washingtonians, Crummell helped form the "Negro-American Society," an organization whose purposes were "the promotion of civilization, progress, and culture among the people of the United States." The society's life, however, was short, lasting only a year. Crummell, a prolific writer, speaker, and organizer, was concerned throughout his career with the need for black moral, intellectual, and industrial development. Long an exponent of various types of industrial education, he also stressed the need for a corps of trained blacks to lead the race in its efforts to achieve wealth, equality, and a sense of identity.[23]

Crogman, following Grimké's suggestion, wrote to Crummell, who, in his reply outlined the form he thought such an organization should take. He envisioned an

African institute composed of say fifty colored scholars, the best we have; devoted to literary, statistical, ethnographical, folklore investigation, pertaining wholly and entirely to Africa and to the world-wide Negro race. It should be both inclusive and exclusive; inclusive of real thoughtful, reading men who have done something; exclusive of all mere talkers and screamers. Its work should be so real and thorough that it would command the respect of the scholarly element outside. I think we have a few ministers, college professors, teachers, artists, writers fitted for such an organization. Many of whom would be glad to undertake the great work.

However, in another part of the letter, Crummell expressed his belief that it would be very difficult "securing and maintaining . . . proper personnel to keep such a group functioning."

23. *Proceedings of the National Convention of Colored People and Their Friends* (Troy, 1847), 32; Akpan, "Alexander Crummell and His African 'Race-Work'," 188–89; Anna J. Cooper, "The American Negro Academy," *Southern Workman*, XXVI (February, 1898), 36; William H. Ferris, *Alexander Crummell, An Apostle of Negro Culture*, ANA Occasional Papers, no. 20 (1920), 8; Hollis R. Lynch, *Edward Wilmot Blyden: Pan-Negro Patriot, 1832–1912* (London, 1967), 38–41; Journal of John W. Cromwell, 1877–1918, in JWCG/M;

Crogman found the reply of the "venerable scholar" encouraging enough for him to write Grimké again, this time sharing Crummell's outline. Crogman urged Grimké to correspond with any of his friends that might be interested in the project, and expressed his intention of writing to a few people he thought would like to be involved. It was his hope, the Clark professor wrote, that the two of them might gather a small "nucleus" to plan the society, and perhaps formally organize it at Atlanta during the Cotton States' and International Exposition in 1895. For, continued the enthusiastic Crogman, "there are to be here at that time several colored organizations." [24]

Nothing more was done, however, for Crummell's doubts became stronger, and more pronounced. In addition to his uncertainty as to whether people could be found to manage the work of the proposed society, he began to feel "the time was inopportune." The failure in 1893 of the Afro-American League, a national coalition of black organizations committed to racial defense, the hand to mouth existence of black publications of the day, and the rapid demise of the black literary society he had helped found in 1877— these and other negative examples may have influenced his thinking, reenforcing fears about the viability of the projected organization. As a result, no further steps were taken and the "African Institute" remained an idea in the minds of several busy men.

Two years later, however, for reasons that are not entirely clear, Crummell's doubts had disappeared and he felt not only that the society was "a possibility, but an imperative necessity." This shift from uncertainty to commitment may have been caused by a growing consciousness that the condition of blacks was deteriorating. Certainly, as Crummell witnessed the political and social rights of his people being steadily pared down, while apologetics justifying their mistreatment emanated from respected intellectual, political, and religious figures, he may have come to believe that an organized group of educated blacks, committed to a reasoned defense of their people, was a necessity. [25]

For a long time, Crummell had believed that black politicians, who were considered by many blacks to be the major leaders and representatives of

---

for a biographical sketch of Crummell, see H. F. Kletzing and William H. Crogman (eds.), *Progress of a Race* (Atlanta, 1897), 496–97; for a discussion of his ideas and intellectual development, see Scruggs, *We the Children of Africa.*

24. Crogman to Grimké, September 24, 1894, in Woodson (ed.), *Works of Francis J. Grimké*, IV, 34–35. Crummell's description is quoted by Crogman in his letter to Grimké.

25. See Cromwell's articles cited in note 20.

their race, were stupid opportunists—men willing to abandon their people's interests for the smallest favors from powerful whites. A dark-skinned man of unmixed African blood, it deeply disturbed him that so many of these same politicians were light-skinned or near-white blacks who prided themselves on their difference in color and background from the mass of other blacks. Crummell's tendency to single out mulatto politicans as especially reprehensible was related directly to clashes earlier in his life with members of Liberia's mulatto governing class. During his twenty years of residence in Liberia, Crummell joined Edward Wilmot Blyden, a distinguished Liberian intellectual and diplomat, in challenging the power and ideas of that country's light-skinned aristocracy which considered itself superior to dark-skinned Liberians. The factional struggles between "educated blacks and the mulatto ruling class" resulted in Crummell's expulsion from his teaching post at Liberia College. These and related experiences made a lasting impression on him. In a letter written the spring of 1896, he vehemently castigated some of the men he saw seeking to become leaders in the black community:

American race prejudice is waxing. Divers indications evidence this fact: but lo and behold, just at this juncture up rise a fanatical and conceited junto, more malignant than white men, pushing themselves forward as leaders and autocrats of the race and at the same time repudiating the race. And what is the basis of their superiority? Bastardy!

To Crummell, the proposed society may also have offered the possibility of providing what he considered authentic and incorruptible leaders for his people.[26]

Another factor that might have caused the clergyman to change his mind was the growing popularity of what he described as "this miserable fad of industrialism." Industrial education for blacks, Crummell wrote a friend in Baltimore in the late 1890s, was something "a lot of white men in the land who pity the Negro but who have never learned to love him" espouse as a "pretext" for placing a "limitation on our brains and culture." In the same letter Crummell expressed his disgust for a "set of black opportunists who will jump at anything a white man says, if it will give him notoriety and help him jingle a few nickles [*sic*] in their pockets." This was a clear reference to black promoters of industrial education such as Booker T. Washington. Al-

26. Alexander Crummell to John Edward Bruce, April 7, 1896, in John Edward Bruce Papers, Schomburg Center for Research in Black Culture, New York Public Library; Lynch, *Edward Wilmot Blyden*, 38–41; Akpan, "Alexander Crummell and His African 'Race-Work.'"

though Crummell himself for many years had stressed the necessity of his race's securing access to various forms of industrial as well as higher education, early in the 1890s, as the clergyman saw manual training coming to dominate the thinking of whites who supported black education (and, as a consequence, the rhetoric of black educators), he began to stress the indispensable role of college-trained blacks in leading the race. It may be that he saw the proposed society as another way of challenging what he viewed as the over emphasis on industrial education. An organization of black men engaged in "literary, statistical, ethnographical, folklore investigation" would demonstrate to whites the intellectual ability of blacks, and to the black community the necessity of possessing a trained body of spokesmen.[27]

A fourth and more personal reason for Crummell's finding the African Institute idea viable in 1896 could have been his retirement from the rectorship of St. Luke's two years earlier. Having labored all of his life for the well-being of his people, Crummell wished to spend his last years writing and speaking in the same cause. Perhaps it seemed to him, as he experienced increased free time after 1894, that the institute he envisioned might be the appropriate focus for these activities. Whether it was one, or all of these reasons, by early 1896 Crummell was ready and eager to take the lead in establishing an African Institute.

From the time Crummell committed himself to the idea, initiative shifted to him and a small group of residents in Washington, D.C., whom he gathered to help him plan the organization. On the evening of December 18, 1896, Crummell met with four men, John Wesley Cromwell, Paul Laurence Dunbar, Walter B. Hayson, and Kelly Miller, to invite their support and cooperation. Miller, a mathematics professor at Howard University, held an A.B. degree from that university and had spent two years at Johns Hopkins University as a graduate student in mathematics and physics. An aggressive, articulate man of great intelligence, he was a rising young academic and essayist. Dunbar had already published three collections of his poetry, *Oak and Ivy* (1892), *Majors and Minors* (1895), and *Lyrics of Lowly Life* (1896), and at twenty-four was well on the way to becoming the leading black poet of his era. Cromwell, a man whose past activities had involved Reconstruction politics in Virginia, a clerkship in the United States Treasury department, and extensive experience as a newspaper publisher,

27. Crummell to George Frazier Miller, July 28, 1898, in Alexander Crummell Papers, Schomburg Center for Research in Black Culture, New York Public Library; Scruggs, *We the Children of Africa*, 8–9; Meier, *Negro Thought*, 94, 222–23.

held a law degree from Howard, and was employed as a teacher in the Washington public schools. A graduate of Oberlin College, Hayson was a Latin teacher in Washington's black high school.[28]

Crummell presided at the meeting, which took place in John W. Cromwell's home. The elderly clergyman explained the purpose of the gathering, inviting the four men to join him in establishing a black learned society. He also shared with them an eight-article constitution he had written. In this brief document the proposed society—called the "African Academy"—was described as "an organization of Colored authors, scholars, and artists." Crummell offered the following set of goals:

a. To promote the publication of literary and scholarly works;
b. To aid youths of genius in the attainment of the higher culture, at home and abroad;
c. To gather into its Archives valuable data, historical or literary works of Negro authors;
d. To aid, by publications, the vindication of the race from vicious assaults, in all the lines of learning and truth;
e. To publish, if possible, at least once a year an "Annual" of original articles upon various Literary, Historical, and Philosophical topics, of a racial nature, by selected members; and by these and diverse other means, to raise the standard of intellectual endeavor among American Negroes.

In terms of membership, Crummell was very precise. The society was to be limited to forty persons and open only to "graduates or Professors in Colleges: Literary characters; Authors, Artists, and distinguished writers." In order to qualify for election suitable candidates had to be recommended by six "enrolled members," and receive the approval of two-thirds of the total membership. Once admitted, the new member would pay an entrance fee, and thereafter annual dues. No amounts were given or suggested for the fees, as this was to be decided by the total membership once the organization was underway.

Following the example of other learned societies, Crummell's constitution permitted the academy to invite "colored authors and writers, members and others," to submit papers for "criticism and judgment." If the

28. For biographical information on Miller see Boris (ed.), *Who's Who*, 142; Walter Dyson, *Howard University: The Capstone of Negro Education, 1867–1940* (Washington, D.C., 1941), 368, 370–73. For Dunbar see Benjamin Brawley, *Paul Laurence Dunbar: Poet of His People* (Chapel Hill, 1936). For Cromwell see Mather (ed.), *Who's Who*, 81; and Cromwell's obituary in the *Journal of Negro History*, XII (July, 1927), 563–66. For Walter B. Hayson see Andrew F. Hilyer (ed.), *The Twentieth Century Union League Directory* (Washington, 1901), 162; "Death of Prof. Walter B. Hayson," Washington *Bee*, August 5, 1905; and "The Hayson Memorial," Washington *Bee*, October 7, 1905.

membership deemed them worthy, they were to be published under the organization's name. Provision was also made for an annual meeting in Washington, D.C., and the final article, an obvious frown at academic pretension, forbade the use of "titles of degrees" by academy members in its publications.[29]

After a lengthy discussion, the five men decided to join together and form the new society. In a series of resolutions they endorsed Crummell's proposal, declared this gathering the primary organization of the academy, adopted the constitution presented to them, and placed their signatures on it as the initial members. Before the signing, however, one change was made in the document: at Dunbar's suggestion, the group agreed that the name of the society should be "The American Negro Academy."[30]

Why Dunbar suggested dropping "African" for "American Negro," and why the others agreed to it is not revealed in any surviving academy records. In his earliest reflections on the society Crummell had called it "the African Institute"; in the provisional constitution, however, the term he used was "African Academy." Like a number of blacks born before the Civil War, Crummell made frequent use of the word "African" when referring to himself or his people, a habit which his years in Liberia had probably reinforced. Dunbar's suggestion may have reflected the decline in popularity of the term "African" among black Americans, as well as the then current feeling among many blacks that the term "Negro" expressed a sense of racial pride and included black Americans of all colors and backgrounds.[31]

Early in the nineteenth century when the American Colonization Society was making great efforts to send blacks to Africa, most free blacks had come to feel that calling themselves Africans supported the society's charge that they were an alien and un-American group. As a result, "Colored" and "Colored American" became the most frequently used words for the remainder of the century. But in the years following the Civil War and Recon-

---

29. No copy of the constitution Crummell composed and presented December 18, 1896, has survived. It is possible, however, to reconstruct it from four sources: 1. three fragile pages of unsigned notes in Crummell's hand on the "Academy" and "African Academy" in JWCG/M; 2. Verbatim account of the March 5, 1897, organizational meeting of the ANA, in JWCG/M; 3. Secretary's minutes of the ANA organizational meeting, March 5, 1897, in *Proceedings of the American Negro Academy*, in JWCG/M, hereinafter cited as *Proceedings*; 4. Proposed Constitution of the ANA, Booker T. Washington Papers, Library of Congress, container 124.

30. *Proceedings*, 1; [Cromwell], "American Negro Academy" *African Times and Orient Review*, 243.

31. Crogman to Grimké, September 24, 1894, in Woodson (ed.), *Works of Francis J. Grimké*, IV, 34–35; [Crummell], unsigned notes on "Academy" and "African Academy," in JWCG/M.

struction a growing discomfort with these words developed. It was probably occasioned, as one writer has observed, "by the tendency of 'the free people of color' to withdraw from the great masses of freedmen." As a consequence, some blacks began to use the word "Negro" to militantly proclaim their connectedness with all black people. It is not surprising that Dunbar, whose poetry celebrated the folkways of the black masses, should have made this suggestion, and that the others should have agreed, thus affirming their identity with all African and African-derived people.[32]

Before adjourning, the group agreed on a plan of organization. Alexander Crummell and John W. Cromwell were charged with the task of having the constitution printed "in a neat four-leafed form." A copy of the constitution, along with a covering letter and an endorsement card, were to be mailed to persons whose "position and qualities" indicated they would be worthy members of the new organization. The endorsement card was to read as follows: "I hereby endorse the constitution of the American Negro Academy, as a member thereof." Below this sentence two lines were to be printed for the signature and address of the recipient. Everyone who returned a signed endorsement card was to be considered a member and invited to a general meeting to be held in Washington, D.C., some time during the presidential inauguration in March, 1897. At the meeting in March the constitution was to be ratified, all of the details concerning fees and operational plans were to be consolidated, and officers elected. The five members agreed to meet ten days later and compile a list of persons to be invited to join the Academy.[33]

When the group assembled again on December 28, four other Washington, D.C., residents, Francis J. Grimké, John Albert Johnson, John L. Love, and Albert P. Miller, were invited to join them as academy members and organizers. Grimké was the Presbyterian minister with whom William H. Crogman had corresponded two years earlier concerning the possibility of founding a learned society. The Canadian-born Johnson, pastor of Metropolitan African Methodist Episcopal Church, was considered one of the finest exegetical preachers in his denomination. Like Walter B. Hayson, Love, who held degrees from Oberlin College and Catholic University, was a teacher in Washington's black high school. Miller was pastor of the Lin-

32. For a brief discussion of names black Americans have called themselves see Lerone Bennett, Jr., "What's in a Name?" in Peter Rose (ed.), *Americans from Africa: Old Memories, New Moods* (New York, 1970), 373–84.
33. Proceedings, 1.

coln Memorial Congregational Church. After graduating from Fisk in 1878, he had spent two years in British West Africa as a missionary. On his return to the United States, he entered Yale Divinity School and received the B.D. degree in 1888. Before coming to Washington, D.C., Miller had pastored in Connecticut and edited a black newspaper in that state.[34]

The constitution was read to Grimké, Johnson, Love, and Miller, who indicated their approval and willingness to join with the others in establishing the organization. At this point the ANA consisted of nine members: a college professor, a poet, three public school teachers, and four ministers. With great dispatch, the men set about taking the next steps. They agreed to meet twice a month between then and the general meeting in early March. In addition, a list was compiled of thirty-one people to be invited to join the ANA and attend the March, 1897, meeting.

Not surprisingly, the men whose names appeared on the list had much in common with the nine who suggested them. They tended to be well educated, with a strong sense of race identity, active and effective leaders, and highly respectable. Seven were college or university professors: J. E. Jones and John Wesley Edward Bowen were on seminary faculties; Jones taught homiletics and Greek at the Baptist Seminary in Richmond, Virginia, and Bowen was an instructor in history and theology at Gammon Theological Seminary, a Northern Methodist institution in Atlanta. William Henry Crogman, another Atlantan and an early exponent of the ANA idea, was professor of Greek and Latin at Clark University. Two of the men, William Saunders Scarborough and Edward A. Clarke, were on the faculty of Wilberforce University, an AME school in Ohio. Both taught Latin and Greek, and Scarborough was head of the classics department. William Edward Burghardt Du Bois was assistant instructor in sociology at the University of Pennsylvania. Lewis Baxter Moore was an instructor in Latin and pedagogy at Howard.[35]

34. Proceedings, 2. These four men may have been invited to the initial meeting on December 8 and, for various reasons, been unable to attend. For biographical information on Johnson see Richard R. Wright, Jr. (ed.), *Centennial Encyclopedia of the African Methodist Episcopal Church* (Philadelphia, 1916), 133–34, and William H. Ferris, *The African Abroad* (2 vols.; New Haven, 1913), II, 777. For Love, see Hilyer (ed.), *Twentieth Century Union League Directory*, 162; and the Washington *Colored American*, November 17, 1900. For Miller see the Washington *Colored American*, October 8, 1898; and Edward F. Goin, "100 Years of Congregationalism in New Haven, Connecticut," *Crisis*, XIX (February, 1920), 178.

35. For biographical information on J. E. Jones see William J. Simmons, *Men of Mark: Eminent, Progressive, and Rising* (Cleveland, 1887), 234–39. For Scarborough, see J. L. Nichols and W. H. Crogman (eds.), *Progress of a Race* (Naperville, Ill., 1920), 427; and Francis P.

Eight of the men on the list headed educational institutions. John G. Mitchell was dean of the AME Church's Payne Theological Seminary, a part of Wilberforce University. Richard Robert Wright, who had suggested to Crogman two years earlier that a learned society be formed, directed the state industrial school for blacks in Georgia. Charles Henry Parrish was principal of Eckstein Institute, a small industrial school in Kentucky. Three of the men, Daniel Jackson Sanders, William Harvey Goler, and Simon Green Atkins were North Carolinians. Sanders was president of Biddle University, a Presbyterian school in Charlotte; Goler headed the African Methodist Episcopal Zion Church's Livingstone College at Salisbury; and Atkins was in charge of a normal and industrial school at Winston, which received some state support. George N. Grisham, principal of the black high school in Kansas City, Missouri, and Inman Edward Page, head of the Colored Agricultural and Normal University in Langston, Oklahoma, were the other two.[36]

Four of the men on the list were lawyers. Clement G. Morgan, a graduate of Atlanta and Harvard Universities, sat on the Cambridge, Massachusetts, city council. Robert Heberton Terrell, a resident of Washington, D.C., was a rising young politician who had held government clerkships and taught in the public school of that city. John Henry Smyth, a former United States minister to Liberia (1878 to 1885) was an active participant in local and national Republican politics, and a strong advocate of juvenile penal reform. Thomas McCants Stewart, who held the A.B. and L.L.B. degrees from the University of South Carolina, had been at various times an AME pastor and a missionary-educator in Liberia. At this time he was practicing law in Brooklyn, New York, where he had recently finished a term on that city's board of education (1891 to 1895).[37]

Weisenberger, "William Saunders Scarborough," *Ohio History*, LXXI, (October, 1962), 2–27, and LXXII, (January, 1963), 15–45. For Clarke see Frederick A. McGinnis, *A History and an Interpretation of Wilberforce University* (Blanchester, Ohio, 1941), 145. For Du Bois, see Boris (ed.), *Who's Who*, 59–60. For Moore see Nichols and Crogman (eds.), *Progress of a Race*, 410.

36. For biographical information on J. G. Mitchell see McGinnis, *Wilberforce University*, 42, 141, 144; and Dorothy E. Hoover, *A Layman Looks with Love at Her Church* (Philadelphia, 1970), 65. For Parrish see Simmons, *Men of Mark*, 1059; and Richardson (ed.), *National Cyclopedia*, 172. For Sanders see D. J. Sanders Memorial Edition, *The Johnson C. Smith University Alumni Journal*, I (April, 1928), 1–3, 6–9. For Goler see David Henry Bradley, Sr., *A History of the A.M.E. Zion Church* (2 vols.; Nashville, 1956, 1970), II, 33. For Grisham see Washington *Colored American*, June 4, 1898, p. 1. For Page see Simmons, *Men of Mark*, 474–80; and Richardson (ed.), *National Cyclopedia*, 357.

37. For biographical information on Morgan see Meier, *Negro Thought*, 175. For Terrell

Ministers were strongly represented among the thirty-one names; their numbers were augmented by the fact that some of the professors were also clergymen. J. W. E. Bowen and J. E. Jones were both ministers, Bowen a Methodist, and Jones a Baptist. The same situation prevailed among the educational administrators. J. G. Mitchell (AME), D. J. Sanders (Presbyterian), W. H. Goler (AMEZ), and C. H. Parrish (Baptist) were all ordained and practicing clergymen. However, seven men suggested for ANA membership worked primarily in church institutions. Three of them, Benjamin Franklin Lee, James C. Embry, and Benjamin Tucker Tanner, were African Methodist Episcopal bishops. Lee, a graduate of Wilberforce, had taught there and served as its president for seven years. After holding the editor's chair of the denominational newspaper, the *Christian Recorder*, for ten years, he had been elected a bishop. Embry, the prime force behind the establishment of the AME publishing house, believed in the press as a means of elevating his race. Tanner was a theologian, essayist, writer, and lecturer who carried on these activities while serving as a full-time church administrator.[38]

Of the four other preachers whose names were listed, three were also AME ministers. Charles W. Mossell, a former missionary to Haiti and author of a history of Toussaint L'Ouverture and the Haitian people, managed a book company. Theophilus Gould Steward, United States army chaplain to the all-black 25th Infantry stationed at Fort Missoula, Montana, had strong interests in Haitian and black American history. Levi Jenkins Coppin edited the *AME Church Review*, a denominational literary magazine. The non-Methodist was Richard Henry Boyd, a Baptist preacher who was in the process of establishing a publishing company in Nashville, Tennessee, to free Negro Baptists from dependence on white concerns.[39]

Although the ministers who were invited to become founding members of the ANA came from a variety of Protestant denominations it was certainly

see Nichols and Crogman (eds.), *Progress of a Race*, 434. For Smyth see Simmons, *Men of Mark*, 373–77. For Steward see Louis R. Harlan (ed.), *The Booker T. Washington Papers* (7 vols.; Urbana, 1972–1977), II, 255.

38. For biographical information on Lee see Wright (ed.), *Centennial Encyclopedia*, 148. For Embry see Wright (ed.), *Centennial Encyclopedia*, 87. For Tanner see Kletzing and Crogman (eds.), *Progress of a Race*, 500.

39. For biographical information on Mossell see Daniel A. Payne, *History of the African Methodist Episcopal Church* (Nashville, Tenn., 1891), 478–80; and N. F. Mossell, *The Work of the Afro-American Woman* (n.p., 1894), 29. For Steward see Mather (ed.), *Who's Who*, 253. For Coppin see Wright (ed.), *Centennial Encyclopedia*, 74–76. For Boyd see Richardson (ed.), *National Cyclopedia*, 414–16.

not a coincidence that seven powerful clergy in the AME Church were invited to connect themselves with the ANA. The AME Church was in this period considered the outstanding example of the ability of blacks to organize, finance, and manage their own affairs. With its numerous schools, two publications, and a publishing house, it was a relatively impressive black organization. In addition, the denomination had produced a number of bishops, such as Daniel A. Payne and Benjamin T. Tanner, who were outstanding race leaders. A few years after the establishment of the academy, W. E. B. Du Bois described the AME Church as perhaps "the greatest voluntary organization of Negroes in the world."[40]

The last five people on the list were engaged in a wide range of activities and occupations. John Edward Bruce was a newspaper correspondent who wrote under the sobriquet, "Bruce Grit." His columns, which appeared in black and white newspapers, were usually trenchant and even blunt in their analyses of people and issues, delighting some and outraging others. William Tecumseh Sherman Jackson taught in the public schools of Washington. Lieutenant Charles Young, a West Point graduate, was instructor in military science and tactics at Wilberforce University. Charles Cattlett Johnson, a physician with a strong interest in public health, practiced in Columbia, South Carolina. William H. Ferris, a graduate of Yale College, was a first-year student in the Harvard Divinity School.[41]

At a session three weeks later, the planners settled several important details. "By an unanimous vote," Alexander Crummell "was assured that it was the 'nine members' expressed wish for him to act as chairman of the informal proceedings" connected with the March organizational meeting. John W. Cromwell, Kelly Miller, and Walter B. Hayson were placed in charge of arrangements for this meeting; and, to expedite their work, an assessment of fifty cents per member was levied to cover "incidental preliminary expenses." Crummell's concern that the organization make every effort to publish a magazine led to the appointment of Francis J. Grimké, Kelly Miller, and Albert P. Miller as a committee to investigate ways of financing and managing it. The group also added six additional names to their list of persons to be invited to join the ANA: John Bunyan Reeve, a Presbyterian min-

40. W. E. B. Du Bois (ed.), *The Negro Church* (Atlanta, 1903), 123–31.
41. For biographical information on Bruce see Boris (ed.), *Who's Who*, 311. For Jackson see Washington *Colored American*, May 4, 1901; and Mather (ed.), *Who's Who*, 151. For Young see Richardson (ed.), *National Cyclopedia*, 527; and McGinnis, *Wilberforce University*, 145. For Johnson see Boris (ed.), *Who's Who*, 105. For Ferris see Boris (ed.), *Who's Who*, 65.

ister and former head of Howard University's theological department, who was pastor of the Central Presbyterian Church in Philadelphia; Matthew Anderson, another Presbyterian clergyman living in Philadelphia and the head of Berean Presbyterian, an "institutional" church engaged in extensive social welfare work; Booker T. Washington, principal of Tuskegee Institute in Alabama; Charles H. Turner, biology instructor at Clark University; Hugh Mason Browne, a teacher in the public schools of Washington, D.C.; and George W. Forbes, a librarian and the editor of a black newspaper in Boston.[42]

The nine planners met two weeks later and agreed that the organizational meeting, scheduled for March 5, 1897, was to be held in A. P. Miller's church, Lincoln Memorial Congregational. They also voted to invite four of the men expected to attend to prepare addresses on topics related to the purpose and goals of the new organization: J. W. E. Bowen was asked to speak on "The Unique Opportunity for the Growth and Development of the Negro Intellect"; W. E. B. Du Bois on "The Duty of Cherishing and Fostering the Intellect of the Race"; B. T. Tanner on "The Special Qualities that Our Race Can Give to the Civilization of the Country;" and W. H. Crogman on "The Special Work of the Educated Professions Aside from the Beaten Path of Their Vocations."[43]

The final business of receiving three additional names for invitation to ANA membership went less smoothly. William Victor Tunnell, rector of King Hall, an Episcopal seminary for blacks, and Charles Chauveau Cook, instructor in English at Howard University, were acceptable to everyone. The third name, however—that of Richard Theodore Greener—"occasioned marked dissent and emphatic opposition." Greener, the first black graduate of Harvard College, had taught at the University of South Carolina (1873 to 1877), earning a law degree there while on the faculty. Later he moved to Washington, D.C., and was dean of Howard's law school (1878 to 1880). During the 1880s and 1890s he was engaged in the private prac-

---

42. Proceedings, 3. Reeve and Anderson were probably suggested by Francis J. Grimké; Washington definitely was. For biographical information on Reeve, see Simmons, *Men of Mark*, 199–201. For biographical information on Anderson, see *Crisis*, XXXV (April, 1928), 117, 139, 298. For biographical information on Turner see Turner to "Dear Sir JW Cromwell," February 20, August 26, and September 7, 1897, all in JWCG/M. For Browne see Harlan, *Booker T. Washington, 1856–1901*, 212. For Forbes see *Crisis*, XXXIV (July, 1927), 151–52. See also Cromwell to Booker T. Washington, January 19, 1897, in Harlan (ed.), *Booker T. Washington Papers*, IV, 255.

43. Proceedings, 4.

tice of law. Greener and his wife, both light-skinned and Caucasian in appearance, were prominent and active figures in the black community.[44]

Though the minutes do not indicate who Greener's supporters were, Crummell led the opposition. He "earnestly opposed" Greener's membership, because, as he wrote to a friend, "for years he has been a white man in New York and turned his back upon all his colored acquaintance." The ambitious lawyer's constant efforts to obtain a "black Republican" political appointment, coupled with Crummell's belief that he passed for white when it suited him, made the man totally obnoxious to the clergyman. He regarded Greener as a prime example of the opportunistic black politicians who despised the race, priding themselves on their racial and social connections with whites, while at the same time demanding recognition as "race leaders." He may pass for white if he wishes, Crummell raged, but "I . . . object to his coming back to our ranks, and then getting on my Negro shoulders, to hoist himself, as a Negro, into some political office."[45]

To Crummell, the ANA was, in part, an effort to challenge and, hopefully, supplant "leaders" such as Greener. Therefore, in his opinion, to have included the lawyer would have contaminated and compromised the organization at the outset. Crummell's objections held and Greener's name was dropped. Then—in what may have been a rebuke to those who had suggested Greener—the name of Peter Humphries Clark, a racial militant who had been active in the antebellum black convention movement and editor of an abolitionist newspaper, was presented and accepted. It is equally possible that this substitution represented the group's agreement with Crummell. And, since the minutes are not absolutely clear on the point, a third possibility exists—that Clark was possibly the fourth name on the list of people

44. *Ibid.*, 4–5. For biographical information on Tunnell see Dyson, *Howard University*, 176, 179, 211. For Cook see "Prof. Cook Drowned," Washington *Bee*, August 27, 1910, p. 4; and Dyson, *Howard University*, 458. For Greener see Richard Bardolph, *The Negro Vangard* (New York, 1959), 117. It is interesting that Crummell, Cromwell, and Greener had all been founders and members of the Negro-American Society in 1877. Greener was president and Crummell first vice-president during its short existence. See. J. W. Cromwell, Journal, in JWCG/M.

45. Crummell to John Edward Bruce, January 21, 1898 in Bruce Papers. Earlier, Booker T. Washington had been interested in the Greener family's racial identity. Responding to a query from the head of Tuskegee Institute, an associate of his living in Washington, D.C., sent the following information: "In regard to Professor Greener's family I have ascertained that Mrs. Greener is a native of this city—being a Miss Fleet before marriage. She is colored and never passes for anything else while here. It is understood here however that she associates only with whites in New York." See Thomas Junius Calloway to Washington, May 5, 1894, in Harlan (ed.), *Booker T. Washington Papers*, III, 415.

considered for membership that evening. But whatever Clark's inclusion represented, the debate on Greener, and his rejection as a member, introduced an issue that was to be intimately connected with the initial discussions in the black community concerning the value and significance of the ANA.[46]

In a final gathering before the general meeting, Cromwell, Hayson, and Kelly Miller presented the group with a detailed program for March 5, which included three sessions. Alexander Crummell was to speak on the significance of the ANA at a morning session; Albert P. Miller and Kelly Miller were scheduled to give addresses at an afternoon session; and W. E. B. Du Bois was to present a paper at an evening session. Because prior commitments made it impossible for J. W. E. Bowen and William H. Crogman to attend the organizational meeting, Albert P. Miller had agreed to take the topic offered to Bowen, and Kelly Miller to present his critical review of a recently published book in place of an address by Crogman. Illness forced Benjamin T. Tanner to decline his invitation to speak, and he was not replaced. The program was approved, individual members were charged with the responsibility for handling final details, and the planning group adjourned *sine die*, having completed its deliberations.[47]

Once Alexander Crummell decided it was an "imperative necessity" that a society to encourage black intellectual activity and defend the Negro race be established, he became the central figure in the attempt to create it. His education, distinguished public role, and lengthy experience as an organizer had made Grimké and Crogman almost instinctively turn to him for advice and encouragement when they first began to discuss such an organization. And, because he was also a dominating personality, his commitment to the idea led to his becoming master of it.

Crummell's years in Washington, D.C., had been filled with efforts to organize and strengthen the life of the black community, and it was natural that the men in that city he gathered to help him initiate the ANA should be activists with a high regard for scholarship and learning. John W. Cromwell had been as energetic as Crummell in the attempt to build strong black in-

46. Proceedings, 4–5. For biographical information on Clark see Simmons, *Men of Mark*, 374–83; and Harlan (ed.), *Booker T. Washington Papers*, II, 383–84.
47. Proceedings, 5–6. (The date given for these minutes in the Proceedings book is wrong. Beside them J. W. Cromwell placed a question mark. Possibly, this meeting took place March 1, 1897, but certainly after February 15, 1897, and before March 5, 1897.) See also J. W. E. Bowen to J. W. Cromwell, February 22, 1897, W. H. Crogman to J. W. Cromwell, February 24, 1897, B. T. Tanner to J. W. Cromwell, January 15, 1897, all in JWCG/M.

stitutions. In 1875 he had founded the Virginia Historical and Literary Society; two years later he joined with Crummell and others in establishing the short-lived Negro American Society. Constantly involved in journalistic ventures, Cromwell was the leading figure in the series of events that led to the creation of the Colored Press Association and was a founder of the Bethel Library and Historical Association in Washington.[48] Francis J. Grimké, less of an organizer than either Crummell or Cromwell, was an oustanding representative of literate ministry and intelligent social concern among the younger black clergy. John Albert Johnson and Albert P. Miller, both supporters of numerous activities for the educational, moral, and social uplift of their people, were men of ability, and, as Grimké did, headed important congregations containing men and women that in Crummell's mind were the stable, honest, hard-working blacks on whom the burden of leading and representing the race fell. Kelly Miller, Dunbar, Love, and Hayson—and in this sense Dunbar was the shining star—were symbols and models of the younger men of genius on whom the future of their people depended.

48. Ferris, *The Negro Abroad*, II, 870; Boris (ed.), *Who's Who*, 24; Cromwell, Journal, in JWCG/M, 5; Thornbrough, *T. Thomas Fortune*, 40; New York *Age*, April 23, 1927, p. 3.

II Beginnings

On March 5, 1897, the one hundred twenty-seventh anniversary of the Boston Massacre where Crispus Attucks, who was believed to have been a mulatto, was the first to die, eighteen black men assembled in the District of Columbia's Lincoln Memorial Church to formally inaugurate the American Negro Academy. This date was chosen because it recalled "an event especially sacred to the Negro." To the men who planned the meeting, Attucks' death in 1770 was a symbol of the patriotic and heroic role black Americans played in the creation of the United States. Consequently, they felt it appropriate that a black society formed to encourage intellectual activity among blacks, and to defend them from "vicious assaults" should begin its public life on this day. March 5 was also the fifth day in the week-long festivities being held to celebrate the inauguration of William McKinley as president of the United States. Many blacks, despite the new Republican president's failure, as a candidate, to speak out in support of their political and social rights, had supported him and saw his victory as that of the party that had emancipated them. Anticipating several black appointments, black politicians journeyed to the city to participate in the councils of their party, fraternize with each other, and enjoy the activities. In addition to its recollection of Attucks' death, the ANA organizers chose March 5 for their meeting because it provided an opportunity to present their association and its goals to the influential blacks visiting the city.[1]

1. John W. Cromwell, "The American Negro Academy," New York *Chronicle*, September 27, 1897, and [Cromwell], "The Negro Academy," Washington *Record* [*ca*. December, 1902],

The nine men who initiated the ANA invited forty-six others to the organizational meeting in Washington, D.C. Although the ANA Proceedings indicate the points at which forty-three of these invitees were nominated, approved, and extended invitations, at some point between February 15 and March 5 three others—John Wesslay Hoffman, Theophilus J. Minton, and Samuel Laing Williams—must also have been extended invitations. Hoffman, a biologist and chemist whose specialty was southern agriculture, taught at South Carolina Agricultural and Mechanical College in Orangeburg. Minton, a founding member and officer of the American Negro Historical Society of Philadelphia, practiced law in that city. Williams, also a lawyer, lived in Chicago. Born in Georgia, he settled in the midwest after graduation from the University of Michigan and the Columbian Law School in Washington, D.C. Ten of those to whom invitations were extended—Richard H. Boyd, Hugh M. Browne, George W. Forbes, William H. Goler, J. E. Jones, Clement G. Morgan, John B. Reeve, Daniel J. Sanders, William V. Tunnell, and Charles Young—sent no reply. Edward A. Clarke, Benjamin F. Lee, John G. Mitchell, and James C. Embry responded negatively to the invitation. Heavy work demands prevented the involvement of Embry and Mitchell. This was also Lee's excuse, as well as his unwillingness to join an organization he could not afford to support financially. Embry and Lee commended the project and Clarke asked to be considered a promoter of their work. Twenty-nine men accepted the invitation to join the Academy and twenty-two of them signed and returned endorsement cards. The seven who did not return cards made a commitment, either through written or verbal replies, to support the organization. This latter group included J. W. E. Bowen, P. H. Clark, C. C. Cook, J. W. Hoffman, L. B. Moore, J. H. Smyth, S. L. Williams, and T. H. Minton. Only eleven invitees—Matthew Anderson, Simon G. Atkins, Charles C. Cook, Levi J. Coppin, W. E. B. Du Bois, William H. Ferris, George N. Grisham, John W. Hoffman, Lewis B. Moore, William S. Scarborough, and John H. Smyth—promised to attend the March meeting. Except for C. C. Cook and L. B. Moore, all of these men lived outside Washington. Ten people sent regrets: John E. Bruce, who had earlier planned to attend, was prevented by his wife's "malignant attack of la grippe"; Benjamin T. Tanner was recovering from an illness and confined to his home; Theophilus J. Minton received the

both in Book of Clippings, in JWCG/M; Cromwell, "The American Negro Academy," *Horizon*, 12; Logan, *Betrayal*, 94–96; Washington *Bee*, February 20, 27, and March 6, 1897.

mailing too late to make plans to come; Peter H. Clark made it clear that attendance at meetings could not be one of the criteria for his membership; Charles H. Turner and Thomas M. Stewart both simply said they could not be present; J. W. E. Bowen, William H. Crogman, Booker T. Washington, and Samuel L. Williams pleaded busy schedules and prior commitments.[2]

Some of the men who signed and returned the endorsement card also sent letters or notes expressing their hopes for the new organization and, in some cases, their concerns. Simon G. Atkins, J. W. E. Bowen, John E. Bruce, Theophilus J. Minton, and Benjamin T. Tanner all responded with great enthusiasm to the idea and the invitation. "It is the most significant step yet taken by the American Negro looking toward his complete vindication as a man," Atkins declared. To Bowen, the association was important because "the larger education of the race" depended on "the men of scholarly temper" establishing a place in the intellectual community for blacks. Minton pronounced the ANA "an excellent idea" and mentioned that some time ago he had suggested the formation of just such a group. "Would you believe me," Tanner's reply began, "I have long wished for such an organization." Bruce pledged to do everything to make "the ANA a fixture among the *great* institutions of this caste-cursed country." George N. Grisham's decision to affiliate was linked to his concern that there be an agency to urge and maintain "a higher standard of literary taste" among blacks. In a cordial, but cautious note Peter H. Clark made it clear that he had joined because of his desire to support the circulation of works produced by black authors, something he believed could only be done "by concerted effort." And Thomas McCants Stewart indicated the tentative nature of his support by writing the following note over his signature on the endorsement card:

2. For biographical information on Hoffman see the Washington *Colored American*, October 7, 1899, p. 1, November 17, 1900, pp. 1, 9, April 4, 1903, p. 16. For Minton see H. Harrison Wayman, "The American Historical Society of Philadelphia, and Its Officers," *Colored American Magazine*, VI (February, 1903), 288–89. For Williams see Spear, *Black Chicago*, 66–67. Clarke to Cromwell, January 29, 1897, Lee to Cromwell, February 8, 1897, Mitchell to Cromwell, February 1, 1897, Embry to Cromwell, February 12, 1897, Anderson to Cromwell, February 4, 1897, Atkins to Cromwell, February 19, 1897, Cook to Cromwell, February 24, 1894[7], Du Bois to Cromwell, February 22, 1897, Grisham to Cromwell, February 2, 1897, Hoffman to Cromwell, February 18, 1897, Scarborough to Cromwell, January 11, 1897, Smyth to Cromwell, February 25, 1897, Bruce to Cromwell, February 26, 1897, Tanner to Cromwell, January 15, 1897, Minton to Cromwell, March 3, 1897, Clark to Cromwell, February 27, 1897, Tuner to Cromwell, February 20, 1897, Stewart to Cromwell, February 25, 1897, Bowen to Cromwell, February 22, 1897, Crogman to Cromwell, February 24, 1897, Washington to Cromwell, February 27, 1897, Williams to Cromwell, March 7, 1897, all in JWCG/M.

"but no obligation as to annual or special assessments—Plan of Governance, sent me, is in blank as to financial feature."[3]

Several correspondents commented on various features of the proposed constitution. Simon G. Atkins was pleased with the "conditions of membership" in Article 3 and the method prescribed for electing new members, but felt that the maximum size of the society should be one hundred rather than forty. Article 3 failed to quiet William S. Scarborough's anxiety that the wrong people might become members; he expressed the hope "that Tom, Dick and Harry *et id omni genus* will not be admitted." John E. Bruce suggested an entrance fee of $5 or $10, payable in two installments, with annual dues of $5. Theophilus G. Steward felt there should be "an annual fee of $5 with no entrance fee for founders." He also declared himself "decidedly opposed to the admission of women to membership" on the grounds that "literary matters and social matters do not mix." It is difficult to know what provoked his last comment, since the proposed constitution sent to prospective members specifically described the ANA as "an organization of . . . men of African descent." Prospective members were not polled on the question of including women, and no other person who returned an endorsement card or replied by letter even referred to this matter. Both James C. Embry, who declined membership in the ANA, and Benjamin T. Tanner, who joined, criticized the organization's name. Embry expressed his distaste for blacks who called themselves "Negroes," a practice he considered "puerile." Tanner, whose concern was different, urged a reversal of the words "American" and "Negro" because "we are Americans. Let the Negro be the adjective and not the noun. We who are of African descent should rate ourselves precisely as do people of European descent."[4]

When the organizational meeting opened Friday, March 5, 1897, eight of the nine Washington members—John W. Cromwell, Alexander Crummell, Francis J. Grimké, Walter B. Hayson, John A. Johnson, John L. Love, Albert P. Miller, and Kelly Miller—plus ten others—Matthew Anderson, Charles C. Cook, Levi J. Coppin, W. E. B. Du Bois, William H. Ferris, George N. Grisham, W. T. S. Jackson, Lewis B. Moore, William S. Scarborough, and

3. Atkins to Cromwell, January 11, 1897, Bowen to Cromwell, February 22, 1897, Minton to Cromwell, March 3, 1897, Tanner to Cromwell, January 15, 1897, Bruce to Cromwell, January 11, 1897, Clark to Cromwell, February 27, 1897, Grisham to Cromwell, February 2, 1897, endorsement card signed by T. McCants Stewart, all in JWCG/M.
4. Atkins to Cromwell, January 11, 1897, Scarborough to Cromwell, January 11, 1897, Bruce to Cromwell, February 19, 1897, Steward to Cromwell, n.d., Embry to Cromwell, January 12, 1897, Tanner to Cromwell, January 15, 1897, all in JWCG/M.

Richard R. Wright—were present; in all, a total of eighteen people. The first session of the meeting opened at 10:30 A.M., with John W. Cromwell presiding. After a few welcoming remarks, Cromwell suggested the election of a temporary chairman and secretary. Alexander Crummell was nominated and elected to the first position, Cromwell to the other. Crummell took the chair and invited Francis J. Grimké "to invoke the Divine blessing" on the assembled group. Following Grimké's prayer, the group elected an official stenographer to make a verbatim report of their meeting, and then listened to an address by Crummell.[5]

Crummell's talk was a discourse on the need of American blacks for "civilization" and the ANA's crucial role in fostering it. In support of his arguments, he drew on ideas and attitudes held by many, if not most, educated blacks regarding the condition of black Americans and black-white relations. To Crummell civilization was a state of being derived from an acquaintance with and commitment to Christianity and the intellectual disciplines. In his several related definitions of the term, he described it as "the action of exalted forces, both of God and man"; as a force which in the "loftiest men . . . bursts forth producing letters, literature, science, philosophy, poetry, sculpture, architecture, . . . all the arts"; and as the expression of intelligent philanthropic concern. A race was, therefore, to be considered civilized only when it produced a sophisticated and regenerative culture of its own. It followed that the individual members of such a race would demonstrate a serious commitment to values, the life of the mind, and religion, as well as to producing advances in these areas. It was Crummell's judgment that American blacks lacked civilization, for it appeared to him that "as a race in this land, we have no art; we have no science; we have no philosophy; we have no scholarship." Unless this situation was changed, he warned, the inevitable result for his people would be "despite, inferiority, repulsion, drudgery, poverty, and ultimate death."[6]

It was important to remember, Crummell continued, that the creation of a "true and lofty race" could only result "from the force and application of the highest arts." There was no short cut to this condition via industrial education, business success, landownership, political power, or social and sexual intermingling with whites. For these were not "fixed factors in so

5. Proceedings, 9; Edward Beckham verbatim account of American Negro Academy Organizational Meeting, March 5, 1897, in JWCG/M, 1, the latter hereinafter cited as Verbatim.

6. Alexander Crummell, "Civilization the Primal Need of the Negro Race," ANA Occasional Papers, no. 3 (1898), 4, 5, 6.

large a thing as the destiny of man." A cultivated moral intelligence was the only force able to enter the life of a people "uplifting the crudeness of laws, giving scientific precision to morals and religion, stimulating enterprise, extending commerce, creating manufactures, expanding mechanism and mechanical inventions; producing revolutions and reforms, humanizing labor; meeting the minutest human needs." The ANA, Crummell told his listeners, was an organization whose purpose was to translate these understandings into programs and actions that would touch the lives of blacks. For this reason he was deeply encouraged by the enthusiasm with which a number of educated blacks hailed the academy.

Crummell saw the gathering that morning as different from any previous meeting of blacks. The difference lay in their purpose, which he defined as "the civilization of the Negro race in the United States, by the scientific processes of literature, art and philosophy." The agents of this process were to be the men gathered there, "scholars and thinkers, who have secured the vision which penetrates the center of nature, and sweeps the circle of historic enlightenment; and who have got insight into the life of things, and learned the art by which men touch the springs of action." It is the work of the "trained and scholarly men" to shape and direct "the opinions and habits of the crude masses," he asserted. This is their responsibility and calling, the activity which makes them more than mere "pedants, trimmers, [and] opportunists." For true scholars, he declared, are also "reformers" and "philanthropists." In closing, the cleric urged his listeners to exhibit a spirit of unselfishness as they went about their task. Unlike those whose goals were political power and social prestige, jealousy and factious hostility must not operate among them, since their very existence demanded a willingness to speedily recognize and generously encourage other talented and able members of the race.[7]

Following Crummell's address, the minutes of the preliminary meetings were read, as well as several supportive letters sent by men unable to be present. The group then decided on a procedure for ratifying the constitution: each article was to be read, discussed, and voted on separately. The lengthy discussion that ensued consumed the remainder of the morning session, and the articles that dealt with membership size, membership qualifications, and the use of degrees occasioned the most significant debate.

Early in the discussion of Article 2, which dealt with membership,

7. *Ibid.*, 3–7.

George Grisham made an eloquent plea for the admission of women to the organization, urging that the ANA concern for the encouragement of talented youth be extended to females as well as males. "In the year of our opening," he declared, there has been "a higher attainment of scholarship . . . by our women then our men." No objections were voiced, and Grisham was assured that women would be admitted. However, nothing was done to change those parts of the constitution which indicated that membership was limited to "men of African descent."[8]

From the time the proposed constitution was circulated, questions had been raised about the appropriateness of forty as a membership limit. In the discussion on Article 2, George N. Grisham, William H. Ferris, Lewis B. Moore, and Crummell insisted that this figure did not allow for the number of able men needed by the academy. Ferris suggested one hundred as more appropriate, but a motion by Moore to raise the limit to fifty was approved.[9] In spite of the optimism expressed by arguments for a higher figure, it was impossible to ignore the small number present, as well as the fact that only twenty-nine out of forty-six people had signed endorsement cards.

Section a of Article 3, which required that ANA members be "graduates, or Professors in Colleges" caused extensive debate. Richard R. Wright opposed it because he thought some of the most useful potential members would fall outside those two categories. W. E. B. Du Bois agreed with him, and offered an amendment changing the section's wording from "Candidates shall be graduates, or Professors in Colleges: Literary characters; Authors, Artists, and distinguished writers" to "Candidates shall be men of Science, Letters, and Art, or those distinguished in other walks of life." This proposed amendment stimulated John W. Cromwell to ask Du Bois if he was attempting to make it possible for "a successful politician" or "a member of Congress" to become a member. Coming from a close friend of Crummell's and one who shared the elderly priest's distaste for most black politicians, this was an important question. Du Bois replied that he was not interested in excluding "statesmen" or any other group, but was concerned that the constitution not define membership in an unnecessarily narrow way.

8. Verbatim, 3, 4, 5. See ANA constitution ratified March 5, 1897, preamble, Article 3, Section a, in JWCG/M.

9. Proceedings, 6, 10; S. G. Atkins to Cromwell, January 11, 1897, in JWCG/M; Verbatim, 3–4, 5. It should be noted that with the exception of Article 8, which involved a tie vote, neither the Verbatim nor the Proceedings gives the figures for any of the votes on the constitution. This may be, as part of the Proceedings suggests, because most of the votes were viva voce.

Walter B. Hayson opposed broadening the qualifications, asserting that the academy was intended to be "an association for men who . . . confine themselves more exclusively to literary matters." Agreeing with him, William H. Ferris expressed the hope that "we not be filled up with preachers and politicians." These statements impelled Francis J. Grimké to remark that an amendment limiting membership to those "distinguished in science, letters, or art" would exclude a number of people present, including himself. This comment from a minister who was one of the best educated and most talented of the younger men present, pointed to the dangers in the position taken by Hayson and Ferris. Reentering the debate, Du Bois contended that the conditions of membership were important only as they served to insure faithfulness to the association's purpose and goals. "You cannot limit the membership of the Academy to men distinguished in Science and Art," he argued, "because we find men who are not distinguished in science or literature or art that are just the men we want."

The matter came to a vote when Hayson moved the following amendment to Du Bois's amendment: "Candidates shall be men of Science, Letters, or Art." This motion lost. Du Bois's original motion was then voted on, and approved.[10]

In connection with Section b of Article 4, which pledged the society "to aid youths of genius in the attainment of the higher culture," Crummell proposed that the ANA annually survey the various college and university campuses in order to discover capable black students who could profitably be sent abroad by the organization for further study. He speculated as to how much stronger the race would have been if ten years earlier this opportunity had been provided for Kelly Miller, or if Du Bois's German studies had been financed by blacks. Since the suggestion was presented as a future possibility, no action was taken.[11]

Consideration of Article 8, which specifically forbade printing an author's degrees in academy publications, produced more heated debate than any other part of the constitution. John L. Love argued that degrees did not indicate scholarly ability, were often fraudulent or purchased, and should, therefore, be ignored. He believed the society could not be burdened with the task of attempting to discriminate between the good and the bad and "that gentlemen who have articles to contribute should be willing to have them published without . . . degrees appended." Du Bois was completely

10. Verbatim, 5–6; Proceedings, 10.
11. Verbatim, 8–9.

opposed, arguing, "I worked hard for my degree, and . . . propose to use it." This matter, in his opinion, was not a legitimate concern of the association. Charles C. Cook, whose remarks were more conciliatory, suggested the question was one of modesty, something which could not be legislated, and urged that the subject be dropped. He was joined by Lewis B. Moore who felt the "matter should be left to the member individually."[12]

At this point Crummell entered the discussion in an attempt to both mediate and clarify the issue as it related to the work in hand. As far as he was concerned

so cheap have become the titles among colored men during recent years, that I have a strong objection to them. I think it decidedly desirable, that an organization should be influential, and not dependent upon arbitrary arrangements. If Dr. Grimké should put his title on his works, I would be pleased to read them. If Mr. Du Bois should place a title on his works, I should be happy to peruse them. But, it seems to me, the less of this is for the better.

He then asked the group to make a decision on the issue. The first poll, done viva voce, was unclear. The standing vote, which followed, resulted in a tie. Since he was presiding officer, and had not voted, Crummell broke it, casting his vote against Du Bois's motion to remove Article 8. Then, in an affirmation of group unity, the sixteen men made the decision unanimous. After which, at Love's request, they struck out those parts of Article 8 permitting authors to use the names of their colleges in academy publications.[13]

Other amendments to the constitution were made with little or no controversy. The preamble was rewritten to bring it into accord with the amended Article 3; provision was made in Article 1 for an annual election of officers; December was selected as the time of the annual meeting mentioned in Article 6; the term "colored" was dropped from Article 5; and $5 was set as the admission fee, with the understanding that this included the first year's dues which, after admittance, were to be $2 per year. Several minor changes were made to improve the document's language, and emphasize that the association was not simply another black literary society, but a body committed to the support of "scientific" scholarship and research. Both of those concerns were expressed in the rewriting of the preamble and Articles 4 and 6. Finally, the constitution was read through and adopted

12. Verbatim, 7; Proceedings, 10–11.
13. Verbatim, 7; Proceedings, 10–11. Although eighteen men were present at various times during the organizational meeting, at the point this vote was taken, Kelly Miller was absent and Crummell presiding. Thus the eight to eight tie. This is the only vote on the constitution where it is possible to know the division figures.

with all amendments. This document, with minor changes, was to be the governing instrument of the society throughout its existence.[14]

With the constitutional work done, Levi J. Coppin, George N. Grisham, and Matthew Anderson were appointed a committee on nominations. The committee withdrew briefly and returned with the following recommendations: president, A. Crummell; first vice-president, W. E. B. Du Bois; second vice-president, J. A. Johnson; third vice-president, W. S. Scarborough; fourth vice-president, S. G. Atkins; corresponding secretary, J. W. Cromwell; recording secretary, L. B. Moore; and treasurer, F. J. Grimké. Though the constitution provided for an executive committe, the nominations committee saw no role for additional officers and recommended that the executive committee consist of the president, first vice-president, corresponding secretary, recording secretary, and treasurer.[15]

Crummell immediately declined nomination as president, citing his age as the major barrier, and urged the election of a younger man. John A. Johnson, first to respond, recalled the history of the society's formation, pointing out that Crummell was the "inspiration" and moving force behind it. The ANA, in his opinion, was the elderly scholar's "child." He begged him to change his decision, assuring him that everything would be done to lighten the work connected with the position. Since, Johnson continued, many of those in the academy had only joined because of Crummell, it would be impossible to elect anyone else president. Du Bois, who spoke next, called the presidency of the ANA a position of honor which should be used to demonstrate—as blacks too seldom did—their "reverence for age and . . . the performance of past duties." On those grounds, he also urged Crummell to accept the office. Francis J. Grimké and George N. Grisham both insisted that without the clergyman heading it, the work of the organization could not be carried on.[16] Though these comments were generated, in part, by personal affection and respect for Crummell, there were also strong practical reasons for them. His education, distinguished and lengthy career, the great respect his views commanded among educated blacks, and the many social and philanthropic contacts he maintained with whites in America and England promised to make his occupation of the presidency an important asset in garnering the necessary black and white support the ANA needed in order to survive and grow.

14. Verbatim, 5–8; Proceedings, 10–11.
15. Verbatim, 8–9; Proceedings, 11.
16. Verbatim, 9–10; Proceedings, 12.

After stating his feelings Grisham made a motion for Crummell's election "by acclamation." Passage was immediate and unanimous. In a brief response accepting the office, the seventy-eight-year-old minister reiterated his earlier reservations. He spoke of his decreasing vitality and a desire to rest until death came. It had been his hope that a younger man with "energy . . . enthusiasm . . . talent and spirit"—someone such as Du Bois, Scarborough, or Kelly Miller—would be elected president. With considerable honesty and bluntness he reminded them that men of his age possessed limited energy for a struggle that required great physical and intellectual vigor. "We have got to meet the minds of this country," he emphasized, "and it is only . . . scientific truth, in every department, that is going to do anything for us." With this issue settled, the rest of the committee's report was adopted, after which the meeting was adjourned for lunch.[17]

The first business of the afternoon session was a report from Albert P. Miller, Francis J. Grimké, and Kelly Miller. These three had been appointed by the Washington members in January to investigate the desirability of publishing a journal. In their report they noted "the growing scholarship of members of our race in America and our inability to give expression to the same." This situation, in the committee's judgment, made it "necessary" that the "academy . . . publish, as soon as it may be practicable, a Journal as an outlet of the best Negro thought in America." They, therefore, recommended the appointment of another committee "to take into consideration, the Publication of a Journal, or such matter, as may best promote the interest and end of this Academy movement among members of our race, who are in sympathy with this effort to broaden the Negro scholarship of the country." Although the report was adopted, Albert P. Miller (who had been chairman of the committee), Du Bois, Wright, and Hayson urged the group to move into this area slowly and with caution. Miller thought publication of a journal should not be attempted before the society had been in operation for a while. The other three urged the group not to make this decision until they had determined such questions as format, method of distribution, and costs. In spite of William H. Ferris' protest that such views were materialistic, and void of "that spirit which the Anglo-Saxon exhibits," A. P. Miller, Kelly Miller, F. J. Grimké, L. J. Coppin, and J. W. Cromwell were appointed a committee to consider further the advisability of publishing a journal. The men of the academy then listened to Albert P. Miller's paper,

17. Proceedings, 12.

"The Development of the Negro Intellect," and Kelly Miller's review of Frederick L. Hoffman's book, *Race Traits and Tendencies of the American Negro*. These two papers were discussed at length, after which they adjourned for dinner.[18]

The final session of the meeting was held that evening at 7:30 P.M. Du Bois's paper, which he entitled, "The Conservation of Races," was scheduled as the first item. However, because of his failure to arrive at the start of the meeting, the question of publications was reconsidered. The decision was made to publish the minutes of the organizational meeting, including Crummell's address, as the first number of the ANA transactions, and Kelly Miller's review as the first occasional paper. In both cases an inexpensive pamphlet was chosen as the form to be used. These actions satisfied members such as Cromwell and Crummell who wished the association to immediately begin "the dissemination of . . . truth and . . . vindication of the race," while the wishes of others, such as Du Bois, A. P. Miller, and Wright, who opposed publication of a journal until there had been careful preparation and research into costs, were also respected. The executive committee was charged with responsibility for this and any future publications, thus making it the organization's board of editors. Du Bois arrived while this business was being transacted and when it was completed delivered his address. After discussing it extensively, the group voted to print "The Conservation of Races" as its second occasional paper. Resolutions of thanks were then voted to the pastor and trustees of Lincoln Memorial Church, to the Washington ladies who served the ANA members lunch, and to William H. Crogman and Charles W. Mossell, both of whom had donated a copy of their most recent books to the society's Archives. Then the academy adjourned sine die.[19]

Considering the many ambitious programs outlined in its constitution and the financial resources they required, the ANA, with only thirty-six initial members, was a small organization. When the American Jewish Historical Society was established, it counted seventy founding members; in the case of the American Irish Historical Society there had been fifty. And, compared to some of the professional societies in which several of its members were

18. Committee report of A. P. Miller, F. J. Grimké, and K. Miller, n.d., in JWCG/M; Verbatim, 10–12; Proceedings, 12–13.

19. Verbatim, 17–19; Proceedings, 14–16. Crogman sent a copy of his *Talks for the Times* (Conn., 1896); and Mossell his *Toussaint L'Ouverture; or, Hayti's Struggle* (Lockport, N.Y., 1896).

active, the academy was literally a midget. In 1897 the American Society of Church History had 175 members, the American Philological Society 463, the American Historical Association 629, and the memberships of the American Academy of Political and Social Science and the National Educational Association ran into the thousands. All of these organizations, including the ethnic cultural societies, published annually, or more frequently, selected papers and addresses delivered at their meetings; and some maintained special research libraries. The academy's membership fees—$5 for a new member and $2 annually thereafter—were lower than any of the groups mentioned except the National Education Association, whose dues were the same. The others had annual fees ranging from $3 to $5 and several offered special memberships at higher rates.[20]

One of the most important things that took place at the ANA's organizational meeting was an attempt by the eighteen participants to develop a common perspective on the meaning and purpose of the black presence in America. The consciousness that educated and thoughtful members of the race needed to address themselves more precisely and aggressively to the task of rebutting racist attacks could only serve as a beginning point for justifying the association. In order to sustain itself, to say nothing of attempting the many tasks outlined in its constitution, the ANA needed an intellectual framework through which it could devise answers to questions concerning the racial identity of black Americans, their role in a predominantly white society, and their relationship to blacks in Africa and other parts of the world. The men who planned the meeting recognized how important it was for the organization to wrestle with these questions. No one was more aware of this than Crummell, whose opening address represented his response to this need. In part, the topics assigned to A. P. Miller and Du Bois also were intended to raise these questions for group consideration.

A. P. Miller's paper, "The Development of Negro Intellect," produced a

20. The ANA should have had thirty-seven members—nine original ones and twenty-nine who accepted invitations to join—but T. J. Minton, for reasons unknown, disassociated himself from the organization. Thirty-six is the number of founding members given by J. W. Cromwell in articles he wrote on the academy, one in 1897, and the other in 1913. See "The American Negro Academy," New York *Chronicle*, Book of Clippings, in JWCG/M; and "American Negro Academy," *African Times and Orient Review*, 243–44. On the other organizations see *Publications of the American Jewish Historical Society*, II (1894), iv, 137; *Journal of the American Irish Historical Society*, I (1898), 5, 13; *Papers of the American Society of Church History*, VII (1897), viii, 301–308; *Transactions of the American Philological Association*, XXVIII (1897), lxxxiii, lxxxiv, lxxxvii; *American Historical Association Handbook* (Baltimore, 1896), 7, 34; *Handbook of the American Academy of Political and Social Science* (Philadelphia, 1897), 7, 83; *Journal of the National Education Association*, XL (1897), 2, 1116.

fragmented and inconclusive discussion that was essentially a series of individual statements concerning the forces affecting the personalities, work, and careers of black intellectuals. It was Kelly Miller's opinion that conditions were excellent for the development and growth of a black intelligentsia because of the relative lack of prejudice on the part of whites in scholarly, literary, and artistic fields. William S. Scarborough agreed that opportunities for achievement existed, but insisted they were negated by the lack of the necessary financial resources for blacks to take advantage of them. In Du Bois's judgment sufficient resources had been made available for the development of "Negro intellect," but they were "dissipated" by being scattered among so many small, poor schools, none of which could "afford to do first class work." Put this money into one institution, he urged, and something significant can be done. William H. Ferris pointed to lack of commitment on the part of black students as the main problem. Walter B. Hayson believd blacks possessed unique abilities for achievement in the musical and literary fields, and that the growth of a black intelligentsia would result from the cultivation of these special aptitudes. John L. Love, who held similar views, interpreted Paul Lawrence Dunbar's success as a demonstration of how necessary it was for educated blacks to turn to their own race and history in order to discern the truth "within." George Grisham contended that the pressures which operated on blacks blocked the effective exercise of their abilities. In his opinion, educated blacks were caught in a cross fire between the conflicting demands of their personal need for fulfillment, their racial community, and white society. The entire situation was exacerbated by the fact that as members of a despised and powerless race any efforts they made at scholarly achievement went unsupported by both blacks and whites.[21]

Du Bois's address, "The Conservation of Races," was a seminal statement, the first in a series of influential arguments by twentieth-century black intellectuals in the United States and abroad, denoting the unique characteristics and qualities of blacks and arguing strenuously for the preservation and cultivation of black racial potential because of the special gifts it offered humanity. It was also the most important statement on the place and role of the academy to emerge from this meeting. Du Bois's definition of the concepts "race" and "intellectual" placed the organization in the context of a worldwide effort by blacks for self-realization, and presented it

---

21. Unfortunately, no copy, review, or summary of A. P. Miller's paper has survived. Verbatim, 14.

with a basic ideology for its work. He believed the idea of race was the dominant force in human history, and the key to all that had happened in the past. To him, a race, "the vastest and most ingenious invention for human progress," was "a family of human beings, generally of common blood and language, always of common history, traditions, and impulses, who are both voluntarily and involuntarily striving together for the accomplishment of certain more or less vividly conceived ideals of life." Each race possessed unique physical, psychological, and spiritual characteristics that were instruments through which it produced a special "message" and "ideal." Blacks, whose potentialities had been presaged in the achievements of Egyptian culture, were one of the great races still waiting to make their full contribution to civilization.[22]

Du Bois saw no way for the black to deliver his "message" unless the entire race was brought to a consciousness of its identity and abilities, a process requiring that blacks develop a sense of group solidarity and reject "absorption by white Americans." As he declared to his audience: "For the development of Negro genius, of Negro literature and art, of Negro spirit, only Negroes bound and welded together, Negroes inspired by one vast ideal, can work out in its fullness the great message we have for humanity." In Du Bois's opinion, the eight million blacks in the United States had been given a crucial opportunity to demonstrate, in the midst of a hostile white society, the unique and original cultural possibilities inherent in their race.

Anticipating objections that white hostility made it impossible for blacks to live up to their full capabilities, Du Bois dismissed race prejudice as a barrier to black development, describing it as simply an expression of the differences in "aims," "feelings," and "ideals" between the two groups. As real as these differences were, because blacks and whites shared certain cultural traits—the same language, religion, and legal system—the prospect of a "fatal collision" was reduced. And, if there was a "satisfactory adjustment of economic life," he believed there was no reason they could not coexist, each group pursuing its own racial ideal. However, at the same time Du Bois argued that white prejudice was a natural expression of valid differences, he admitted that its effect, together with the experience of slavery and the consequent economic weakness of his race, had been to create a situation in which blacks possessed "only one means of advance, our belief

22. W. E. B. Du Bois, *The Conservation of Races*, ANA Occasional Papers, no. 2 (1897), 7–10. In the address, Du Bois expressed the opinion that if Egyptian civilization "was not wholly Negro it was certainly very closely allied."

in our great destiny." As the initial step in seeking to fulfill that destiny he urged the establishment of strong black organizations, among them a Negro Academy or "intellectual clearinghouse."

The tasks Du Bois outlined for this "intellectual clearinghouse" were numerous and complex. Through its membership and activities it had to be the highest expression of black intellect and the chief "exponent of race ideals." It would be the responsibility of its members to bring into communication with each other those educated blacks "scattered in forgotten nooks and corners throughout the land," and provide them with a public voice. Du Bois challenged the ANA to become a national strategy center, determining "the broad lines of policy and action for the American Negro" in regard to issues such as political disfranchisement, school segregation, and discrimination in public accommodations. Who, he asked, was better equipped than they to conduct such essential research projects as the compilation of federal and state laws regarding blacks. He also saw it as part of their task to function as a moral agency, challenging any false and dishonest self-perceptions held by the race, and seeking ways to stem the rising incidence of disease, criminality, and sexual immorality among their people. In closing, Du Bois presented a seven-point summation of his address, offering it as the "Academy creed." [23]

At the conclusion of the paper there was enthusiastic and prolonged applause. However, in the discussion that followed several members questioned Du Bois's emphasis on preserving racial identity. William H. Ferris felt that the ablest blacks had to be recognized on terms that went beyond race, something that could not be achieved "by developing all that is Negro, but all that will be useful to civilization." Richard R. Wright wondered how the race could maintain its group identity when so many blacks were attempting to disperse themselves among whites. William S. Scarborough found it impossible to "conceive of two races . . . equal in every particular, living side by side, without intermingling." George N. Grisham argued that it was not racial characteristics that should be preserved, but the characteristics of the race's "best human specimens." To him it seemed ridiculous to urge a backward people to concentrate on preserving their racial identity when they were surrounded by a "great civilization." If you put a Negro "under the refining influence of the 19th Century," he affirmed, "he is no longer a Negro."

23. *Ibid.,* 10–15.

Other members disagreed sharply with these comments. Kelly Miller maintained that "Providence" had placed blacks in this country with a special end in view. Like the Jews they had to be faithful to their identity in order to make their unique contribution to mankind. Albert P. Miller told the group that his years as a missionary in Africa had convinced him that black advancement was dependent on American blacks making themselves equal to whites, and then returning to Africa. However, he believed none of this could be accomplished without the cultivation of "Negro manhood" and "race Pride." John L. Love declared himself amused to hear black intellectuals advocate "race destruction"—something he believed no comparable group of whites would ever do. In his opinion this was a clear demonstration of the need for "race enthusiasm." Alexander Crummell and Matthew Anderson both challenged the relevance of Scarborough's statement that two races could not coexist without intermingling. They insisted that no amount of intermingling could diffuse or destroy racial continuity because race was a divinely ordained category of human existence.[24]

Kelly Miller's critical review of Hoffman's *Race Traits and Tendencies of the American Negro* was different in focus and aim from the papers delivered by A. P. Miller and Du Bois, both of which had dealt with topics related to the purpose and goals of the new organization. Miller had been asked to present his review when three of the four men originally invited to address the meeting sent regrets. His paper, a persuasive and effective challenge to Hoffman's argument that Negroes were degenerate and on the verge of extinction, was intended to be a model for future efforts by the ANA to defend blacks.[25] The men of the academy expressed their belief in its effectiveness by voting to print it as their first occasional paper.

When the organizational meeting closed the evening of March 5, 1897, a great deal of work had been done. The ANA had been formally inaugurated, a constitution ratified, and a strong and impressive slate of officers elected. The papers presented and the discussion they precipitated had provided an opportunity for a group of concerned, educated blacks to have a dialogue with each other about the problems confronting their race, its future, and their role in its development. Two of those papers had been deemed such important and effective pieces that they were to be distributed as the acad-

24. Verbatim, 19–23.
25. Kelly Miller, *Review of Hoffman's Race Traits and Tendencies of the American Negro,* ANA Occasional Papers, no. 1 (1897).

emy's first publications. It was with a feeling of excitement and anticipation that the members awaited public response to their newly formed society and its first actions.

In the months that followed the organizational meeting, articles discussing the academy and its occasional papers appeared in a number of newspapers. The Philadelphia *Tribune* gave the new society extensive coverage, and the *Chronicle*, a New York paper edited by John E. Bruce, a founding member of the ANA, carried a lengthy article by John W. Cromwell giving the history, membership, and purpose of the new society. Brief notices also appeared in the *Reformer*, a journal in Richmond edited by John H. Smyth, another founding member of the ANA; the *Star of Zion*, the African Methodist Episcopal Zion Church's denominational paper; and the Indianapolis *Freeman*. William H. Crogman, one of the originators of the academy idea and a staunch supporter of its work, included a brief essay by Alexander Crummell, "The Prime Need of the Negro Race," in *Progress of a Race*, a book he coedited. The essay, with its stress on the necessity for an elite of college- and university-trained blacks, was, in many ways, a paraphrase of Crummell's inaugural address. There was a difference in stress, however. In the revised version, Crummell used his arguments to refute the idea that "industrialism" was "the solution of the Negro problem." The volume appeared in late 1897 and Crogman's editorial comment on the essay reflected his nervousness in the face of the growing intensity of the industrial versus higher education debate among blacks. Attempting to minimize the difference between the two points of view he made the following conciliatory statement: "There is probably no dissent from the . . . opinion of Dr. Crummell. Even the leaders in industrial education have repeatedly declared themselves in favor of the broadest culture possible. While there may be differences of opinion in the practical working, yet all are laboring diligently for the one great end—the elevation of the race." Especially gratifying to ANA members were the articles, editorials, and notices that appeared in two foreign newspapers, the *Advocate* of Kingston, Jamaica, and the British West African newspaper, the Lagos *Weekly Record*. While all of these were black or black-oriented publications, a few white newspapers also noticed the ANA's appearance.[26]

26. Cromwell, "The American Negro Academy," New York *Chronicle*, in Book of Clippings, and John Henry Smith to Cromwell, February 25, 1897, both in JWCG/M; *Star of Zion*, December 16, 1897, p. 4; Kletzing and Crogman (eds.), *Progress of a Race*, 361–67; Lagos *Weekly Record*, July 5, 1897. In his corresponding secretary's report to the first annual meeting

Fannie Barrier Williams, a black writer who discussed the ANA in the Chicago *Times-Herald*, perceived it as a quest by black intellectuals for a more conscious role in resolving issues confronting their people. She felt the membership was composed of genuine scholars, men with a reputation for "perfect sanity of purpose." If, she prophesied, they could carry out the work they proposed, it would constitute a real contribution to the "best thought" on black-white relations. In a short review of Miller's paper, the Washington *Times* discussed its challenges to Hoffman's study. Mildly positive, it recommended "the brochure . . . to anyone interested in the economic future of the South." The article, which also described the academy and mentioned Du Bois's paper, closed with the following positive comment: "The future development of the South depends in large measure on the way in which the race problem is settled, and it may as well be admitted that the educated negro is going to assist in its solution. These papers are interesting as giving his side of the case, which cannot very well be settled without his help." An even shorter article, announcing the formation of the academy, giving a list of its officers, and outlining its goals, appeared in the Washington *Post*. The Boston *Evening Transcipt* devoted an impressive amount of space to an analysis of Miller's paper, expressing agreement with practically all of his criticisms. The ANA, however, received only the briefest mention.[27]

Crummell, who visited England during the summer and fall of 1897, actively publicized the academy and its two occasional papers. In his letters to John W. Cromwell he told of his long talk about the society with Henry Mason Joseph, an American black living in London, and his attempts to draw attention to Occasional Paper No. 1. One of the public figures to whom he sent a copy was Sir Edward Russell, editor of the Liverpool *Daily*

---

of the ANA, Cromwell made the following observation: "It is worthy of remark that the colored press, with the exception of 'The Philadelphia Tribune' has taken but the scantiest notice of our Academy work" (Proceedings, 27–28). The *Star of Zion* article was a reprint from the Indianapolis *Freeman*. The article on the ANA that appeared in the *Advocate* is mentioned in John Edward Bruce to Cromwell, November 29, 1897, in JWCG/M. In a column written by Bruce, which appeared in the *Star of Zion*, he identified Dr. J. Robert Love as editor of the Jamaica *Advocate*. Love, who had written a book entitled *Romanism Is Not Christianity*, was described as "one of the blackest and most scholarly men in Jamaica." "He is," Bruce told his readers, "as proud of his beautiful black skin as a boy with his first pair of boots." (*Star of Zion*, December 16, 1897, p. 4).

27. Chicago *Times-Herald*, (undated clipping in J. W. Cromwell Scrapbook, in John Wesley Cromwell Papers, Moorland-Spingarn Research Center, Howard University, Washington, D.C.); Washington, D.C., *Times*, September 12, 1897, p. 17; Washington *Post*, March 6, 1897, p. 4; Boston *Evening Transcript*, November 5, 1897, p. 8.

Post and a former Liberal Member of Parliament. Russell later talked with Crummell about the "Academy and the 'Negro cause' in general."[28]

While in London Crummell also spoke to "three law students" about the organization. These men, black natives of British dependencies in the West Indies and Africa, were disturbed and angry about the brutal methods then being employed by London officials to bring the sub-Saharan Africans under their control. After Crummell returned to the United States, at least two of these men—H. Sylvester Williams of Trinidad, West Indies, and T. J. Thompson of Sierra Leone—were leaders in the formation of the "African Association of London." Composed of "educated and prosperous Africans," the group's goals were "to encourage a feeling of unity; to facilitate friendly intercourse among Africans in general; [and] to promote and protect the interests of all subjects claiming African descent." When news of the association reached Crummell he felt that his description of the ANA and its publications had provided part of the impetus for it. At his request, in December, 1897, the first annual meeting of the academy passed a motion hailing "with delight the organization of the Central British African Association in the city of London."[29]

It was, however, an article by T. Thomas Fortune in the New York *Sun*, a white newspaper, which created the widest interest in the academy. Fortune, who was the leading black journalist of the period, the editor of the New York *Age*, a widely circulated black weekly, and the foremost proponent of the term "Afro-American" as the appropriate designation for all blacks, attacked the society for its use of the word "Negro," a term he considered applicable only to persons of unmixed African descent. In a direct reference to Du Bois's paper, "The Conservation of Races," Fortune also rejected as totally impractical the idea that global Pan-Africanism was essential "for

28. Crummell to Cromwell, June 15, October 5, 1897, in Crummell Papers.

29. Crummell to John E. Bruce, January 21, 1898, in Bruce Papers. In one of his newspaper columns, J. E. Bruce suggested a different cause and effect relationship between the ANA and the African Association of London. It was his opinion that "the British African Association received its inspiration and encouragement . . . from perusing the able and comprehensive description of the work and scope of the National Negro Academy from the pen of Prof. John W. Cromwell of Washington, D.C., . . . published in a New York paper, copies of which found their way to various parts of Europe and Africa." Bruce was referring to the article on the academy written by Cromwell, which appeared in the *Chronicle*, a paper he edited. See Clarence G. Contee, "The Emergence of Du Bois as an African Nationalist," *Journal of Negro History*, LIV (January, 1969), 48–61, for a brief history of the African Association and a description of H. Sylvester William's work in bringing about the London Pan-African Congress in 1900; also "The African Association," Lagos *Weekly Record*, undated clipping in Book of Clippings, in JWCG/M; Proceedings, 35 (the Proceedings do not state whether or not a copy of the resolution was sent to the "Central British African Association").

the development of Negro genius, of Negro literature and art, of Negro spirit." This "sounds well enough," the editor of the *Age* commented, "but is absolutely unattainable in a country where Anglo-Saxon ideals of literature and art and everything else predominate and will to the end of the chapter, absorbing to themselves all that makes for national beauty and strength." [30]

Moreover, Fortune charged that the new organization, by stressing "Negro" identity, would accentuate the color line that existed in the black community and further alienate from each other the "black" and "mulatto" members of the race. In the article, the journalist traced the tensions between these two groups back to experiences in slavery when, he contended, lighter-skinned Negroes had had more contact with and received better treatment from whites, thus making them more prepared for freedom. Fortune, himself a light-skinned man with Caucasian features, found it strange that dark-skinned blacks should be disturbed by their light-skinned brothers' continuing to reap the benefits of earlier treatment and occupying many of the leading political and social roles in the black community. In his judgment, this more favored group had always functioned as a buffer, reducing the impact of white prejudice on the mass of blacks and interpreting the needs of the entire race to whites. In Fortune's opinion the ANA would only exacerbate intra-group tensions, creating a situation similar to that prevailing in parts of the West Indies where blacks divided themselves into factions along complexional lines. [31]

To some academy members, the most enraging part of the article was Fortune's attempt to buttress these last assertions by pointing to complexional differences between them and their wives. "An amusing phase of the matter," he wrote, "is that Mr. Du Bois is not black at all, but brown and did not take a black woman to wife. Dr. Crummell and Mr. Cromwell are both unmixed in blood, but both of them married mulatto women; and it is very generally the case that those black men who clamor most loudly and persistently for the purity of the Negro blood have taken to themselves mulatto wives." Fortune's article was republished in *Liberia*, the magazine of the American Colonization Society, in the Lagos [Nigeria] *Weekly Record*, and in numerous black-American newspapers. [32]

---

30. T. Thomas Fortune, New York *Sun*, May 16, 1897, sec. 3, p. 3.
31. *Ibid.* See also Thornbrough, *T. Thomas Fortune*, 131–34.
32. Fortune, New York *Sun*, May 16, 1897, sec. 3, p. 3; *Liberia*, Bulletin no. 11 (November, 1897), 60–65; Lagos *Weekly Record*, July 24, 1897, p. 6; J. E. Bruce to J. W. Cromwell, November 29, 1897, in JWCG/M.

Shortly after Fortune's article appeared, John W. Cromwell, in his capacity as corresponding secretary of the ANA, sent a letter of rebuttal to the editor of the *Sun*. In it Cromwell categorically denied that the "work of this organization will tend to separate the colored people of African descent into two hostile parties." There was, he insisted, nothing "either in the constitution and avowed purpose of the organization or in its personnel" to support Fortune's allegations. Of the group's eight officers "only two would be classed as Negroes of pure lineage, while three are mulattoes"; and, he pointed out, the same division existed among the members. Referring to Du Bois's paper, "The Conservation of Races," which Fortune had judged one of the strongest proofs of the academy's pro-Negro antimulatto sentiments, Cromwell observed that: "During the discussion on the . . . paper . . . two of the blackest members, both educators, contended that it was very difficult, if not impossible, to maintain a race identity in this land, while the most eloquent advocates of race ideals were men in whose blood there was not only visible admixture but a predominance toward the Aryan race." Cromwell's reply was calm, matter of fact, and devoid of any personal references to Fortune.[33]

Privately both Cromwell and Crummell were enraged. In an earlier draft of his letter Cromwell had described Fortune's article as "ludicrous and absolutely unreliable," containing "garbled" quotations and "unfair inferences." Fortune he referred to as an "opportunist" who thought he was white. However, in the revised version which was mailed to the *Sun*, Fortune's charges were repudiated in a way that presented Cromwell and the ANA as being above engaging in personal attacks. Crummell thought the article a "contemptible, jesuitical and lying" piece of journalism. What upset him most were the references Fortune had made to his and other members' "personal and domestic affairs," actions which he considered clear signs of Fortune's "gross mendacity." In a letter to John E. Bruce, Crummell rejected the assertion that there was a connection between a man's "race devotedness" and his wife's racial background. "But," he added, "my wife is not a mulatto and the fellow knows she is not."[34]

Fortune's article and Cromwell's letter precipitated a brief debate in a few black newspapers about the utility and appropriateness of the academy, but usually discussion centered around the relations between so-called pure

33. J. W. Cromwell, Letter to the Editor, New York *Sun*, May 24, 1897.
34. J. W. Cromwell, handwritten draft of a reply to T. T. Fortune, n.d., in JWCG/M; Crummell to Bruce, December 15, 1897, in Bruce Papers.

blacks and their mixed brothers. John E. Bruce, in a rambling, disjointed reply to Fortune, which appeared in the *Star of Zion*, charged that mulattoes had created the color line in the black community by their overbearing, superior, and prejudiced attitude toward those with darker skin. In West Africa, the Lagos *Weekly Record* printed an editorial which described the academy as an expression of the rising culture of black Americans and their new willingness to "halt . . . amalgamation," demand recognition of their "manhood," and protest mistreatment. Fortune's arguments were rejected by the editorialist as the typical shortsighted objections raised by the "lighter colored" who were unable to see that the most important issue facing all African and African-derived people was the future development of blacks. West Africans took so intense an interest in this debate that in subsequent issues of the *Record* Du Bois's occasional paper was serialized and Fortune's article reprinted in full.[35]

All in all, the academy received small attention from the press, scarcely any from white papers and, with a few exceptions, only the most cursory notice from black publications. Besides the Washington *Post*, no major paper in either racial community discussed the ANA and none speculated editorially as to its future. Sadly enough, this was also true of the two black newspapers in Washington. It is quite possible that if Fortune had not attacked the organization it would have gotten even less publicity. The members were extremely disappointed, but remained convinced that it was a significant achievement to have established the organization and published two papers, which, as Crummell observed in December, 1897, had been "noticed in Europe, Africa [and the] West Indies, as well as in . . . America."[36]

35. J. E. Bruce to J. W. Cromwell, November 29, 1897, in JWCG/M; J. E. Bruce, *Star of Zion*, December 2, 1897; Lagos *Weekly Record*, July 3, 17, 24, 31, 1897.
36. Crummell to J. E. Bruce, December 9, 1897, in Bruce Papers.

III *Nurturing the Seed*

During the eighteen months that Alexander Crummell was president of the ANA, he was an active and dominating figure in the fledgling organization. Except for a short period during the summer and early autumn of 1897, when he was traveling in England, Crummell presided at every meeting of the ANA's executive committee. At these sessions—usually convened in his home—his was a strong voice (at times the strongest) in shaping this body's decisions. It was not that Crummell was domineering or overbearing; his fellow officers, men of equally strong opinions who did not hesitate to make themselves heard, would not have tolerated such behavior, even from him. Rather, it resulted from their conviction that in numerous areas his judgment was not only authoritative but sound as well. It was this feeling that motivated a competent and decisive man such as ANA corresponding secretary John W. Cromwell to write to Crummell in England, asking his suggestion for topics to be considered at the next annual meeting, and sharing his anxiety at the members' slowness in forwarding their dues.[1]

Crummell actively and enthusiastically publicized the organization among his friends and acquaintances. Mention has already been made of his conversation with Sir Edward Russell, editor of the Liverpool *Daily Post*. In the summer of 1897, probably stimulated by similar exchanges with one or two whites in New York, an article on the ANA appeared in the *Mercantile and Financial Times*. Whenever Crummell came in contact with

---

1. Crummell's attendance at ANA executive committee meetings and the frequency of their assembling in his home is documented in the ANA Proceedings, March, 1897, to June 18, 1898, 17–44; see also Crummell to Cromwell, October 5, 1897, in Crummell Papers.

blacks who struck him as being both intelligent and concerned about the well-being of their race he told them of the academy. While in England this had been one of the themes in his conversations with the American expatriate Henry Mason Joseph, from whom he obtained the promise of an article for the hoped-for Annual, with Paul Laurence Dunbar, who promised to contribute a poem; and with the three law students he met in London. He was responsible for bringing James Theodore Holly, an Anglican bishop and head of his church's work in Haiti, into a relationship with the ANA as a corresponding member. Stopping in New York during the summer of 1898, the "conspicious talent" of Maritcha B. Lyons, a public school teacher, caused him to invite her "to write a paper for our annual meeting." Communicating his action to Cromwell a few days later, he asked, self-consciously, "Did I take too great a liberty?" The question reflected Crummell's nervous anticipation of possible negative reactions from some members of the all-male ANA. No second thoughts were experienced, however, after urging his old friend John E. Bruce, who lived in Albany, New York, to get together "a strong paper as a contribution" and spend part of his Christmas holiday attending the ANA annual meeting.[2]

The author of three books and numerous sermons, articles, and addresses, Crummell was committed to the academy's establishing itself as a black publishing center. With this end in mind, he and the executive committee labored to create a structure, secure content, and obtain financial backing for an annual or quarterly publication that would contain "the very best original articles, stories, and poems, illustrative of the scholarly and literary attainments of the race." As early as June, 1897, when their paths crossed in England, Crummell had suggested to Dunbar that upon returning to the United States, he make Washington his home and become editor of a proposed "monthly magazine . . . for purely Negro literature." Following this conversation, in a lengthy letter to John W. Cromwell, Crummell outlined the steps by which such an enterprise could be organized and sup-

2. William Shennessy to Cromwell, July 21, 1897, in JWCG/M. In this letter Shennessy speaks of "the enclosed . . . typewriter proof of an article on the Academy which we are about to print in an early issue of this paper." No copies of the *Mercantile and Financial Times* for 1897 have survived. Joseph and Dunbar are mentioned in Crummell to Cromwell, June 15, 1897, the meeting with three law students in Crummell to Bruce, January 21, 1898, both in Crummell Papers. At Crummell's suggestion, Holly was elected a corresponding member at the first annual meeting, December 28–29, 1897. See Proceedings, 35. Maritcha B. Lyons is mentioned in Crummell to Cromwell, August 5, 1898, the invitation to Bruce in Crummell to Bruce, December 9, 1897, both in Crummell Papers.

ported. In February, 1898, "under the suggestion and direction" of the president, the executive committee distributed among the members an appeal for an endowment to finance a periodical.[3]

Crummell believed in the importance of the American Negro Academy, and expressed it in numerous ways. When Cromwell shared with him a concern over the "tardiness of incoming fees," the cleric, in an answer shaped by long experience as an organizer in the black community, replied that he was not surprised. "For some time," he pointed out, "this will be a difficulty and hindrance to our work. We have as yet no wide stable basis of race feeling to work upon: it has got to be created." The first president of the academy saw the creation of "race feeling" as one of the society's most necessary tasks. It was his firm belief that confronting his people's detractors—whatever their complexion—with the undeniable fact of black intellectual ability would help to do this. For this reason, he strongly encouraged the association to distribute regularly its occasional papers to schools, libraries, "representative educators and men in our [black] professional life"; and it was with pleasure that he saw the practice initiated during his tenure as president. Crummell's hope that the academy would be a force in creating race feeling and his belief that its activities demonstrated black intellectual ability were reflected in a note he sent to John E. Bruce describing the December, 1897, meeting. After assuring Bruce that "our meeting was a notable affair," Crummell indicated what he considered one of the most important ways in which the ANA was demolishing obstacles that blocked achievement of its goals. "It happened," he gleefully told his friend, "that every speaker was a Negro, pure and unadulterated. There was no discrimination in the appointments. Some three or four eminent mixed men were appointed and at the last could not come. So you see that—'it happened'."[4]

Crummell's color consciousness, like that of many other dark-skinned blacks, was, in part, related to a persistent view, articulated by some northern whites in the years before the Civil War, that blacks with Caucasian blood were not only the fortunate possessors of superior physical features,

3. Executive committee discussions of an annual or quarterly publication while Crummell was president appear in the Proceedings, 17, 18, 19, 20, 25, 26, 39, 40, 41. See also J. W. Cromwell, "The American Negro Academy," New York *Chronicle*, September 27, 1897, in Book of Clippings, in JWCG/M; Crummell to Cromwell, June 15, 1897, in Crummell Papers; "Secretary's Report," second annual meeting, Proceedings, 59–60; ANA appeal for endowment fund, n.d., in Bruce Papers.

4. Crummell to Cromwell, October 5, 1897, Crummell to Bruce, January 21, 1898, both in Crummell Papers; "Secretary's Report," first annual meeting, Proceedings, 27.

but were more intelligent, spirited, and rebellious than those who were dark skinned and unmixed. His antipathy to such views reinforced his commitment to the ANA's goal of publicizing the achievements of black intellectuals, especially those whom he believed to be "pure Negroes." Although he did not consider himself hostile to blacks of mixed ancestry per se, Crummell's comment to Bruce, as well as similar statements to other friends and associates, suggests that this lifelong foe of white racist attitudes had views on mixed and lighter-skinned blacks that reflected his entrapment in an equally pernicious form of prejudice—complexional racism.[5]

During the eighteen months he headed the ANA, Crummell's public opposition to the widely held view expressed by Booker T. Washington, that industrial education was the complete solution to the economic and moral problems of blacks, became more intense. In an essay published in late 1897, he affirmed the necessity of continued efforts to increase the number of college- and university-trained blacks, and argued that the race's development was dependent on them. In his letters to his friend, George Frazier Miller, a black Episcopal priest in Brooklyn, New York, he expressed himself even more frankly, identifying the supporters of industrial education as whites hostile to black "brain" and "culture," and their self-serving black allies. He had no doubt of the two groups' willingness to sacrifice his race's welfare to their own ends. That Crummell perceived Booker T. Washington as one of the most important and harmful of these black "opportunists" is suggested by a comment he made to John W. Cromwell in one of his letters from England. "Yesterday," he confided to Cromwell, "I was talking with a noted and somewhat famous English clergyman. He told me he had visited the states several times. . . . He remarked, you have a tremendous fight before you, but one great difficulty in your way is the 'white man's nigger.' Some of your own men will betray and sell you. There is that Booker Washington who constantly betrays your cause to please the South!!!" In his last address to the academy in December, 1897, Crummell attacked the racism and "cheapness" masked by white support of industrial education, interpreting it as a sign "that even now, late in the 19th century, in this land of

5. It is interesting that in the postwar years the more dominant and popular view among whites (and one buttressed by Darwinist thinking) was that products of interracial matings or miscegenation were sterile, weak, and even more prone to extinction than pure blacks. By the 1890s the mulattoes were being depicted by some whites as the most dangerous kind of black, because of their supposed proclivity for rape and crime. See Frederickson, *The Black Image in the White Mind* for discussion of both theories, especially 117–18, 121, 161–62, 163n, 234–35, 277–78.

learning and science the creed is—'Thus far and no farther,' i.e., for the American black man." [6]

Crummell's death on September 10, 1898, came as a blow to the members of the new organization he had done so much to bring into being. Both as a person and as a symbol they felt dependent on him. His loss, at a time when practical procedures for carrying out the society's various programs were still being developed, when the society's officers were still learning how to work effectively with each other, and when a fund-raising campaign was in progress, made the members even more conscious of the immensity and difficulty of the work they had set out to do. No one expressed the feelings of his fellow academy members, and especially those who were officers, better than John W. Cromwell, who included the following reflection in his report to the second annual meeting: "Ripe though he [Crummell] was in years the Academy was the infant who still needed the parental care and affection of its progenitor. That those who have succeeded to the trust and responsibility of managing its interests have been perplexed and embarrassed need not be questioned." [7]

During the approximately four months between Crummell's death and the election of a new president in December, 1898, the executive committee worked diligently to keep the organization functioning. Monthly meetings were held in which plans for the coming annual meeting of members were completed, and applications for membership processed. At the first executive committee meeting after Crummell's death a memorial resolution was passed, copies of which were sent to the Crummell family, read at the funeral in New York City (to which three ANA representatives were sent), and incorporated into several of the numerous memorial services held in Washington. It was also decided that one of the sessions of the 1898 annual meeting would be a memorial to Crummell. The deceased clergyman's friend, James T. Holly, Anglican bishop of Haiti, was invited to give the eulogy. [8]

AME minister John Albert Johnson, second vice-president of the ANA

6. Alexander Crummell, "The Prime Need of the Negro Race," in Kletzing and Crogman (eds.), *Progress of a Race*, 361–67; Crummell to Miller, July 20, 28, 1898, Crummell to Cromwell, October 5, 1897, in Crummell Papers; Alexander Crummell, "The Attitude of the American Mind toward the Negro Intellect," ANA Occasional Papers, no. 3 (1898), 13.

7. Proceedings, 60.

8. *Ibid.*, 45–52. The role of the academy and various members of the society in Crummell's funeral and other memorial services held in his honor can be traced in articles appearing in Washington's two black newspapers, the *Colored American* and the Washington *Bee*, from September 17, to November 5, 1898.

and the society's highest ranking officer resident in Washington, presided at executive committee meetings, thus solving the immediate question of leadership succession. However, in deference to the nonresident first vice-president, W. E. B. Du Bois, since the autumn of 1897 professor of economics and history at Atlanta University, Johnson was referred to as the acting first vice-president. At its meeting on October 7, 1898, the executive committee directed John W. Cromwell, the corresponding secretary, to advise Du Bois "as to the duties incumbent on him in connection with the annual meeting." Accordingly, a letter was sent asking the first vice-president to preside at the annual meeting, give the customary presidential address, and to send to the executive committee any suggestions he might have regarding the meeting. Cromwell also urged, perhaps on his own initiative, that Du Bois present some of the findings from his current research on black economic life.

In his reply Du Bois said he would be unable to attend the December meeting because the Atlanta University schedule gave him no Christmas vacation. He would, however, send "a series of economic tracts as per recommendation." He made the following suggestions to the executive committee: include on the program a sketch and "estimate" of Crummell's life "by someone familiar with him" and publish it; schedule a summer meeting, which he could attend, "where we could, if we wished spend a month together and talk and plan"; ask someone else to give the presidential address. On the last suggestion he was flexible, and promised, if they thought it best, to "send one in to be read." The committee followed up on his first proposal by the Holly invitation, tabled the second, and voted formally to invite him to give the "annual presidential address." True to his promise Du Bois mailed the address, "The Wings of Atalanta," which was read for him by John W. Cromwell.[9]

Despite his absence, Du Bois was elected president of the ANA "by acclamation" at the December, 1898, annual meeting. Kelly Miller made the nomination and Francis J. Grimké seconded it. In early November, a brief notice had appeared in the Washington *Colored American* informing those who did not know that "J. W. Cromwell, the well-known educator and historian," had been in charge of the organization since Crummell's death.

9. Proceedings, 45–52; Du Bois to Cromwell, November 5, 1898, in JWCG/M. "The Wings of Atalanta" appears as Chapter V in W. E. B. Du Bois, *Souls of Black Folk* (Chicago, 1903).

"He is likely," the notice concluded, "to be elected president at the December meeting." Whether Cromwell desired or sought the office is not known. Given his closeness to Crummell and his devotion to the cause of the academy, it would not have been surprising. It is interesting that when "a committee of three on nominations of officers was asked for" Kelly Miller made a motion that eliminated this procedure in favor of nominations from the floor. Perhaps it was not a coincidence that Miller also offered the one and only name considered for the highest office. Whatever Cromwell's ambitions may have been, those academy members attending the meeting wanted a president who, like Crummell, was known and respected in both the black and white communities as well as the possessor of a distinguished educational background and scholarly credentials. Du Bois's striking address at the organizational meeting in March, 1897, plus his Harvard degrees and the scholarly work he had done on the African slave trade and the black community of Philadelphia, made him the natural choice. With the exception of some shifting of positions among the various vice-presidents, all of the other officers were reelected.[10]

Du Bois was neither a strong nor an effective president of the ANA. The years he held the office (1898–1903) were among the busiest and most creative of his long career as an intellectual and public figure. The many demands on his time, combined with the fact of his residence in Atlanta—far removed from the executive committee (all of whose members lived in Washington)—made it almost impossible for him to give the academy much of a place amongst his myriad activities. During these years Du Bois taught full time, engaged in research on the economic status of southern black farmers, directed the annual Atlanta University Conference on Negro Problems, and edited for publication several of the conference's reports. He was a constant contributor to numerous national publications, among them the *AME Church Review, Outlook, Atlantic Monthly, Independent,* and the

10. Proceedings, 53; Washington *Colored American*, November 5, 1898, p. 8. Du Bois held an A.B. (1888) from Fisk University, as well as an A.B. cum laude (1890), A.M. (1891), and Ph.D. (1895) from Harvard. In 1891 he had been the first black American to deliver a paper before the American Historical Association. The address, "The Enforcement of the Slave Trade Laws," was based on research for his dissertation, which was published in 1896 under the title, *The Suppression of the African Slave Trade to the United States of America, 1638–1870.* From 1892 to 1894, Du Bois was a student in Germany, where most of his time was spent at the University of Berlin. After returning to America, he taught for two years at Wilberforce University, leaving that institution to conduct a study of the Philadelphia black ghetto for the University of Pennsylvania. In the fall of 1897, he joined the Atlanta University faculty. Two years later his Philadelphia research was published as *The Philadelphia Negro* (Boston, 1899).

New York Times Magazine. In April, 1903, the last year he headed the society, a collection of his writings appeared under the title, *Souls of Black Folk.*

Between 1898 and 1901, Du Bois attempted to carry out his obligations to the ANA with some regularity. He corresponded with Cromwell three times in 1899 suggesting persons to be invited to join the academy and giving his estimate of names offered by others. In one of these letters he also listed prominent whites he thought should receive academy publications. When a business trip carried him through Washington, he arranged beforehand to meet with the executive committee. In letters to Cromwell, who remained corresponding secretary during the years he was president, Du Bois periodically requested information on the status of ANA publications, finances, and programs, offering in return advice and help. At his urging the words, "Alexander Crummell, Founder," were placed on all ANA stationery. In 1901, when Du Bois was given the responsibility of assembling the Negro section of the Paris Exposition, he was able to promote the work of the academy by including in the exhibit the academy's publications, biographical sketches of Alexander Crummell, and a list of ANA members.[11]

After 1901, however, the demands of Du Bois's other activities seemed to leave him even less time for the ANA. As early as March, 1900, after he had taken three months to appoint a working committee, Du Bois began or concluded almost all of his letters to Cromwell with an apology or an excuse. Either an anticipated or recently ended "absence from home had prevented an earlier reply," or the press of work made a request impossible. The most glaring sign of Du Bois's difficulties with his office (and the one probably most offensive to ANA members) was his irregular attendance at their annual meetings, coupled with the failure to forward a presidential address when he was unable to be present. To this group of equally hard-working and overburdened men struggling to perpetuate a black learned society, the maintenance of form was almost as important as attendance. Of the five annual meetings that occurred during his years as president, Du Bois attended and addressed two, in the latter case coming in barely under the wire, since he arrived during the last session. In 1899, 1902, and 1903 he failed to appear or mail an address, sending instead a telegram apologizing for his ab-

11. Du Bois to Cromwell, February 29, March 25, November 17, December 9, 1899, November, 1900, June 7, 1901, n.d. [late summer, 1901?], October 11, 1902, in JWCG/M. For Du Bois's involvement in the Paris Exposition see Herbert Aptheker (ed.), *The Correspondence of W. E. B. Du Bois* (2 vols.; Amherst, 1973), I, 45n.

sence. No attempt was ever made to remove him from office (Du Bois was always reelected unanimously), but in 1902 the members assembled for the annual meeting expressed their irritation by voting "that the annual address be delivered by the ranking vice-president in the absence of the President." [12]

In a letter written to Cromwell in late fall of 1903, Du Bois opened the way to a resolution of his and the organization's dilemma. "I had hoped," he informed the corresponding secretary,

to be with the Academy this year, but I cannot. I think we have both too many duties for our offices and I particularly am too far from Washington to do my work properly. I am going to decline, therefore, any candidacy for reelection although of course I shall be eager to do all I can in the ranks. We need a president, resident in Washington, a secretary with a considerable amount of time at his disposal and an enlarged membership.

Du Bois also communicated this decision to the ANA membership in a telegram sent to the seventh annual meeting on December 28, 1903: "Greeting to the Academy: Recommend entire change of officers. Refuse reelection absolutely. Urge united effort for future success. Movement must not fail." [13]

Clearly, in Du Bois's opinion, he was not the only officer who needed to resign. His advice to Cromwell that he give up the office of corresponding secretary, and his recommendation to the members of the ANA that they elect a completely new slate of officers was direct to the point of bluntness. Although Du Bois made it clear in his letter to Cromwell that he believed him to be too busy to be an effective corresponding secretary, it is unclear why, by December, 1903, he had decided an "entire change of officers" would be an improvement. Who did he have in mind as replacements for Kelly Miller, John A. Johnson, William H. Crogman, Matthew Anderson, George M. Lightfoot, Francis J. Grimké, Walter B. Hayson, John L. Love, and Cromwell? And why was he unwilling to participate personally in the selection of a more able team of officers? Because there is no evidence to answer either of these questions, one is forced to speculate. Nothing has survived in Du Bois's papers, in those of other ANA members, or in the academy records to indicate that he had any specific people in mind whom he wished to see running the society. As for the second question, his telegram seems to have been the last of a series of signs that although he still considered the ANA and its work important, the society had ceased to be an

12. Du Bois to Cromwell, March 5, 1900, n.d. [late summer, 1901?], October 11, 1902, October 25, 1903, in JWCG/M. Proceedings, 71, 74, 83, 85, 94, 107, 108, 112.
13. Du Bois to Cromwell, October 23, 1903, in JWCG/M; Proceedings, 112.

activity in which he wished to invest a large amount of time and interest. There is no doubt that Cromwell and his fellow officers were involved in too many activities to give the academy the attention it needed—they themselves would have admitted it—but unless there were suitable replacements for them, their withdrawal from positions of leadership would have meant the dissolution of the association. Because of these realities, the men attending the seventh annual meeting probably found Du Bois's advice both gratuitous and irresponsible. And, since the other officers of the academy had been more faithful than the president in carrying out their responsibilities, it is hard not to wonder if he was questioning the effectiveness of others because of the poor job he had done.

In the academy's constitution the executive committee was described as a body "of five persons who shall perform the usual duties." Since this description was essentially an exercise in nondefinition, the emergence of the executive committee as one of the association's two most important instruments of governance (the other was the annual meeting), implied that even though no guidelines were given, the founders had a fairly clear idea of what they wanted it to do. At the organizational meeting, instead of selecting five additional people, the committee on nominations recommended that the executive committee consist of the president, first vice-president, corresponding secretary, recording secretary, and treasurer. This recommendation, which was accepted, created an executive committee whose only non-Washington, D.C., member was W. E. B. Du Bois, the first vice-president. Because it was understood that Washington would be the headquarters of the society, this was a conscious decision. The organizational meeting also designated the executive committee as the association's board of editors, and charged it with the responsibility for the academy's publications. This action initiated a practice continued throughout the society's existence. Whenever a decision was made, the executive committee was responsible for its implementation.[14]

Although the first committee on nominations recommended that the executive committee be composed of the officers of the academy, membership on that committee did not inhere in the office that one held. Consequently, the annual meeting elected the executive committee, and usually elected to it those officers resident in Washington. Thus, Crummell was elected a member, and served as presiding officer until his death. Francis J. Grimké

14. Articles 1 and 6, ANA Constitution (1897), 2, 3, in JWCG/M.

and John W. Cromwell were also elected to it, and from 1898 to 1903, they were regularly reelected while holding the offices of treasurer and corresponding secretary, respectively. From Crummell's death to the second annual meeting in December, 1898, John Albert Johnson, second vice-president, presided at executive committee meetings. After that year the committee elected its own chairman. During Du Bois's presidency, because he lived in Atlanta, the head of the ANA did not regularly attend executive committee meetings. Du Bois was present, however, and may have presided, at special "call meetings" held when he was visiting Washington or passing through. Under Crummell the executive committee quickly developed into the organization's administrative staff and an advisory council to the annual meeting. It continued to carry out these functions during the years Du Bois was president.[15]

With the exception of John W. Cromwell, who as corresponding secretary received the munificent sum of $25 per year, the executive committee was an unsalaried group of volunteers. All of them were engaged in demanding careers, many with other, equally exacting, civic, religious and social commitments.[16] Given their busy lives the amount of work done by these men was impressive. In addition to editing the occasional papers and arranging for their publication, advertisement, and sale, they developed a format and administrative structure for the proposed ANA periodical and conducted two fund-raising campaigns to finance it. As the responsible body between annual meetings, they allocated Cromwell's salary, authorized the payment of academy bills, and admonished members who were remiss in fulfilling their obligations. It was their duty to plan the annual meeting, including such details as selection of speakers, program arrangement, advertisements, meals, and a meeting place. The executive committee also kept the members in communication with each other and transmitted the organization's work to outsiders. They did the first by printing and distributing

15. Proceedings, 30, 53, 74, 86, 95, 108–109, 113. In 1903 the five members elected to the executive committee included Francis J. Grimké, but not J. W. Cromwell. The Proceedings, however, referred to Cromwell as a member ex officio (113). Probably, the participation of the corresponding secretary had quickly come to be considered essential and at some point prior to the 1903 annual meeting the holder of this office was made an ex officio member. For mention of John Albert Johnson as presiding officer of the executive committee, see Proceedings, 45. See also Du Bois to Cromwell, March 25, 1899, in JWCG/M.

16. Financial report of the corresponding secretary to first annual meeting, December 27, 1897, Proceedings, 29. After December 30, 1901, Cromwell's salary was ten dollars per year, "with two dollars and a half in addition for every occasional paper issued" (Proceedings, 97). For a discussion of civil, professional, religious, and social involvements of the members of the ANA, see Chapter IX.

the occasional papers, the constitution, and the transactions (minutes) of the annual meetings, plus any other information deemed essential; the second by disseminating the various ANA publications, meeting announcements, and statements to black and white scholars, philanthropists, newspapers, educational institutions, and anyone else interested in its work.

In the area of general administration the executive committee was responsible for carrying out the decisions of the annual meetings; the distribution and tallying of ballots in membership elections; the recommendation of distinguished foreign blacks for election as corresponding members; and responding to general inquiries about the organization. The competent management of these and many other tasks thrust the executive committee into still another role—as the recommender of policy. The impetus for this came from two sources: the committee itself, which found it necessary to recommend specific actions to the annual meetings, and from the annual meetings, which, due to the committee's special role and experience, referred numerous matters to it for consideration. Because policy questions were so frequently considered, the committee developed a special procedure for handling them. Usually a subcommittee drawn exclusively from the membership of the executive committee was appointed to study an issue and bring in a report. After approval by the full committee a recommendation was presented to the next annual meeting. This practice meant that a tiny group of Washington, D.C., members dominated the society's decision-making process.

Crummell's death and the election of Du Bois as his successor led to the transformation of the executive committee from the president's cabinet and staff into the executive body of the organization. Du Bois's written communications with the corresponding secretary, while he was president, were essentially a series of letters expressing his approval of executive committee decisions. His inability, perhaps at times, his unwillingness, to involve himself deeply with the ANA made him marginal to its decision-making processes. The result was a tacit assumption by the Washington-based executive committee of exclusive responsibility for planning and directing the work of the academy between annual meetings, a situation very different from that which had prevailed under Crummell. This shift also resulted in John W. Cromwell's emergence as the most dominant figure in the academy during Du Bois's presidency.

A busy man with multiple interests, Cromwell was a teacher in the Washington public school system and editor of the Washington *Record*. He was also an amateur historian and an avid collector of books and art related to the black experience. Among his many activities, however, his commitment to the academy came closest to being total. A tireless concern for the development of the ANA and the efficient handling of his post as corresponding secretary quickly made him a key figure in the organization. Devoted to Crummell, both as a personal friend and a race leader of integrity and insight, Cromwell worked closely with the minister and, after Crummell's death, strove to keep the society functioning, as well as faithful to its founder's goals.

Cromwell's office entailed an immense number of duties that were constantly being amplified, primarily as a result of his willingness always to do more. He handled the details regarding all materials printed and distributed by the ANA, including stationery, constitutions, transactions, fund-raising appeals, and occasional papers. In part, because of his journalistic background, he worked with every committee concerned with the establishment of a periodical, a venture he believed essential to the academy's work. In 1898, he began to urge the society to issue an annual or yearbook that would give statistical "information respecting all our [the Negro race's] varied interests, educational, material, and religious—also political in the enlarged sense." Not only was Cromwell invariably on the subcommittee to arrange for the annual meetings but he was usually responsible for scheduling the program. His role in the annual meetings was equally prominent since he presented an annual secretary's report that was to all intents and purposes a state-of-the-academy address, including recommendations for future courses of action. Because he was responsible for communicating decisions and requests to the members, Cromwell became the link between the larger membership and the governing bodies of the organization. So much so, that for many people, both in and outside the society, his name became synonymous with the ANA. This tendency was accentuated by his activity as the chief interpreter and defender of the association in the newspapers. Not only did he respond to T. Thomas Fortune's attack on the ANA, but six months after the founding of the academy he wrote a lengthy article for the New York *Chronicle* giving the history behind the society's establishment and a description of what it was attempting to do. A similar article appeared over his signature in the Washington *Record* on the eve of the sixth annual meeting in December, 1902.[17]

17. Proceedings, 28; Cromwell, "The American Negro Academy," New York *Chronicle*

Under both Crummell and Du Bois, Cromwell was responsible for carrying out most of the decisions of the executive committee and the annual meetings, but there was a difference in his relationship with each of these men. He depended heavily on Crummell's judgment and regularly consulted him, both personally and, when the clergyman was away from Washington, by letter. Du Bois he knew and respected, but the Atlanta professor's physical distance and lack of involvement both forced him, and gave him the opportunity, to function with greater autonomy. The executive committee also experienced the difference in leadership style under Du Bois, and it was Cromwell who took the lead in shaping its response to the new situation. His willingness to take the initiative may also have been related to the fact that in 1898 (the year Du Bois was elected president) he was fifty-three and Du Bois thirty. It is hard to imagine the Washington *Colored American* article, which described Cromwell as having "general charge" of the ANA and predicted his forthcoming election as president, appearing without the seed being planted, even if unconsciously. Cromwell may have been a guiding force during the interim between Crummell's death and the election of a new president, but John Albert Johnson headed the executive committee and, at no time, did that body's minutes record a change in the status of the corresponding secretary.

By December, 1898, eight of the academy's thirty-six original founders had been dropped from its membership list because of failure to pay dues. The eight were John Wesley Edward Bowen, Paul Laurence Dunbar, John Wesslay Hoffman, Charles W. Mossell, Inman E. Page, Charles H. Parrish, Charles H. Turner, and Booker T. Washington.[18] It is difficult to say with certainty why these men, after signing an endorsement of the new organization, almost immediately disassociated themselves from it. For a few, the $5 admission fee and $2 yearly dues might have been a deterrent, though it is difficult to see this as a problem for any but the most financially hard-pressed. And most of the eight could easily have afforded these fees. Others, specifically Hoffman, Page, Parrish, and Washington—all of whom were educators in institutions committed to industrial education—may have felt that the academy's goals, which put great stress on the value of "artistic, literary, and scientific" activity, were, if not at odds with their work, mar-

---

and [Cromwell], "The Negro Academy," Washington *Record*, both in Book of Clippings, in JWCG/M. For a discussion of Fortune's attack on the ANA, see Chapter II.

18. Proceedings, 61.

ginal to it. Certainly, as educated blacks in the late 1890s divided themselves into differing groups on the related issues of industrial versus higher education, and militancy versus accommodation, the decision to join or not to join the academy was probably viewed by most, if not all, prospective members, in terms of its consistency with their public positions on these two issues. The purpose, goals, and most active founding members of the academy left no doubt that it would be committed to a strong public support of black intellectual advancement and a militant defense of black rights. For this reason, it was surprising that Booker T. Washington, the major black spokesman for industrial education and black accommodation to the racial program of the New South, signed and returned the academy's endorsement card. Whatever his reasons for doing so, after further reflection he probably decided that membership in the academy would not only appear to contradict several of his public positions, but would link him with a group of men with whom he would find it difficult to pursue common goals. Hoffman, Page, and Parrish may have come to the same conclusion.

The defection of these eight men was significant, for all were important figures in the black community—some would become even more so in future years—and their allegiance would have greatly strengthened the new academy's possibilities of success. It is hard to avoid the conclusion that, for a variety of reasons, they had little or no real interest in the goals of the organization. Whatever the cause for these withdrawals, such early signs of disinterest from important blacks augured poorly for the ANA's future. Unfortunately, the problem of member defection was one that would plague the association throughout its existence.

Over the next five years others fell away. William Tecumseh Sherman Jackson, a Washington schoolteacher, was inactive after 1901, and after 1902, the same was true of Charles Cattlett Johnson, a Columbia, South Carolina, physician; Lewis Baxter Moore, a Howard University professor; and Richard Robert Wright, head of the Georgia State Industrial School. Johnson had been an active and enthusiastic member of the organization from its inception. In October, 1899, a month before he was scheduled to present to the third annual meeting his research on "Consumption among American Negroes," his house and all its contents were destroyed by fire. As a consequence, Johnson became preoccupied with his own affairs and, though he continued to pay dues for the next three years, he never became as involved again, ceasing, after 1902, to be a member. Moore, a young instructor in Latin and pedagogy at Howard, allowed his membership to lapse because "other obligations" made it impossible for him to afford the dues.[19] The reasons for Jackson's and Wright's withdrawals are not known. Thus, by December, 1903, the number of active founding members was twenty-three.

The membership of the academy grew slowly. During the first six years of its existence only thirteen new members were elected. They included Hightower T. Kealing (1898), an educator and prominent Methodist layman who was editor of the *AME Church Review*; Orishatukeh Faduma (1899), principal of Peabody Academy in Troy, North Carolina; Archibald H. Grimké (1899), a lawyer, former United States consul to Santo Domingo, and the brother of Francis J. Grimké; Albert Witherspoon Pegues (1899), a Baptist minister and professor of theology at Shaw University, Raleigh, North Carolina; Charles E. Bentley (1899), a Chicago dentist active in his profession and in various black equal-rights groups; Thomas Washington Talley (1899), instructor in science at Alcorn (Mississippi) Agricultural and Mechanical College; George Washington Henderson (1899), professor of theology and pastor of the University Church, Straight University, New Orleans; James Major Colson (1899), principal of the Dinwiddie Agricultural and Industrial School in Petersburg, Virginia; Alexander Walters (1899), an AMEZ bishop and the president of the Afro-American Council; Daniel Jackson Sanders (1899), a Presbyterian clergyman who headed Biddle University in Charlotte, North Carolina; Thomas Junius Calloway (1900), former principal of Helena (Arkansas) Normal School, who was, at the time of his election, United States special commissioner to the Paris Exposition; John Hope (1900), a teacher at the Atlanta Baptist College in Georgia; and George Morton Lightfoot (1901), professor of Latin at Howard University.[20]

19. Johnson to Cromwell, November 6, 1899, Moore to Cromwell, June 11, 1902, "Blotter of Dues," all in JWCG/M.

20. For biographical information on Kealing see Wright (ed.), *Centennial Encyclopedia*, 144; for Faduma see Yenser (ed.), *Who's Who*, 145–46. For Grimké see Boris (ed.), *Who's Who*, 82. For Pegues see Yenser (ed.), *Who's Who*, 330–33. For Bentley, see Spear, *Black Chicago*, 57–58. For Talley see Mather (ed.), *Who's Who*, 258–59, and W. M. Brewer's life sketch of Thomas Washington Talley, *Journal of Negro History*, XXXVIII (April, 1953), 251–53. For Henderson see Washington *Colored American*, March 25, 1899, p. 1, and J. W. Cromwell, Corresponding Secretary's Report to the thirteenth annual meeting [untitled], December 28, 1909, in JWCG/M. For Walters see Obituary of Alexander Walters, *Crisis*, VI (March, 1917), 223, and Stephen R. Fox, *The Guardian of Boston: William Monroe Trotter* (New York, 1970), 110. For Sanders see D. J. Sanders Memorial Edition, *Johnson C. Smith University Alumni Journal*. For Calloway see Yenser (ed.), *Who's Who*, 210, and Harlan (ed.), *Booker T. Washington Papers*, III, 177. For Hope see Yenser (ed.), *Who's Who*, 218. For Lightfoot see life sketch of G. M. Lightfoot, *Journal of Negro History*, XXXIII (January, 1948), 119–20.

Two of these thirteen, Sanders and Calloway, "never qualified," that is, neither ever paid an entrance fee or annual dues. As a result, they were both eventually removed from the academy roster. In a letter written six years after his name had been dropped, Sanders explained to Cromwell that work pressures had prevented him from fulfilling the membership requirements in 1899. The reason for Calloway's negligence remains obscure. George Henderson's deep involvement in the equal rights struggles of the New Orleans black community, plus his duties as a teacher and clergyman, made it impossible for him to attend annual meetings or to contribute papers. He, therefore, resigned from the ANA in 1902.[21]

The majority of these men were recruited on the suggestion of persons who were already members. When an individual was recommended to the corresponding secretary, Cromwell wrote that person (sometimes, however, only after making his own inquiries), describing the organization and inviting an application for admission. Five of the men elected during these years—Bentley, Colson, Talley, Calloway, and Hope—were brought to Cromwell's attention by W. E. B. Du Bois. Sanders, Henderson, and Archibald Grimké were suggested by members of the executive committee, at one of that body's meetings. A similar process of informal recommendation led to Faduma's and Pegues's induction, and was probably responsible for kindling Walters' and Kealing's interest in the society.[22]

There was usually little controversy in these membership elections. This was due, in part, to the constitutional requirement that an applicant had to be endorsed by six members. Thus, once the endorsements had been obtained, even if the candidate was unknown to most members, his election was almost assured. W. E. B. Du Bois did oppose Faduma's admission, arguing that he was "in no sense eligible." Faduma's endorsers, however, included five founders—Crummell, Albert P. Miller, William H. Ferris, John Albert Johnson, and Levi J. Coppin. Du Bois's was the only vote recorded against him.[23]

---

21. Sanders to Cromwell, November 13, 1905; Henderson to Cromwell, December 16, 1901; "Blotter of Dues," all in JWCG/M.

22. Du Bois to Cromwell, February 29, 1899, April 17, May 7, 1903, Faduma to Cromwell, February 17, 1898, Pegues to Cromwell, March 10, 1898, Walters to Cromwell, November 27, 1899, Kealing to Cromwell, February 7, 1898, all in JWCG/M; Proceedings, 47. In addition to Sanders, Henderson, and Grimké, five other persons who never became members of the ANA were suggested by the executive committee: the Reverend Messrs. W. H. Weaver, H. H. Proctor, W. H. Goler, and Harvey Johnson, and Mr. C. W. Luckie.

23. Du Bois to Cromwell, November 11, 1898, and December 27, 1898, Faduma to Cromwell, April 20, 1899, all in JWCG/M.

The early membership elections were characterized by lengthy waiting periods before the results could be determined. Many members failed to return the ballots promptly and, in some cases, not at all. To alleviate this problem, the second annual meeting voted in 1898 that "unless members notified of votes on applications for membership . . . responded within thirty days they will be construed as voting in favor of the applicant or applicants."[24] While this action apparently made the election process operate with more dispatch, it actually reduced its significance by making it possible for members to escape the responsibility of deciding for or against a candidate.

The thirteen men elected to the academy represented only a little over a third of the total number of names suggested for membership. Du Bois urged Cromwell to write the following men, urging them to apply for membership: Charles Waddell Chesnutt, a Cleveland lawyer whose short stories had been published in the *Atlantic Monthly* and by Houghton Mifflin; George W. Forbes, former editor of the Boston *Courant* and a member of the Boston Public Library staff; Clement G. Morgan, a lawyer who sat on the Cambridge, Massachusetts, city council; Daniel Hale Williams, founder of Chicago's Provident Hospital and one of the most distinguished surgeons in the United States; William H. A. Moore, a newspaperman connected with the Chicago *Record*; and Andrew H. Hilyer, an accountant employed by the federal government, who was supervising, on his own time, the compilation of a Washington, D.C., "directory of Negro business."[25]

Du Bois did not know that Forbes and Morgan had previously declined membership in the ANA at its founding. In a letter responding to his other suggestions, Cromwell conceded Hilyer's abilities, but opposed the idea of approaching him on the grounds that there were already too many Washington members. Du Bois, sensing that Cromwell's opposition was more complex, replied, somewhat archly, "If Hilyer is worthy, his misfortune to live in Washington ought not to debar him." Nevertheless, Hilyer's name was dropped. Cromwell also questioned Moore's suitability for membership, but eventually wrote him, only, however, after he obtained a favorable opinion from Chicago ANA member Samuel Laing Williams. Moore, who expressed great interest in joining the society, put much effort into gathering six endorsers, but his name never appeared on any record as a member. Chesnutt's reply to Cromwell's letter was gracious, but it was a clear refusal

24. Proceedings, 58.
25. Du Bois to Cromwell, February 29, 1898, November 17, 1899, both in JWCG/M.

to involve himself. "I do not know," he wrote, "that my achievements in the field of letters are as yet of sufficient importance to qualify me for such an honor." Chesnutt's polite rejection of the invitation was almost certainly related to his disapproval of any stress on the uniquely "Negro" heritage of American blacks and of separatism as a solution to the race issue, both positions legitimately associated with the academy, even though they were not accepted by all members.[26] There is no evidence that Daniel Hale Williams ever replied to the letter from the corresponding secretary.

Other academy members also passed on names to Cromwell. George N. Grisham recommended Edward Augustus Johnson of Raleigh, North Carolina, a lawyer, businessman, and school principal whose *School History of the Negro Race in America* had gone into its third edition in 1893. Samuel L. Williams thought W. L. Martin, Edward E. Wilson, and Spencer Dickerson "would be desirable members." All three lived in Chicago, where the first two were lawyers, active in city politics, and the third was a physician. When Cromwell, acting on advice from Matthew Anderson, attempted to interest Episcopal clergyman Henry L. Phillips, rector of Philadelphia's Church of the Crucifixion, in the ANA, the minister expressed his "hearty accord" with its aims, but declined because he was "so overburdened with work of all kinds." William H. Crogman sent the names of "two young men, both graduates from Atlanta University," Charles W. Luckie, a teacher of English literature and history, in the Prairie View State Normal School, Prairie View, Texas, and Paul E. Spratlin, a physician practicing in Denver, Colorado. In response to a request from Cromwell for a list of possible candidates Orishatukeh Faduma sent the names of twelve men, one of whom, Charles H. Boyer, teacher of mathematics, Greek, and English in St. Augustine's College, Raleigh, North Carolina, became a member in 1905. Only one person, William R. Sinclair, financial secretary to Howard University, applied directly to the association for admission. Although he made application in 1900, Sinclair was not admitted until 1906, a year after his book, *Aftermath of Slavery*, an able attack on white supremacist thought, was published.[27]

26. Du Bois to Cromwell, December 9, 1899, Williams to Cromwell, December 8, 1899, Moore to Cromwell, December 22, 1899, and March 10, 1900, Chesnutt to Cromwell, March 29, 1899, all in JWCG/M. For a discussion of Chesnutt's opinions on these issues and his feelings toward Du Bois see Frances Richardson Keller, "Toward Human Understanding: The Life and Times of Charles Waddell Chesnutt" (Ph.D. dissertation, University of Chicago, 1973), 539–52, 570–86.

27. Grisham to Cromwell, November 15, 1899, Williams to Cromwell, December 8, 1899,

Not surprisingly, John W. Cromwell was the organization's most active recruiter. Besides frequently requesting the names of potential candidates from the general membership and conducting the correspondence with them, he introduced the ANA to numerous men he considered talented and reflective. During Du Bois's first term as president Cromwell sought the Atlanta university professor's opinion of four Bostonians, all of whom were lawyers: Butler Wilson, William H. Lewis, James H. Wolff, and Edward Everett Brown. Du Bois thought Wilson and Lewis "good material," Wolff a very "questionable addition," and Brown "entirely out of the question." Later Cromwell wrote to David Augustus Straker, a Detroit lawyer who had played an important role in South Carolina politics during Reconstruction, attempting to draw him into the society. Straker, author of *New South Investigated* (1888), a critique of social, political, and economic conditions in that region, promised to follow up on the invitation "as soon as convenient."[28] With the exception of Charles H. Boyer and William R. Sinclair, none of these men ever became members of the academy.

In spite of the fact that over forty-eight persons were suggested as candidates or invited to apply for admission, only thirteen new members were inducted between the founding of the society and 1903. In his secretary's report to the first annual meeting, Cromwell asked the members to help him build a wider interest in the work of the academy. They could do this, he informed them, by providing him with the name and address

of at least one energetic enthusiastic unselfish worker in every institution for the higher education of the race and in every town and city having an aggregate of 5000 Negro population . . . of some sympathetic physician in every city possessing ten thousand or more of our population; of a trained lawyer in every densely populated community and of at least one minister of each denomination in every southern state who believes the social welfare of the race is of sufficient importance to justify the investigation and consideration of social and economic problems as well as the enforcing of moral and religious duties.

A year later, at the second annual meeting, Cromwell made a similar plea, this time specifically urging his listeners to bring the organization to its full membership of fifty. He assured them that there were "scores of men with the necessary scholarship, culture, the consecration of purpose, the integrity

Anderson to Cromwell, December 25, 1897, Phillips to Cromwell, November 17, 1898, Crogman to Cromwell, February 29, 1898, Faduma to Cromwell, February 4, 1902, Sinclair to Cromwell, January 18, 1900, all in JWCG/M.

28. Du Bois to Cromwell, December 9, 1899, Straker to Cromwell, February 2, 1903, both in JWCG/M.

of character and devotion to our ideals" to fill out the ranks of the group. This last appeal may have had some small effect. Whereas in 1898 the society had only been able to produce four candidates for membership, six new members were elected in 1899. These ten new faces, however, replaced about an equal number of dropouts. The three men inducted between 1900 and 1903 had the same effect. Clearly, despite the importance of the academy and its work, it was proving difficult to raise its membership to the constitutional limit.[29]

Despite the fact that George N. Grisham had argued for the admission of women at the ANA's organizational meeting, and had, after great effort, exacted an assurance that they would be eligible for membership, no efforts were made by any academy member (including Grisham) to recruit black women who were "Authors, Scholars, Artists . . . [or] distinguished in other walks of life." When in December, 1897, Anna J. Cooper, a prominent member of Washington's black intellectual elite, wrote an article on the academy for the *Southern Workman*, it was her understanding that its membership was "confined to men." The only ANA member to behave as if women might have a place in the association was Alexander Crummell, who in August, 1898, invited Maritcha B. Lyons to present a paper at the second annual meeting. Lyons, who was the first black female graduate of the public high school in Providence, Rhode Island, had been a teacher in the Brooklyn public schools since 1869. After Crummell's death in September, 1898, the executive committee reaffirmed his invitation to her. Unable to attend the meeting, Lyons sent a paper, "Afro-American Literature," to be read at the meeting. Presumably because the author was a woman, the committee invited a Washington woman, E. D. Barrier, to read it. This was the first and the last meeting in which a paper written by a woman was presented to the society. Although the black community produced some outstanding female artists, educators, and civic leaders during the late nineteenth and early twentieth centuries—figures such as Fanny Jackson Coppin, Ida Wells-Barnett, Mary Church Terrell, Lucy Laney, Nannie Burroughs, Meta Warrick Fuller, and Alice Dunbar-Nelson—nothing was done to draw them into a relationship with the American Negro Academy.[30]

29. Proceedings, 28, 61.
30. Cooper, "American Negro Academy"; Proceedings, 50, 57. See Chapter II for discussion of Grisham's efforts to insure the admission of women to the ANA. For biographical information on Maritcha B. Lyons, see New York *Age*, February 2, 1929, p. 1.

At the first annual meeting in December, 1897, the Academy had voted to admit, as corresponding members, foreigners of "great distinction." Such persons had to be recommended by the executive committee and approved by two-thirds of the members present at an annual meeting. This provision, which became By-Law No. 6, expressed the hope of many ANA members that their academy would function as a cultural and intellectual link between black Americans and blacks in other parts of the world. No larger statement outlining the specific expectations that lay behind this decision was ever made, but it is clear that the ideas of Alexander Crummell and W. E. B. Du Bois were very important in shaping it. One of the major themes in Crummell's life and writings was his conviction that black Americans had a unique role to play in the destiny of Africa and its people. Du Bois was of the same opinion, and also believed that all Africans and African-derived peoples shared a common identity and destiny. Both were constant and forceful proponents of these views, many of which, with various modifications and additions, were shared by other ANA members.[31]

Between 1897 and 1903 the academy elected eight corresponding members. After passing By-Law No. 6, the 1897 annual meeting temporarily suspended the section that required candidates be recommended by the executive committee. This made possible the immediate election of Edward Wilmot Blyden, a Liberian writer, teacher, and statesman; James Theodore Holly, Anglican bishop of Haiti; Sir Samuel Lewis, an African lawyer and politician who had served as Queen's Advocate and Chief Justice in Sierra Leone (British West Africa); and Henry Ossawa Tanner, an American painter who had won numerous prizes in Europe and America for his art work. Tanner, who was also the son of ANA founding member Benjamin Tucker Tanner, had, in his early thirties, gone to Paris to study and, after 1899, settled there permanently. This was the basis for his being considered a "distinguished foreigner." Lewis was nominated by John Henry Smyth, who had become acquainted with him while serving as United States minis-

---

31. Proceedings, 34–35. For Crummell's ideas on the relationship between black Americans and Africa see his "Civilization as a Collateral and Indispensable Instrumentality in Planting the Christian Church in Africa," in J. W. E. Bowen (ed.), *Africa and the American Negro* (Atlanta, 1896), "Hope for Africa" in his book *The Future of Africa: Being Addresses, Sermons, etc. Delivered in the Republic of Liberia* (New York, 1862), and "Our National Mistakes and the Remedy for Them" (1870) in the collection of his writings entitled *Africa and America* (Springfield, Mass., 1891). Du Bois's ideas in this connection, especially for the time period under discussion, are expressed in his first address before the academy, *The Conservation of Races*, ANA Occasional Papers, no. 2 (1897), see especially 7–10.

ter to Liberia. Kelly Miller suggested Blyden and Tanner, both of whom were much admired by educated black Americans. Bishop Holly was nominated by his old friend, ANA president Alexander Crummell.[32]

All four men accepted their election, but Holly's long, effusive reply must have been especially gratifying to the members of the association. He assured them that the importance of their "Academic organization in moulding the future of the American Negro" could not be exaggerated. Thereby, his letter continued, the "race seems to gather to itself, in an embryonic focus, its select, highest, and best vital forces." He congratulated himself on being a part of this intellectual effort that would shape the "brain" of the "forthcoming new Negro race," and declared the movement to be nothing less than "a special inspiration of Divine Providence." In his letter of acceptance Henry O. Tanner said that he was "highly honored" by his election, but asked to be informed of the "privileges" and "duties" of the position. In response to a request that accompanied his letter of notification, Tanner promised to furnish copies of any of his pictures for reproduction in the proposed ANA quarterly magazine.[33]

A year later, on the recommendation of the executive committee, the academy's second annual meeting elected two Haitians as corresponding members: Antenor Firmin, a leading politician in his country, and Louis Joseph Janvier, a diplomat and scholar who was chargé d'affaires of the Haitian mission in London. Theophilus G. Steward, a founding member of the academy, suggested Firmin's election. Bishop Holly did also, at the same time strongly recommending the same honor for Janvier. Because the independent black nation of Haiti was a symbol of freedom to black Americans, Firmin's skillful blockage, in 1891, of an attempt by the United States to gain control of Môle St. Nicolas, one of Haiti's harbors, made him a hero to the small circle of black Americans aware of the incident. Holly described Firmin as "one of the most brilliant Negroes intellectually now living—of unmixed blood"—and the author of a "learned work on anthropology" which had been praised in Europe. At the time of his election, less was known of Janvier, who held a medical degree from the University of Paris

32. Proceedings, 35. For biographical material on Blyden, see Lynch, *Edward Wilmot Blyden*; for Holly see George F. Bragg, *History of the Afro-American Group of the Episcopal Church* (Baltimore, 1922), 192; for Lewis see John Desmond Hargreaves, *A Life of Sir Samuel Lewis* (London, 1958); for Tanner see Marcia M. Matthews, *Henry Ossawa Tanner* (Chicago, 1969).

33. Holly to Cromwell, January 20, 1898, Tanner to Cromwell, n.d., both in JWCG/M. Replies from Blyden and Lewis have not survived.

and was a graduate of the École de Politique in the same city. He was also a member of numerous French learned societies and had written articles on medicine, racial theory, Haitian literature, politics, and history. Both of these men, on Holly's recommendation, had earlier been elected members of the American Academy of Political and Social Science.[34]

Both Firmin and Janvier sent letters of acceptance, but Firmin's has not survived. Janvier, in his reply, expressed great pride in the "honor conferred upon me by this noble institution of which the power will be felt . . . for the benefit of our Race all over the world." He also sent, for the academy library, a copy of his book, *Constitutions of Hayti from 1801 to 1885*.[35]

Three men were elected corresponding members during W. E. B. Du Bois's presidency, Thomas Greathead Harper, Henry Mason Joseph, and Samuel Coleridge-Taylor. Harper, an Episcopal clergyman, had been ordained in 1885, and served for several years as rector of St. Philip's Church in Newark, New Jersey. Later he moved to London, where he was living when, sometime between 1898 and 1902, the academy elected him one of its corresponding members. Joseph, who was born in the West Indies, taught at St. Augustine's School in Raleigh, North Carolina, during the early 1880s. While there he was ordained into the ministry of the Protestant Episcopal Church. Several years later he resigned his teaching post and emigrated to England. Alexander Crummell visited Joseph in London during the summer of 1897, at which time the two men discussed the future of the newly established academy. Joseph promised to contribute a paper to the organization's proposed quarterly magazine, but because of Crummell's death the next year and the failure of the magazine to materialize, the offer was never followed up. In December, 1899, the academy acknowledged Joseph's interest in its work by electing him a corresponding member.[36]

Four years later Samuel Coleridge-Taylor, an impressive young musician, was chosen a corresponding member. The son of an African man and an

34. Proceedings, 55. For a description of Firmin and the Môle St. Nicolas incident see Rayford W. Logan, *Haiti and the Dominican Republic* (New York, 1968), 110–12, 117–25, and Logan, *Diplomatic Relations of the United States with Haiti, 1776–1891* (Chapel Hill, 1941), 438–57; information on Janvier is given in Logan, *Diplomatic Relations*, 279, and the Washington *Colored American*, June 24, 1899, p. 6. See also Holly to Cromwell, January 20, 1898 (postscript marked "private"), Steward to Cromwell, n.d., both in JWCG/M.

35. Janvier to Cromwell, May 19, 1899, in JWCG/M; Washington *Colored American*, June 24, 1899, p. 6.

36. For biographical information on Harper see Bragg, *History of the Afro-American Group*, 121, 269; Proceedings, 105. For Joseph see Bragg, *History of the Afro-American Group*, 175, 269.

English woman, he was born in London in 1875. Coleridge-Taylor studied music under private tutors and at the Royal College of Music. Although some of his earlier compositions had been performed in public, the first part of what would become his most famous work, "The Hiawatha Trilogy," was presented in 1898 at the Royal College of Music. Over the next five years he produced a series of orchestral and choral works that were favorably received in England. Though his works were less familiar to American audiences, he was widely acknowledged in the United States as a talented musician and composer. Black Americans took a special pride in his career; and in Washington, D.C., one of the leading black choirs was called the Samuel Coleridge-Taylor Choral Society. In a brief note of acceptance the composer assured the academy of his "deepest sympathy" with its goals and "great interest" in the work of the organization.[37]

Two corresponding members, while on brief visits to the United States, took part in programs sponsored by the academy. In 1900, when James Theodore Holly, who had been born in Washington, came to the city to see family and friends, "the resident members" of the ANA "tendered . . . [him] a complimentary banquet." At this affair, Holly delivered an address on politics and political leaders in Haiti, his adopted country. Two years later, Thomas Greathead Harper, who lived in London, attended the sixth annual meeting of the organization and delivered a paper on the "Contemporary Evolution of the Negro Race."[38]

In the six years following its organization the academy held seven annual meetings. With the exception of the fourth, which was convened in March, 1901 (at the time of William McKinley's second inauguration), all of these gatherings took place during the last week of December. The first six meetings were held in the Lincoln Memorial Congregational Church and the seventh in the Metropolitan AME Church. Usually a meeting lasted two days, during which time two to four public sessions were held, the number depending on how many addresses were to be read. Since six was the usual number, there were normally three sessions. The papers, ordinarily written by ANA members, dealt with topics assigned by the executive committee or accepted by it after consultation with the author. Generally, each paper was

37. Proceedings, 114. For biographical material on Coleridge-Taylor see W. C. Berwick-Sayers, *Samuel Coleridge-Taylor, Musician* (London, 1915), and Washington *Bee*, March 18, 1911, p. 6. See also Coleridge-Taylor to Cromwell, n.d., in JWCG/M.
38. Washington *Colored American*, November 10, 1900, p. 14; Proceedings, 105.

followed by a discussion of its contents and related issues. By rule, only ANA members participated in the discussion, but from time to time a distinguished or prominent nonmember was allowed to speak, "by permission of the academy," and, on a number of occasions, some were invited to do so. Every annual meeting also included one or two business sessions open only to members. During these sessions elections were held, dues collected, reports made, and outstanding concerns related to administration and programs discussed, with new policies and programs sometimes emerging.

Papers presented at the early annual meetings lacked any topical or thematic connection beyond the fact that they all touched on the problems and concerns of black Americans. As a result, those present listened to a series of diverse and often discrete papers and discussions. Beginning with the sixth annual meeting in 1902, a change was made. Early in the year, the executive committee, believing that the coming meeting would be improved by consideration of one subject from different points of view, decided on "Religion and the Negro" as its overall theme. The result was considered a success and, though this format was not used the next year, it eventually became standard practice.[39]

The executive committee created the program for the annual meetings, including the selection of the various people invited to speak. In most years, an equal amount of time was spent reworking the program because of invitations declined or a previously announced speaker's sudden cancellation. Du Bois, for reasons discussed earlier, was a constant offender in this last regard, but he was not alone. John W. Hoffman, who taught in South Carolina's Agricultural and Mechanical College at Orangeburg, was scheduled to speak at the first annual meeting on the "Outlook of Scientific Work among the Negroes," but "the illness of the president of the State University" prevented his being present. Richard R. Wright, requested by the executive committee to give a paper at the fourth annual meeting, agreed to read one he had written earlier, "Negro Companions of the Spanish Conquistadores." He was, however, unable to attend the meeting and the paper was never delivered. Francis Louis Cardozo, former secretary of state and treasurer of South Carolina, promised to "prepare and read a paper . . . on the part of the Negro in the reconstruction of South Carolina" for the fourth annual meeting. However, neither Cardozo nor his paper made an appearance. Illness kept John H. Smyth away from the fifth annual meeting,

39. Proceedings, 97.

where he was scheduled to speak on "Christian and Moral Influences of Reformatories." In 1902 both William H. Ferris and Alexander Walters failed to deliver papers that had been advertised in public notices for the sixth annual meeting. Ferris was to have given "A Historical and Psychological Account of the Genesis and Development of the Negro's Religion" and Walters to have answered the question, "Is the Negro Church Fulfilling Its Mission?"[40]

The excuses for declining offered by persons invited to speak ranged from understandable to specious. AME bishop Benjamin T. Tanner informed the committee he could not prepare a paper for the first annual meeting because he was "hard at work on a new book." The biologist, Charles H. Turner, asked to contribute a paper at the same meeting, refused because he was recovering from a severe attack of "remittant fever." In 1898 the committee twice extended an invitation to Dr. Charles B. Purvis, a physician who had been surgeon-in-chief of Freedman's Hospital, to speak on "Environment vs. Heredity, Scientifically Considered." Purvis apprised the committee that he saw no conflict between the two but, because he had recently suffered "much disturbance" and felt "out of joint," it was impossible for him "to muster up the energy necessary to a . . . discussion." When the same request was made of Dr. Furman L. Shadd, another prominent Washington physician, he also sent regrets. One of the committee's greatest disappointments was Bishop James T. Holly's gracious but definite refusal to deliver the eulogy at the ANA memorial service for Alexander Crummell. Holly's excuse was his lack of familiarity with the details of Crummell's public career and intellectual work. An invitation was extended to Booker T. Washington to address the second annual meeting on a subject of his choice. Though Washington assured the academy that he was "not unmindful of the compliment," he refused because his many previous engagements made acceptance impossible. George F. T. Cook, former Superintendent of the Colored Schools of Washington, was asked to prepare a paper on the history of the Washington public school system, but he declined, feeling there was not enough time between the request and the meeting at which it was to be presented. The record holder, however, was Francis J. Grimké, who refused four separate invitations to deliver a paper before various annual meetings.

40. Washington *Post*, December 30, 1897, p. 3; Wright to Cromwell, February 2, 1901, announcement card, fourth annual meeting, Smyth to Cromwell, December 30, 1901, Walters to Cromwell, October 9, 1902, announcement card, sixth annual meeting, all in JWCG/M; Proceedings, 78, 79, 83–88, 105–111.

Since Grimké, an able public speaker, was ANA treasurer and a member of the executive committee, his behavior is difficult to understand.[41]

Many of those invited to read papers were overburdened with work. This was especially true of Du Bois, Tanner, Wright, and Francis J. Grimké, all of whom had numerous involvements and constant invitations to lecture, preach, and orate. In addition, these men regularly produced written pieces for newspapers and periodicals. There were other academy members who operated under the same pressures. However, the large number of people who failed to appear and who declined to read papers suggests that there were other reasons. Though the executive committee rarely issued an invitation to present a paper less than two months before the meeting for which it was scheduled, to men whose busy lives left little room for scholarship it must have frequently seemed as if there was not enough time in which to get something written. Many of the subjects the academy wanted discussed demanded not only interest and involvement but scholarly background, intellectual insight, and much preparation. Some of the people invited to speak had experience in preparing and delivering learned papers, but for those who did not the challenge may have seemed overwhelming, to say nothing of the prospect of facing comments and questions from academy members.

Occasionally, the executive committee was very specific in terms of what it wanted or did not want to hear from a speaker. When, at the height of the controversy stirred up by T. Thomas Fortune's attack on the academy and its use of the term "Negro," William S. Scarborough declared his willingness to present a paper entitled "Afro-American or Negro—Which?" the committee informed him "they would prefer that he select another topic." Scarborough, who complained to Cromwell that "the attitude of our executive committee makes no sense," withdrew both the paper and himself from the program. In a similar action the executive committee decided that it "would be inexpedient" for John H. Smyth to present a paper on juvenile reformatories at the December, 1898, annual meeting. Presumably, this was because part of the meeting was a memorial to Crummell and the topic was considered inappropriate. Seeking to set some limits on what they anticipated would be a controversial paper, the academy sent the following com-

41. Proceedings, 22, 23, 44, 50, 66, 78, 79, 98; Tanner to Cromwell, October 15, 1897, Turner to Cromwell, October 26, 1897, Purvis to Cromwell, July 10, November 19, 1898, Shadd to Cromwell, November 25, 1898, Holly to Cromwell, November 25, 1898, Washington to Cromwell, October 22, 1898, and announcement cards for first, second, third, and sixth annual meetings, all in JWCG/M. For biographical information on Purvis and Shadd, see Helen Buckler, *Daniel Hale Williams, Negro Surgeon* (New York, 1954), 98–99, 104, 127.

munication to John L. Love shortly before the second annual meeting: "The executive committee will be glad to have you present a paper upon the constitutions recently adopted in several of the Southern states: but would request that it might be wise to refrain from a judicial criticism of the opinions of the Supreme Court of the US." Conversely, in July, 1900, the executive committee asked Kelly Miller to "make a careful and critical examination of the recent address of Mr. Charles Dudley Warner . . . before the American Social Science Association." Warner, president of the association, had argued in an address delivered May 7, 1900, that higher education had not only failed to bring about the personal and social elevation of the black masses, but had instead "bred idleness, indisposition to work, a vaporous ambition in politics, and that sort of conceit of gentility of which the world has already enough." To elevate effectively the "character and position" of blacks he recommended a system of "elemental teaching," coupled with "moral instruction and training in industry and habits of industry." Miller's reply, delivered at the fourth annual meeting, was entitled, "Education of the City Negro." [42]

At the first annual meeting Francis J. Grimké, Lewis B. Moore, and John H. Smyth were appointed to be a committee on constitutional revision. In their report, which was presented on the second day of the meeting, they recommended adoption of three amendments: to increase the number of officers in Article 1 by adding a "statistician" to the list, with the stipulation that this be a salaried post "when onerous duties are judged to demand it"; and insertion in Article 7—which dealt with fees—of a provision for ouster from the organization if a member failed to pay dues two years in succession. The first and second recommendations demonstrated the committee's support of Cromwell's proposal that the academy publish a yearbook containing statistics on all phases of black American life, a project he had pushed strongly in his secretary's report. The third was an indication of how difficult it was to obtain dues from some members. In spite of strong

42. Scarborough to Cromwell, October 9, 1897, Cromwell to Love [*ca.* early December, 1898], both in JWCG/M; Proceedings, 21, 49, 52, 78, 88. For Fortune's attack, see Chapter II. The Proceedings give the title of Kelly Miller's address as "The Education of the City Negro," while the announcement card for the fourth annual meeting states it as "The Anglo-Saxon as a Civilizer of Backward Races." Miller also presented a paper challenging Warner's views at a meeting of the American Social Science Association held in Washington the week of April 20, 1901. (See Washington *Colored American*, May 4, 1901.) See also Charles Dudley Warner, "The Education of the Negro," *Journal of Social Science*, XXXVIII (June, 1900), 1–14.

pressures for passage of the proposed amendments to Article 1, the annual meeting rejected them, but approved the change in Article 7.[43]

The same three-member committee also recommended adoption of the following eight by-laws, five of which were designed to strengthen the already powerful role of the executive committee:

1. Special Meetings of the Academy may be held at the call of the Executive Committee when and where they may decide.
2. The general arrangement of the proceedings of the meetings of the Academy shall be directed by the Executive Committee.
3. Abstracts of all papers to be read before the Academy must be submitted to the Executive Committee before reading and their decision regarding such papers shall be final.
4. Papers and other literary productions brought before the Academy shall be limited to thirty minutes except in the case of the annual address by the President to which this By-Law shall not apply.
5. Publications of the Academy of whatever kind shall be made only under authorization of the Executive Committee.
6. Foreigners of great distinction may be elected corresponding members of the Academy by a ⅔ vote of the members in attendance upon any regular meeting of the Academy, on condition that such persons have been recommended by the Executive Committee.
7. Amendments to the Constitution and By-Laws may be made by a ⅔ vote of members at any regular meeting subsequent to that in which they have been proposed.
8. All meetings of the Academy shall be opened with prayer.

All suggested by-laws, except 2 and 6, were adopted as presented. Number 2 was rejected in toto, while 6 passed after a minor wording change.[44]

Besides academy members, it is difficult to know how many people attended the annual meetings. The members present ranged from a high of nineteen at the third annual meeting in 1899 to a low of seven in December, 1903, when the seventh annual meeting was held. Fourteen members were present in December, 1897; thirteen in December, 1898; twelve in March, 1901; eight in December, 1901; and thirteen in December, 1902. Usually most of the members present were Washington residents. The two exceptions, each different from the other, were the meetings held in December, 1899, and December, 1902. At the former the group was almost evenly di-

43. Proceedings, 28, 30, 34–35, and "Blotter of Dues," in JWCG/M. The annual meetings were always hesitant to create new officers. When, during the fourth annual meeting K. Miller made a motion to create the post of "historian," he was persuaded to withdraw it and the executive committee made responsible for the work that would have been connected with the proposed position. See Proceedings, 84.
44. Proceedings, 34–35.

vided, with ten Washington members present and nine from other places. The meeting in 1902 was the only time members from outside the District of Columbia were in the majority; seven came from elsewhere and six from Washington. The fact that after December, 1897, all the members of the executive committee, as well as two-thirds of the officers, were Washingtonians made these figures even more significant.[45]

Assumption by Washington members of a major role in the direction of the society had been anticipated by the organizers. Article 6 of the constitution designated Washington as the seat of the academy. There had been a number of reasons that seemed to justify this decision: the founder lived there; Washington was centrally located for blacks interested in the ANA; and the strong cultural and intellectual resources of the city's black community. In addition there was the practical reality that whatever city was chosen as national headquarters those members living in other places would have neither the time nor the means (for frequent travel) to allow any but limited involvement. No one, however, either anticipated or desired annual meetings that reflected so little of the society's character as a national black institution.[46]

One observer, who attended the public sessions in December, 1897, noted that each one "drew crowds of interested outsiders, men and women, from all walks of life who showed by sympathetic applause how close to their hearts were the subjects handled." Another spectator described the public sessions on the first day as "largely attended and marked by great interest and enthusiasm." And, in commenting on the two held the second day, the same person noted that they were "attended by representative Negro citizens to the full capacity of the Church." One of the attendants was Richard T. Greener, the man whose membership in the academy Crummell had successfully opposed. In a letter to John E. Bruce, Crummell described his behavior. Greener, he told his friend, "attended our public meeting and got

45. There were seven annual meetings from the time the ANA was organized to the end of Du Bois's presidency: December, 1897, December, 1898, December, 1899, March, 1901, December, 1901, December, 1902, and December, 1903. The reason for the relatively large number of members present in December, 1899, is discussed earlier in Chapter III. Probably the low attendance at the two meetings held in 1901 was the result of scheduling two national meetings in one year.

Formal records of attendance have survived for only two annual meetings during these years, the third and fourth. See Proceedings, 76; "Summary of the Proceedings of Third Annual Session"; and "Fourth Annual Session" (the last two are printed documents), in JWCG/M. Figures for members present at the other annual meetings have been obtained by counting those mentioned in the Proceedings and in newspaper accounts.

46. ANA Constitution (1897), in JWCG/M.

into a state of bitterness. He has been perambulating Washington denouncing me on account of my hatred of mulattoes. 'Dr. Crummell don't want any mulattoes in the Academy. He has striven to keep them out' and etcetera." In the same letter, Crummell denied Greener's charges, pointing out, as John W. Cromwell had in his reply to similar accusations leveled against the ANA, the sizable number of mixed and almost white Negroes who were members. Whatever the general effect of Greener's criticisms they angered Crummell so deeply that he was still furious almost a month after the incident.[47]

Although there is even less information on nonmembers present at the other annual meetings, various accounts do supply scattered bits and pieces of information. Several of Washington's black ministers were usually in attendance. Frequently, a local cleric of some importance or a denominational official visiting the city was invited to open one of the public sessions with prayer. In December, 1902, when the academy focused on "Religion and the Negro," black clergy made up a sizable portion of the audience. Some, by permission of the academy, were major participants in the discussions following the various papers. Another participant in 1902 was William H. H. Hart, a professor in Howard's Law School and a man with strong religious and philanthropic interests. Two whites, present at the second annual meeting, offered their opinions (again with permission) when the addresses delivered at that meeting were discussed. One, William Augustus Croffut, a writer and journalist who opposed American imperialistic tendencies, was identified in the ANA Proceedings as "a well-known friend of the Negro." The other, Ainsworth R. Spofford, was a former Librarian of Congress. In a brief review of the third annual meeting the Washington *Colored American* blamed "inclement weather" for the fact that "all the meetings were somewhat slimly attended." Beyond these few sporadic details, little else is known about either the content or size of the audiences that gathered to hear the academy papers read and discussed.[48]

Press coverage of the academy was sparse and scattered. The only magazine to notice the society was Hampton Institute's publication, the *Southern Workman*, which, in February, 1898, printed an article describing the acad-

47. Cooper, "The American Negro Academy," 35; Washington *Post*, December 29, 1897, p. 8, and December 30, 1897, p. 3; Crummell to Bruce, January 21, 1898, in Crummell Papers. For a discussion of Crummell's opposition to Greener's membership in the ANA see Chapter I.
48. For references to clergy at the annual meetings see Proceedings, 31, 45, 55, 56, 58, 59, 74, 75, 76, 106, 107, 108, 113, 114; for Hart see Proceedings, 107; for Croffut and Spofford see Proceedings, 56, 57.

emy's first annual meeting. Shortly before this meeting, the Philadelphia *Times*, a leading daily in that city, printed a notice giving its date and location, the titles of scheduled papers, and their authors. A week after the sessions ended an editorial appeared in the Washington *Colored American* praising the academy for its support of "the higher education of the Negro . . . as the basis upon which . . . he must stand and be judged." The success of this gathering, the editorial continued, "will be gratifying to colored men everywhere, and will give the Association an importance that is national in character." The piece concluded with a wish for the organization's "long life and abundant success." Washington's two major newspapers, the *Post* and the *Evening Star*, were both fairly generous in the space they provided for reports on the meeting. Each printed three separate articles containing a short history and description of the society, brief synopses of the addresses, and a summary of the business transacted. In content the two sets of articles were similar. The *Evening Star*, however, also devoted an editorial to the academy, the only attempt by a major white publication to assess the significance and potential of the ANA.[49]

"Wide possibilities," in the opinion of the editorialist, existed for an organization seeking "the elevation of the negro race through educational enlightenment." Praising the academy's concern with "statistics," "investigation," and the scholarly perspective, he offered the judgment that it "should develop into a conservative, serviceable factor," especially since "there does not appear any sign of a disposition to accentuate the race feeling in any section." At this point the editorial made an interesting shift. Booker T. Washington's educational work at Tuskegee was introduced as "one of the most remarkable achievements of the latter part of the century" because of its positive effect on the "academic and industrial" development of blacks. However, even more remarkable, to the writer, was "the spirit with which the work is regarded by the people of the South." There was, he believed, a message for the ANA in Washington's approach. "This new Academy," the editorialist advised, "can well foster the spirit with which the white people regard this [Tuskegee] and similar works among negroes." After observing that the organization "seems now to be in careful hands" (Du Bois had just

49. Cooper, "The American Negro Academy," 35–36; Philadelphia *Times*, December 25, 1897, p. 24; Washington *Colored American*, January 1, 1898, Robert Heberton Terrell Papers, Library of Congress, Box 6, Scrapbooks (it is likely that Terrell, a founding member of the ANA, wrote the editorial; his name is handwritten, in pencil, at the bottom of the clipping); Washington *Post*, December 27, 1897, p. 10, December 29, 1897, p. 8, December 30, 1897, p. 3; Washington *Evening Star*, December 28, 29, and 30, 1897.

been elected Crummell's successor), the editorial closed with a cautious benediction for the work of the ANA.[50]

The editorial suggests that under Crummell's leadership the academy was perceived by some as a challenge to Washington's work as well as the basis on which he received support from southern whites. A letter written to the editor of the *Evening Star* two weeks later also made reference to Booker T. Washington, this time, however, as part of a direct and immediate criticism of the association. The writer, who signed himself, "A Hewer of Wood," attacked the ANA for its lack of concern with the needs of the black masses, while praising Washington for his interest in the welfare of the entire race.[51]

After the first annual meeting press coverage became even smaller. The Washington *Colored American* carried notices of all the annual meetings between 1897 and 1903. In most years it printed an advance announcement giving the date, place, and program of the various sessions as well as subsequent articles reporting who the officers were for the coming year and listing the "distinguished" members who had attended. Coverage was always brief, with little or no information on the content of the addresses delivered or the opinions expressed in the discussions following them. Two weeks before the third annual meeting a short article on the academy appeared in the Boston *Transcript*. In spite of the fact that it was written by John E. Bruce, a committed and active ANA member, there was little difference, either in form or content, from the typical Washington *Colored American* announcement. In January, 1902, George Grisham wrote to John W. Cromwell requesting "a full list of members and an account of prospective doings" for the Kansas City *Journal*, which wanted to do a "write-up" on the academy. The information was sent, but Grisham failed to pass it on to the paper.[52]

A more positive occurrence, however, and one which indicated the seriousness with which some black leaders viewed the ANA was the fraternal visit of the leading delegates of the Afro-American Council to its third annual meeting. The council was a national coalition of black leaders and

50. Washington *Evening Star*, December 29, 1897, p. 6.
51. "Needs of the Negro Race," Washington *Evening Star* (the letter is dated January 14, 1898), Book of Clippings in JWCG/M.
52. Washington *Colored American*, November 5, 1898, p. 8, December 10, 1898, p. 4, December 17, 1898, p. 4, December 24, 1898, p. 4, January 7, 1899, p. 9, February 4, 1899, p. 7, January 6, 1900, p. 11, December 29, 1900, p. 5, March 16, 1901, p. 8, December 14, 1901, p. 9, December 28, 1901, p. 7, December 20, 1902, p. 16, January 3, 1903, p. 1, January 10, 1903, January 2, 1904. Once an article appeared solely to announce the names of newly elected members. See Washington *Colored American*, March 25, 1899. See also Boston *Transcript*, December 12, 1899, p. 9; Grisham to Cromwell, January 8, 1902, and February 24, 1902, in JWCG/M.

organizations committed to race defense. In December, 1899, the ANA's annual meeting and that of the council's executive committee overlapped. Among the men who were prominent members of both organizations and present for the two meetings were W. E. B. Du Bois, president of the ANA, Alexander Walters, president of the council, Kelly Miller, John E. Bruce, John W. Cromwell, and Albert P. Miller. At the close of the two groups' separate sessions, a committee of prominent black Washingtonians, headed by Daniel Murray, a member of the Library of Congress staff, sponsored a joint reception for them.[53]

As the ANA began its sixth year in 1903, many members were concerned because the organization had achieved so little. Besides occasional papers and annual meetings there was little else to which to point. But even more alarming were a series of patterns that seemed to be constants; small growth in membership; steady loss of new and old members; failure of members to pay dues; poor attendance by members and the general public at annual meetings; the inability to find financial resources for an expanded program; and lack of public interest in the group's activities and goals. As a result, by the fall of 1903, most of the members who were concerned about the survival and development of the ANA had decided that its main problem, and one which, if rectified, would probably solve the others, was its uninvolved president, W. E. B. Du Bois.

53. Washington *Colored American*, January 6, 1900, pp. 11, 13, 16.

IV *Quest for an Audience*

Shortly after its founding in 1897 the ANA commenced to publish, in the form of occasional papers, short essays written by members of the society. Usually these essays had been delivered earlier as papers at one of the annual meetings. They were selected for publication because the academy believed them to be excellent examples of black intellectual ability, correctives to distorted or prejudiced opinions concerning their race, and significant contributions to the general body of knowledge about black Americans. Over the course of its thirty-two years of existence, the ANA published twenty-two occasional papers, some of them containing more than one essay.

The first two occasional papers, published by the ANA in 1897, found a small, but deeply interested body of readers who, through these pamphlets or reviews of them, became aware of the organization. The appearance of Occasional Paper no. 1, Kelly Miller's *Review of Hoffman's Race Traits and Tendencies of the American Negro* was heralded by "reading Notices" in the New York *Age* and the Washington *Bee*, two widely circulated black newspapers. Shortly afterwards, the Washington *Times* and the Boston *Transcript*, both major newspapers in their respective cities, discussed the Miller article. In the months following the organizational meeting, Miller read his piece before Washington's Bethel Literary and Historical Association and the Hampton (Virginia) Institute Summer Conference. This last appearance led to the printing of a summarized version in the institute's magazine, the *Southern Workman*. At the request of John W. Cromwell, Robert Russa Moton, commandant of the Hampton cadets, agreed to act as a salesman for the ANA's papers. Moton, who thought Miller's pamphlet "well gotten up" and a "credit to the Academy," sold at least twenty-six copies in Virginia.[1]

George E. Stevens, pastor of the Bethany Baptist Church in Syracuse, New York, and Charles A. Sheldon, general manager and treasurer of the Consolidated Car Heating Company in Albany, New York, each wrote directly to the ANA to purchase a copy of Occasional Paper no. 1. In his letter, Stevens expressed a desire "to come in closer touch with the American Negro Academy." Sheldon requested, in addition to the paper, "some information as to who Professor Miller is, and what are his qualifications for speaking authoritatively upon this subject."[2]

George W. Henderson, pastor of the chapel at Straight University in New Orleans, and Peter H. Clark, principal of a black high school in St. Louis, both shared their opinion of Miller's paper in letters to John W. Cromwell. To Henderson, a future member of the ANA, Miller's criticism of Hoffman's book represented the kind of vigorous and intelligent defense which blacks needed. "I have been pained," the black Congregationalist minister wrote, "as doubtless many others have been, that we [black Americans] have not been able to answer with adequate learning and scholarship the constant attacks and criticisms upon us and our rights, with which the public press teems, especially the Southern press. Mr. Miller's article is the right thing, and admirably done. We need to do more of this kind of work." Clark, a veteran black activist and founding member of the ANA, was less satisfied. In his opinion, Miller had picked "a flaw or two in Hoffman's book" but failed to disprove the main charges. "Who," he asked Cromwell, "will be the next to ride a tilt against Hoffman?"[3]

Occasional Paper no. 2, W. E. B. Du Bois's essay, *The Conservation of Races*, was commented on and reprinted in full by the Lagos *Weekly Record* in Nigeria; T. Thomas Fortune took issue with parts of it in an article in the New York *Sun*, criticizing the motives behind the founding of the ANA; and, early in 1898, the *Southern Workman* summarized the paper. Peter H. Clark's reaction to part of it was very positive. He was so impressed with Du Bois's stress on the need to eliminate "immorality, crime and laziness

1. Proceedings, 39; Washington *Bee*, September 4, 1897, p. 4; "Review of Mr. Hoffman's Book by Professor Kelly Miller," *Southern Workman*, XXVII (September, 1897), 180; Moton to Cromwell, August 18, September 27, 1897, in JWCG/M.

2. Stevens to Cromwell, November 9, 1897, Sheldon to Cromwell, September 28, 1897, in JWCG/M.

3. Henderson to Cromwell, December 26, 1898, Clark to Cromwell, February 12, 1898, in JWCG/M.

among the Negroes" that he sent a copy to Ralph Tyler, a black on the staff of the Columbus (Ohio) *Dispatch*, asking him to give the paper a notice. Clark purchased a dozen copies "for distribution among my friends," and asked Cromwell to send him "as many extras as you can spare" for circulation throughout St. Louis. On the other hand, Clark felt that Du Bois, through the critical analysis of black weaknesses and failings, pleaded "guilty to [Frederick] Hoffman's charges" of black inferiority, but suggested neither "a cause for the evil nor a remedy." Du Bois's paper aroused some interest among the faculty and friends of Hampton Institute, but not half as much as Miller's paper did. Moton sold only eight copies of Occasional Paper no. 2.[4]

The officers and members of the ANA took great pride in Occasional Papers nos. 1 and 2. George N. Grisham of Kansas City, Missouri, was of the opinion that if the organization did "no more next year, its existence will be fully justified." Even Peter H. Clark, who had been equally generous with both criticisms and compliments, pronounced himself "pleased with the publications of the year 1897, though not satisfied." Speaking as a friend of the society, Robert R. Moton of Hampton Institute assured Cromwell in the spring of 1898 that "the two publications so far have been most excellent." And, in his presidential address to the first annual meeting in December, 1897, Alexander Crummell described "the deep interest" aroused by the appearance of these two papers. Crummell informed his listeners that not only did they "reach the circles of scholars and thinkers in this country," but they "attracted interest and inquiry where the mere declamatory effusions, or, the so-called eloquent harangues of aimless talkers and political wire-pullers would fall like snowflakes upon the waters." The ANA did distribute the papers widely among intellectuals, but the available evidence suggests that neither paper excited wide interest in either the black or white community. It was true, however, that a small circle of readers, which included members of both races, had welcomed them as significant contributions to the body of literature on race relations.[5]

At the first annual meeting in December, 1897, John W. Cromwell reported on the distribution of Occasional Papers nos. 1 and 2, and that five

---

4. "The Conservation of Races," *Southern Workman*, XXVII (February, 1898), 2; Clark to Cromwell, May 11, May 19, 1897, February 12, 1898, Moton to Cromwell, November 16, December 21, 1897, March 4, (no year, but probably 1898), all in JWCG/M.

5. Grisham to Cromwell, November 24, 1897, Clark to Cromwell, February 12, 1898, Moton to Cromwell, April 1, 1898, all in JWCG/M. Crummell, "The Attitude of the American Mind toward the Negro Intellect," ANA Occasional Papers, no. 3 (1898), 17–18.

hundred of each pamphlet had been printed. Strenuous efforts by the corresponding secretary to place them in the hands of members, "representative educators, . . . men in our public life," and the general public had produced the following results: 135 copies of no. 1 and 70 copies of no. 2 had been mailed for review and as complimentary copies; 72 copies each of nos. 1 and 2 had been distributed to members; 97 copies of no. 1 and 37 copies of no. 2 had been sold; 27 copies of no. 1 and 25 copies of no. 2 had been given to agents; and 169 copies of no. 1 and 300 copies of no. 2 were on hand. Cromwell had received purchase requests for the two pamphlets from the Boston Public Library and individuals unknown to him in Baltimore, Milwaukee, New York City, Syracuse, and Albany. In two or three places he also sold them through agents who were not ANA members. One, the bookseller at Wilberforce University in Ohio, was only able to dispose of a few. Cromwell's agent in Baltimore reported eight sales, all of Kelly Miller's paper. "Have many promises," he explained, "but [they] fail to take. All stand on price." Occasional Paper no. 1 was being offered for $.25, no. 2 for $.15. Among the recipients of complimentary copies of the two occasional papers was Collis P. Huntington, president of the Southern Pacific Railroad, Drew Theological Seminary, the New York Public Library, and the Hartford Theological Seminary.[6]

In March, 1898, the executive committee decided to publish two papers written by Alexander Crummell: "Civilization, the Primal Need of the Negro Race," the address he delivered at the ANA's organizational meeting; and "The Attitude of the American Mind Toward the Negro Intellect," his presidential address at the first annual meeting of the ANA. The two were issued as Occasional Paper no. 3. In the second paper, Crummell discussed white hostility toward black intellectual activity, tracing the origins of this form of racism back to the earliest appearance of blacks in the English colonies. He also pointed to the current enthusiasm for industrial education as the newest manifestation of the continuous hostility toward black intellect. Both of these themes were marshaled to support his argument that the ANA was a unique and important institution. The unchanging pattern of

6. Proceedings, 27; Herbert Putnam to Cromwell, November 19, 1897, Cushing and Company to Cromwell, September 10 and September 22, 1897, DesForges and Co. to ANA, October 18, 1897, E. D. Chapman to Cromwell, June 3, 1897, G. P. Putnam's Sons to ANA, June 10 and June 11, 1897, Chas A. Sheldon to Cromwell, September 28, 1897, E. S. Clarke to Cromwell, December 27, 1897, A. Theo. Luca to Cromwell, October 19, 1897, C. P. Huntington to Cromwell, September 29, 1897, S. G. Ayres to "Dear Sir," October 23, 1897, S. G. Ayres to ANA, October 29, 1897, A. T. Perry to Cromwell, July 21, 1897, all in JWCG/M.

white hostility to black genius meant that the blacks had to assume responsibility for the "cultivation and fostering of . . . [their] own race-capacity." And this, Crummell stressed, was what the ANA was engaged in doing through its meetings and publications.[7]

The ANA had one thousand copies of Occasional Paper no. 3 printed, of which ten were given to each member and thirty-five to the author. Others were distributed by the corresponding secretary to libraries, educational institutions, prominent individuals, and newspapers. In addition, John E. Bruce, a New York member of the organization, sent copies of the pamphlet to Democratic and Republican politicians in the northeast.[8]

Despite the fact that it was distributed widely, with one exception, all of the reaction to the occasional paper came from members of the society. William H. Crogman included a paraphrase of "Civilization, the Primal Need of the Negro Race," in *Progress of a Race*, a book he coedited in 1897. The paraphrase also appeared when another edition of the book was published in 1902. Crogman, a consistent advocate of higher education for blacks, did this because the paper contained ideas with which he strongly agreed. William H. Ferris felt Crummell's two papers to be the best existing critique of "the fad of industrial education for the Negro," an idea he believed had "been engendered by Booker T. Washington in his desire for the 'good will' of the Southern white man." "Dr. Crummell's paper," he wrote Cromwell, "in its humorous satire upon the advocates of extreme industrialism for the Negro seems to me to be as effective as Cardinal Newman's powerful lectures on Anglican difficulties."[9]

The only newspaper to comment on the occasional paper was the Washington *Colored American*. "Civilization, The Primal Need of the Negro Race," in the opinion of its reviewer, "touched the root of the intellectual problem of the Negro in this country." "In every sentence," the review continued, "there appears new thought, formidable reasoning, and true con-

7. Proceedings, 43; Crummell, "The Attitude of the American Mind toward the Negro Intellect," 13–14, 16. At the organizational meeting on March 5, 1897, the academy had decided to publish "Civilization, the Primal Need of the Negro Race," along with the minutes of that meeting as the first number of the ANA transactions. The minutes of the meeting were published, but "Civilization" was not included with them, probably because the executive committee later realized that this would have buried an important paper in a business document. Certainly publication as an occasional paper promised to give it wider circulation.

8. Proceedings, 44, 60, 63; Bruce to Cromwell, June 26, 1898, in JWCG/M.

9. Kletzing and Crogman (eds.), *Progress of a Race*, 361–67; J. W. Gibson and W. H. Crogman (eds.), *Progress of a Race* (1902), 385–91; Ferris to Cromwell, December 20, 1899, in JWCG/M.

clusions." The content of the second paper was described as "the most unique and powerful presentation of the position taken by the white people, principally the scholars and better classes, toward educated colored persons." The reviewer also expressed strong agreement with Crummell's criticisms of industrial education, which he felt made clear "the difference between labor and thoughtful labor, a new idea entirely." [10]

Crogman's actions, as well as the comments by Ferris and the Washington *Colored American*, were gratifying, but the absence of any reaction from leaders in the country's academic, intellectual, religious, and philanthropic circles was very disappointing to the ANA. In a report to the second annual meeting in December, 1898, John W. Cromwell noted, with disappointment, that even though no. 3 was "distributed more liberally than [1 and 2] the previous year," there had been little public interest. The following month, the executive committee, motivated partly by the many copies of Occasional Papers nos. 2 and 3 still in its possession, ordered that they "be sent to libraries of colored educational institutions." Copies of no. 1, however, were reserved "for sale, except in rare cases." [11]

Charles Cook, the author of Occasional Paper no. 4, *A Comparative Study of the Negro Problem*, had originally entitled it "A Study of the Conditions Attending upon the Entrance of England and Japan upon the Progressive Stage as a Part of Determining the Point of Equilibrium between the White and Colored Peoples of America." Although the essay was essentially a series of reflections on the problems of blacks in America, its most consistent theme was the search for an adequate response by blacks to their situation as a powerless, oppressed minority. Rejecting militancy, business enterprise, and passive acquiescence as solutions, Cook argued that blacks should demonstrate a moral, religious, and patriotic superiority over whites. This, in his opinion, would allow them to challenge white prejudice by demonstrating its contradictions. Delivered at the second annual meeting in December, 1898, Cook's paper was then published by the *Southern Workman* in early 1899. Subsequently, because the ANA wished to distribute the paper under its own name, the executive committee contracted with the magazine for five hundred reprints of the article. [12]

10. Washington *Colored American*, July 9, 1898, p. 5.
11. Proceedings, 60, 62.
12. "A Comparative Study of the Negro Problem by Charles C. Cook," *Southern Workman*, XXVIII (February, 1899), 46, and XXVIII (March, 1899), 92; Proceedings, 64; Alice M. Bacon to Cromwell, January 27 and February 6, 1899, C. W. Betts to Cromwell, February 8, 1899, all in JWCG/M.

Published in 1899, Occasional Paper no. 5, *How the Black St. Domingo Legion Saved the Patriot Army in the Siege of Savannah, 1779*, was a careful and accurate discussion of the role of a Haitian regiment (part of the French military forces that fought alongside the American revolutionary army) in preventing the capture of Savannah, Georgia, by British troops. Its author, Theophilus G. Steward, an AME minister who had been, for a time, a missionary in Haiti, learned of the incident while living in that country. At the time he wrote the paper, Steward was chaplain to the all-black 25th United States Colored Infantry, and stationed at Fort Logan, Colorado. Consequently, he mailed the manuscript to the ANA and it was read at the second annual meeting in December, 1898, by John H. Smyth. Kelly Miller, a member of the subcommittee that recommended publication of the paper, felt that it "treated of an important historical occurrence." Shortly after it appeared in print, the academy received a request for a copy of "your famed new publication" from John H. Toomer, an employee of the Savannah Board of Tax Assessors and Receivers. Toomer indicated his intention to donate it to Savannah's public library. James T. Holly, a corresponding member in Haiti, also considered it an important historical study. After reading it, he purchased a dozen copies.[13]

Theophilus G. Steward, however, was very displeased with the printed version of his paper. A careful and in many ways meticulous writer, he felt that, as published, the occasional paper presented a poor impression of him and the society. These feelings were communicated directly to the executive committee. He pointed out indignantly, "The note put to Sergeant Jasper's banner belongs to Count Pulaski's banner and should have been on p. 11. 'Anxiety' is divided in the wrong place; 'Hessian' is robbed of its *capital*. These things do not speak well for the 'Negro Academy' nor do I think the paper or the style of printing, generally up to the dignity of the august organization. Lift the Booklets to a higher plane." No correction was ever made of the errors Steward pointed out because neither he nor the academy could afford the cost of a second printing.[14]

Occasional Paper no. 6, *The Disfranchisement of the Negro*, was the third tract issued by the ANA in 1899. In it, John L. Love examined the procedures being used to disfranchise southern Negroes, traced the history of this movement, scrutinized the revised constitutions of Mississippi,

13. Proceedings, 56; Steward to Cromwell, n.d., Miller to Cromwell, November 13, 1898, Toomer to Cromwell, July 8, 1899, Holly to Cromwell, November 27, 1901, all in JWCG/M.
14. Steward to Cromwell, June 16, 1899, in JWCG/M.

South Carolina, and Louisiana, and analyzed the effect on blacks of changes in these states' fundamental laws. Francis Garrison, son of the abolitionist William Lloyd Garrison, and a member of the Boston publishing firm, Houghton Mifflin, was sent a complimentary copy of the pamphlet. Garrison found it so impressive that he returned a letter with an order for seven more, which he planned to distribute. It was, he wrote to Cromwell, his "wish that many thousand might be circulated." ANA member Alexander Walters agreed. He believed the paper "the best production on the subject" in print. In addition to quoting extensively from Love's article in a Boston speech, Walters sought permission for the Afro-American Council, of which he was the president, to purchase and distribute a thousand copies. William H. Ferris thought Occasional Paper no. 6 an excellent means of counteracting "the idea that it was a mistake to give the Negro the ballot and that the Negro had better surrender his political and civil rights." In his opinion, Love's paper, along with several other ANA publications, gave "facts which might cause those who sympathize with the South to pause and take breath," possibly even supplanting their "apathy and indifference" toward the problems of blacks with "a thoughtful noble spirit." And, it was probably the publication of *Disfranchisement of the Negro* that prompted Charles Winter Wood, a teacher of elocution and drama at Tuskegee, to write directly to Love requesting "the full set of the occasional papers." [15]

As the year 1899 drew to a close, John W. Cromwell and John E. Bruce both made special efforts to remind the general public of the papers that the ANA had published that year, as well as earlier. In November, 1899, Cromwell was negotiating with *Howard's American Magazine*, a black publication based in Pittsburgh, Pennsylvania, for the purchase of advertising space. Though the evidence is unclear as to how Cromwell planned to use the space, he probably wanted the magazine to print a list of the ANA papers available for purchase, along with an announcement of the society's forthcoming annual meeting. Unfortunately, so few copies of *Howard's American Magazine* have survived that it is impossible to know whether the advertisement appeared, and, if so, what it said. In December, 1899, an article on the American Negro Academy written by Bruce appeared in the Boston *Transcript*. In it, he recommended to the *Transcript*'s readers the "valuable papers" which the association "occasionally" published and sold "at a nominal price." "If," Bruce promised, "our white friends in the North

---

15. Garrison to Cromwell, March 6, 1899, Walters to Cromwell, October 4, 1899, Ferris to Cromwell, December 20, 1899, Wood to Love, September 14, 1899, all in JWCG/M.

who are anxious to know what the Negro is doing toward the solution of the racial problem—what the thinkers of the race are contributing to that end—would subscribe to the literature of the academy they would find that these earnest Negro scholars have an intelligent grasp of the great questions which not only concern Negroes, but the nation of which they are a part." Bruce also used the article to publicize the third annual meeting scheduled to meet in two weeks.[16]

One of the papers delivered at that meeting was an address by W. E. B. Du Bois entitled "The Present Outlook for the Dark Races of Mankind." In June, 1900, the executive committee voted to print this paper as Occasional Paper no. 7, knowing at the time that it was scheduled to appear in the July issue of the *AME Church Review*. The situation almost guaranteed that the pamphlet would sell poorly. The ANA could not get its publication out before July, and it lacked the block of subscribers and guaranteed purchasers that the *Review*, a church-sponsored magazine, could take for granted. The executive committee's motivation for this decision was almost certainly the desire to lay claim to what it considered an ANA paper no matter what the consequences.

When Du Bois was informed of this decision, he wrote to John W. Cromwell, questioning its wisdom. "I am," he informed Cromwell, "doubtful of the expediency of publishing my last year's address. Those colored people who may want it can find it in the *Review*. For others the matter is a little old and the Academy has already published one of my papers. You will of course follow your own and the committee's decision." It is not clear whether Du Bois made arrangements with the editor of the *Review* to print his paper before or after he read it at the meeting in December, 1899. If the latter, his action may have reflected a low regard for the ANA's occasional papers as a vehicle for his writings. In any case, the committee must have been impressed by Du Bois's logic, for they decided to publish another paper as the ANA's next occasional paper.[17]

In 1901, *Right on the Scaffold or the Martyrs of 1822* appeared as Occasional Paper no. 7. This paper, which had been read by its author, Archibald H. Grimké, at the third annual meeting in December, 1899, was a history of the unsuccessful slave insurrection plotted by Denmark Vesey, a free black

16. Thomas Wallace Swann to Cromwell, November 2, 1899, James W. H. Howard to Cromwell, November 6, 1899, both in JWCG/M; Boston *Transcript*, December 12, 1899, p. 9.

17. Proceedings, 74, 77. The July, 1900, issue of the *AME Church Review* is no longer extant, making it impossible to see if the essay appeared. See also Kealing to Cromwell, March 15, 1899, Du Bois to Cromwell, November, 1900, both in JWCG/M.

of Charleston, South Carolina. Unlike a historian who later wrote on this same subject, Grimké believed that Vesey was the mastermind behind a well-conceived and potentially successful slave uprising. Although the decision to issue the paper was made in June, 1900, lack of funds prevented action for several months. By March, 1901, it had been printed, for the executive committee directed, on the sixteenth of that month, that "200 copies . . . be distributed among members and libraries and 25 to the author." [18]

Grimké, who had a wide circle of friends and acquaintances, frequently shared with them copies of articles he had written, including his papers published by the ANA. One of his white friends who received "the Martyrs of 1822" was Richard Price Hallowell of Boston, a wealthy businessman and philanthropist, who in his youth had been an abolitionist. In return, Hallowell sent a note of thanks for

a bit of history of which, I must confess, I have hitherto been almost entirely ignorant. I knew that Denmark Vesey had plotted an insurrection which ended in disaster to him and his companions, but that is all. . . . He is a hero of your race. . . . The record of such men ought to be kept fresh in the minds of colored men of every succeeding generation. It should be an incentive to resistance of the tyranny and persecution of the present day. Fortunately, secret plotting is no longer necessary, but the spirit that inspired it is the same that demands today a full recognition of not only the manhood but the civil, political, and social rights of the colored man.

Another white Bostonian, Albert E. Pillsbury, who was a member of a well-known family of reformers, a distinguished constitutional lawyer, and a former attorney general of Massachusetts, also received a copy, though several years after the paper had been in print. In his acknowledgment, Pillsbury, who possessed a keen sense of judgment and who was apparently familiar with Grimké's writings, told him that "as a piece of pure literature . . . it is probably your high-water mark." [19]

There was an interval of four years between the time Occasional Paper no. 8, *The Educated Negro and His Mission*, was delivered and its appearance in print. Presented by William S. Scarborough at the meeting in December, 1899, under the title, "Higher Education: Its Relation to the Fu-

18. Richard C. Wade has suggested in his essay, "The Vesey Plot: A Reconsideration," *Journal of Southern History*, XXX (May, 1964), 143–61, that the Vesey plot existed only in the minds of hysterical whites.
19. Hallowell to Grimké, May 21, 1903, Pillsbury to Grimké, October 15, 1913, both in A. H. Grimké Papers, Moorland-Spingarn Research Center, Howard University, Washington, D.C.

ture of the Negro," it was an argument for the indispensability of black scholars and college graduates in shaping the healthy social, economic, and political development of black Americans. In December, 1901, a subcommittee of the executive committee recommended its publication, conditional upon revisions by the author. Accordingly, the paper was returned to Scarborough who held it for almost a year before making changes and returning it in October, 1902. The executive committee had originally planned to publish the paper in a pamphlet containing papers written by other ANA members. This plan had to be abandoned when Scarborough made it clear that it was totally unacceptable to him. "I cannot," he informed the executive committee, "consent to have my paper appear with any other—that is under the same cover. If it appears *at all it must* appear alone and must go forth on its *own* merits. No other plan will meet my approval." In December, 1902, the executive committee, after receiving a favorable report on Scarborough's revised manuscript from its subcommittee, voted to publish it "as soon as funds . . . [became] available." By January, 1903, the organization had enough money to print the paper, and five hundred copies were ordered. The size of the order, however, was doubled at Scarborough's request. Of the thousand copies printed, five hundred were reserved for the author, who agreed to pay the ANA $10 as his share of the publication costs.[20]

Scarborough received the five hundred occasional papers he had been promised, but failed to send the $10. In a letter to John W. Cromwell written in late December, 1903, he assured the corresponding secretary that he would send "that $10 . . . soon," attributing his failure to do so eleven months earlier to a lack of cash as a result of his recent European trip. Cromwell, who, by this time, was very angry with Scarborough because of his failure to pay the bill (and who may have feared that it would never be paid), shared the problem and his concerns about it with the members of the academy who met in Washington that month for the seventh annual meeting. The members referred the matter to the executive committee. At a meeting in February, 1904, the committee directed Cromwell to correspond with Scarborough in order to "secure prompt adjustment of the obligation"; and passed a motion "that no publication . . . be undertaken in be-

20. John L. Love and Kelly Miller to Cromwell, December 10, 1901, Scarborough to Cromwell, December 23, 1901, December 20, 1902, January 20, 1903, all in JWCG/M; Proceedings, 77, 100, 101.

half of any member until the amount pledged by him has actually been paid." Still the debt went unsettled.[21]

To eliminate the possibility of this happening again, the executive committee offered the following amendment to Article 7 of the constitution at the eighth annual meeting in March, 1905: "failure [by any member] in payment of [an] obligation voluntarily assumed for two years, shall cause membership to cease." Because the rules of the ANA required that a constitutional amendment be voted on at the annual meeting subsequent to that in which it had been proposed, no decision was made until December, 1905, when the amendment was approved.[22]

Since Scarborough failed to pay his debt, he ceased to be a member of the ANA either in December, 1905, or in December, 1907, depending on how the amendment was interpreted. Scarborough was never an affluent man, and given his numerous memberships in professional and learned societies, plus the frequent trips he took to educational and religious meetings, there must have been a number of times when his financial obligations exceeded his income. Nevertheless, it is hard to believe that he could not have paid the ANA $10 sometime between 1903 and 1905. For some reason he was not only unwilling to pay that sum, but was not interested in doing anything to placate the members of the ANA, such as agreeing to make small payments over a period of time. In 1924, nineteen years after the organization had passed the amendment to Article 7, Arthur A. Schomburg, who knew nothing about the cause of Scarborough's separation from the ANA, met him at a gathering in New York City. He took the occasion to remind Scarborough of the ANA and its work, urging him to actively "support . . . the principles which hold it together." In a letter describing this meeting to John W. Cromwell, Schomburg said that Scarborough told him "He didn't know whether he was in or out." For good reason, Schomburg found this an unsatisfactory answer. This feeling was reflected in his summary comment to Cromwell: "If he [Scarborough] can support the white organizations to which he belongs, greater by right must he do something with those of his own race."[23]

21. Scarborough to Cromwell, December 28, 1903 in JWCG/M; Proceedings, 113, 116.
22. Proceedings, 116, 121–22, 132–33.
23. For an excellent introduction to Scarborough's very active life as a scholar, churchman, and educational politician see Francis P. Weisenberger, "William Saunders Scarborough," *Ohio History*, LXXII (October, 1962), 2–27, and LXXII, (January, 1963), 15–45. Schomburg to Cromwell, March 5, 1924, in Arthur Alfonso Schomburg correspondence to John Wesley Cromwell, Moorland-Spingarn Research Center, Howard University, Washington, D.C., hereinafter cited as SC/MSRC.

Between 1897 and 1903, through the publication, sale, and distribution of the first eight occasional papers, the ANA created a small audience for its work and established a public identity. The Buffalo (New York) Public Library, the library of the Department of the Interior's Bureau of Education, the Newberry Library in Chicago, the New Hampshire State Library, the public library in St. Louis, and the library of Oberlin College were, after 1897, among the regular recipients of the occasional papers. These and a number of other public and private libraries were initially presented complimentary copies of Occasional Papers nos. 1 and 2. As a result, most of these institutions asked to be placed on the organization's list of paying subscribers. Complimentary copies of the papers were also sent to a selected group of whites thought to be interested either in black-white relations or the writings of black Americans. At the request of John W. Cromwell, various ANA members submitted lists of people, who, in their opinion, fitted either or both categories. Only one of these lists is still extant. It was compiled by W. E. B. Du Bois in 1899, and included the names of nine white Philadelphians whose work or philanthropic activities linked them to the black community or to issues that affected it.[24]

Though the total number of people who read the papers seems to have been small, the ANA received several letters that were indications of their effectiveness as a means of introducing the society and the ideas of its members to a larger public. The occasional papers probably stimulated Jasper C. Barnes of Maryville College in Maryville, Tennessee, to write to the academy in 1898, asking for "statistics, literature, or suggestions" that would aid him in preparing "a paper on the influence of the Past and Present Industrial Systems of the South on the Development of Personality in the Afro-Americans." A year later the ANA received a very gratifying communication from its former antagonist, T. Thomas Fortune, editor of the New York *Age*. After acknowledging receipt of Occasional Paper no. 5, Fortune complimented the ANA on the "good work" it was doing in the "pub-

---

24. Brown to Cromwell, December 27, 1899, Bureau of Education, U.S. Department of Interior to Cromwell, June 13, 1899, F. V. Cheney to Cromwell, January 30, May 13, 1899, January 10, 1900, Arthur H. Chase to ANA, November 26, 1900, F. M. Crunden to "Secretary, ANA," February 27, 1899, Azariah S. Root to Cromwell, September 15, September 29, 1899, Du Bois to Cromwell, November 17, 1899, in JWCG/M.

All of the persons on the list Du Bois compiled were Philadelphians involved in some form of educational or philanthropic work that brought them into contact with members of the black community. The following names appeared on Du Bois's list: Charles C. Harrison; Susan P. Wharton; Professor Spiers; Samuel McCune Lindsay; Silas Weir Mitchell; Talcott T. Williams; Robert C. Ogden; Isaac Hallowell Clothier; and Julia Farrington.

lication of these pamphlets." In 1902, when Kate Brousseau, a teacher of psychology and pedagogy in the State Normal School at Los Angeles, requested "definite information" on "the social condition of the Negro," she was sent copies of Occasional Papers nos. 1–4. Brousseau, a candidate for the doctoral degree at the University of Paris, was gathering materials for her thesis, "The Problem of Negro Education in the United States." After reading the papers, she wrote a second time to express her thanks and to share her opinion in regard to the debate as to whether blacks were best suited for industrial training or higher education. "While," she reflected, "the majority of both races must do manual work, I cannot understand why a Negro who had literary or artistic tastes should not be encouraged to follow his natural bent. I imagine that the Dumas, Mr. Tanner, Prof. K. Miller, Prof. Du Bois would have made very indifferent blacksmiths or carpenters."[25]

The scattered newspaper notices, the requests by major public and private libraries for copies, and the letters of inquiry produced by the occasional papers pleased the ANA, but this interest did little to alleviate its growing concern and disappointment at the general lack of enthusiasm shown by most black and white publications, and at the limited sales of the occasional papers. In an attempt to give papers considered worthy of distribution a wider circulation, the third annual meeting passed a motion in 1899 authorizing the executive committee to arrange "with the editor of the *AME Church Review* or other magazine as may be desirable for the publications of the Academy." Two manuscripts were sent to the *Review*, but the opposition of members who wanted the organization to issue its own papers, brought a quick halt to the practice. These same members also accelerated their efforts to get the society to publish its own magazine.[26]

Several months before the third annual meeting authorized negotiations with "the *AME Church Review* or other magazine," Hightower T. Kealing, editor of the *Review*, had asked John W. Cromwell for a list of the ANA's members. He wished "to communicate with them in an effort to secure their

25. There is no way of knowing or of even estimating how many people read the academy's publications. If, as is likely, the ANA kept records of the sales and distribution of the various occasional papers published between 1897 and 1924, they have not survived. Barnes to "Gentlemen," September 19, 1898, Fortune to Cromwell, June 16, 1899, Brousseau to Cromwell, April 2, 1902, August 27, 1902, all in JWCG/M. Brousseau's thesis was published under the title *L'education des nègres aux Etats-Unis* in 1904, the same year the University of Paris awarded her a doctoral degree.

26. Proceedings, 72, 77. For reasons that will be discussed later, their efforts were unsuccessful.

co-operation, by contribution and otherwise, in making the Review the broadest and most scholarly publication ever issued by the race." In the same letter, Kealing told Cromwell he would "be glad" to have the academy use his magazine to speak "to a larger audience than any present medium at its command allows," and assured the corresponding secretary that the *Review* "was intended to be the highest expression for the whole race and such I am laboring to make it."[27]

Although there is no evidence that Cromwell sent Kealing a list of ANA members, it is hard to imagine how he legitimately could have denied it to him, since the editor of the *Review* was himself a member of the society. However, Kealing's letter sheds an interesting light on the motion passed at the third annual meeting. Kealing himself proposed this motion because he needed articles for the magazine he was editing and wanted to use the ANA membership as one of his sources. It was at Kelly Miller's insistence that the motion was amended to include other publications besides the *Review*. In 1899, even its most committed members were discouraged about the ANA's inability to give its occasional papers wider distribution or to finance a magazine. Nevertheless, Cromwell, Kelly Miller, Francis J. Grimké, Walter B. Hayson, and others must have realized that to allow their papers to be printed in the pages of another organization's journal meant not only abandonment of a major goal, but that the papers would cease to be clearly identified as products of the ANA.[28]

Of the ANA's various public activities, the occasional papers were the most important in stimulating a growing public consciousness of the society's existence. One sign of this was the individual requests for information or help which the association received. In March, 1898, A. J. Carter wrote to the executive committee, requesting the ANA's assistance in gaining admission to the United States Military Academy at West Point. The minutes record, tersely, "no action taken thereon." Two months later, an article on the ANA and its publications prompted S. J. Taylor, "A. B., Principal, Epiphany Hall, Cuttingham near Cape Palmas, Liberia," to send John W. Cromwell the following letter, which expressed his deep appreciation of the ANA's goals, and his desire to subscribe for its publications:

I trust you will sympathize with the presumption that shows itself in my writing you, a perfect stranger, to inquire about the "American Negro Academy" of which you are the corresponding secretary.

27. Kealing to Cromwell, March 15, 1899, in JWCG/M.
28. Proceedings, 72.

My main reason for taking such step is because, as a Negro, I feel that nothing that is undertaken to develop my race anywhere should ever be foreign or uninteresting to me.

Then laboring in this part of Africa, I deem it the greatest privilege to be in touch with such enlightened minds that can conceive and organize any scheme whose object is "to uplift the race to higher planes of thought and action."

I would therefore be very grateful if you can send me some information about your "academy" and also let me know whether its publications are obtainable by any one who is not one of its *bona fide* members.

Thanking you in anticipation for your kindness and wishing every possible success to your most laudable and patriotic efforts.

It is difficult to believe that Taylor's letter did not result in his receipt of the published occasional papers and a place on the academy's mailing list.[29]

From its beginning, one of the chief goals of the American Negro Academy was to publish its own journal. When the decision was made at the organizational meeting in March, 1897, to print Du Bois's and Miller's papers as occasional papers, this was viewed as a temporary expedient because the association did not yet have a publication. At the time no one doubted that the situation would soon be changed. In the months following the organizational meeting the executive committee was continuously engaged in creating a structure and format for the proposed magazine. All members were requested to contribute articles, limits were set on the length and number of pieces to be included, and prizes were to be awarded "for the best essays on literary and scientific topics." These proposals, plus a recommendation that the magazine be a quarterly instead of an annual, were presented to the December, 1897, meeting. Absence of funds to support the venture led to the appointment of a subcommittee consisting of Charles C. Cook, Kelly Miller, and John W. Cromwell to consider methods of financing it. The committee considered a "benefit entertainment" and an endowment fund appeal. Nothing came of the idea of a benefit, but in March, 1898, letters appealing for contributions to an ANA endowment fund were distributed to potential donors. The appeal, which described the academy as "an organization whose aim is the promotion of literature and art," sought to raise $1,000. The appeal pointed out that $100 "had already been subscribed in our circles here." At the second annual meeting in December, 1898, a report on the appeal revealed there had been "little or no response."[30]

29. Proceedings, 43 (the Proceedings give no information on Carter other than his name and request); Taylor to Cromwell, June 8, 1898, in JWCG/M.

30. Proceedings, 18, 19, 20, 25, 26, 39, 40, 41, 43; Cook to Cromwell, January 27, 1898,

In January, 1899, the executive committee decided to seek the advice of "friendly whites" in the literary and publishing fields concerning the best method of getting their papers into journals with an interracial and national readership. Consequently, Cromwell wrote to George Washington Cable, a distinguished southern writer and an outspoken opponent of the oppression of blacks; to John Vance Cheney, director of Chicago's Newberry Library; to Thomas Wentworth Higginson, author, abolitionist, and colonel of the all-black 1st South Carolina Volunteers during the Civil War; and to Francis J. Garrison, son of the abolitionist William Lloyd Garrison and a member of the Boston publishing firm, Houghton Mifflin. Of the four letters, only a copy of the one to Cable has survived. Probably in outline and content it was the standard form for the others. The ANA secretary opened the letter with a paragraph praising Cable for his "chivalric and able championship of the right of the Negro to equality of civic rights and to a fair and impartial hearing at the bar of an enlightened public opinion." Describing himself and the other ANA members as 'earnest but patient, determined though conservative," Cromwell explained that they were "convinced that a duty devolves upon the race itself to furnish its own champions to vindicate its claims to equal citizenship and to [gain?] recognition in the higher realms of culture and art, as well as to repel the covert and open assaults made against it by leaders of thought and action." After referring Cable to the ANA's constitution and Occasional Papers nos. 1, 2, and 3 for further information (sent "under separate cover of this date"), Cromwell stated his reason for writing:

Except in the rarest cases, we have but few men so well known that the publishers of such established quarterlies and monthlies as the Atlantic Monthly, the Forum, and North American Review, will give respectful consideration to any contribution we might make. Yet, we have not a few among us whose scholarship and literary ability would be creditable to any race.

To learn how best to secure an opportunity to direct these contributions, oft in sheer self-defense, is an object of this communication.[31]

Replies were received from Garrison, Higginson, and Cheney. Garrison suggested that the ANA submit its papers to the *Atlantic Monthly* ("which is published by the firm [with] whom I have long been connected"), pointing out that this magazine had "welcomed contributions from Prof. Du Bois, Hon. John S. Durham, Booker T. Washington, and Mr. Chas. W.

---

in JWCG/M. ANA appeal for endowment fund, n.d., in Bruce Papers. No list of those who contributed the hundred dollars described in the appeal letter has survived.

31. Proceedings, 63; Cromwell to Cable [copy], January 23, 1899, in JWCG/M.

Chesnutt." In a sweeping assessment of the then current situation on the American literary and publishing scene, the publishing executive expressed the opinion that "Literature knows neither race nor sex, and articles, stories, and books will not lack opportunities for publication on account of the color of the writers, especially in these days of numberless periodicals and sharp competition for good material on the part of the magazines and of press syndicates. Opportunity was never so great as now for securing a market for good work. The magazine editors, who have become the sieves through which most new writers have to pass and test their work, cannot know anything about the color or sex of the writers who send them manuscripts." Then, recalling the name and special concerns of the organization for which Cromwell was inquiring, Garrison allowed himself, for the space of a sentence, to become entangled in the problems that had led to this exchange of letters. "Doubtless," he continued, "the treatment of certain subjects bearing on the relationship of the races would betray by the standpoint of the writer his identification with one or the other race, but even then the attitude of the Atlantic, and I think also of the Century, Forum, and North American Review, show that they seek on any question of vital importance or great immediate interest the opposite view of those especially affected." Closing his letter with a reminder that Frederick Douglass had always gotten his opinions before the American people, Garrison assured Cromwell that the able black men of their day would also find "channels" open to them.[32]

Although Garrison's letter offered little that was helpful, it was the most serious reply received. Higginson's letter contained advice and comment on issues related to the ANA, but failed to even address the publishing question. "Keep writing and keep sending to publisher," was Cheney's one sentence response. It was not long after this that the ANA tried its brief experiment with the *AME Church Review*.[33]

Periodically, individual members reminded the society of its original commitment to publishing a magazine, but the failure of the 1898 appeal discouraged any further action until March, 1901, when the fourth annual

32. Garrison to Cromwell, March 6, 1899, Higginson to "Dear Sir," May 11, 1899, Cheney to Cromwell, January 30, 1899, all in JWCG/M. Logan in *Betrayal*, especially Chapter 13, "The Negro as Portrayed in the Leading Literary Magazines," presents an analysis that raises serious questions about the tone and content of Garrison's reply.
33. Garrison to Cromwell, March 6, 1899, Higginson to "Dear Sir," May 11, 1899, Cheney to Cromwell, January 30, 1899, all in JWCG/M. For a discussion of the ANA's brief experiment with the *AME Church Review*, see earlier this chapter.

meeting convened. At this meeting, John L. Love, a founding member, was the chief figure in an effort to get the ANA to attempt a second appeal. After extensive discussion, the idea was approved, and in June, 1901, letters requesting "subscriptions to a fund to guarantee the publication of a magazine for one year or until the same could be self-sustaining" were mailed to ANA members. Several pledges to the fund and $35 in cash were received. A letter opposing the project from Peter H. Clark of St. Louis was also received. However, most members even failed to reply. In early December, 1901, realizing that the appeal was also a referendum, the committee sent special "slips" to those who had not replied. When the fifth annual meeting assembled on December 30, 1901, the question of whether or not there would be a magazine was one of the ANA's main concerns.[34]

The matter came up during the meeting's business session. As part of the discussion, John W. Cromwell shared Peter H. Clark's letter. The opposition of the St. Louis educator was based on his belief that "the Afro-American public" would sustain "no literary ventures, not even those publications, which containing only misinformation and cringing politics, are conducted on a level with the development and aspirations of that public." As proof, Clark pointed to the limited sales of the occasional papers. The alternatives he suggested—"publication of approved papers in the AME Review," in periodicals "of national reputation" such as the *Independent* and *Arena*, and in "metropolitan papers of national circulation" and "reputation"—were the very approaches that were proving so unsatisfactory. The issue was discussed until John Love moved that the ANA instruct the executive committee "to return all funds and cancel all pledges." The motion was approved, but in an amended form which allowed the executive committee to make the final decision as to when this was to be done. Thus the second effort to raise funds for a magazine ended as unsuccessfully as the first.[35]

Although the fifth annual meeting had directed the executive committee to "return all funds and cancel all pledges," this order was not carried out. Possibly a shortage of funds made this impossible until dues had again built

34. Henderson to Cromwell, December 26, 1898, reveals that, in spite of the failure of the 1898 appeal the corresponding secretary had not given up the idea of publishing a magazine; another example of continued support for the idea is Grisham to Cromwell, December 15, 1899 (both of these letters are in JWCG/M). See also Proceedings, 87–88, 89, 90, 91; Grisham to Cromwell, September 3, 1901, Henderson to Cromwell, December 6, 1901, Clark to Cromwell, July 23, 1901, all in JWCG/M. The only donors to the appeal revealed in the ANA records are George N. Grisham and Orishatukeh Faduma.

35. Clark to Cromwell, July 23, 1901, in JWCG/M; Proceedings, 94.

up in the treasury. Possibly supporters of the magazine idea hoped for a reconsideration of the decision. Whatever the reason, the executive committee also failed to communicate to the members who had not been at the meeting in December, 1901, that the idea of publishing a magazine had been abandoned. Notice was not even sent to those members who had contributed to the appeal, but who had not been present. This poor handling of a delicate piece of business produced at least three letters from uninformed contributors, who asked for some information on the status of the proposed publication.[36]

Early in 1903, when the Capitol Savings Bank, the one black financial institution in Washington, D.C., failed, the situation regarding the contributions to the magazine appeal fund became even more complicated. Although the ANA did not keep all of its monies in this bank, the contributions to the appeal fund were on deposit there; and they were lost. However, it was not until February, 1904, that the executive committee explained to the various contributors that the magazine project had been abandoned and their money lost. Perhaps the executive committee was waiting to see if the bank's depositors would receive any of their money back. If so, the wait was in vain. The executive committee promised to repay the contributors to the appeal fund as soon as the ANA could afford to do so. In December, 1906, the association fulfilled its promise.[37]

Attempts by the ANA to become a publishing center met with little success during the years Cromwell and Du Bois headed the organization. In addition to issuing the occasional papers and making strenuous efforts to finance a literary magazine, the society also gave serious consideration to the publication of a yearbook containing pertinent statistics on the black American community; a series of economic tracts; and an annual "handbook . . . of the universities, colleges, and academies engaged in the instruction of colored youth." All of these projects were endorsed by an annual meeting, but none came to fruition. Besides the occasional papers, the association was only able to print copies of its constitution, minutes of three national meetings, and membership lists.[38]

36. Proceedings, 94; Grisham to Cromwell, January 8, 1902, Faduma to Cromwell, June 20, 1902, and December 29, 1903, in JWCG/M.
37. The failure of the Capitol Savings Bank is mentioned in Constance M. Green, *The Secret City: A History of Race Relations in the Nation's Capital* (Princeton, N.J., 1967), 160. It was also discussed by "Bruce Grit" (John Edward Bruce) in his column which appeared in the Washington *Colored American* on January 24, 1903, pp. 1, 4. See also Proceedings, 116, 140.
38. Proceedings, 28–29, 40, 55, 93; Du Bois to Cromwell, n.d. [*ca.* December 26, 1898], in JWCG/M.

Alexander Crummell (1819–1898). Founder and first president of the American Negro Academy. *Courtesy of Moorland-Spingarn Research Center*

W. E. B. Du Bois (1868–1963). Second president of the American Negro Academy.
Courtesy of Moorland-Spingarn Research Center

Archibald H. Grimké (1849–1930). Third president of the American Negro Academy. *Courtesy of Moorland-Spingarn Research Center*

John W. Cromwell (1846–1927). Corresponding secretary of the American Negro Academy from 1897 to 1919 and its fourth president.

From Daniel Wallace Culp, Twentieth Century Negro Literature *(Naperville, Ill.: J. L. Nichols and Company, 1902).*

Francis J. Grimké (1850–1927). Treasurer of the American Negro Academy from 1897 to 1919. *Courtesy of Moorland-Spingarn Research Center*

Kelly Miller (1863–1939). An active and influential member of the American Negro Academy from its inception until its demise.

Courtesy of Moorland-Spingarn Research Center

Carter G. Woodson (1875–1950). Major figure in the attempt to reform the American Negro Academy in 1920–1921. *Courtesy of Moorland-Spingarn Research Center*

Jesse E. Moorland (1863–1940). An active member of the American Negro Academy during the years 1906 to 1919. *Courtesy of Moorland-Spingarn Research Center*

Alain L. Locke (1886–1954). One of the few major figures in the black intellectual community active in the American Negro Academy during its final years.

Courtesy of Moorland-Spingarn Research Center

Arthur A. Schomburg (1874–1938). Fifth and last president of the American Negro Academy.

Courtesy of Schomburg Center for Research in Black Culture, New York City Public Library

V *Struggle for Maturity*

On December 29, 1903, Archibald H. Grimké was unanimously elected the third president of the American Negro Academy. A graduate of Lincoln University in Pennsylvania (A.B., 1879; A.M., 1872), and of the Harvard Law School (1874), he had settled in Boston after completing his education and had become a respected member of that city's legal profession. Beginning in 1883, and for the next two years, he and a former law partner, Butler R. Wilson, published and edited the *Hub*, a black newspaper. An independent in politics, Grimké was appointed United States consul to Santo Domingo by Democratic President Grover Cleveland. He held this post from 1894 to 1898. After his return to this country, Grimké divided his time between Boston and Washington, D.C. He had strong family and friendship ties in both cities and, though at first more deeply involved in the cultural and civic life of Boston, he became an equally prominent figure in Washington's black community. Grimké was the author of two biographies, *Life of William Lloyd Garrison, the Abolitionist* (1891) and *Life of Charles Sumner, the Scholar in Politics* (1892), as well as numerous articles on the antislavery movement, African colonization, and social and political concerns of black Americans. Some of the latter had appeared in the Boston *Herald*, the Boston *Traveler*, and the *Atlantic Monthly*. Like his predecessors, Crummell and Du Bois, Grimké was well educated, a clear and forceful writer and speaker, strongly committed to higher education as a key tool for black development, and a figure known and respected by blacks and whites.[1]

1. Allen Johnson and Dumas Malone (eds.), *Dictionary of American Biography*, VII,

The strong possibility exists that Grimké had been sounded out as to his willingness to accept the presidency of the ANA and to faithfully carry out its responsibilities well before he was elected. The difficulties and disappointments created by Du Bois's behavior as president made it crucial to ensure that the next executive would be able and willing to give the society a major share of his time. From at least 1901, John W. Cromwell seems to have quietly conducted a search for someone to take Du Bois's place. One of the men he attempted to interest in the office was William S. Scarborough, head of the classics department at Wilberforce University and an important scholar in his field. In a letter written to Cromwell a week before the fifth annual meeting, Scarborough urged the corresponding secretary to support Du Bois's reelection for the following reasons: "He [Du Bois] is both able and capable and has made a good officer. Let him remain. Let good enough alone. In my opinion—the race has not yet produced a more *thoroughly* scholarly young man than Du Bois. He is an honor to the race—to the country." Though he agreed with Scarborough's general assessment of Du Bois, Cromwell knew better than anyone the poor quality of his performance as head of the ANA. In November, 1903, the corresponding secretary assured Richard R. Wright, president of the Georgia State Industrial College, of his support if he would become a candidate for the presidency of the ANA. Wright, already heavily committed to several organizations, thanked Cromwell, but declined. These two overtures suggest that a similar, and more successful, proposal was made to Grimké sometime before the meeting in December, 1903.[2]

As president of the ANA, Grimké was an active and publicly visible figure who rarely missed an annual meeting and took great pleasure in delivering his presidential address each year. In spite of other, and sometimes conflicting, obligations he presented sixteen papers and addresses before the ANA, more than any other member. Six of these were published as occasional papers. Grimké was also a frequent attendant at executive committee meetings. Even when he was absent, however, his brother and close friend, Francis J. Grimké, was usually present. Francis, who had been elected treasurer of the ANA and a member of the executive committee in March, 1897, continued to hold these offices throughout Crummell's, Du Bois's, and his

---

632–33; Angelina W. Grimké, "A Biographical Sketch of Archibald H. Grimké," *Opportunity*, III (February, 1925), 44–47; Lerner, *The Grimké Sisters*, 358–66.

2. Scarborough to Cromwell, December 23, 1901, Wright to Cromwell, November 17, 1902, both in JWCG/M.

brother's presidencies, relinquishing them only when Archibald ceased to head the association in 1919. As long as Archibald was president of the ANA, Francis was an important communication link between him and the executive committee.

Grimké was president of the ANA for sixteen years, a period equal to half the life of the society. During the time he headed the association it continued to experience crises and frustrations but, despite its problems, these were the years in which the ANA did its most creative and significant work. In retrospect, these years would stand out as the period of greatest stability. Recalling Grimké's election many years later, one member of the ANA described it as an event that gave the organization "a new lease of life."[3] Certainly, the election of a president who could allot a significant portion of his time and energy to the society was a real improvement. Even the fact that Grimké, during his first years in office, spent a good part of his time in Boston was an asset, for it allowed the executive committee and the ubiquitous corresponding secretary—both accustomed to operating with the president at a distance—to incorporate him into the governance structure gradually.

During Grimké's presidency, the ANA inducted forty new members, a marked increase over the thirteen gained under Crummell and Du Bois. However, despite the fact that there were thirty-three members in 1903, any possibility of a dramatic increase in size was vitiated by the significant number of old and new members who dropped out.

Death eliminated four members: Walter B. Hayson, a Latin teacher in Washington's black high school (1905); John H. Smyth, former United States minister to Liberia and director of the Virginia Manual Labor School (1908); James M. Colson, principal of the Dinwiddie Agricultural School (1909); and Charles C. Cook, head of Howard University's English department (1910).

By 1913, the following men had all terminated their relationship with the society: Charles E. Bentley, Peter H. Clark, Levi J. Coppin, Hightower T. Kealing, George N. Grisham, Albert P. Miller, Albert W. Pegues, Thomas W. Talley, Benjamin T. Tanner, Alexander Walters, and Samuel Laing Williams. Tanner resigned because the demands of his office made it impossible for him to attend the annual meetings regularly. The polite and regretful tone of the letter of resignation he wrote in 1905 contrasted sharply with the one

3. William H. Ferris, *Alexander Crummell, an Apostle of Negro Culture*, ANA Occasional Papers, no. 20 (1920), 9.

written by Walters in 1913. Responding to a bill for unpaid dues, the AMEZ prelate brusquely told Cromwell that he had informed him "a long time ago that I desired to have my name stricken from your roll, stating that it was impossible for me to attend meetings during the holidays." Refusing to pay the bill, Walters declared himself in debt to the ANA for nothing except his "prayers and best wishes." Williams, who never attended an annual meeting and declined several invitations to present a paper, resigned in 1904, "having," as he put it, "forfeited my right to be considered any longer a member." In 1906, Grisham informed Cromwell he was thinking of resigning. By 1908, he had come to a decision. "For several years," he reminded the corresponding secretary, "I have deemed myself too faraway for active participation in the work of the body and I am perfectly willing to yield my place to someone able and willing to do effective work." Coppin's and Miller's withdrawals probably were related, in part, to new work assignments. In 1900, Coppin was elected a bishop and sent to head the AME Church in South Africa; Miller, who had been pastor of the Lincoln Memorial Church since the mid-1890s, left Washington in 1901 to take a church in Grand Rapids, Michigan.[4]

Sometime between 1913 and 1920, Simon G. Atkins and John Hope also ceased to be members. As early as 1901, Atkins described to Cromwell the repeated separations from "desk and books" imposed on him by constant fund-raising efforts. "To build up a school like mine and keep it going," he complained, "reduces one almost to a condition of slavery and largely unfits him for critical work. And this is the only kind the Academy can afford, as in the past, to accept." These pressures, undoubtedly, played a part in causing his withdrawal. Hope, who became president of the Atlanta Baptist College in 1906, may have felt the need to focus his energies in that setting.[5]

For members of the ANA such as Benjamin T. Tanner, Levi J. Coppin,

---

4. See "complete roster" of members of the academy in [J. W. Cromwell], "American Negro Academy," *African Times and Orient Review*, 144. The list of members contained in this article omitted the names of Matthew Anderson and Robert H. Terrell, two founders who were life-long members of the ANA. See also Tanner to Cromwell, October 11, 1905, Walters to Cromwell, January 30, 1913, Williams to Cromwell, December 9, 1904, Grisham to Cromwell, April 25, 1906, and December 16, 1908, all in JWCG/M. For Miller see Washington *Colored American*, July 6, 1901, p. 9, and Washington *Bee*, July 13, 1901, p. 8; for Coppin, see Wright (ed.), *Centennial Encyclopedia*, 74. No evidence has survived that explains the withdrawal of Bentley, Kealing, Pegues, and Talley.

5. See list of "directors or managers," "Articles of Incorporation of the American Negro Academy," January 30, 1920, Instrument #15583 in incorporation *Liber* 35 at Folio 443, Office of Recorder of Deeds, Washington, D.C.; and Atkins to Cromwell, November 20, 1901, in JWCG/M. For information on Hope see Yenser (ed.), *Who's Who*, 218.

George N. Grisham, and Simon G. Atkins, who attempted to be responsible participants in the groups they joined, the restriction of the ANA's membership to fifty probably had some influence on their decision to withdraw from the society. It is possible that these men, as well as some others, may have felt that they were occupying spots that could be filled by persons able to be more active.

Most of the forty new members who entered the ANA during these years were recruited through individual contact. John W. Cromwell, Archibald H. Grimké, and the executive committee were the chief figures in this activity. The annual meetings and the society's publications also played a part in attracting potential members, as well as the simple desire on the part of some candidates to associate themselves with a prominent group of men.

By the end of Archibald H. Grimké's third year as president, ten—and possibly eleven—new names had been added to the organization's membership list. In 1904 Arthur Ulysses Craig, director of the Armstrong Training School in Washington, whose election had been strongly and repeatedly urged by W. E. B. Du Bois, became a member. Others elected that year were Butler R. Wilson, Archibald Grimké's former law partner; Benjamin Franklin Lee, an AME bishop who had been president of Wilberforce University; and Owen Meredith Waller, a physician in Brooklyn, N.Y., who was also an Episcopal clergyman and a former rector of St. Luke's Church in Washington, D.C.. The following year, Charles H. Boyer, dean of St. Augustine's College, Raleigh, North Carolina; John Robert Clifford, a lawyer in West Virginia who was editor and publisher of the Martinsburg *Pioneer Press*; and AMEZ bishop George Wylie Clinton joined the ANA. (Boyer's name initially had been suggested by Orishatukeh Faduma.) Three Washington residents—Roscoe Conkling Bruce, assistant superintendent of city schools; Jesse Edward Moorland, general secretary of programs for blacks conducted by the Young Men's Christian Association; and William Albert Sinclair, field secretary of the Constitution League, a biracial group organized to promote equal rights for blacks through legal action, entered in 1906. Moorland and Sinclair both received strong endorsements from Atlantan John Hope. Although the exact date of his entrance is unclear, sometime between 1905 and 1907 William Victor Tunnell, rector of King Hall, an Episcopal seminary for blacks that was affiliated with Howard University, also became a member.[6]

6. Du Bois to Cromwell, April 17 and May 5, 1903, Wilson to Cromwell, November 30, 1904, Faduma to Cromwell, February 4, 1902, Moorland to Cromwell, December 26, 1905,

Each succeeding year, at least one new name was added to the list of academicians, and often three or four. In 1907, the executive committee invited Joseph J. France, a physician in Portsmouth, Virginia; Marcus Fitzherbert Wheatland of Newport, Rhode Island, also a physician; Charles M. Thomas, a teacher in the Washington Normal School; Richard Robert Wright, Jr., research fellow in sociology at the University of Pennsylvania; and James Robert Lincoln Diggs, president of the Virginia Theological Seminary and College in Lynchburg, to deliver papers dealing with social problems in the black community, provided that they also apply for membership in the academy. France, Wheatland, and Wright accepted the conditional invitation. That same year Solomon Carter Fuller, psychiatric resident at the Westborough (Massachusetts) Insane Asylum, joined the society. Archibald H. Grimké, who served on the board of trustees of the Westborough Asylum from 1884 to 1894, was a friend of Fuller and the person responsible for drawing him into the ANA. The following men were received into the association in 1908: James Emman Kwegyir Aggrey, teacher of English, Latin, and New Testament Greek at Livingstone College in North Carolina; Herbert Clay Scurlock, professor of physiology and biochemistry in Howard University's School of Medicine; and Jesse Max Barber, founder and editor of an important and widely read periodical, *Voice of the Negro*. Barber's election, of which Archibald H. Grimké was a strong advocate, was strenuously opposed by Joseph J. France, who communicated to Cromwell his judgment that the editor of the *Voice* was more a "demagogue" than a "calm judicious . . . recorder of events."[7]

Hope to Cromwell, April 23, 1906, all in JWCG/M; Proceedings, 117, 125, 132, 199. For biographical information on Craig see Nichols and Crogman (eds.), *Progress of a Race* (1920), 354–56; Washington *Colored American*, March 9, 1901, pp. 1, 12; Washington *Bee*, September 15, 1917, p. 1; Arthur A. Schomburg to J. W. Cromwell, November 26, 1919, in SC/MSRC. For Wilson see John Daniels, *In Freedom's Birthplace* (Boston, 1914), 95, 103, 302, 456. For Lee see Wright (ed.), *Centennial Encyclopedia*, 148. For Waller see Bragg, *History of the Afro-American Group*, 272; Washington *Colored American*, June 20, 1903, pp. 1, 5. For Boyer, see Boris (ed.), *Who's Who*, 3–6. For Bruce see Nichols and Crogman (eds.), *Progress of a Race* (1920), 343. For Moorland see Boris (ed.), *Who's Who*, 145. For Sinclair see Otto H. Olsen, "Introduction" to W. A. Sinclair, *Aftermath of Slavery* (New York, 1969), v–x. For Tunnell see Dyson, *Howard University*, 176, 179, 211; and Bragg, *History of the Afro-American Group*, 163, 178.

7. Proceedings, 143, 144, 153, 155; Barber to Cromwell, July 16, 1908, France to Cromwell, September 14, 1908, both in JWCG/M. Only France, Fuller, and Wright delivered papers at the eleventh annual meeting in 1907. See Proceedings, 144. In a letter written seven years after his election, Aggrey told W. E. B. Du Bois that "Mr. J. E. Moorland of Washington and Mr. Cromwell had me elected member of the American Negro Academy." See Aptheker (ed.), *Correspondence of W. E. B. Du Bois*, I, 184. For biographical information on France, see cata-

During the next six years the ANA gained twelve new members: James R. L. Diggs of the Virginia Seminary and College (1909); Lorenzo Z. Johnson (1909), a Presbyterian minister in Baltimore; Lafayette McKeen Hershaw (1910), an employee of the United States Department of the Interior and a member of the District of Columbia bar; Ernest Everett Just (1911), biology professor at Howard University; Edward Christopher Williams (1911), principal of Washington's black high school; and George William Cook (1913), dean of Howard University's Commercial Department. Sometime after 1913, Charles Victor Roman, professor of eye, ear, nose, and throat diseases in Meharry Medical College, Nashville, became a member. In 1914, the following men were added to the academy's ranks: Walter Henderson Brooks, pastor of Washington's Nineteenth Street Baptist Church; Freeman Henry Morris Murray, a printer and an employee of the United States War Department; Neval Hollen Thomas and Carter Godwin Woodson, teachers in Washington's black high school; and Arthur A. Schomburg, a Puerto Rican-born bibliophile who was employed by a New York banking concern.[8]

Nine new people were admitted during the next five years. William Pickens, dean of Morgan College in Baltimore, was elected in 1915. The following year three new members were chosen: James Weldon Johnson, a poet, songwriter, and former diplomat, who was an editor and columnist for the New York *Age*; Robert Wellington Bagnall, rector of St. Matthew's Episco-

loguer's notes on letter from France to Carter G. Woodson, November 3, 1921, in Carter G. Woodson Papers, Library of Congress, and John A. Kenney, *The Negro in Medicine* (n.p., 1912; rpr. Ann Arbor, 1973), 34. For Wheatland, see Boris (ed.), *Who's Who*, 218. For Thomas, see Thomas to Cromwell, November 4 and December 30, 1914, both in JWCG/M. For Wright, see Boris (ed.), *Who's Who*, 230–31. For Diggs, see Nichols and Crogman (eds.), *Progress of a Race*, 363–64. For Fuller, see Kenney, *The Negro in Medicine*, 14–15. For Aggrey, see Edwin W. Smith, *Aggrey of Africa* (New York, 1930). For Scurlock, see Boris (ed.), *Who's Who*, 181.

8. Proceedings, 144, 168, 170, 180, 197; corresponding secretary's report to the thirteenth annual meeting, December 28, 1909, p. 4, Just to Cromwell, January 14, 1911 (2 separate letters), and n.d., Cook to Cromwell, December 15, 1913, Woodson to Cromwell, December 18, 1913, all in JWCG/M; Schomburg to Bruce, May 26, 1914, in Bruce Papers. For biographical information on Johnson, see *Hilltop* (student magazine of Howard University), January 26, 1949, p. 1, and Washington *Star*, January 16, 1949, p. 26. For Hershaw, see Mather (ed.), *Who's Who*, 208. For Just, see Yenser (ed.), *Who's Who*, 254. For Williams, see E. J. Josey, "Edward Christopher Williams," paper presented at American Library Association History Round Table, June 24, 1968. For Cook, see Dyson, *Howard University*, 368–70. For Roman, see Kenney, *The Negro in Medicine*, 13–14. For Brooks, see Boris (ed.), *Who's Who*, 24–25. For Murray, see "Analysis of F. H. M. Murray Papers," in "Analysis of Manuscript Collections," Moorland-Spingarn Research Center, Howard University, Washington, D.C. For Thomas, Woodson, and Schomburg, see Boris (ed.), *Who's Who*, 200, 227–28, 179.

pal Church in Detroit; and Charles Douglass Martin, pastor of a Moravian Brethren Church in Harlem. Thomas Montgomery Gregory, professor of public speaking and director of dramatic arts at Howard University; William Ashbie Hawkins, an attorney in Baltimore; and former Haitian diplomat John Hurst, who was an AME bishop, joined in 1917. Only one new member—Monroe Nathan Work, director of the department of records and research at Tuskegee Institute—was elected in 1918. In 1919 Robert Tecumtha Browne, an author and translator who was president of the Brooklyn Negro Library Association, and Robert A. Pelham, a clerk in the United States Census Bureau, were added to the society's roster. Martin and Browne were recruited by Arthur A. Schomburg and John E. Bruce, while Hawkins' interest in the ANA was stimulated by his fellow Baltimorean, William Pickens. Pelham, whose chief supporter seems to have been John W. Cromwell, had been an unsuccessful candidate for membership in 1917. Since the election procedure used by the ANA counted unreturned ballots as favorable votes, for him to have been rejected, over half the membership must have participated in the election that year, with the majority casting their votes against him. There was opposition to his election when his name was put forward again in 1919, but this time he secured enough votes to gain admission.[9]

In 1914, Charles M. Thomas made a strong bid for admission to the ANA. Earlier, Thomas, along with four other people, had been invited to apply for membership and to deliver a paper at the eleventh annual meeting in December, 1907. At that time he expressed no interest in either proposal. Seven years later, he had changed his mind and was eager to become part of the ANA. In a letter to the executive committee, Thomas praised the work of the organization, and offered to deliver, at the next annual meeting, a paper he had written on African customs and laws. After reading it, how-

9. Pickens to Cromwell, March 25, and July 27, 1915, Johnson to Cromwell, January 7, 1916, Bagnall to Cromwell, July 15 and September 26, 1916, Du Bois to Cromwell, January 12, 1916, Gregory to Cromwell, December 26, 1916, Hawkins to Cromwell, December 27, 1916, Hurst to Cromwell, November 14, 1917, all in JWCG/M; Schomburg to Cromwell, October 4, 1917, in SC/MSRC; Work to Cromwell, February 12 and May 7, 1918, Schomburg to Cromwell, February 2 and July 20, 1919, Browne to Cromwell, August 11, 1919, all in JWCG/M; J. E. Moorland to A. H. Grimké, January 10, 1919, in A. H. Grimké Papers. For biographical information on Pickens see Boris (ed.), *Who's Who*, 158. For Johnson see Boris (ed.), *Who's Who*, 8. For Martin see Mather (ed.), *Who's Who*, 184–85. For Gregory see Boris (ed.), *Who's Who*, 81. For Hawkins and Hurst, see Boris (ed.), *Who's Who*, 88, 100. For Pelham see Francis H. Warren, *Michigan Manual of Freedman's Progress* (Detroit, 1915), 87–92. For Work see Boris (ed.), *Who's Who*, 229. For Browne see Mather (ed.), *Who's Who*, 46.

ever, the executive committee decided the paper was unsuitable for presentation and, in what was probably a related action, tabled Thomas' application for membership. The committee also failed to inform him of their reasons for rejecting his paper. Extremely disappointed, Thomas wrote to John Cromwell, defending both the quality of his research and his "loyalty to race ideals." In addition, he asked to be informed in what way he had failed "to satisfy the demands of the executive committee." Cromwell's response has not survived, but the executive committee's action ended Thomas' candidacy.[10]

Two years later, Arthur A. Schomburg, who had entered the academy in 1914, discovered that his friend Alain L. Locke, professor of philosophy at Howard University, was not a member. Since Locke was not only qualified (he held three degrees from Harvard University, including the Ph.D., had been the first black-American Rhodes scholar, and had written a number of highly praised books and articles) but maintained close friendships with John W. Cromwell and several other leading members of the organization, Schomburg was surprised. In a letter written to Locke shortly after making this discovery, Schomburg asked him, "Why don't you join?" In his reply Locke made it clear that he was not sure the involvement would be worth his time and trouble. Because his letter has not survived, there is no way of knowing exactly why he felt this way. However, a second letter Schomburg sent attempting to diminish the importance of Locke's objections suggests that it was Locke's contention that there would have to be changes in the way the ANA functioned organizationally, as well as in the quality of its members' participation, before he could consider connecting himself with the society. But whatever the specific reason or reasons for Locke's objections to seeking admission to the ANA, Schomburg's arguments did not change his mind.[11]

By 1920, thirteen of the forty new members admitted to the ANA between 1904 and 1919 had left the organization. A list of members of the society compiled in 1913 omitted the names of Benjamin F. Lee, Owen M. Waller, Butler R. Wilson, Charles H. Boyer, George W. Clinton, and Henry C. Scurlock. Seven years later, when another list was compiled, William V.

---

10. Proceedings, 143; Thomas to Cromwell, November 4, 1914, and December 30, 1914, both in JWCG/M.

11. Schomburg to Locke, December 31, 1916, January 1, 1917, both in A. L. Locke Papers, Moorland-Spingarn Research Center, Howard University, Washington, D.C.

Tunnell, William A. Sinclair, Solomon C. Fuller, Marcus F. Wheatland, Richard Robert Wright, Jr., J. Max Barber, and James R. L. Diggs were not on it.[12]

There were thirty-three members of the ANA when Grimké became president in 1903. With forty new members, the society should have expanded well beyond the constitutional limit of fifty. However, the dropout of eighteen old members (men elected before 1903) and thirteen new members (men elected after 1903)—a total of thirty-one persons—meant a net increase of only nine. This was reflected in the forty-two names on the membership roster in 1920.[13] This high attrition rate took its toll on the society. To lose thirty-one members—many of them distinguished and influential persons—severely weakened its programs, finances, morale, and prestige. It also meant that the organization was being rejected repeatedly by the very men to whom it ought to have had the most appeal.

The most basic reason for this was the failure of the association to realize its goals. Because the ANA was unable to secure the resources for effectively publishing and disseminating the works of black scholars and writers, the occasional papers continued to be its only public offering. It was unsuccessful in its search for ways to influence the institutions responsible for the instruction of black youth and, because it lacked the funds, was unable to develop its own programs in this area. The founders had also talked of providing scholarships for exceptionally talented black students, but the project never materialized. Efforts were made to create a black-American historical archive but this too was an unsuccessful project. The indifference of both the black and white public to the ANA's presence and programs literally nullified its attempt to function as the vindicator of black Americans "from vicious assaults, in all the lines of learning and culture." These programmatic difficulties all combined to prevent the ANA from establishing itself as an important intellectual center, thus making it increasingly less attractive to educated black men in search of institutions that provided affirmation for their work and a public platform for their ideas.

At the same time, some of the society's goals were being preempted by other organizations. By 1905 the black agricultural and mechanical colleges had formed a national association, which had as one of its sections a re-

---

12. [Cromwell], "American Negro Academy," *African Times and Orient Review*, 244; "ANA Articles of Incorporation."

13. [Cromwell], "American Negro Academy," *African Times and Orient Review*, 244; "ANA Articles of Incorporation."

search department; a Negro Society for Historical Research was founded in New York state in 1911; three years later a group of black social scientists began efforts to form a society of researchers; and, in 1915, the Association for the Study of Negro Life and History was formed in Chicago. Two other organizations founded during these years, the National Association for the Advancement of Colored People (1909) and the National Urban League on Urban Conditions among Negroes (1911), were essentially committed to objectives and activities quite different from those of the ANA, but both of them, by establishing lively, well-edited publications which printed a range of materials, including articles by and about black artists, scholars, and scientists, drew attention to the ANA's lack of a journal and the limited impact of its irregularly published occasional papers. Since various members of the ANA were active figures in the establishment of each of these organizations, their involvement in them had the effect of cutting down on the time and energy they had to give to the ANA and its programs. Some men may have left the ANA, and others may have chosen not to seek membership in it, because they believed the work of these other associations to be more directly related to the issues and problems that affected them.

The financial weakness of the ANA made it impossible for the organization to move into the area of educational philanthropy by establishing a fund to provide scholarships "to encourage and assist youthful, but hesitant scholars" and "to aid youths of genius in the attainment of the higher culture at home or abroad." Such a program, if instituted, might have made it possible for the ANA to establish ties with black institutions of higher education similar to those enjoyed by a number of religious denominations and by educational foundations such as the Peabody Education Fund, the John F. Slater Fund, the General Education Board, the Anna T. Jeanes Fund, the Julius Rosenwald Fund, and the Phelps-Stokes Fund, all of which provided direct financial support to selected black schools. These foundations, whose interests and sizable resources were directed toward the support of education, exercised vast influence in quarters of the black and white communities where practical and theoretical decisions concerning the education of black Americans were being made. Because the religious denominations had numerous projects that demanded their interest and financial support, their influence was not as strong. Although the grants made by the churches and the foundations to black institutions were used in a variety of ways, these gifts helped finance, both directly and indirectly, the education of black students as well as further educational training for black college graduates.[14] If the ANA had possessed even a modest scholarship fund this would have increased its importance in the eyes of many educated blacks, thus strengthening the allegiance of those who became members and increasing its appeal to some of the men it sought to draw into the organization.

The ANA also suffered from the fact that its work was not viewed positively by Booker T. Washington, the principal of Tuskegee Institute. Washington, because of his support of industrial education and his implicit endorsement of black accommodation to southern racial practices, was the figure in the black community most frequently consulted by whites seeking to know what black institutions, causes, or individuals were worthy of support. Although, in 1897, Washington had signed a card endorsing the constitution of the ANA "as a member thereof," his failure to pay his initiation fee and his refusal to appear as a guest speaker before the society indicated how slight an interest he took in the organization and its work. And, as a rule, the organizations he favored prospered, and those he opposed failed. From 1903 until his death in 1915, Washington was deeply involved in struggles with educated blacks who disagreed with his educational views, his racial philosophy and the use he made of his power in the black community. While the ANA, as an organization, was never directly involved in this controversy, many of those who challenged Washington were founders, members, or officers of the society. While there is no evidence that Washington ever directly criticized the ANA, it is possible that this may have turned what, on his part, had been a disinterest in the ANA into a more negative attitude. As the line between his supporters and critics was drawn more sharply after 1903, the Tuskegeean's ability to help or hinder the careers of aspiring blacks probably caused many of them to view membership in the ANA as fraught with liabilities. Some of the withdrawals from the society, as well as its difficulties in attracting members, may have stemmed from this situation.[15]

During the sixteen years of Grimké's presidency, the ANA frequently had to concern itself with membership issues. When, in 1905, the executive

14. John Hope Franklin describes the complex role of religious denominations and foundations in the field of Negro education in *From Slavery to Freedom*, 277–84, as do August Meier and Elliott Rudwick in *From Plantation to Ghetto* (New York, 1970), 200–202. For an in-depth discussion of the role and activities of the Southern Education Board and the General Education Board see Louis R. Harlan, *Separate and Unequal* (Chapel Hill, 1958), 75–101.

15. For a discussion of Washington's disagreements and clashes with other black leaders, see Meier, *Negro Thought*, 100–118, 190–206, 207–47.

committee sent letters to men who had become inactive, inviting them to put themselves in good standing again, only three people responded: Daniel J. Sanders, Paul Laurence Dunbar, and Lewis Baxter Moore. Moore, who had dropped out in 1901, was reinstated in 1906 and his back dues remitted. Although Sanders promised to pay his entrance fee—something he had failed to do when elected in 1899—there is no record that he ever did. Dunbar, who was to die a year later, expressed thanks for the offer but described himself as a "helpless and almost confirmed invalid." He asked the corresponding secretary to convey his "fair greetings and long love to the old association," with the assurance that "my heart, if not my body, or my pocketbook, is with them." [16]

Regular financial support of the ANA was such a problem for many active members that the executive committee was forced repeatedly to urge those in arrears to pay their back dues. Some few may have experienced difficulty in producing $2 per year, but for the majority of delinquents, this reflected a lack of interest. In 1909, the problem became so acute that it was discussed at the annual meeting, where it was decided to send a special communication to offenders urging them to put themselves in good standing. This action was repeated again in 1913 and this time the communication was accompanied by copies of Article 7 of the constitution which provided for the cessation of membership if fees went unpaid for two years. These efforts produced mixed results. Some recipients—such as Alexander Walters—terminated their connection with the ANA; others—William H. Crogman was an example of this group—told the executive committee of their financial difficulties, and promised to pay as soon as possible. In spite of these efforts to confront members with their financial responsibilities to the association, unpaid dues continued to be a problem. As a result, the ANA's difficult financial situation became even worse. [17]

In 1917, when another reinstatement offer was made, William H. Crogman and John L. Love, both founding members, were the only persons who responded. The offer requested payment of $5 in return for which a former member was restored to good standing and his back fees forgotten. Crogman sent a check to Francis J. Grimké, treasurer of the ANA, and in the

16. Proceedings, 139; Sanders to Cromwell, November 13, 1905, Dunbar to Cromwell, February 27, 1905, both in JWCG/M.

17. Proceedings, 174, 176, 194, 130, 144; A. H. Grimké and J. W. Cromwell to ANA members, January 17, 1914, Walters to Cromwell, January 30, 1913, Crogman to Cromwell, December 4, 1911, all in JWCG/M.

note which accompanied the payment, he told Grimké, "It is a joke that one of the founders of the Academy should allow his name to be dropped because of delinquency in payment of dues, but the sinner ought to be punished." For Grimké, Cromwell, and the other members who were struggling to keep the organization alive, the need for punishment was clear but the humor in the situation must have been elusive. A former resident of Washington, D.C., Love, who at this time lived in Kansas City, Missouri, accepted the offer and promised to send $5 sometime in the near future. Two years later he had still not sent the money, but, in a letter to Cromwell, he affirmed both his continued interest in the ANA and the intention of sending the fee. Consequently, Love was kept on the membership list.[18]

A slightly different, but related, issue was the failure of some new members to pay their $5 entrance fee. As opposed to the matter of dues, this problem was resolved with complete success. In a move which eliminated the opportunity for defaulting, the annual meeting held in December, 1914, decided that "applications for membership [in] the future shall be accompanied by the fee of five dollars and the secretary be instructed to notify all applicants that their application must be accompanied by the initiation fee of five dollars, which will be returned if unfavorable action be taken."[19]

As corresponding secretary, John W. Cromwell was the ANA's agent in the various negotiations with delinquent members. He wrote the communications requesting payment of overdue fees and handled any collateral correspondence that resulted. Even when Archibald H. Grimké or members of the executive committee worked on a communication with him, the final version usually reflected his tone and carried his phrasing. By a skillful combination of persuasion and appeal to duty, Cromwell kept a number of wavering members in the organization. So long as a man continued to express commitment to the ANA and its ideals—whether his dues were paid regularly or not—Cromwell did not give up hope of restoring him to active involvement.

The financial problems plaguing the ANA were not unique to the society. During the years when Grimké headed the society, the Afro-American Council, the Niagara Movement, the National Negro Suffrage League, the Negro American Political League, and the Equal Opportunity League, all

18. Crogman to Grimké, September 20, 1917, in Woodson (ed.), *Works of Francis J. Grimké*, IV, 196; Love to Cromwell, February 27, 1917, and April 12, 1919, both in JWCG/M; "ANA Articles of Incorporation."
19. Proceedings, 198.

associations concerned with the protection of the political and social rights of blacks, limped along, unable to garner enough money to pursue effectively the goals that had inspired their establishment. As a result, these groups, whose membership, like that of the ANA, was all black, had very short lives.[20]

By contrast, the same time period was one of expansion for black fraternal organizations and mutual benefit societies, whose memberships and treasuries grew steadily. These organizations used their dues to purchase or construct buildings as meeting places and investments, to provide accident, health, and life insurance to their members, and, in some areas, to organize banks. This was also a period of expansion for black churches, which grew both in size and income. Although the activities of the churches frequently included programs similar to those conducted by the fraternal and benefit societies, they made their unique contribution to the black community through the athletic, charitable, educational, and social welfare programs which they conducted. The general hostility of most Americans toward blacks, the popularity of industrial education among whites who took an interest in blacks, and the stultifying influence of Booker T. Washington's dominance of the black community all worked to discourage black Americans who were interested in the pursuit of political, social, or intellectual equality, causing many black leaders to put their strongest energies into the support of organizations committed to economic and moral uplift. In part, the lack of interest in the ANA shown by those members who repeatedly failed to pay their dues, was a reflection of this mood.[21]

Three men, Duse Mohamed, Joseph Ephraim Casely Hayford, and James Carmichael Smith were elected corresponding members during Archibald H. Grimké's presidency, all of them in 1912. Duse Mohamed, an author and journalist, was the son of an Egyptian army officer and his Sudanese wife. Though he was born in Alexandria, Egypt, from the age of nine Mohamed was educated in England. After studying history at King's Col-

---

20. No individual studies of these organizations have been written, but their histories can be traced through the mentions they received in the following books: Meier, *Negro Thought*, Thornbrough, *T. Thomas Fortune*, Fox, *Guardian of Boston*, Spear, *Black Chicago*, and Francis L. Broderick, *W. E. B. Du Bois: Negro Leader in a Time of Crisis* (Stanford, 1959), 75–79.

21. For information on the fraternal organizations, mutual benefit societies, and black churches, see Du Bois, *Efforts for Social Betterment Among Negro Americans*, Atlanta University Publications, no. 14 (1898), and his *The Negro Church*, Atlanta University Publications, no. 8 (1903); Franklin, *From Slavery to Freedom*, 296–99; Meier and Rudwick, *Plantation to Ghetto*, 193–200.

lege, London University, he traveled extensively in Europe, America, and Asia Minor as part of a troupe of actors. In 1911, his book, *In the Land of the Pharaohs*, a statement of pan-African and pan-Asian nationalistic sentiments, appeared. The following year he brought out the first issue of the *African Times and Orient Review*, a London-based journal which, under his editorship, was influential in nourishing the nascent nationalism of Africans and Asians, especially in parts of the world ruled by Great Britain. Mohamed was acquainted with John Edward Bruce, a black-American journalist and ANA member, who may have given his name to the executive committee. When informed of his election, Mohamed sent a warm letter of thanks in which he pledged to support the association. From John W. Cromwell he requested an article on the society, plus pictures of "the founders and officers, and the building or room in which it meets," offering to publish them in his magazine because, as he wrote, "Institutions of this kind cannot be too widely known." True to his word, the article on the ANA appeared in the November/December, 1913, issue of his publication. Besides being the only article printed on the ANA which contained photographs of its founders and members, it was one of the most extensive and best-written descriptions to appear.[22]

J. E. Casely Hayford, a West African lawyer and author, played an important role in the development of African national independence movements. W. E. B. Du Bois was familiar with his writings as early as 1904, when Hayford sent him a copy of his book, *Gold Coast Native Institutions, with Thoughts upon a Healthy Imperial Policy for the Gold Coast and Ashanti*, and an address, "Africa and Africans," which he delivered at a dinner held in London to honor Edward Wilmot Blyden, a distinguished West African who had been elected a corresponding member of the ANA in 1898. In 1911 Hayford's book, *Ethiopia Unbound: Studies in Race Emancipation*, appeared, attracting considerable attention in Great Britain and West Africa. John W. Cromwell, who may have become acquainted with Hayford's writings through Du Bois, wrote the West African lawyer in 1904 complimenting him on the quality of his published work. There is no evidence of further correspondence between Hayford and other members of

22. Proceedings, 188; Duse Mohamed, *In the Land of the Pharaohs* (London, 1968). For biographical information on Mohamed see the introduction to the second edition of his book by Khalil Muhmud; and E. David Cronon, *Black Moses: The Story of Marcus Garvey and the Universal Negro Improvement Association* (Madison, Wisc., 1955), 15, 43. See also Bruce to Cromwell, December 29, 1913, Mohamed to Cromwell, February 26 and July 30, 1913, all in JWCG/M; [Cromwell], "American Negro Academy," *African Times and Orient Review*, 244.

the ANA after 1904, but his election indicated the society's high esteem for him as a public figure and as an intellectual.[23]

James Carmichael Smith was born in the West Indies, taught school in New York state from 1872 to 1876, and then moved to West Africa where he became a prominent public figure. From 1896 to 1900 he was assistant postmaster general of Sierra Leone, and from 1900 to 1911 he managed the Sierra Leone Savings Bank. In 1909 the executive committee of the ANA recommended his election as a corresponding member, but, for some reason, no action was taken. A man of scholarly interests, Smith had by 1912 produced nearly a dozen books on economic questions. At the time of his election as a corresponding member of the ANA, he was already a member of several English learned societies. Smith returned a gracious letter of thanks to the ANA but, in an enclosed note—prompted, no doubt by his lack of knowledge concerning the organization—asked what was expected of a corresponding member, and requested a list of the ANA's past and present membership.[24]

Although no other corresponding members were elected between 1903 and 1919, three other men were suggested for the honor. In April, 1908, Edward Wilmot Blyden of Liberia wrote to John W. Cromwell, apprising him of the forthcoming visit to the United States of J. J. Dossen, vice-president of Liberia. "Mr. Dossen, I think," he confided to Cromwell, "would like to become a member of the 'American Negro Academy,' which you so ably and worthily represent." Dossen visited the United States that year but was not elected a member of the ANA, perhaps because he lacked scholarly, literary, or artistic qualifications. The following year the executive committee recommended for election I. Bud-M'Belle, "interpreter in native languages to the high court of Griqualand in South Africa." Speaking for the committee, John W. Cromwell described him to the thirteenth annual meeting as the author of " 'Kafir Scholar's Companion', a volume of

23. Hayford to Du Bois, June 8, 1904, in Aptheker (ed.), *Correspondence of W. E. B. Du Bois*, I, 76; three works by J. E. Caseley Hayford: *Gold Coast Native Institutions* (London, 1903); *Africa and the Africans, Proceedings on the Occasion of a Banquet, Given at the Holborn Restaurant, August 15, 1903, to Edward W. Blyden, by West Africans in London* (London, 1903); *Ethiopia Unbound* (London, 1911). See also Hayford to Cromwell, July 27, 1904, March 24, 1913, in JWCG/M. For biographical information on Hayford, see *Crisis*, XXXVIII (June, 1931), 198, and Aptheker (ed.), *Correspondence of W. E. B. Du Bois*, I, 76.

24. For biographical information on Smith see Ferris, *African Abroad*, II, 605; "Biography of James Carmichael Smith," *African Times and Orient Review*, III, (July 21, 1914), 419–21; J. W. Cromwell, untitled six-page report, December 28, 1909, Smith to Cromwell, February 27, 1913 (2 separate letters), all in JWCG/M.

180 pages which includes a bibliography covering more than two hundred years of publications and dealing with the Native Races of South Africa." Bud-M'Belle's name, however, never appeared on a membership list. No other names were put forward until 1916, when Arthur A. Schomburg informed Cromwell that he would soon be nominating Pedro C. Timothee, professor of Latin at the University of Puerto Rico. Timothee, he told Cromwell, had received an A.B. degree from the Institute de Instruction in San Juan, Puerto Rico (Schomburg's alma mater) and was a highly regarded French translator, and a trained pharmacist and lawyer. Perhaps Schomburg failed to follow through on the nomination since Timothee was not elected a corresponding member.[25]

Corresponding members were supposed to be links between the ANA and black intellectuals abroad but their affiliation produced few tangible results. When Samuel Coleridge-Taylor, the black English composer, came to Washington to conduct his work, "Hiawatha," the executive committee sent him a message which offered the "felicitations" of the society on the occasion of his visit. Neither the Proceedings nor the correspondence of the ANA contain any evidence of a response from Coleridge-Taylor. Between 1903 and 1919, only one of the ANA's twelve corresponding members, Henry Mason Joseph, an American-born Episcopal priest, living in England, actively involved himself with the association. On December 27, 1905, at the ninth annual meeting, Joseph, who was visiting the United States, delivered a paper on "The Moral Power of Education." And in December, 1908, when he again returned to the United States, Joseph participated in a panel discussion at the twelfth annual meeting.[26]

The ANA's only other international effort was the occasional correspondence of its secretary John W. Cromwell with a few foreign intellectuals. In 1904, Cromwell sent letters to the influential West African nationalist, J. E. Casely Hayford, and to Alan Kirkland Soga, a prominent figure in South Africa's Bantu community. Soga, who was a leader in efforts to raise the political consciousness of black South Africans, was editor of *Izwi Labantu* (The Voice of the People), a "Kaffir-Sesutho English Weekly," in East London, Cape Colony. In part, the letters were intended to introduce the ANA and to this end Cromwell enclosed a set of occasional papers in each one. But the corresponding secretary also expressed the society's desire to coop-

25. Blyden to Cromwell, April 3, 1908, J. W. Cromwell, untitled six-page report, December 28, 1909, both in JWCG/M.
26. Proceedings, 135, 160.

erate with black African leaders and requested each man to outline the differences he perceived in the way black Americans and Africans viewed themselves and their future.[27]

Both men responded positively to the corresponding secretary's letter. Hayford—who eight years later was elected one of the ANA's corresponding members—expressed thanks for the ANA publications and referred Cromwell to the introduction of his recent essay, "Africa and the Africans," for his opinion concerning "the difference between the Afro-American . . . and the West African school of thought." In turn, he requested that Cromwell and other "leading Afro-American thinkers" share their views on the subject with him. Hayford also promised to bring the association's publications "to the notice of West Africans" and sent the names of the Rev. Attoh Ahuma of Accra, Gold Coast and the Rev. Mark C. Hayford of Cape Coast, Gold Coast, for inclusion on the society's mailing list. Soga expressed thanks for the publications and his regret that "distance interferes so greatly with the free expression of our views." There was, he told Cromwell, "so much required by your letter that I will have to postpone a fuller reply." Soga also described himself as "struggling with a book which will embody all the information you are seeking." He did, however, affirm the resolve of the ANA to cooperate, as he put it, "with your brothers in Africa who need the guidance of their fellow countrymen in America at this critical time," and pointed to the "growing rapproachement between the best intellects among the blacks and coloured of both countries" as a new development with positive implications for the future. In addition, Soga promised to send the names and addresses of native African editors who would be interested in the ANA and its publications.

In spite of the warmth of these communications no continuous exchange of information resulted in either case. There was no further correspondence between Hayford and Cromwell until 1912 when the secretary sent the West African an announcement of his election as a corresponding member. The following year, Hayford, in a note of thanks, promised to periodically "supply . . . litrature [*sic*] as will help you follow the work we are doing on

---

27. For biographical information on Soga see Monica Wilson and Leonard Thompson (eds.), *Oxford History of South Africa, 1870–1966* (2 vols.; New York, 1971), II, 355, and Stanley Trapido, "African Divisional Politics in the Cape Colony, 1884 to 1910," *Journal of African History*, IX (1968), 97. Copies of Cromwell's letters to Hayford and Soga have not survived. The description of what he said to them is based on references in their return letters to him. See Hayford to Cromwell, July 27, 1904, and Soga to Cromwell, August 27, 1904, both in JWCG/M.

this side." He also sent his two latest publications and promised a copy of one written earlier. There was still communication between Soga and Cromwell up to 1906 for in that year the ANA official passed on to Bishop Holly of Haiti a suggestion of Soga's that an "ecumenical Negro Congress" be convened. Holly expressed interest in the plan and asked to have more information on it. "It is a pleasing sight," the aged churchman wrote, "to see the educated natives of Africa, our Motherland, taking up the cause of the race of Ham." [28]

In a manner reminiscent of Crummell's early activity on behalf of the ANA, John Edward Bruce, in 1906, referred Theophilus E. Samuel Scholes, an English writer, to the executive committee for help in publicizing a book he had recently written. Scholes's work, *Glimpses of the Ages*, was, in his words, an "exhaustive" discussion of the "subject of the alleged superiority of the white race, and the alleged inferiority of the coloured races." Scholes wanted his study brought to the attention of the American public and asked the committee, through John W. Cromwell, "to bring the work before the readers of your papers." There is no evidence as to how the executive committee dealt with the request, but, if the members thought the book of any worth, disseminating it certainly fitted into the ANA's goal of promoting mutual exchanges and support between black Americans and their brothers and friends abroad. [29]

There were many reasons why the ANA did so little in the foreign field. Its members were physically far removed from their counterparts in Africa, Latin America, the West Indies, and Europe. Most of them had never met or mingled with educated blacks in these places, and even the few who had, as well as those who followed developments in black communities abroad, frequently had only limited understanding of the cultures, governmental systems, or concerns of their inhabitants. However, the chief reason was the ANA's constant preoccupation with basic survival, in terms of poor membership participation, limited funds, and lack of a full-time staff. At no point did the organization function with enough ease, resource, or predictability to make possible serious program development in regard to promoting international contacts.

28. Hayford to Cromwell, March 24, 1913, Holly to Cromwell, July 26, 1906, both in JWCG/M.
29. Theophilus Scholes to Cromwell, April 21, 1906, in JWCG/M.

There were eighteen formal meetings of the ANA in Washington, D.C., during the sixteen years that Archibald H. Grimké was president. Fifteen of those were held during the last week of December. The three exceptions were the eighth annual meeting and two special meetings held in 1911. The eighth annual meeting, which convened on the second and third of March, 1905, was scheduled to coincide with the second inauguration of Theodore Roosevelt as twenty-sixth president of the United States. Deeply concerned about the recent triumphs of the various southern movements to disfranchise blacks, the ANA chose as its theme, "The Negro and the Elective Franchise." Roosevelt's appointment of a handful of black officeholders during his first term (1901–1905), and his few kind words for black Americans during the recent election campaign raised hopes that the ANA's program might gain the attention of the many important black and white politicians visiting the city. The society held two meetings in 1911 to commemorate the one hundredth birthdays of two deceased white Americans, Charles Sumner and Wendell Phillips, both of whom had defended black people before and after the Civil War.[30]

Prior to 1904, the ANA held all but one of its formal sessions at the Lincoln Memorial Congregational Church, but from 1904 until 1911, this was only one of several meeting places. Three meetings did take place at Lincoln (December, 1905, December, 1908, and December, 1909), but two were convened on the campus of Howard University (December, 1906, and December,1907), one at the Fifteenth Street Presbyterian Church (January, 1911), and two at the Metropolitan AME Church (March, 1905, and November, 1911). Beginning in December, 1912, and on through to the end of Archibald H. Grimké's tenure in December, 1919, all meetings were held in the YMCA Branch building on 12th Street, between S and T Streets, N.W. This structure, which was completed in 1912, was built to serve the black community, and its director, Jesse Edward Moorland, was a member of the ANA. The reasons for these shifts in meeting place are not clear. At times they may have reflected a desire for a large auditorium. Not only did the ANA anticipate sizable crowds for the meetings held at the time of Roosevelt's inauguration and the Sumner and Phillips Centenary observances, but the black churches in which they met on these occasions were chosen because of their importance in the community. Part of the motivation for holding two meetings on Howard's campus could have been to at-

---

30. Proceedings, 117, 122–23, 179; "Centenary of Wendell Phillips" announcement card, in JWCG/M. Roosevelt's attitude toward blacks is briefly discussed in Logan, *Betrayal*, 386.

tract faculty and students. And, at times, meeting choices may have simply reflected practical considerations. Before the YMCA building became available, it was often difficult to know very far in advance what meeting space would be available in the black community.[31]

The ANA meetings, which continued to be under the executive committee's direction, were usually programmed around a general theme. As previously mentioned, the one in March, 1905 (eighth annual meeting), dealt with "The Negro and the Elective Franchise." In December of that year a series of papers were delivered on the "Education of the Negro" (ninth annual meeting). The concern of the papers presented in December, 1906 (tenth annual meeting), was the "Economic Phase of the Negro Problem." Although the executive committee chose "Criminal Statistics on Vital Problems" as the topic for December, 1907 (eleventh annual meeting), the inability of the scheduled speakers to appear forced a revision. The theme was changed to "Physical Aspect of the Negro in America" and four loosely related papers were presented under that title. The general topic for the December, 1908, meeting (twelfth annual) was educational and employment opportunities. As usual, the subject was introduced through a series of formal papers, but there was also a round-table discussion by Archibald H. Grimké, William V. Tunnell, Henry M. Joseph, Orishatukeh Faduma, Lafayette M. Hershaw, and Jesse E. Moorland on the question, "Is Enthusiasm in Education on the Wane?" During the course of the panel discussion "the presence of Miss Charlotte Putnam, a pioneer teacher in Virginia, led to a request for words from her lips as to the burning question." Miss Putnam's compliance made this the second and last occasion on which a woman participated in a meeting of the ANA as a peer of its male members and guests. The format of papers along with a panel was considered so successful that it was repeated the next year when the general theme was the "Social Status of the Negro in America" (thirteenth annual meeting).[32]

Most of the meetings convened from 1910 to 1919 had a specific focus or theme, but there were some exceptions: the Sumner Centenary in January,

31. Proceedings, 121, 131, 171; announcement cards for tenth, eleventh, twelfth, and fourteenth annual meetings, "Centenary of Wendell Phillips" announcement card, annual meeting announcement cards for December, 1912, December, 1913, December, 1914, December, 1915, December, 1918, and December, 1919, all in JWCG/M; Washington *Bee*, December 25, 1915, p. 4, December 16, 1916, p. 1, December 22, 1917, p. 7; Green, *The Secret City*, 179.
32. Proceedings, 117, 128, 160–62, 166, 172; also announcement cards for the tenth, eleventh, and twelfth annual meetings, all in JWCG/M. For the other occasion on which a woman participated in a meeting of the ANA see Chapter III.

1911 (fourteenth annual meeting), and the Phillips Centenary in November of that year were essentially memorial services, with addresses on the lives and achievements of these men also presented. The December, 1911, gathering (fifteenth annual meeting) had no public program and was devoted exclusively to ANA business. In December, 1912 (sixteenth annual meeting), the society discussed "The Present-Day Negro." However, the following three annual meetings (seventeenth, eighteenth, and nineteenth) lacked an overall theme and the organization reverted to its earlier practice of listening to a variety of papers on diverse and often discrete topics. This shift may have reflected the executive committee's general discouragement because of shrinking attendance at the public sessions and the many difficulties experienced in finding members and nonmembers who would prepare papers for the meetings.[33] In December, 1916 (twentieth annual meeting), the centenary of Frederick Douglass' birth was observed, but not in the form of a memorial service. Instead, five papers were delivered on various aspects of the deceased black leader's life and career. A year later (twenty-first annual meeting) the ANA gathered to discuss the "Migration of the Negro" and, in 1918 (twenty-second annual meeting), its concern was the place of black Americans in the postwar world. The fact that the December, 1919, meeting (twenty-third annual)—Archibald H. Grimké's last one as president—had no general theme was probably the result of tensions between the president and other ANA executive committee members.[34]

As in previous years the executive committee or one of its subcommittees selected the individuals who were invited to deliver papers before the ANA annual meeting. When a meeting had a theme, persons invited to speak were often given the freedom to write on any subject of their choosing that related to it, but just as frequently the executive committee would devise the topics for the papers to be given and assign them. These procedures represented little or no change from the pattern that had been established under Crummell and Du Bois. One difference, however, was the committee's increasing preoccupation with the members' poor participation in the life of the ANA, especially in regard to preparing papers and attending the annual meetings.

33. Program announcements for the fifteenth, sixteenth, seventeenth, eighteenth annual meetings in JWCG/M; Proceedings, 156, 169, 170, 174, 182, 190.
34. Washington *Bee*, December 16, 1916, p. 1, and December 22, 1917, p. 7; twenty-second annual meeting announcement card, in JWCG/M.

Between 1904 and 1908, at least a third of the persons asked to address the society either declined or agreed to and then failed to appear at the appointed time. Sometimes their reasons were unassailable, as in March, 1905, when illness prevented Kelly Miller from giving his paper on the relationship between the migration of blacks and their voting power. More often, the excuses were similar to the one offered by Samuel Laing Williams of Chicago when he declined, five months after it had been extended, his fourth invitation to address the ANA. Though he wrote, as he said, "with a sense of shame," he simply told the executive committee that his plans for a trip to Washington were "shattered." There was no mention of sending a paper to be read.[35] By 1908, the problem had become so acute that the organization attempted to do something about it.

In September, 1908, the executive committee discussed at length ways "to interest the members of the Academy in their meetings." No specific proposals emerged, but it was agreed that the problem should be presented to the annual meeting scheduled for December. When the issue was raised at that meeting discussion turned on the question of the best method "to stimulate discussion on the papers . . . read before the Academy." Eventually a motion was passed "that each member . . . be requested to be present in person at our annual meeting or to send a letter discussing briefly some phase of the subject selected by the Academy or to make some suggestion bearing on the general scope of the work of the Academy."[36]

It is not clear how soon after this meeting this plan was put into operation, but it would have been inconsistent with John W. Cromwell's previous behavior if he did not begin polling members in regard to the next annual meeting. There is no doubt that he was doing so by 1912, for in April of that year he sent a letter to the members informing them that the theme of the forthcoming meeting (December, 1912) would be "The Present-Day Negro." The letter also listed the six papers the executive committee had agreed on and that were to be discussed. A reply, within thirty days, offering "any suggestions or contribution that may promote the end in view was requested."[37] Polling members in this way did not solve the problem of general participation for the issue surfaced again in 1913.

At the seventeenth annual meeting John W. Cromwell submitted an amendment to the ANA's constitution which, if approved, would have al-

35. Proceedings, 123; Williams to Cromwell, December 9, 1904, in JWCG/M.
36. Proceedings, 154, 157.
37. Cromwell to "Dear Sir," April 20, 1912, in JWCG/M.

lowed the executive committee, on application of one-third of the enrolled membership, "to hold meetings of the Academy in places other than Washington." Though it was not specifically mentioned in the Proceedings, Cromwell also wished to see greater experimentation in the time of year annual meetings were held. As early as 1898, W. E. B. Du Bois and Kelly Miller had made similar suggestions. While he was president of the ANA, Du Bois found it difficult and, at times, impossible to attend the annual sessions of the organization and had urged the society to schedule meetings in the summer in a place other than Washington, D.C. At the second annual meeting in December, 1898, Miller made a similar recommendation, but the matter was referred to the executive committee, where it died. The desire for a meeting time other than the last week of December had frequently been voiced by other members and several who had withdrawn from the ANA cited dissatisfaction with the time of annual meetings as one of their reasons. Cromwell's amendment represented an attempt to make some adjustment in both of these areas. No action was taken, however, because of By-Law 7, which required that a constitutional amendment be voted on at the annual meeting subsequent to that in which it had been proposed.[38]

When the amendment was again presented at the eighteenth annual meeting in December, 1914, the fifteen members of the ANA who were present decided to defer a vote on it for another year. This may have been because of opposition to the idea or possibly a desire to get a clearer notion of how the full membership felt. In any case, when the ANA met in December, 1915, Cromwell was determined that there would be a vote, and he took the lead in successfully pushing for a final consideration of the amendment. Arthur U. Craig, a resident of Washington, D.C., opposed the change because, as he told his fellow members, no other meetings should be held than "at the time and place named in the constitution." Craig's opinion was challenged by Matthew Anderson of Philadelphia, who argued that a mid-summer meeting would "increase interest in the Academy idea." Lorenzo Z. Johnson of Baltimore and Arthur A. Schomburg of New York both supported Anderson on similar grounds. When the amendment was put to a vote it was unanimously approved by the thirteen members present.[39] In spite of this constitutional change, the problem of lagging interest on the part of mem-

38. Proceedings, 55, 194; Du Bois to Cromwell, November 5, 1898, in JWCG/M. For complaints concerning the meeting time of the ANA see the following: Henderson to Cromwell, December 16, 1901, Tanner to Cromwell, October 11, 1905, Walters to Cromwell, January 30, 1913, all in JWCG/M.
39. Proceedings, 170, 182, 198.

bers continued to plague the association. It is impossible to know whether changes in meeting time and place might have improved the quality of the ANA's annual meetings because, as long as Archibald H. Grimké was president, they continued to be held in Washington, D.C., during the last week of December. Grimké may or may not have been a key factor in preventing the selection of other meeting times and places, but it seems significant that the first change in this regard took place the year after he was replaced as president.

Another problem troubling the ANA as much as participation of members was the poor public attendance at the ANA's open sessions. At times the executive committee saw these two concerns as related, believing that if more members attended meetings discussions of the papers would be more exciting, thus producing increased public attendance. Notices were placed in the black newspapers of Washington, D.C., and New York and printed announcements were distributed each year but nothing seemed to eliminate the problem, which increased to such a degree that the small public attendance at the open sessions of the seventeenth annual meeting in December, 1913, was a severe embarrassment to the association. At an executive committee meeting a month later, "means for drawing out larger meetings . . . and exciting . . . greater interest" were discussed extensively, without any satisfactory solution. However, in the interval between the introduction and passage of Cromwell's constitutional amendment to allow greater freedom in regard to selection of the time and place of general meetings, many members came to believe that this might be the means of more effectively presenting the work and concerns of the ANA to a larger audience.[40] The fact that the amendment was not used until after 1919 prevented any test of that theory.

Information on the number of people, members and nonmembers, who attended the ANA's annual meetings, is not more abundant for this period than for its early years. The bits of information that have survived indicate that between 1904 and 1919 the average number in attendance was thirteen. The lowest attendance occurred in March, 1905, and December, 1912, when only eight members appeared; the high point was December, 1919, when twenty-two members were present.[41]

40. *Ibid.*, 130, 157, 182.
41. J. W. Cromwell did record the members of the academy present at a few annual meetings between 1904 and 1915 but failed to do so on a regular basis. His lists are found in Pro-

Although John W. Cromwell, from time to time, listed in the Proceedings the names of members of the ANA present at an annual meeting, he left no record of the size of the audiences that attended the public sessions of the meetings. Once in a while—but not consistently—he mentioned the non-members who attended a meeting, but usually only if they had been specially invited or if they spoke during a discussion following a paper. Newspaper accounts would sometimes make reference to the size of an audience at a meeting, but this was more unusual than typical. The paucity of such references, since the newspapers and journals that printed news about the ANA were usually sympathetic to it, may be an indication that the public attendance was quite small—a fact these publications probably chose to discreetly pass over.

An observation recorded by John W. Cromwell in his journal shortly after the twelfth annual meeting in 1908 supports this view. "As usual," he wrote, "the number [present] was small—not more than 75 different people at the different sessions, the average [number at each] being less than one half [32?]." The statement also indicates that seventy-five was the approximate attendance for many, if not most of the previous meetings. Because of their special character the centenary observances held three years later to honor Charles Sumner (January 6, 1911) and Wendell Phillips (November 29, 1911) probably drew more of an attendance than the average annual meeting. This was undoubtedly true of the Sumner memorial for *Crisis* magazine and the Washington *Evening Star* both noted that there were "several hundred colored people" present plus "a number of white people."[42]

No other newspaper commented on attendance until December, 1915, when the Washington *Bee* described the twentieth annual meeting as "largely attended." The reason, the article pointed out, was the "popular interest" in the subjects treated. That year four papers were read, all by ANA members: Archibald H. Grimké spoke on "The Sex Question and Race Segregation"; Theophilus G. Steward on "The Message of the Santo Domingo Negro to the Negro Race"; Lafayette M. Hershaw on "Negro Citizenship Prior to the Civil War"; and John W. Cromwell presented a bibliographical essay on books and articles dealing with black Americans which

ceedings, 123, 195, 200. It gives figures on attendance for meetings from 1904 to 1915, and the break-down between residents of Washington and those from other parts of the country.

42. Cromwell, Journal, 132, in JWCG/M; *Crisis*, I (February, 1911), 5.

had appeared in print that year. Because Grimké and Hershaw were prominent militants whose opinions were highly regarded, the widespread concern among blacks regarding the aggressively anti-Negro mood of the country increased interest in what they had to say. The topical nature of Steward's subject was due to recent efforts by the administration of President Woodrow Wilson to coerce the warring political factions in Santo Domingo—a country with a sizable black population—into acceptance of a series of agreements that would make their nation a protectorate of the United States. However, the fact that the article in the Washington *Bee* supplied an explanation for the sizable audiences that came to hear these papers implied that attendance at the typical annual meeting was usually smaller. Available sources provide even less information in this regard concerning the four successive meetings.[43]

From time to time prominent persons who were not members of the ANA appeared at its meetings. In March, 1905, when the ANA discussed "The Negro and the Elective Franchise," the Rev. William Jefferson White of Augusta, Georgia, was present. White, almost certainly in the city for Roosevelt's inauguration, was a leading black Baptist minister. During Reconstruction he had begun a career that involved him in education, journalism, politics, and the equal rights movement. The founder of Augusta Baptist Institute, he also edited the Georgia *Baptist*, a newspaper of broad concerns, which had considerable influence outside its denomination. In 1906 when the ANA met in the Small Chapel of Howard University, Wilbur Patterson Thirkield, a white Methodist clergyman who was president of the institution, conducted the "devotional exercises" at one of the public sessions. At the conclusion of the meeting Thirkield "congratulated the Academy on its ideals and its work." The next year the ANA held its annual meeting in the "Main Building" at Howard and Thirkield again gave the invocation. On request, he also reacted to a paper by Archibald H. Grimké on "The Economic Condition of the Negro," and participated extensively in

43. Washington *Bee*, January 8, 1916, p. 1. Grimké and Hershaw were both forthright proponents of political and social rights for blacks. Grimké's career as an essayist and public speaker was built on activities directed toward this end. He also gave expression to these concerns through a vigorous involvement with the NAACP. Hershaw was part of the Du Bois-led Niagara Movement, helped edit *Horizon*, a magazine published by the Niagara Movement, and was active in the NAACP. For brief discussion of the two men in this regard see Aptheker (ed.), *Correspondence of W. E. B. Du Bois*, I, 91, 229n. Selden Rodman discusses the policy of the United States with regard to Santo Domingo from 1914 to 1916 in *Quisqueya: A History of the Dominican Republic* (Seattle, 1964), 106–127.

the ensuing discussion. Thirkield attended one of the sessions of the annual meeting in 1908 and took part in a general discussion of Orishatukeh Faduma's paper, "Social Problems in West Africa from the Standpoint of an African." The following year he again appeared at one of the sessions of the annual meeting and opened it with prayer.[44]

When the Charles Sumner Centenary observance was held in 1911, two of the addresses were delivered by whites—Wendell Phillips Stafford, a justice of the District of Columbia Supreme Court, and ex-Senator William E. Chandler of New Hampshire. Both men had long histories as courageous supporters of the black struggle for political rights and equal treatment under the law. Later that year Stafford was the guest speaker at the memorial for Wendell Phillips.[45]

In 1915, Oswald Garrison Villard, a white philanthropist who was a grandson of William Lloyd Garrison and one of the founders of the NAACP, attended part of the nineteenth annual meeting. Archibald H. Grimké may have been responsible for Villard's presence since the president of the ANA was at the time head of the Washington, D.C., chapter of the NAACP and, as was Villard, a member of its national board. At the conclusion of the final session of the meeting, Villard was introduced and, in a brief address, expressed great optimism concerning the future of blacks in the United States.[46]

A year later, when the ANA heard a series of papers on the life and work of Frederick Douglass, T. Thomas Fortune, former editor of the New York *Age*, and Thomas B. Patterson, an agricultural specialist on the faculty of Livingstone College in Salisbury, North Carolina, were present. In the 1880s, when he was a young man, Fortune had met Douglass and developed a respect for him which was lifelong. But the real drawing card must have been the chance to visit, chat, and debate with old acquaintances such as ANA members John E. Bruce, John W. Cromwell, and Robert H. Terrell. These were men Fortune had known since young manhood and two of the three (Bruce and Terrell) presented papers on aspects of Douglass' career. Patterson had initiated, with notable success, many programs to improve the life of black farmers around Salisbury. The fact that his close friend and

---

44. Proceedings, 123, 140, 149, 150, 158, 172. For biographical data on White see Meier, *Negro Thought*, 156, 176, 221–22. For a biographical sketch of Thirkield, see Harlan (ed.), *Booker T. Washington Papers*, III, 279.
45. Proceedings, 179; and "Centenary of Wendell Phillips" program card, in JWCG/M.
46. Proceedings, 190.

fellow Livingstone faculty member, James E. K. Aggrey, was an enthusiastic member of the ANA probably influenced his decision to attend.[47]

In December, 1919, A. Philip Randolph, a young black activist, delivered a paper on "The New Radicalism and the Negro" at the twenty-third annual meeting of the ANA. Randolph, who was a socialist and the coeditor of the *Messenger*, a New York-based magazine which took an avowedly Marxist position in analyzing the causes of prejudice and discrimination, was not a member of the ANA. Two months before the annual meeting, the executive committee invited him to come to Washington, D.C., as the guest of the ANA and address its members on this subject. Randolph was a well-known and controversial figure in the black community, but his invitation to appear before the ANA probably came because his magazine had printed Archibald H. Grimké's poem, "Her Thirteen Soldiers," a protest against the United States Army's execution of a group of black infantrymen in 1917 on charges of murder and rioting. The poem had first been offered to *Atlantic Monthly* and *Crisis* magazines, but these two publications rejected it. Many blacks, including Grimké, considered the dead soldiers heroes who had vindicated black manhood and paid the ultimate price for doing so. Because Randolph and Chandler Owen, coeditors of the *Messenger*, shared this opinion they printed the poem in their magazine.[48]

The executive committee's invitation to Randolph disturbed and angered Jesse E. Moorland, one of its members. Moorland, a Congregationalist minister who was national director of the YMCA's programs for blacks, was outraged that a man with Randolph's opinions should have been invited to address the ANA. Two other things further incensed him: the decision to invite Randolph had been made at a meeting of the executive committee which he had been unable to attend; and he had not been informed about the decision immediately after the meeting. A week before Randolph was scheduled to speak, Moorland communicated his feelings to Francis J. Grimké, treasurer of the ANA and also a member of the executive committee. Why Moorland wrote to Francis and not to his brother Archibald, who

47. T. Thomas Fortune, "Washington Letter," New York *Age*, December 28, 1916, p. 2. For biographical information on Fortune see Thornbrough, *T. Thomas Fortune*; for Patterson see Smith, *Aggrey of Africa*, 92.

48. Cromwell to Randolph, October 8, 1919, Randolph to Cromwell, October 14, 1919, both in JWCG/M; *Messenger*, III (October, 1919), 25–26. For biographical information on Randolph, see Jervis Anderson, *A. Philip Randolph: A Biographical Portrait* (New York, 1972). Anderson (p. 113) discusses the incidents that led to the publication of Grimké's poem in the *Messenger*.

was president of the ANA, or to the executive committee as a whole, is unclear. It may have been because he felt certain that Grimké, who was his close friend and a Presbyterian clergyman, shared his feelings about Randolph and the invitation. In his letter, Moorland protested the fact that the decision to invite Randolph to speak had been made when he was not present, and charged that such an invitation was "inconsistent with the dignity" and "purpose" of the ANA. To him, the invitation was an endorsement of the activities and ideas of Randolph and Owen, men who, in his opinion, were opposed to everything the ANA represented. Moorland reminded Grimké that the two were enemies of the Christian religion, editors of a publication that disseminated radical propaganda, and bitter critics of several members of the ANA, whom they attacked repeatedly in the *Messenger.*[49]

Randolph and Owen advocated socialism, the unionization of black workers, and militant opposition to racism. They also used the columns of their magazine to attack the majority of black political, social, and religious leaders whom they charged with ignorance of the real causes of poverty and racism, preoccupation with their own welfare, and a willingness to ally themselves with whites who were the worst enemies of the black community. In articles with titles such as "The Failure of the Negro Leaders," "Negro Leaders Compromise as Usual," and "The Failure of the Negro Church," they repeatedly called for "new leaders with a more thorough grasp of scientific education, and a calm but uncompromising courage." Neither man had any qualms about naming the men they wished to see displaced from leadership roles. Members of the ANA most frequently criticized, attacked, and denounced were W. E. B. Du Bois, Kelly Miller, William Pickens, Archibald H. Grimké, James Weldon Johnson, Robert H. Terrell, and John E. Bruce. Though biased, Moorland's description of Randolph and Owen was generally accurate. Whether their beliefs and opinions constituted valid reasons for refusing to permit either man to address the ANA was another question.[50]

49. Moorland's letter to F. J. Grimké has not survived. However, much of its content is indicated in the reply which Grimké sent. See Grimké to Moorland, December 22, 1919, in Woodson, *Works of Francis J. Grimké,* IV, 262–63. Several passages of Grimké's letter suggest that part of Moorland's objection to Randolph and Owen may have stemmed from attacks the two men had made on him. There are, however, no references to him in the *Messenger.*

50. *Messenger,* II (January, 1918), 23–24; II (July, 1918), 27–28; III (March, 1919), 21–23; III (May–June, 1919), 26–27; III (July, 1919), 16–21; III (September, 1919), 7–8, 16–17; III (October, 1919), 6, 17–18, 20; III (December, 1919), 20–21.

Francis J. Grimké's reply was a polite but frank refutation of all the objections Moorland raised. After expressing surprise at the "tenor" of his friend's letter, Grimké described the meeting of the executive committee "at which Mr. Randolph was invited to address the Academy": "All the members were present, as I remember except yourself; Prof. Miller presided and the vote was unanimous. No one seemed to feel that there was anything inconsistent with the dignity or purpose of the Academy in inviting him." Sharply disagreeing with Moorland's assessment of the two journalists and their publication, Grimké defended all three in glowing terms. "Both the editors of the *Messenger*," he told Moorland, "are young men of unusual brain power and are thoroughly trained men. The *Messenger* is decidedly the ablest Negro journal that is published; it has more brain to the square inch than any other Negro publication that I know of. These young men by the forceful and clean-cut presentation of the claims of the colored people are attracting more and more to themselves the attention and respect of the thoughtful and more progressive Negroes all over the country."

In Grimké's opinion, Moorland's "criticism of the action of the Executive Committee" indicated that he had "entirely misunderstood the purpose of the Academy." As a corrective, the treasurer of the ANA offered the following clarification:

1. It [the Academy] is not a religious organization. It was not founded with apologetic intent—I use the term as the chief cause—as a means of buttressing up religion. Its members may all be Christians; but as an Academy it has no religious tenets.
2. It has stood, and I trust always will stand for the freest discussion of all subjects of human interest. What it ought to seek is to encourage the free exchange of thought; it ought to be a kind of clearing house for the best thought of the best brains of the race. It would be a sad mistake to shut out from our discussions any line of honest thinking. What we need is light, and never mind from what source it comes, it ought to be welcomed. The attempt to restrict discussion belongs not to this age, but rather to the dark ages. The American Negro Academy would soon become a back number, if such should be its policy.
3. The American Negro Academy never has and I trust never will concern itself about attacks made upon gentlemen who happen to be members of it. . . . If . . . [any member] cannot defend himself, if he is such an intellectual weakling that somebody else must come to his defense, the reflection on the Academy is not that it doesn't come to his defense, but that it should have such a member on its list. The Academy has nothing, absolutely nothing to do with attacks made on men who happen to be identified with it. And it is strange that you should assume that it has. Membership in the American Negro Academy doesn't put a man above or beyond criticism, does it? The Academy would simply make itself ridiculous if it acted upon any such assumption.

There is no way of knowing exactly how Moorland reacted to this letter, or whether he was present when Randolph delivered his paper. Even though he remained a member of the ANA, after 1919 Moorland ceased to play an active role in the organization.[51]

Randolph delivered his paper on December 30, 1919, at an evening session of the twenty-third annual meeting. In it, he denounced American capitalism and proclaimed the usefulness of the bourgeois leadership of the black community at an end. The description of the address, which appeared in the Washington *Bee*, was the lengthiest article that newspaper ever printed on an annual meeting of the ANA. According to the newspaper's reporter,

Mr. Randolph very philanthropically, carefully, charitably and clearly pointed out the fact that the "old crowd" leaders [who] have guided the Negro race as well as their ability would permit, but owing to the fact that a great proportion of their education had been devoted to the less essential things in life, the study of Greek and Latin, etc., at the expense of the more essential studies, the economical, political, and social history of the various races of the human family, this "old crowd" order of leaders, which is classified under the head of the "right wing" and the "center order" of society is not in the position to give advice to the Negro which will be of value to him, because of their lack of valuable knowledge and valuable information.

Mr. Randolph [asked] the Negro to consider well the side he was going to line up with when the inevitable arrives in full blast, and left with the audience the portrayal of the picture of the Negro lined up with the capitalists, the Republican and Democratic parties, who have been exploiting him and the poor white man since the abolition of slavery, and who will continue to exploit them both as long as either of these parties are in power, as against the Labor party, to become a part of the ruling power in the future history of the world.

Randolph's paper, which the *Bee* described as a "splendid oration," produced "many responses," including a large number of spirited defenses of both the "right wing" and the "center order of society." Although the article did not indicate the size of the audience or name all of the people who commented on the paper, it implied that an impressive number were present, and that several persons who were not members of the ANA participated in the ensuing discussion. According to the *Bee*, when "Prof. Carter Woodson, author of 'The Journal of Negro History,' took the floor and uttered the five simple words, 'Mr. Randolph is a prophet.' . . . The audience burst forth in such continued vociferous applause that Prof. Woodson was unable to speak another word for ten minutes." The audience shouted,

51. Grimké to Moorland, December 22, 1919, in Woodson, *Works of Francis J. Grimké*, IV, 262–63.

"Enough said. You have said it all. The Negro will line up with the 'left-wing,' the radicals, the Labor party."[52]

Academy member John E. Bruce, a prominent journalist whom Randolph and his associate Owen repeatedly criticized in their magazine, had quite a different reaction to the paper, and was probably among those seated in the audience, who, during the discussion, defended "the 'right wing' and the 'center' order of society." Bruce thought Randolph's address a series of "bitter attacks on all things not socialistic," and was especially offended by the young radical's consignment, "to overlasting perdition [of] the old leaders, political and spiritual, despite the fact that without these old leaders' efforts in the past in blazing a path for the younger leaders to tread, they would not now be treading in this path." In this regard, the socialist's opinions reminded him of "the snake in Aesop's fable, biting the hand that gave it warmth." Although Randolph's performance as a speaker impressed Bruce as "brilliant, masterly, [and] eloquent," in his opinion, the editor of the *Messenger* provided no "proofs as to its [Socialism's] efficacy as a solvent of all the social, political, and economic evils of which humanity is heir." Nothing in Randolph's analysis of the United States and the situation of black Americans made a positive impression on Bruce, who left the session convinced that his aversion to the theories of Marx and his various disciples, orthodox and heretical, was the better part of wisdom. "I have," he confided to his diary, "no faith in socialism and its propagandists. It has occupied the attention of thinkers for centuries past and no three of them seem to agree as to its efficacy as a solvent for the ills of the body politic. Socialists are themselves divided and there can never be unity in division."[53]

Neither the records of the ANA nor the papers of its members provide any indication of the ways in which other academicians evaluated Randolph's paper. In light of the exchange between Francis J. Grimké and Jesse Moorland, it would be especially interesting to know how the Grimké brothers reacted to it. One possible hint as to the impact it had was the absence of any effort on the part of any officer or member of the society to have "The New Radicalism and the Negro" published as an occasional paper. However, in spite of the fact that nothing in the ANA's constitution or by-laws forbade publishing the works of nonmembers, only papers written

52. Washington *Bee*, January 10, 1920, p. 6. The address is mentioned in the *Messenger*, IV (March, 1920), 13.

53. Peter Gilbert (ed.), *The Selected Writings of John Edward Bruce: Militant Black Journalist* (New Yor, 1971), 156.

by men who belonged to the society had been printed. In the years following the society's establishment an unstated policy of closing its occasional
papers to all but members may have come to be the rule.

The coverage that the ANA received from the newspapers in Washington
between 1904 and 1919 was, on the whole, even sparser and less substantive than during the first five years of its existence. The *Bee*, the city's black
newspaper, and its two leading white dailies, the *Post* and the *Evening Star*,
almost always took note of the society's annual meetings and special observances, but their articles usually were brief and superficial. Occasionally,
one of these newspapers would draw their readers' attention to a particular
address that had been given, but this was more unusual than typical.

One of the most interesting exceptions to this pattern took place following the eighteenth annual meeting in December, 1914, when an editorial
appeared in the Washington *Bee*, ridiculing the ANA for the meaningless-
ness and irrelevancy of the "scientific standpoint" from which the organization attempted to relate to the black and his problems. However, the editorial's real concern was revealed by its suggestion that Archibald H.
Grimké and the ANA "secure a few of Dr. Booker T. Washington's books
. . . and . . . discuss the Negro and all his belonging from a commonplace
point of view." The reason for the *Bee*'s attack was not concern about the
ANA's methods of inquiry, but the opposition of Grimké and many of the
members of the ANA to Washington's educational theories, racial philosophy, and use of his powerful role as advisor to influential white philanthropists and politicians to harass his critics. One of Washington's chief supporters in the nation's capital was the editor of the *Bee*, William Calvin
Chase, who used his newspaper to censure any person or organization who
fell into disfavor with the principal of Tuskegee. Indeed, the "fine hand" of
Washington may have been behind the poor press coverage the ANA received in the District of Columbia and other parts of the country.[54]

Although it varied, some of the coverage the ANA received in publications outside of Washington, D.C., had greater depth than the articles carried by the local press. *Horizon*, one of the short-lived organs of the
Niagara Movement, which was led by W. E. B. Du Bois, argued in an editorial printed in 1908 that the ANA should merge with several racial defense organizations, but the suggestion had little appeal for the men who

54. Washington *Bee*, January 9, 1915, p. 4. See also August Meier, "Booker T. Washington
and the Negro Press," *Journal of Negro History*, XXXVIII (January, 1953), 65–82.

were officers of the society. Two years later, perhaps to affirm the unique character of the ANA's work, John W. Cromwell wrote a lengthy article for *Horizon*, discussing the association's history, structure, and scholarly publications. After the NAACP established *Crisis* magazine as its journal in 1910, W. E. B. Du Bois, its editor, seemed uncertain whether or not he wished to give the ANA regular coverage. In 1911 the magazine carried a short description of the Charles Sumner Centenary observance, but there was no other mention of the ANA until 1916 when a brief review of the nineteenth annual meeting (December, 1915) appeared. Beginning in 1918, and each year thereafter, however, *Crisis* began to print a short article on the society following its December annual meeting. The most informative piece on the organization written during these years was the article Cromwell prepared for the November–December issue of the *African Times and Orient Review* in 1913. In 1915 the society received a rare bit of attention from a white newspaper when the Boston *Herald*, in an editorial, quoted extensively from, and strongly praised, Archibald H. Grimké's essay, "The Ultimate Criminal," a critique of white racism which had been his presidential address at the eighteenth annual meeting in December, 1914. Because of Brooklynite Arthur A. Schomburg's increasing involvement with the ANA after 1916, he was responsible for the appearance of several articles on the ANA in the New York *Age*.[55]

One of the most affirmative responses to the ANA was an unidentifiable article which appeared shortly after the twenty-second annual meeting in December, 1918, where a series of militant papers demanding equal treatment for blacks in postwar America had been delivered. However, the writer of the article noted bitterly, "the meeting might as well have been held in Timbuctoo as in Washington for all the attention it got from the white population of the capitol." If, the reporter continued, the "eloquent and vigorous thinking" at this meeting really represented postwar black attitudes "then lively times lie ahead for states and cities—not to mention the Nation—that discriminate against the Negro." Picking up the tone of the speakers, the writer made the following declaration: "The Negro race's record of bravery in the war, as a generous donor to Liberty loans and [the]

55. *Horizon*, III (June, 1908), 4, V (February, 1910), 11–12; *Crisis*, I (February, 1911), 5, VI (February, 1916), 165, VII (February, 1918), 191, IX (February, 1920), 213; [Cromwell], "American Negro Academy" *African Times and Orient Review*, 243–44; Boston *Herald*, June 2, 1915, p. 10. Grimké's address was published as ANA Occasional Paper no. 17 (1915). See also New York *Age*, December 28, 1916, p. 2, December 29, 1917, p. 5, and January 10, 1920, pp. 1, 2.

Red Cross and the Seven Agencies' Fund, and as a supporter of the War for Democracy is not to be allowed to go forgotten or as it was for naught; and if there is no Caucasian appreciation of it, in the form of a more decent, humane treatment of the black democrat by the white democrat, then the man who fought superbly in France may find ways of fighting bravely in Alabama—or the District of Columbia." In rhetoric that fairly shouted, this observer pointed out that such ideas had not formed any part of the "Gospel" Booker T. Washington had "preached," but, he continued, "he is dead . . . a war had been fought, and the Negro intellectuals are now saying boldly that which when Washington lived they only muttered." [56]

Although the article implied that the death of Booker T. Washington removed the chief obstacle which had kept blacks from speaking freely about their treatment in the United States, the new mood of black Americans after 1918 was largely due to their anger, disillusionment, and frustration. Black Americans, though second-class citizens in every sense of the word, were loyal supporters of the American cause during World War I. In the capacities of soldiers, war workers, and financial contributors, they endured constant mistreatment and abuse, believing that by "joining ranks" with other Americans and demonstrating their patriotism by forgetting, for a time, their grievances, whites would be persuaded, after the war, to cease to deny them economic opportunities and civil rights. However, instead of improvement in their situation, the postwar period brought even greater repression and racial hostility. Many blacks, including some recently returned soldiers were lynched, and there were widespread attacks on the black community in the form of race riots. In many cases blacks fought back by doing battle with their attackers and, across the nation, articulate blacks protested their mistreatment, ridiculed the democratic pretensions of their countrymen, and expressed their hatred for white racism with an unparalleled frankness. [57] The ANA's proceedings during the twenty-second annual meeting reflected the impact on black thought of the war and all its related experiences.

56. This article minus author, publication, and date, can be found in J. W. Cromwell's Book of Clippings, in JWCG/M.
57. Franklin, *From Slavery to Freedom*, 333–67.

VI *Addressing the Issues*

During Grimké's presidency, the academy published nine occasional papers, numbers 9 through 18/19. Occasional Paper no. 9, *The Early Negro Convention Movement* by John W. Cromwell, appeared in 1904. In preparing the paper, Cromwell drew on primary sources that had not been used before, including information solicited from Peter H. Clark and James T. Holly, both of whom had been involved in these important antebellum gatherings of black Americans. At the close of his paper, Cromwell made clear that the concept of industrial education as a valuable form of training for blacks was espoused by a number of black leaders before either Frederick Douglass or Booker T. Washington publicly supported it. Holly was especially pleased with the paper and, when two years later his copies were stolen, he wrote the academy asking for seconds.[1]

Defects of the Negro Church, an essay written by Orishatukeh Faduma, was also published in 1904. Issued as Occasional Paper no. 10, it contained a strong critique of the black-American religious community. Faduma, a minister himself, pointed to the following practices as faults and deficiencies which undermined the efficacy of black churches: "worldliness" or a general "tendency to lay stress on outwardness rather than inwardness"; "the neglect of rural communities"; personal and institutional problems experienced by clergy; the "worldliness" of the laity; and "excessive emotionalism in worship." The author directly charged black ministers with being poorly educated, frequently guilty of "sexual unchastity," and overly involved in

1. John W. Cromwell, *The Early Negro Convention Movement*, ANA Occasional Papers, no. 9 (1904), 13–14, 20–21; Holly to Cromwell, July 26, 1906, in JWCG/M.

fund-raising and church administration—all to the detriment of their role as religious leaders. Many of the laity, in his opinion, were "self-centered and self-seeking," without any authentic missionary spirit or "concrete" commitment to religious virtues. In addition, he felt that they lacked practical knowledge of "business-methods," a situation which led to inefficient church management, especially in the area of finances. Though he called for changes, Faduma felt that the religious condition of blacks deserved as much "pity" as "censure" because of the "two hundred years" they had spent "in the house of bondage," during which their "wild, primitive nature was left untrained." He believed education to be the best resource for promoting "the proper religious development of the Negro."[2]

Initially, despite the executive committee's belief that Faduma's paper was an accurate description of several basic problems plaguing black religious institutions, they felt some anxiety about publishing it, fearing that the paper might be viewed simply as an attack on black ministers and the black church. Such an interpretation, besides being inaccurate, would have embarrassed those academy members who were clergy and offended many black churchmen whose support the society sought. Though the executive committee had no doubts as to the quality of the paper, it voted, in February, 1904, that the manuscript, "be referred to the president for report as to the advisability of its publication." The president, Archibald H. Grimké, recommended that the academy publish the paper, and, by June, Occasional Paper no. 10 was being distributed to members, libraries, and newspapers.[3]

Shortly after the executive committee made its final decision to print *Defects of the Negro Church*, its author sent John W. Cromwell a check for $10.95 to pay for several hundred copies he planned to distribute personally. When Faduma received them he was furious because errors he had noted on the galley proofs sent to him several months earlier had not been corrected. As Theophilus G. Steward had done five years earlier, he registered a sharp complaint. In a letter to Cromwell, who handled most of the business connected with the publication of papers, Faduma made it quite clear that he held him personally responsible for what had happened. The corresponding secretary's reply has not survived nor is it possible to determine whether the academy ever made the corrections Faduma demanded.[4]

2. Orishatukeh Faduma, *Defects of the Negro Church*, ANA Occasional Papers, no. 10 (1904), 4, 6, 8, 13, 14, 17.
3. Proceedings, 116, 125.
4. Faduma to Cromwell, June 23, 1904, in JWCG/M.

There is little evidence regarding public reaction to *Defects of the Negro Church*, but from what is known the paper seems to have excited public interest for several years. James T. Holly thought it an important statement on the black church and always tried to keep several of the pamphlets in his possession. In 1911, responding to a request from Faduma, the executive committee agreed to reprint his paper. Both the costs and the total number of papers printed were divided between the academy and the author. And, in 1913, at the request of the executive committee, Faduma gave permission for a second reprinting of his paper.[5]

In 1904 the academy published, as Occasional Paper no. 11, five papers and a sermon, all of them discussions of a general theme, *The Negro and the Elective Franchise*. Four of the papers—"The Meaning and Need of the Movement to Reduce Southern Representation" by Archibald H. Grimké; "The Penning of the Negro or the Negro Vote in the States of the Revised Constitutions" by Charles C. Cook; "The Negro Suffrage in the States Whose Constitutions Have Not Been Specifically Revised" by John Hope; and "The Potentiality of the Negro Vote, North and West" by John L. Love—had been read at the eighth annual meeting in March, 1905. The fifth paper, "Migration and Distribution of the Negro Population as Affecting the Elective Franchise," had been scheduled for presentation at the same meeting, but illness prevented the author, Kelly Miller, from delivering it. The sermon, "The Negro and His Citizenship," was preached by Francis J. Grimké at a religious service in Washington.[6] The papers by Archibald Grimké, Cook, Hope, and Love formed part of the period's small but growing challenge by black Americans to the white South's defense of disfranchisement and the subordination of southern blacks. Beginning in the 1930s many of the interpretations offered in these papers would find a place in revised histories of events in the South during the last quarter of the nineteenth century. Francis Grimké's sermon was a classic example of the arguments used by many blacks to express their continuing commitment to social and political equality for black Americans.

In the first paper, "The Meaning and Need of the Movement to Reduce

5. Proceedings, 183; Holly to Cromwell, July 26, 1906, Faduma to Cromwell, May 28, 1913, all in JWCG/M. When they first appeared in 1904, copies of both Occasional Papers nos. 9 and 10 were sent to ANA members and to "libraries and represented [representative] newspapers." During Archibald H. Grimké's administration, the ANA usually printed five hundred copies of a paper. This was probably the size of the first edition of Faduma's paper. It is impossible, however, to even speculate as to what the size of the second and third editions were.
    6. Proceedings, 122–23, 125.

Southern Representation," Archibald Grimké traced the history of the "slave representation clause" in the United States Constitution, arguing that this provision, which gave the South "the right to count five slaves as three freemen in the apportionment of representatives," was the basic cause of the Civil War. By their rebellion and defeat southerners lost this privilege but, Grimké pointed out, through their disfranchisement of the blacks, they regained it on an even larger scale, due to the fact that after the ratification of the Fifteenth Amendment in 1870, all blacks were considered citizens. This amendment allowed the southern aristocracy to obtain control over an even larger block of representative power. Grimké believed the chief effects of disfranchisement would be threefold: political and economic disaster for blacks; the ultimate "degradation of white labor"; and the eventual subversion of "free institutions in the Republic." To restore the voting rights of blacks and punish the South, he called for a reduction in the congressional representation as provided for in the Fourteenth Amendment.[7]

Charles C. Cook's essay, "The Penning of the Negro," presented two motives as an explanation for the white South's disfranchisement activities: the desire to create a powerless black industrial labor pool, and a determination to eliminate black Americans as a decisive factor in political clashes between whites. In the course of his paper, Cook reviewed the Republican party's platform statements on black suffrage from 1868 to 1904. He found that although the party consistently expressed support for blacks in their struggle to maintain the right to vote, during those years the movement to eliminate black voters only became stronger and more effective. This, Cook believed, was the result of an increasing affinity between the North and South, especially with respect to their views on social and moral issues. He saw the North moving to make "slaves" of its white laborers and, as a result, no longer opposed to the South's reenslavement of blacks. "The gulf," he wrote, "which widened into bitter civil war, is now closing; the two types [white northerners and southerners] are drawing nearer; the divorce between sections is shifting around to a divorce between classes." As he surveyed the social scene in America, Cook saw retrogression rather than progress. For this reason he attacked as meaningless slogans Americans' stated belief in republican government as a virtuous form of rule, the Constitution as the ultimate hope of wronged groups in America, the idea of "New World" innocence, and other standard American pieties of his day. How-

7. Archibald H. Grimké, "The Meaning and Need of the Movement to Reduce Southern Representation," ANA Occasional Papers, no. 11 (1905), 3–14.

ever, despite his pessimism, Cook made a plea to the Republican party not to abandon blacks; and, at the conclusion of his paper, exhorted his race to remain within that party, to continue to be hopeful, to engage in self-help activities, to reject violence and subversive groups, and to continue to strive for all their rights, including "social equality."[8]

In spite of its title—"The Negro Suffrage in the States Whose Constitutions Have Not Been Specifically Revised"—John Hope's paper only dealt with developments in the state of Georgia. Hope explained that through the use of the "white primary" Georgia had been as successful in eliminating black voters as those states that had amended their constitutions. Behind this activity he perceived "a hatred for Colored people and a determination to have white supremacy at any cost of life and honor." The body of Hope's paper was devoted to presenting detailed proofs that Georgia's "white primary" had brought about the political and social emasculation of blacks. Responding to those blacks who advised accommodation with this situation, he urged his people to continue to vote, and to fight for the right to vote. "Better welcome disfranchisement as men," he concluded, "than suffer from it as cowards."[9]

In his paper, "The Potentiality of the Negro Vote, North and West," John L. Love argued that even though the number of blacks in those sections of the country was numerically small, when an election was evenly, or nearly evenly, divided between the political parties black voters could decide the outcome. The ballot, in Love's opinion, was "the surest means of securing a 'square deal'." But before the "three hundred thousand Negro voters of the north and west" could begin to utilize it toward that end, it was first necessary for them "to recognize its value" and to learn how to use it in the same way "all other aggrieved elements of the body politic" did, that is, by voting only for their friends and always against their enemies. To realize "the effectiveness and potentiality of the Negro vote" Love called for "an absolute and courageous disregard of traditions." By this he meant that blacks would have to cease voting automatically for Republican candidates and, instead, make the two parties bid for their assistance. Love urged blacks in the North and West to cease their habitual support of the Republican party and begin to consider their "well-being and safety identical with the well-being

8. Charles C. Cook, "The Penning of the Negro," ANA Occasional Papers, no. 11 (1905), 22–31, 39–40, 46–50.

9. John Hope, "Negro Suffrage in the States Whose Constitutions Have Not Been Specifically Revised," ANA Occasional Papers, no. 11 (1905), 51–60.

and safety of the republic," requiring "all men who seek [their] vote to consider it likewise." But, he stressed, without "intelligent, honest, straightforward, and unselfish [black] leadership"—a resource lacking in many places—blacks would not have the necessary skill and sophistication for bipartisan politics.[10]

Kelly Miller's paper, the shortest of the six, was more significant for its statistical tables than for its arguments. The tables contained statistics on the growth of the black population from 1790 to 1900; on the number of blacks living in the South and in the North; on the number of black males of voting age in the northern states; and on the number of black males of voting age in northern cities. In the brief interpretation which accompanied the tables, Miller expressed the belief that as long as blacks were one-tenth of the American population there would be a racial problem. "From the foundation of our government," he noted, "the Negro has constituted a serious political problem, mainly because of his unequal distribution." "If," he continued, "agricultural and economic conditions had been uniform, and the slaves had been evenly scattered over the whole area of the United States [,] the political phase of the race problem would have been far different from what it is and has been throughout our national life. The fact that the bulk of this race has been congested in one section has constituted the cause of political friction from the foundation of the constitution till the present hour." Miller was also of the opinion that in spite of the steady migration of blacks to the North and West, the greater number would choose to remain in the South. Nevertheless, he felt, as Love did, that the significance of the northern migration, because of the potential it created for new forms of black political power, was "out of all proportion to its absolute weight."[11]

Francis J. Grimké's sermon, "The Negro and His Citizenship," was a discussion of the importance of blacks continuing to defend the legitimacy of their hard-won status as American citizens. Grimké's biblical text, Acts 22:25–29, was the story of St. Paul's encounter with Roman officials in Jerusalem. Paul was arrested for provoking a public disturbance and scheduled for examination by flogging. However, when the apostle told his jailors he was a Roman citizen, they abandoned their plans to interrogate him by

10. John L. Love, "The Potentiality of the Negro Vote, North and West," ANA Occasional Papers, no. 11 (1905), 61, 63, 65–66.

11. Kelly Miller, "Migration and Distribution of the Negro Population as Affecting the Elective Franchise," ANA Occasional Papers, no. 11 (1905), 72–77, 79, 84.

torture because it was illegal to examine a citizen of the empire in this way. Grimké pointed to his text as a model of how blacks should behave whenever their rights as American citizens were infringed. Citizenship, in his estimation was "a sacred thing . . . to be prized . . . [and] highly esteemed"; especially so by black Americans, who, despite their "length of residence . . . unstinted toil . . . [and] great sacrifices of blood" had been denied this status in America for 250 years. Grimké urged three forms of resistance to what he saw as a growing "determination on the part of our enemies to prove that we are utterly unworthy of this great boon of citizenship": a strong attempt by all black Americans to develop themselves "intellectually, morally, spiritually, and . . . materially"; efforts by blacks to "promote the general good" on "municipal, state, and national" levels; and an unrelenting demand on the part of the race's elite and masses for all the privileges of American citizenship, including the "right to life, liberty, and the pursuit of happiness"; the "right of receiving equal accommodations"; the right "of serving in the Army and Navy"; the right "of suffrage"; and the right to hold "office . . . to be voted for . . . and to be appointed to positions of honor and trust by the executive power." Grimké also made clear his opposition to those who urged blacks to make some accommodation to racism. "We are," he reminded black Americans, "citizens, clothed with citizenship rights; and, there is no thought or intention on our part of ever surrendering a single one of them. Whatever others may think of it, or desire in regard to it, we do not propose to retreat a single inch, to give up for one moment the struggle. I say, *we* and in this, I believe I speak for those who represent the sentiment that is taking more and more firmly hold of the heart of the race. I belong to what may be called the radical wing of the race, on the race question: I do not believe in compromises; in surrendering, or acquiescing, even temporarily, in the deprivation of a single right, out of deference to an unrighteous public sentiment." [12]

The academy's decision, in March, 1905, to publish these six papers in one occasional paper forced the executive committee to begin looking for a printing company that would charge the least. The expense of the earlier occasional papers, which had only contained one or two papers, had been a serious drain on the organization's treasury because there was little financial return by way of sales. As a result, the executive committee thought it imperative to keep the printing cost of Occasional Paper no. 11 as low as

12. Francis J. Grimké, "The Negro and His Citizenship," ANA Occasional Papers, no. 11 (1905), 72–77, 79, 84.

possible. Despite an extensive canvassing of printing companies, the committee was unable to find one whose price the society could afford. In June, 1905, the committee resolved the problem by voting "that the expense of printing the paper [would] be divided equally between the Academy and the contributors," with each contributor paying one-sixth of the total cost. All of the contributors agreed to these terms and each was assessed $8.33.[13] Thereafter the executive committee made it standard practice for all authors of papers chosen for publication to pay one-half of the expenses or, when several papers were published in one occasional paper, an equivalent portion.

Like the ten previous publications, Occasional Paper no. 11 was sent to "the leading libraries of the country" and an especially strenuous effort was made to get it before the public. Despite the committee's efforts, neither blacks nor whites seemed interested. The most affirmative response the organization received was a comment by Albert E. Pillsbury in a speech he delivered before a racially mixed audience in Boston. "I have," Pillsbury said on that occasion, "read within a few days a pamphlet on this subject [*The Negro and the Elective Franchise*] produced by colored men, in which there is more logic, more philosophy, and more statesmanship than the whole white race North and South has developed since the time of the constitutional amendments." The members of the executive committee felt so grateful for this tribute that Pillsbury's statement was entered into the society's official minutes. No positive comment about any of the ten earlier occasional papers had been treated in this way.[14]

Occasional Paper no. 12, which appeared in 1908, was the presidential address delivered by Archibald H. Grimké at the academy's eleventh annual meeting in December, 1907. Though originally entitled "The Economic Condition of the Negro," for publication it was renamed *Modern Industrialism and the Negroes of the United States.*[15] The central idea of the paper was Grimké's argument that the southern states were undercutting their efforts to industrialize, and consequently reducing their ability to compete with the North, by restricting the economic and political rights of their black citizens. He believed that by undoing Reconstruction the white South had forced blacks into "serfdom," and returned the section to the inefficient form of industrialism and industrial labor which had made it possible for

13. Proceedings, 126–27.
14. Proceedings, 127, 129.
15. Proceedings, 149.

the North to win the Civil War. This, Grimké argued, was utter folly, for "the south cannot, economically, eat its cake and have it too. It cannot adopt a policy and a code of laws to degrade its Negro Labor, to hedge it about with unequal restrictions and proscriptive legislation, and raise it at the same time to the highest point of efficiency. But it must as an economic necessity raise this labor to the highest point of efficiency, or suffer inevitable industrial feebleness and inferiority." He attributed much of the North's industrial strength to the fact that it had a body of free laborers, characterized by "intelligence, skill, self-reliance, and power of initiative." In his opinion, these characteristics of northern labor were the fruit of that section's commitment to "universal education and popular suffrage." For its own welfare, Grimké urged the South to cast off "its chimerical fears of Negro domination" and "educate and emancipate" its black workers.

Copies of Grimké's paper were sent to members of the academy, to one hundred libraries, to leaders in the black community, and to prominent whites interested in "the Negro question." One of the blacks who received the pamphlet was Emmett J. Scott, private secretary to Booker T. Washington. Scott acknowledged receipt of the article, but made no comment on its contents. One of the most positive reactions came from Albert E. Pillsbury. "If any other writer," he wrote Grimké, "has looked as deeply or clearly into this question, it has not come to my notice. It is one of the best things you have ever done." [16]

Five years after its publication, Pillsbury still felt so positive about *Modern Industrialism and the Negroes of the United States* that he wrote to W. E. B. Du Bois, editor of *Crisis*, "calling his attention to its great power . . . for missionary purposes in the South." Pillsbury, a member and financial supporter of the NAACP, hoped that Du Bois would print the paper in the *Crisis*. Du Bois made no response, failing to even acknowledge the letter. In March, 1915, a year and a half after he had first written to Du Bois, Pillsbury sent the editor of the *Crisis* a sharply written note, again calling the matter to his attention. He demanded,

Please have the goodness to inform me, by a word on the enclosed card, whether you have received a letter which I wrote you considerably more than a year ago about Mr. Grimké's Modern Industrialism—and about the same time a copy of my Lincoln and Slavery sent you—and oblige,

Yours very truly,

16. Proceedings, 154; Scott to Grimké, December 16, 1908, Pillsbury to Grimké, January 18, 1909, both in A. H. Grimké Papers.

Two days later Du Bois responded. He told Pillsbury:

I do not find the letter to which you allude in my files and yet I seem dimly to remember it. Was it unanswered? The editorial department is seriously undermanned and we cannot help mistakes and ommissions sometimes.

Very sincerely yours,

"Undoubtedly," Pillsbury wrote to Grimké, "he [Du Bois] received them both—and it is not worth my while, nor probably yours, to speculate upon his silence." [17]

Even if Pillsbury's mailing failed to reach Du Bois's desk, it is hard to believe that he had not seen and probably read Occasional Paper no. 12. As a former president of the academy, and a member in good standing, he should have been sent two copies. Possibly, Du Bois was not impressed by Grimké's paper, or, even if he thought well of it, he may have felt that there was no reason to reprint it in *Crisis*. However, his response to Pillsbury—indifferent to the point of discourtesy—conveyed an unwillingness to take seriously either Grimké's paper or Pillsbury's interest in it. Du Bois's reply is also open to being interpreted as hostile towards Pillsbury or Grimké or both. The stiff, distant tone of his letter takes on even more significance in light of the fact that Grimké, during the time these exchanges took place, was president of the Washington, D.C., chapter of the NAACP and a member of the organization's national board. [18]

Early in 1909, the executive committee considered for publication four papers presented at the twelfth annual meeting in December, 1908. One, "The Demand and Supply of Increased Efficiency in the Negro Ministry" by Jesse E. Moorland, was eventually approved and it appeared later that year as Occasional Paper no. 13. The other three were turned down by a majority of the committee. The three papers rejected for publication were "Negro Ideals and Ambitions," Archibald Grimké's presidential address; "Social

17. Pillsbury to Grimké, October 6, 1913, Pillsbury to Oswald Garrison Villard, June 2, 1915 (copy), Pillsbury to Grimké, November 26, 1913, Pillsbury to Grimké, May 17, 1915 (letter contains copies of a March 11, 1915, note from Pillsbury to Du Bois; and of a March 13, 1915, note from Du Bois to Pillsbury), all in A. H. Grimké Papers. Pillsbury's book, *Lincoln and Slavery*, which he also sent to Du Bois along with a copy of Grimké's *Modern Industrialism*, was published by Houghton Mifflin of Boston and New York in 1913. The Boston attorney may have felt that his writings had "missionary power" too.

18. Proceedings, 154. It is impossible to say for certain whether or not *Crisis* received copies of the ANA occasional papers since no academy mailing or distribution lists have survived. However, the special place which this magazine occupied in the early decades of the twentieth century as the leading black publication, makes it hard to imagine that the ANA would not have sent copies of the occasional papers to its editorial offices.

Problems in West Africa from the Standpoint of an African," by Orishatukeh Faduma; and one by Arthur U. Craig, "The Work of the Negro
Land Grant College." Grimké's paper called on white Americans to treat
blacks as equals because the two races shared the same "ideals and ambitions," that is, they both desired to be economically independent, as well as
"strong, intelligent, and dominant." Faduma's treatise was a discussion of
tribal life among West Africans, and especially of their practice of polygamy. He took the position that polygamy was "at present a necessary evil"
in that part of the world, and asserted that since there was a "dearth of
men" in West Africa, the ultimate result would be a restoration of the "equilibrium between the sexes." In his paper, Craig compared the educational
programs of the land-grant colleges that trained black students with those
that trained white students, arguing that the existence of both was equally
important and must be continued.[19]

It is clear that "Social Problems in West Africa," which contained a defense of polygamy, was not published because it was considered too controversial. There was probably a fear that it would be interpreted as a defense
of sexual immorality by many clergy and devout laymen who were ANA
members, as well as by those black and white friends of the society who on
religious or other grounds considered monogamy an intrinsic part of morality and civilization. In addition, the very self-conscious "race leaders" who
made up the membership of the academy and its executive committee felt
tremendous internal and external pressure to always present their concerns
and those of their people in accord with the strictest canons of respectability. Thus, in spite of the fact that Kelly Miller and Charles C. Cook,
"severe critics both, acknowledged the scholarship of the author," this was
not enough to allay the fear that publication would have a negative effect on
the image of the academy and black intellectuals.[20]

Lack of evidence makes it difficult to say for certain why the other two
were rejected, so it is necessary to speculate. Grimké's paper seems little different in basic content and tone from his three other papers the ANA had
previously published. Since "Negro Ideals and Ambitions" would have been
his fourth occasional paper, and in 1909 no other academy member besides
Grimké had had three of his papers published, that rejection may have re-

19. Cromwell, untitled six-page report, December 28, 1909, in JWCG/M; Washington
Evening Star, December 29, 1908, p. 18.
20. Cromwell, untitled six-page report, December 28, 1909, Cromwell, Journal, 132, both
in JWCG/M; Proceedings, 159.

flected a belief that, for the time being, enough of this author's work had been presented. Craig's paper seems to have been written to dramatize the importance of preserving the principle of "separate but equal" in the apportionments to black and white land-grant colleges under the Morrill Act of 1890. To this end he called for an improvement in the teaching, administration, and curricula of black institutions receiving funds. Craig, and those who admired his paper, feared that unless the quality of the black land-grant schools was raised their public monies might be taken away, thus destroying them. Though only a few administrators or teachers in these schools were members of the academy in 1909, a majority of the members of the executive committee may have felt that the paper was an unfair attack on an important group of black educators who were doing the best they could under adverse conditions. They may also have believed that it was unwise to criticize, in so public a way, a group of people whose ability to hinder the work of the ANA was enormous.[21]

John W. Cromwell was especially impressed with Faduma's and Craig's papers when he heard them in December, 1908. Following the annual meeting, he recorded in his journal his reactions to the two. He wrote: " 'Social Problems in West Africa from the standpoint of an African' was a revelation to many for the scholarship shown and the novelty of the arguments in behalf of polygamy for the West African. . . . 'The Work of the Negro Land Grant Colleges' was prepared with unusual thoroughness and thoughtfulness. If published it may work reform." Because Cromwell had been so positively impressed by these papers, he was angered by the executive committee's refusal to publish them, and by the grounds on which they justified their decision.[22]

Consequently, at the annual meeting in December, 1909, Cromwell, in his corresponding secretary's report, discussed the occasional papers extensively, including the executive committee's decision not to print the papers read by Faduma, Craig, and Grimké. Though he had not mentioned Grimké's paper in his journal the previous year, Cromwell may have been impressed with it also, and equally disappointed at the committee's decision

---

21. By 1909 the ANA had already published the following three papers written by Archibald H. Grimké: *Right on the Scaffold, or the Martyrs of 1822,* ANA Occasional Papers, no. 7; "The Meaning and Need of the Movement to Reduce Southern Representation," ANA Occasional Papers, no. 11; *Modern Industrialism and the Negroes of the United States,* ANA Occasional Papers, no. 12. See also Cromwell, untitled six-page report, December 28, 1909, in JWCG/M.
22. Cromwell, Journal, 132, in JWCG/M.

not to print it. Or, it may have been political shrewdness that caused him to mention the president's paper along with the other two. He opened the subject by noting that the association had published very little during the previous year. Even though, he told the members of the society, the management of the "publication department" was delegated to the corresponding secretary, responsibility for the lack of activity was not his. If the executive committee had made some different decisions, the association could have issued four occasional papers instead of one. Citing the committee's rejection of papers by Grimké, Faduma, and Craig, Cromwell called on the members to formulate a definite policy to deal with the question of "whether we are to be held responsible for the individual views set forth in our publications." Only then, he told them, could the executive committee "steer between the Sylla [*sic*] of inanity and the Charybis [*sic*] of destructive adverse criticism." Without a clear policy in this regard, Cromwell warned his listeners, it would be difficult, if not impossible, to assist through publications in "the dissemination of the truth and the vindication of the Negro race from vicious assaults." [23]

There were two other references to the occasional papers in the corresponding secretary's report. Cromwell informed the members that, at the direction of the executive committee, in July, 1909, he had written to a total of "ninety different colleges and libraries . . . to ascertain to what extent . . . they would preserve our 'occasional papers'." Forty-five of these institutions, including "the University of Georgia at Athens and Trinity College, Durham, North Carolina," had promised, in their replies, to add the ANA papers to their permanent collections. In return, Cromwell had placed them on the society's mailing list. The corresponding secretary also used his report to express great dissatisfaction with the academy's practice "of printing . . . editions of five hundred occasional papers each, one half to go to the author of the paper and three copies to each member." This had created an accumulation of papers totaling "more than two hundred copies of different numbers [,] barring . . . 1 and 10," which were out of print. Because he no longer had the "household space to store so large a number of pamphlets free from dust and dirt," Cromwell asked the academy to make funds available for the storage of these papers in a more appropriate place. [24]

The eleven members at the thirteenth annual meeting showed no interest in further clarifying the organization's policy on publications, or in chal-

---

23. Cromwell, untitled six-page report, December 28, 1909, pp. 1–3, in JWCG/M.
24. *Ibid.*

lenging the executive committee's decision not to publish the papers by Grimké, Faduma, and Craig. They did, however, attempt a response of sorts to Cromwell's concern about the storage of occasional papers. The corresponding secretary was instructed to send an additional copy of each pamphlet in storage to every member of the academy.[25]

In spite of the academy's action in regard to surplus copies of occasional papers, this continued to be a problem, especially for John W. Cromwell. Two years later, at the fifteenth annual meeting in December, 1911, Cromwell informed the members that copies of occasional papers were continuing to accumulate and that their storage was still a problem. In response, the members "voted that [only] 6 copies [of an occasional] be retained thereafter." How the unsold and undonated extras of past and future occasional papers were to be disposed of was not recorded in the Proceedings. For some reason, this still did not eliminate the problem. In January, 1913, at Cromwell's urgent request, the executive committee tried its hand at formulating a solution. The corresponding secretary was given permission to use his membership dues as "an allowance for the storage of the publications of the Academy." In addition, Cromwell was authorized to procure "a packet or other filing device for Mss. of the Academy." It is not absolutely clear, but this last provision may have been for the protection of manuscript copies of papers delivered before various annual meetings.[26]

A year after he gave the report at the thirteenth annual meeting, Cromwell, in an article which appeared in *Horizon* magazine, declared that the ANA's occasional papers were "eagerly sought for in representative college libraries where they are in demand whenever inter-collegiate discussions of the Race Problem take place." As proof, he pointed to "the correspondence of the Academy" and "the special requests" he received "for data on various phases of this absorbing question."

To put it kindly, this was an exaggeration of the facts. The academy's correspondence reveals that between 1897 and 1910, a small number of institutions sought the occasional papers for their collections, and that, from time to time, an even smaller number of individuals and organizations expressed an interest in them or sought data from the association. Cromwell's report in 1909, with its description of his letter to "ninety different colleges and libraries," made it clear that the executive committee felt a need to increase the number of institutions that were receiving its occasional papers.

25. Proceedings, 171, 174.
26. Proceedings, 184, 191.

This and the related problem of surplus papers were major concerns of the executive committee in 1911 and in 1913. Clearly, Cromwell's statement in *Horizon* was made in the interest of public relations rather than accuracy.[27]

Although in 1909 the executive committee rejected three papers proposed for publication, it acted favorably on a fourth, "The Demand and Supply of Increased Efficiency in the Negro Ministry," which was issued as the ANA's thirteenth occasional paper. Its author, Jesse E. Moorland, presented the paper at the ANA's twelfth annual meeting in 1908, hoping that it would promote reform. Moorland believed that the most important thing about a race or nation was the quality of its religious beliefs and practices, and that this was the standard by which it was judged progressive or backward. For this reason he felt the production of "efficient ministers" had to be a crucial concern among black Americans. No other group of individuals, in his estimation, possessed the power of helping or hindering the race's progress as did black clergy. In his experience, the blacks in communities where there was a "well-trained, honorable, upright and efficient minister," showed "marked improvement . . . along every line," but where there was an "immoral, ignorant minister the community was full of despair." Moorland pointed out that the problem of reprobate and uneducated ministers was exacerbated by the fact that blacks, unlike whites, had such a small pool of educated men from which to recruit men into this profession. He perceived several factors which demanded that a strong effort be made to draw intelligent, creative, and committed men "into the Master's service": the "increased intelligence of the [black] people"; the small number of black men currently in training for the ministry; the generally low "average in scholarship and natural force" of blacks currently in theological schools; the materialism of the time which had influenced many talented men to choose more lucrative professions; the fact that men of ability, disgusted by examples of bad ministers, were rejecting the profession as a career choice; and the loss of Christian faith among the able black graduates of northern schools. Moorland was certain that the most effective responses to this series of interrelated problems would be a reform of the curriculum in the theological seminaries; the encouragement by Christian families and individual congregations, of able young men to enter the ministry; a commitment, on the part of the churches, to financially support ministerial candidates while they were being trained; and agreement among the denomi-

27. Cromwell, "The American Negro Academy," *Horizon*, 11–12; Proceedings, 184.

nations active in the black community not to accept into their ministries men who were not trained intellectually.[28]

Surprisingly, there seems to have been little reaction to Moorland's paper in either the black or white religious and secular press of the day. This is especially odd since many of the members of the academy were clergy, and several were editors of church newspapers. Perhaps the issues Moorland raised were so controversial that most blacks who heard or read the paper preferred to react to it privately.

The general theme of the thirteenth annual meeting in December, 1909, was "the social aspect of the Negro problem." Two months later, the executive committee voted to publish as occasional papers three of the five papers which had been delivered at that assembly. They were "The Effect of Social Prejudice upon the Negro" by James Robert Lincoln Diggs; "The Social Evolution of the Black South" by W. E. B. Du Bois; and "The Social Status of the Negro in the North" by Richard Robert Wright, Jr. Digg's study was an analysis of the ways in which the "caste spirit" in the United States had strengthened the belief that black Americans were morally and intellectually worthless. Because this attitude permeated the country, he urged blacks not "to dwell on its cause, but to ferret [it?] out and pursue its remedies." In his paper, Du Bois used evidence from his studies of rural and urban blacks in the South to prove that "the city . . . Negroes" were the most progressive. As proof, he pointed to the region's black urban communities which had responded to "Jim Crow" laws by devising ways to meet many of their social, cultural, religious, and economic needs within the framework of an all-black or predominantly black social setting. Wright's address was based on his Ph.D. dissertation for the University of Pennsylvania, as well as his experiences as a minister in Chicago and Philadelphia. Both his research and direct contacts with urban black communities indicated that the general problem faced by northern blacks was their inability to earn a decent living due to the implacable discrimination they faced from prospective employers and labor unions.[29]

John W. Cromwell wrote to Diggs, Du Bois, and Wright, informing them of the executive committee's decision, and "requesting them to submit their

28. Jesse E. Moorland, *The Demand and the Supply of Increased Efficiency in the Negro Ministry*, ANA Occasional Papers, no. 13 (1909), 3–7, 9–11.

29. Washington *Evening Star*, December 26, 1909, p. 2, December 29, 1909, p. 4; Proceedings, 172–73, 176; Washington *American*, January 1, 1910, copy in Cromwell Papers, Moorland-Spingarn Research Center.

revised manuscripts." Because he was unwilling to pay half the printing costs, as required by the ANA's rules, Du Bois's answer was no. "I think," he told the executive committee, "the terms are all right but I can get my pamphlets published for nothing pretty easily and do not feel that I ought to spend the money. I am sorry." Du Bois did not add, as he could have, that his national reputation as a scholar and commentator on racial relations made it relatively easy for him to get his paper published free in one or more of the northern white literary or scholarly journals, as well as in almost any of the black periodicals, religious or secular. However, this response, coming as it did from a founder and former president, was particularly cold.[30]

Though the details are obscure, negotiations with Wright and Diggs were equally unsuccessful. Since Wright had been occasionally contributing articles on blacks in the North to the *Southern Workman*, he may have felt a special commitment to continue to send his work to this magazine; or its larger audience, which included a sizable number of influential whites, may have made it a more attractive forum to him. There is also a possibility that Wright implicitly made publication of his paper conditional on the academy's agreement to a plan of his. Whatever the deciding factor, his paper was not published by the ANA. Between March, 1910, and June, 1912, Wright did, however, contribute four articles to the *Southern Workman* on "Negroes in the North." There are no clues to the reason or reasons why Diggs's paper was not published.[31]

At the same time Cromwell was negotiating with Wright and Du Bois about the publication of their papers, both of these men were attempting to persuade the ANA to assist them in their work with another organization. Wright, who, in 1909, became business manager of the AME Church's Book Concern, was deeply involved in turning what had been a bankrupt and inefficiently run enterprise into a profitable and well-managed agency of his denomination. In the late fall of 1909, he wrote to Cromwell, describing his efforts to build a "constituency" for the future publications of the Book Concern, and suggesting a proposition he believed would aid the Book Concern and the ANA. He asked:

Why can not we [the AME Book Concern] become the agents for the Academy? If the Academy would be willing to pay the cost price of getting out the literature, I

30. Proceedings, 176; Du Bois to Cromwell, October 18, 1910, in JWCG/M.

31. Wright's articles in the *Southern Workman* began to appear while he was a research fellow and Ph.D. student at the University of Pennsylvania (1905–1911). See issues of the *Southern Workman* from April, 1906 to June, 1912.

would give to them the same number of copies of each of their publications which they usually have in order to supply their constituency, for the privilege of printing an equal number for the supply of a new constituency which I am building up. Thus, they would get their printing done at a much less rate than they would otherwise have it done. They would also extend their influence to a much greater number of people than they have yet reached, and also, through us, build up a demand for their literature which would help us dispose of even their supply a great deal better.

Wright expressed regret that he could not pay the academy for the privilege of publishing its occasional papers, but indicated that once he had created "a demand for this literature" the ANA could look forward to receiving a "royalty." This process, however, would take a "few years." [32]

Despite the fact that the ANA had not been pleased with an earlier cooperative relationship with the *AME Church Review*, and had dissolved it shortly after it was approved, Cromwell expressed interest in the suggestion. Perhaps he felt that this arrangement, unlike the earlier relationship with the *Review*, might work better because the ANA would not have to give its papers to the journal of another organization for publication. He might also have been intrigued by the possibility that the Book Concern could reduce the ANA's printing costs and broaden its audience. There is, however, some question as to the sincerity of Cromwell's interest in the offer, for at the time he was engaged in establishing a new scholarly publication, American Negro Monographs, which would make its appearance in 1910. The corresponding secretary's receptiveness to a discussion of Wright's offer may not have reflected a genuine interest in it, but rather his desire to keep Wright in a frame of mind that would cause him to allow the academy to print his paper, "The Social Status of the Negro in the North," as an occasional paper.

In January, 1910, Wright responded to a request from Cromwell for a more definite statement of the financial terms that went with his plan, and an inquiry as to when a copy of the revised manuscript of his paper would reach the corresponding secretary. In reply to the first matter, Wright offered to "do the Occasional Papers of the American Negro Academy for One dollar and twelve cents per page, with the understanding that we [the AME Book Concern] be allowed to take five hundred copies and give five hundred copies to the Academy." Using the fourteen-page Occasional Paper no. 13 as a standard, Wright estimated that five hundred pamphlets would cost the Academy $20.16. In regard to his own paper, he told Cromwell, "I

32. Wright to Cromwell, December 25, 1909, in JWCG/M.

should like to revise it as soon as possible though I could not promise definitely when I could get it in shape for print. It was hurriedly gotten together and I should not, of course, care to print it as it is." The business manager of the AME Book Concern was undoubtedly a busy man, but it is impossible not to wonder if he was saying, indirectly, that his interest in having the paper published by the ANA was dependent on the academy's accepting the Book Concern as its printer and agent.

Cromwell did not answer this letter, and Wright wrote the following month, inquiring about the state of their negotiations. In his communication he told the corresponding secretary, "I did not hear from you about the Academy Occasional Papers. I have already received two orders for my own, 'Negro in the North,' and just as soon as I return from the Bishops' Council I shall begin to get it in proper shape. I think I can do so about the middle of March and will be ready to put it on sale at that time." Wright's mention of his plan and his paper in the same paragraph again suggests that he was linking the two together. There was no further correspondence between Wright and Cromwell regarding the printing and distribution of the occasional papers, or the publication of "The Social Status of the Negro in the North." However, the final resolution of both matters is certain. The AME Book Concern never printed or distributed any ANA occasional papers; and Wright's paper was never published by the academy.[33]

The academy also received a business proposition from W. E. B. Du Bois, who, like Wright, was getting used to a new role and new responsibilities. In 1910, after functioning as one of the major figures in the formation of the National Association for the Advancement of Colored People, Du Bois resigned his professorship at Atlanta University and accepted the new organization's invitation to become "research director." As one of his first major efforts, he persuaded the NAACP's board of directors to establish a magazine to be called *Crisis*, of which he became editor. In October, 1910, Du Bois wrote to the academy, inviting it to purchase advertising space for its

33. Wright to Cromwell, January 4, 1910, February 3, 1910, both in JWCG/M. It is interesting to compare the price quoted by Wright with the amounts the ANA paid for its occasional papers just before and shortly after he made his offer. In 1908, the ANA paid $33 for five hundred copies of the eighteen-page Occasional Paper no. 12; in 1910, $20 for the fourteen-page Occasional Paper no. 13 (the Proceedings do not say, but presumably for five hundred copies); and in 1911, $26 for five hundred copies of the twenty-page Occasional Paper no. 14. (See Proceedings, 165, 177, 186.) Although the academy, throughout its existence, used several printing companies, most of its work was done by Robert L. Pendleton, whose business was located in Washington, D.C.

occasional papers in the first issue of *Crisis*. He added the following post-script to his letter: "You'll have to rush—our space is going rapidly to my great surprise." Despite this warning, the executive committee did not even discuss the matter, and the first issue of *Crisis* appeared without any academy advertisement. Whether this was deliberate or because of the committee's preoccupation with other business is unclear.[34]

Early in November, Du Bois wrote again, calling the executive committee's "attention to the *Crisis* magazine as an advertising medium for books on the race problem such as the Publications of the American Negro Academy." In addition he told them that his office received "hundreds of inquiries" concerning such books, that "the distinguished names" on *Crisis'* general committee gave the magazine's recommendations "weight," and that the staff expected, "through our magazine[,] to extend this department" in the near future. The letter closed with an appeal to the ANA to take out an advertisement for the December issue. Two weeks later, the executive committee decided that "the suggestion to advertise the occasional papers in *Crisis* was not . . . a good business proposition." There are no clues as to the basis on which this decision was made.[35]

However, by March, 1911, the committee had a "change of heart" and, in an "about face," voted "that an advertisement . . . covering ½ single column" should be placed in "*Crisis'* Easter number." This shift may have been caused by the strong positive response to the NAACP and *Crisis* on the part of educated blacks and many whites. As a result, advertisements for the ANA's publications appeared in the April, May, and June, 1911, issues of *Crisis*. The total cost to the academy for all three was $4. They must not have boosted sales because after June, 1911, the executive committee ceased to purchase advertising space. Despite the fact that the academy continued to issue papers until 1924, no other ads for its publications appeared in *Crisis*.[36]

The fourteenth occasional paper, which appeared in April, 1911, was a "Historical address" by Archibald H. Grimké on the life and career of Charles Sumner, who from 1850 to 1874 was United States senator from Massachusetts. In what was essentially a brief eulogy—the address was delivered at a June, 1911, memorial service for Sumner—Grimké reviewed his

34. Du Bois to Cromwell, October 17, 1910, JWCG/M.
35. Du Bois to Cromwell, November 14, 1910, in JWCG/M; Proceedings, 176.
36. Proceedings, 179; *Crisis*, I (April, 1911), 32, 33, I (May, 1911), 41, I (June, 1911), 8.

subject's involvement in the antislavery and free-soil movements, his efforts to convince Lincoln and the Republican party to make the abolition of slavery one of the objectives of the war against the Confederacy, and his championship of "Negro citizenship and suffrage" in the years after the Civil War. Grimké's address was based on a biographical study of the Massachusetts senator that he had written several years earlier.[37]

After the distribution of the pamphlet, Grimké received notes of commendation from Booker T. Washington and his old friend, Albert E. Pillsbury. Washington complimented Grimké on the "masterful way" in which he had sketched Sunner's "activities as one of the great citizens of Massachusetts." He also assured Grimké that publication of the address would give it a "wider hearing than the one received upon the occasion of its delivery." Pillsbury, who had participated in several memorials for Sumner in 1911, informed Grimké that he had not seen or heard "any other address on so high a level of thought or literary merit" as Occasional Paper no. 14. "It strikes me," the Boston lawyer continued, "as the best thing of yours I have ever seen."[38]

In the same letter, Pillsbury described himself as "a little surprised at the tone of your allusions to Lincoln." There were two references to the sixteenth president of the United States in Grimké's address. The first contrasted Lincoln's policy of expediency in regard to emancipation with Sumner's commitment to freedom for the slaves.

Mr. Lincoln and the Republican party started out to save the Union with slavery. It is the rage now, I know, to extol his marvellous sagacity and statesmanship. And I too will join in the panegyric of his great qualities. But here he was not infallible. For when he issued his Emancipation Proclamation, the South too was weighing the military necessity of a similar measure. Justice was Sumner's solitary expedient, right his unfailing sagacity.

The second reference was a comparison of Sumner's plan of reconstruction with that of Lincoln and others:

How ought local self-government to be reconstituted in the old slave states at the close of the war. Sumner had his answer, others had their answer. His answer he framed on the simple basis of right. No party considerations entered into his

---

37. Archibald H. Grimké, *Charles Sumner Centenary Historical Address*, ANA Occasional Papers, no. 14 (1911); Archibald H. Grimké, *Life of Charles Sumner, the Scholar in Politics* (New York, 1892).

38. Washington to Grimké, May 19, 1911, Pillsbury to Grimké, May 18, 1911, both in A. H. Grimké Papers. Booker T. Washington, in his letter to Grimké, also acknowledged a copy of Occasional Paper no. 14, which had been sent to his private secretary, Emmet J. Scott.

straightforward purpose. He was not careful to enfold within it any scheme or suggestion looking to the ascendency of his section. It was freedom alone that he was solicitous of establishing, the supremacy of democratic ideas and institutions in the newborn nation. He desired the ascendancy of his section and party so far only as they were the real custodians of national justice and progress. God knows whether his plan was better than the plans of others except in simpleness and purity of aim. Lincoln had his plan, Johnson his, Congress its own. Sumner's had what appears to me might have evinced it, on trial, of superior value and wisdom, namely, the element of time, indefinite time as a factor in the work of reconstruction.

Pillsbury, who had recently written an article which offered different interpretations of Lincoln's responses to these issues, enclosed a copy of it, "in order," he wrote, "that we may compare views."[39]

In January, 1913, the executive committee made the decision to publish as occasional papers two papers which had been presented the previous December during the sixteenth annual meeting. They were Archibald H. Grimké's presidential address, "The Ballotless Victim of One-Party Government," and a scientific paper by Ernest Everett Just, "The Mendelian Theory of Inheritance and the Skin Color of the Present Day American Negro." The committee directed John W. Cromwell to have five hundred copies of each paper printed, after the authors complied with the "customary conditions of the payment of one-half of Publication [costs]." However, Grimké's paper was not published until 1915, and Just's never appeared as an occasional paper. Quite possibly, in 1913 the two men may have been unable or unwilling to pay their share of the costs. Or the decision to print the papers might have been temporarily abandoned because the academy later found it lacked the necessary funds due to the sharp increase between 1912 and 1914 in the number of members who failed to pay their dues. Unfortunately, the organization's records contain nothing which even suggests why no other attempt was made to publish Just's paper, and why Grimké's was not issued until two years later.[40]

Lafayette M. Hershaw's paper, *Peonage*, was published in 1915 as Occasional Paper no. 15. Two years earlier, it had been presented at the seventeenth annual meeting under the title, "The Status of the Negro Laborer before the Law." The paper was an attack on those statutes in southern states that made the abrogation of a labor contract by a worker a criminal offense. By compelling blacks to work for white employers against their wills, such

39. Pillsbury to Grimké, May 18, 1911, in A. H. Grimké Papers; Grimké, *Charles Sumner Centenary Historical Address*, ANA Occasional Papers, no. 14 (1911), 15, 16.
40. Proceedings, 191, 189. I have been unable to locate a copy or review of Just's paper.

laws, Hershaw charged, stripped them of "freedom of labor" and "freedom of contract," two basic rights guaranteed by law "in all English-speaking countries," and constituted a form of legalized "peonage." Hershaw classified the most blatant of these discriminatory laws under five headings: those regulating "contracts of employment; enticement of laborers to quit their employers; violation of a contract with a surety by one convicted of a misdemeanor; the laws of vagrancy; and the laws relating to immigrant agents." He also noted "other laws, perfectly proper on their face," which were "perverted to reduce persons to a condition of peonage." These laws included "false pretense or false promise laws; absconding debtor laws; billboard laws; and in fact every ordinance, regulation, or statute defining a misdemeanor or crime." Moving beyond his discussion of specific statutes, Hershaw made clear the fundamental reason southern whites were allowed to victimize blacks in this way. He pointed out: "The real foundation of peonage . . . was the refusal to regard him [the black] as a man having rights as other men have them. So far has wrong, and injustice, and oppression gone that not only is the Negro outside of the consideration of the law of the land, but practically outside of the humane and kindly regard of a majority of the white race in the United States. Not only are laws perverted and given a special twist and interpretation in cases where the Negro is a party to litigation, but even words in ordinary use lose their accepted meaning when applied to him." Because these attitudes were so deeply rooted in the minds and emotions of whites, Hershaw saw little hope for a change in the "peonage" laws or the social reality they reflected.[41]

Except for a brief comment in a letter from ANA member James R. L. Diggs to John W. Cromwell, there is no evidence as to how Hershaw's paper was received. Diggs thought it a "fine contribution" which presented "the many subterfuges resorted to to deprive men of color of their liberty."[42]

The academy published two other occasional papers in 1915, both written by Archibald H. Grimké. *The Ballotless Victims of One-Party Government*, Grimké's presidential address at the sixteenth annual meeting in December, 1912, was issued as Occasional Paper No. 16; and *The Ultimate Criminal*, his presidential address the next year, followed it as Occasional Paper No. 17. In *The Ballotless Victims of One-Party Government* Grimké

41. Proceedings, 196; Lafayette M. Hershaw, *Peonage*, ANA Occasional Papers, no. 15 (1915), 6–10, 11–13.
42. Diggs to Cromwell, July 13, 1915, in JWCG/M.

traced the inability of southern blacks to migrate from one part of the country to the other; their entrapment in a segregated "Jim Crow" world; their deprivation of the rights of freedom of speech, freedom of the press, and public assembly; and their lack of protection from violence to a single source—disfranchisement. To him, disfranchisement was an expression of the "old slaveholders'" refusal, after the Civil War, to accept blacks as fellow citizens. But, he pointed out, by depriving the freedmen of their political rights, the planter aristocracy paid a price. They had prevented any possibility of establishing an alliance with the blacks, thus opening the way to their own loss of power to "another class of whites, risen since the war, who distrust and hate them." Grimké also charged that the North, through its compromise with the South over the presidential election of 1876, gave up on Reconstruction, and removed any remaining obstacles to black disfranchisement. It was after 1876, he noted, that "the stream of reaction against the Negro set in strongly . . . and it has gathered volume each succeeding year since."

Grimké believed that the only way blacks could improve their situation was by possession of the ballot. But the struggle to regain it was hindered by lack of support from the North, which was engaged in "exploiting the South industrially." The sectional ties which resulted from this new economic relationship had led the North to abandon blacks and to accept their political and social isolation in the South. But here again, Grimké warned, the white South would pay a high price, "For the whites cannot advance in law and order, in private and public morals, in wealth and in industrial intelligence and efficiency with the speed commensurate with their social and sectional opportunity if they persist in wasting so much of their individual and collective energies in keeping the Negro down at the bottom of their social and political fabric without regard to his merits and abilities."

Grimké saw the appearance of the Progressive party as the one sign of hope for blacks. He argued that because it was not associated with the victory of the Unionists over the Confederates it would be able to attract "to itself Southern white men in sufficient numbers to make it a formidable party of opposition in Southern affairs." But, in order to create such a place for itself in southern politics, Grimké felt that, below the Mason-Dixon line, it would have to be a segregated party, run by whites. In defense of this belief, he went so far as to justify Theodore Roosevelt's refusal, at the Progressive party's convention in 1912, to support civil rights for blacks in the

South, and his rejection of black delegates from southern states. Grimké was convinced that Roosevelt's actions were not racist, but a necessary accommodation to southern realities by a party leader seriously bidding for support in that region. In his estimation, they did not indicate hostility to black voting rights, but were necessary first steps in initiating the process which would eventually lead to reenfranchisement of blacks.[43]

The Ultimate Criminal criticized the way in which white Americans used crimes which had been committed, or which they suspected had been committed, by individual blacks to make "an omnibus indictment against the moral character of the whole race." Those who did this, Grimké charged, were "monstrously unjust and wicked." Noting that there was very little black crime during slavery and the Civil War, he ascribed its rise to black Americans' "new and bitter experiences of wrong at the hands of whites" after 1865. The experiences he referred to were the laws passed by southern states at the end of the Civil War which forced the freedmen into a "new species of bondage"; "the violence and lawlessness" practiced against blacks in the South and North which had created a climate in which violence and crime seemed permissible to members of both races, and possibly even normative; the frequently corrupt "carpet-bag governments," which "initiated them [southern blacks] promptly by the power of example into the great and flourishing American art and industry of graft"; the creation, during the post-Reconstruction years, of two separate legal and moral systems in the South, one for whites and one for blacks; "the Southern policy of civil and political repression and oppression of its colored population in order to keep them within their caste of inferiority and subordination to whites"; the enforced poverty of black laborers; the congested, disease-filled, hopeless, and depressing ghettoes of the cities where blacks were forced to live; and the conscious efforts on the part of the white South to provide as little education as possible for blacks, so as to keep them as ignorant as possible. "Who then," Grimké asked, "in these circumstances are the ultimate criminal, those who are unwillingly poor and ignorant, or those who make and keep them so by bad and unequal laws, by bad and unequal treatment?"[44]

There was no public reaction to *Ballotless Victims*, but *The Ultimate*

43. Archibald H. Grimké, *The Ballotless Victims of One Party Government*, ANA Occasional Papers, no. 16 (1915), 4–7, 8, 10, 14–18.

44. Archibald H. Grimké, *The Ultimate Criminal*, ANA Occasional Papers, no. 17 (1915), 3, 4, 5, 6–14.

Criminal attracted a fair amount of interest. Several members of the ANA, who also belonged to Washington's Bethel Literary and Historical Association, thought its message so important that Grimké was invited to read it again at one of Bethel's meetings in January. And shortly after the occasional paper appeared in early April, 1915, the author began receiving letters of praise from some of the persons to whom copies were sent. Mary White Ovington, a white socialist and social worker, who was among the chief founders of the NAACP, was "profoundly impressed" with the pamphlet. "I wish," she wrote Grimké, "I could send it broadcast. Certainly it ought to be in the hand of the Bd. of Censorship that passed the Birth of a Nation. I will speak of it at the NAACP." Arthur B. Spingarn, a distinguished lawyer who was head of the NAACP's legal committee, also liked the paper, which he told Grimké he had read "with great profit and enjoyment." One of the most affirmative messages came from Burt Wilder, a retired professor of neurology and vertebrate zoology at Cornell University. Wilder stated in very clear terms the impact the paper had on him and his wife. "We have," he wrote, "read the latter paper with mingled admiration, indignation and shame; the first for your logical and eloquent statement of the case; the second at the rongs [*sic*] of your race; the third at the responsibility of ours." [45]

Albert E. Pillsbury complimented Grimké on the essay, which he described as a piece "up to the highest level of the best thought bestowed on this subject." Pillsbury's appreciation for the paper rekindled his desire to see his friend's writings appear in *Crisis*. In the same letter, he shared this concern with Grimké and sought the name of someone powerful enough to force Du Bois to take such a suggestion seriously. "How can the NAACP," Pillsbury asked, "do better than to give wide circulation to such literature as this and the Modern Industrialism. If you know of anyone who has sufficient influence with DuBois to get him to answer a letter, I should like to have the question put to him. It should have a much wider circulation than I suppose your Academy papers achieve. Did you offer it to DuBois? I presume not, but the Crisis would, I presume, have multiplied its circulation if accepted." [46]

45. Washington *Bee*, January 9, 1915, p. 5. Ovington to Grimké, April 13, [1915?], Spingarn to Grimké, April 16, 1915, Wilder to Grimké, June 7, 1915, all in A. H. Grimké Papers. Burt G. Wilder was an advocate of "simplified spelling." This was the reason for the odd, but phonetically correct spelling in his letter.

46. Pillsbury to Grimké, May 27, 1915, in A. H. Grimké Papers.

Grimké's response to this letter has not survived, but four days later Pillsbury sent the following letter to Oswald Garrison Villard, former chairman of the NAACP's national board:

A year and a half ago or so I wrote DuBois about Grimke's "Modern Industrialism," sending him a copy though presuming that he had seen it, calling his attention to its great power, as I thought, for missionary purposes in the South. He paid no attention to it; indeed my letter was never anwered. Recently Grimke has produced a study of the cause of negro criminality under the title "The Ultimate Criminal." I presume you have seen both of these pamphlets. They ought to have a wide circulation, especially in the South. If you have read them you know that they are wholly out of the common class—profound, clear, direct and convincing; indeed if there is any better thinker or writer than Grimke on the negro question he is unknown to me. Can the NAACP do better than to put such literature as this into wide circulation? This is real constructive work, and I am bound to say that I think that it would be more effective than any the Association is doing to my knowledge. The Crisis is admirable in its way, but what is it really doing in the field? Is it really much of anything more than an embellished record of current events? Grimke's pamphlets expose the fallacies and dangers both of the economic and of the social situations, with a clearness of thought and lucidity of statement that must carry conviction. It seems to me that the Association is missing an opportunity in allowing seed to go to waste that may be sown to such a harvest as I think these pamphlets are capable of producing if put where they ought to go.

Not surprisingly, Pillsbury's letter, with its snide and carping references to the content of *Crisis*, failed to open the pages of the NAACP's journal to Grimké's essays. However, sometime after this letter was written, the NAACP distributed 110 copies of *The Ultimate Criminal*, but no excerpts or reprints of this or any other occasional paper ever appeared in the magazine. There is no way of knowing for certain, but Villard was probably instrumental in getting the NAACP to distribute Grimké's essay. It is also likely that this was done without Du Bois's approval. The editor of *Crisis* distrusted Villard and, on an earlier occasion, had made clear his lack of interest in Grimké's writings.[47]

Pillsbury's concern that Grimké's paper have "a much wider circulation" may have been instrumental in causing the Boston *Herald* to take notice of it. A month after he wrote to Grimké, the *Herald* printed an editorial which mentioned, with great respect, Grimké's background and accomplishments, expressed agreement with his analysis of black criminality and its "ultimate" cause, and quoted extensively from the occasional paper. The author

47. Pillsbury to Villard, June, 1915 [unsigned copy], in A. H. Grimké Papers. The 110 copies distributed by the NAACP are mentioned in a letter from Freeman Henry Morris Murray to John W. Cromwell, July 8, 1915, in JWCG/M.

was introduced as "a gentlemen of means and education residing in Washington, D.C., who formerly held a high position in the foreign service of the government." His paper was described as "a study . . . which, for depth of insight and power of foresight, would enhance the reputation of any statesman or college president capable of producing it." The editorial quoted extensively from those sections of the paper which discussed the vulnerability of southern blacks at the end of the Civil War, and their defenselessness, after 1876, in the face of political, economic, and sexual exploitation by whites. In the opinion of the editorialist, if the paper had been written by a white man its arguments would be "unanswerable." But, because its author—a man "of distinguished ancestry which his white relatives, well-known citizens of Boston, freely acknowledged"—had African blood and was classified as black, his views were disregarded or rejected.[48]

The academy records, for the years for which they exist, provide little detailed information on how the executive committee decided which papers were and were not to be published. In 1915, however, after the committee rejected one of the papers under consideration, its author questioned the decision and, by doing so, produced a letter which sheds some light on the way in which the selection process operated at that time.

The paper in question, James Robert Lincoln Diggs's essay, "The Aesthetic Education of the Race through the Church," was read at the eighteenth annual meeting in December, 1904. The following spring, the executive committee decided not to publish it. As corresponding secretary, John W. Cromwell wrote Diggs to inform him of this decision. In the letter, Cromwell shared with Diggs the criticisms of the paper which had been made by Archibald H. Grimké and Kelly Miller. Presumably, the opinions of these men had strongly influenced the executive committee's decision. In revealing to Diggs the comments of two fellow members of the executive committee, Cromwell may have been functioning more in the capacity of a friend then as an officer of the society.[49]

48. Boston *Herald*, June 2, 1915. Grimké was the natural son of "a wealthy South Carolina planter," Henry Grimké, and Nancy Weston, "a beautiful family slave." Through his father, Grimké was also the nephew of the two female abolitionists and reformers, Angelina and Sarah Grimké. These women, who left South Carolina and eventually became part of prominent reform circles in New England, acknowledged their relationship with Archibald Grimké and his brother Francis while the two were students at Lincoln, and provided financial assistance for the education of both men. (See *DAB*, VII, 623–33.)

49. Proceedings, 200; Diggs to Cromwell, July 13, 1915, in JWCG/M. Three other papers were presented at the eighteenth annual meeting besides Diggs's: "The Evolution of the Negro

Diggs received Cromwell's letter prior to the publication of the three occasional papers issued by the ANA that year. However, he did not respond to it until after the appearance of Occasional Paper no. 15. Though he felt that Lafayette M. Hershaw's paper on *Peonage* was excellent, its similarity to previous occasional papers, in terms of approach and content, convinced him that he should challenge the executive committee's decision not to print his own study. In a letter to Cromwell, Diggs argued that his paper—"prepared last December very hurriedly"—had been "carefully revised" and, if published, would be a unique and valuable addition to the annals of the academy. "You see," he told the corresponding secretary, "but little about the aesthetic growth of peoples in American works [,] even in those on philosophy." As for the criticisms made by Grimké and Miller, he dismissed them on the grounds that they were not related to the subject he had discussed:

Mr. Grimke said he regretted that the paper did not deal with the rich musical endowment of the race. Mr. Miller evidently expected a statistical or mathematical treatment from the standpoint of the plantation songs, etc., if I understand him. If I had followed the line of treatment suggested by these criticisms the discus. would have had no relation to, or bearing upon, the subject. How can one treat The Musical Endowment of the Race with the subject we had? It would have been bad rhetoric and worse judgment. Now it may be that those gentlemen have given their time to the historical, the social, the political, economic types of essays, and have not studied the phase of race life treated in the paper.

In the final paragraph of his letter, Diggs offered a battery of minor reasons for printing his paper: it was shorter than Hershaw's by 950 words; he would "gladly" pay his share of the printing costs; and, if published, he could dispose of at least one hundred copies in Baltimore where he was president of Clayton Williams University and pastor of Trinity Baptist Church. Despite Diggs's protestations, the executive committee did not reverse its decision.[50]

Occasional Paper no. 15 also provoked a strong reaction from Freeman Henry Morris Murray, who used its appearance as an opportunity to put into writing some of his opinions about what was wrong with the ANA's publication policy. In a letter to John W. Cromwell, Murray conceded that Hershaw's paper was "*very* excellent as far as it goes," but declared it a "pity" and a "shame" that the author of *Peonage* "could not have been en-

---

Church" by Walter Henderson Brooks; *The Ultimate Criminal* by Archibald H. Grimké; and "Educating the Negro before 1860" by Carter G. Woodson.

50. Diggs to Cromwell, July 13, 1915, in JWCG/M.

couraged to get up a full book—a treatise—on the matter; complete, authoritative, and frank, and have it published at the expense of the Academy." Why, he asked, had not the ANA encouraged the writing and publication of books on crucial topics such as southern disfranchisement and the black voter, or paid for the publication of the books recently written by its members, John W. Cromwell, Theophilus G. Steward, and Carter G. Woodson? Why was it not making possible the publication of other worthwhile books by encouraging potential black authors, and assuring them of financial support when their manuscripts were completed? "If," Murray asserted, "the Academy was even remotely what it ought to be such would be its task and its reason for existence."

A good deal of Murray's desire to see the ANA publish books, as well as his concern about the organization's failure to encourage potential authors by assuring them "of financial support" was related to his personal experiences as a researcher and writer, as well as the fact that he and his sons owned a printing business in Washington. At the same time, he believed that the members of the academy and other educated blacks had failed to encourage and support him while he was completing a lengthy study on blacks in American art; and he was depressed and angry because no major publisher had been willing to accept his finished work.[51]

Cromwell's reply to these criticisms and questions has not survived, but bits and pieces of it are hinted at in a lengthy rebuttal Murray wrote in response to the corresponding secretary's answer. After expressing "regret" that Cromwell's "efforts seem[ed] to be mainly directed to excusing and defending the present innocuous desuetude of the Academy," Murray rejected the ANA officer's indisputable argument that the association's main problem was a lack of funds to support extensive publishing activities. "The fundamental trouble," Murray declared, "is that the Academy is run and has been for many years by a combination of self-seekers and fakers." As proof, he pointed to Hershaw's paper: "Now, no one knows better than you that Hershaw was given an opportunity to read and his paper was published for reasons wholly independent of his supposed ability or the worth of the pa-

---

51. Murray to Cromwell, July 8, 1915, in JWCG/M. Murray was referring to the following three books: John W. Cromwell, *The Negro in American History* (Washington, 1914); W. Steward and T. G. Steward, *Gouldtown* (Philadelphia, 1913); and Carter G. Woodson, *The Education of the Negro Prior to 1861* (New York, 1915). Although Cromwell's book said that it was published by the academy, he paid the printing costs for it himself.

In 1916 Murray was successful in getting his study published. It appeared under the title, *Emancipation and the Freed in American Sculpture* and was published by his and his sons' printing company, Murray Brothers of Washington.

per. It is true he has ability and what is of far more importance[,] industry and a scholar's pride. But it was not these—known or suspected—that put him on the program or on the executive committee. If you cannot see that—well, there is no use in my using paper and ink in an effort to put a little life in the (Academy) endeavor."

Murray believed that the "combination of self-seekers and fakers" was headed by Archibald H. Grimké and that Grimké was the person who decided whose papers would be read at annual meetings and published as occasional papers. He was equally convinced that Grimké eliminated from consideration those who were not his supporters and admirers, thus insuring that most of his papers were printed. The fact that *The Ultimate Criminal*, Grimké's presidential address at the December, 1914, meeting, was to be published as Occasional Paper no. 17, seemed to Murray incontestable proof of all his charges. In his opinion, Grimké's paper had been one of the poorer ones presented that year. "I heard," he informed Cromwell, most of "Grimké's paper on the 'Ultimate Criminal' but it never occurred to me that an institution supposed to—and boasting to—represent the *scholarship* of the race would sponsor such a dissertation—at least not until all else that represented real scholarship and effort has been printed and put out. If the Academy must—put out pamphlets—nothing more—why could it not put out the best that offers each year? Why, any two sheets—taken at random—of Dr. Brooks's paper were worth—to the Academy—and the race—more than a hundred essays on the order of Grimké's and Diggs—and they were not bad at all, as essays. They sounded good. I liked them—but it pained me to think what might have been read there if the Academy represented what it ought to and sincerely made effort to obtain."

It is difficult to say with certainty whether or not Murray's view of Archibald H. Grimké was an accurate one, or in what ways it was accurate. Grimké knew he was an able speaker and writer, was certainly eager to present his writings to the public, and, in 1915, he may have conspired with his friend Albert E. Pillsbury to pressure W. E. B. Du Bois to open the pages of *Crisis* to his essays. It is interesting that out of the twenty papers published by the ANA while he was its president, six, almost one-third, were pieces he wrote. No other member had as many papers published during the entire existence of the organization. When one considers that between 1903 and 1919 (the years of Grimké's presidency), from thirty-six to forty-two men were members of the academy, and that many of them were able scholars and essayists, the number of occasional papers by Grimké does seem large. On the other hand, many of the academy's members declined to write papers for the organization—some found the task too difficult, others did not have the time, and still others, such as Du Bois and R. R. Wright, Jr., at times preferred to have their work published elsewhere. It is also impossible to know how many members' papers were not published because they could not afford or refused to pay half the cost of printing them. Whatever the answers to the unanswerable questions raised by Murray's letter, the eventual efforts of men such as John W. Cromwell, John E. Bruce, Arthur A. Schomburg, and others to unseat Grimké, lend some credence to Murray's charges that he was self-serving.[52]

At the same time, one must look carefully at the source of these charges. Murray was honest enough to admit in his second letter to Cromwell that he was still very angry because the executive committee, for reasons that are now obscure, had turned down his request to deliver, at the meeting in December, 1914, a paper he had written. The subject and content of his paper are unknown, but given his lifelong interest in the black American as depicted in representational art, it is reasonable to assume that it dealt with this topic. This incident had strongly influenced his attitude toward the society. "I know full well," he told Cromwell, "that all this sounds like the snarling of a disappointed man—that I am 'sore' because I was turned down, etc., etc. Well let it go so. I am sore—sore because my paper was refused. But not sore because *my* paper was refused but because my *paper* was refused. I should have been even more sore had I known of the refusal of such a paper from any other hand. I am sore most of all because the Academy has become a 'personally conducted' machine—actually in the way of—but why go on?"[53] Despite the distinction he made between "*my* paper" and "my *paper*" Murray's tone was that of a man who felt not only that his work had been disparaged, but that he had been personally insulted. For reasons that were probably as much emotional as objective, he charged Grimké with running the academy in a way that resembled Booker T. Washington's political "machine." Whatever truths Murray voiced about the academy and Grimké in his two letters, his charges were as much products of the negative reactions to his writings and his lack of power in the ANA as the genuine expression of a concern for the general welfare of the society.

In 1916 the ANA issued a pamphlet containing six papers: "The Sex Ques-

---

52. Between 1901 and 1924, the ANA published eight of A. H. Grimké's papers. One was issued before he was elected president, and one after he had left office.
53. Murray to Cromwell, July 13 and 14, 1915, in JWCG/M.

tion and Race Segregation" by Archibald H. Grimké; "Message of San Domingo to the African Race" by Theophilus G. Steward; "Status of the Free Negro Prior to 1860" by Lafayette M. Hershaw; "Economic Contribution by the Negro to America" by Arthur A. Schomburg; "Status of the Free Negro from 1860 to 1870" by William Pickens; and "American Negro Bibliography of the Year" by John W. Cromwell. Like Occasional Paper no. 11, all of the essays were printed in one booklet, but for some reason the organization denoted it as "Occasional Papers nos. 18 and 19." The six papers presented in what was, apparently, a double occasional paper had been delivered at the nineteenth annual meeting in December, 1915.

At the heart of Archibald Grimké's insightful analysis of "The Sex Question and Race Segregation" was his belief that as long as one race ruled another both the oppressors and the oppressed would experience "moral deterioration." For southern blacks and whites, he noted, this process had begun in 1619, when the first cargo of African slaves arrived, and it had led, inevitably, to the development of a "double moral standard" for white men and black women in the south. To Grimké, the consequences of this moral breakdown were reflected in the region's present inability to regulate fairly or effectively sexual conduct between males of the dominant and females of the subordinate race. This moral paralysis stemmed from southern society's unwillingness to place restraints on white males by providing protection for black women or to demand that white males accept responsibility for the consequences of their sexual relations with black women. Grimké used blunt language to make absolutely clear that sexual contacts between black women and white men in the South were shaped and dominated by the predatory and exploitative tendencies of white men. "Neither the law nor public opinion," he charged, "puts an equal value on the chastity of the women of the two races. Female chastity in the so-called superior race is rated above that in the so-called inferior race. Hence the greater protection accorded to the woman of the first class over that accorded to the woman of the second class."

This situation, Grimké pointed out, was extremely offensive and disturbing to black men, for it was a constant reminder of their powerlessness. They could neither protect black women from the aggressions of white males, nor did they have similar access to white women. It also stimulated black men to imitate, within their own racial community, the worst sexual behavior of their white counterparts. Thus, Grimké reasoned, "the vital connection . . . between the morals of the two races" necessitated that "moral regeneration of either . . . include both." As a starting point, he recommended "abolition of the double moral standard, and the substitution in law and public opinion of a single one, applicable alike to the conduct of both [races]."

Grimké also attacked southern white women for their efforts to reform the men of their race through activities that had the effect of further degrading the legal and social standing of their black sisters. "Is it not," he asked, "the white women of the South more than any other agency, or than all other agencies put together, who are responsible for the existence of a public sentiment in the South which makes it legally impossible for a colored girl to obtain redress from the white man who betrayed her, or support from him for his bastard child?" Such an attitude, continued Grimké, only added "immensely to the strength of the white man's temptation by making . . . illicit intercourse safe for him to indulge in." It was impossible, he argued, for "the white women of the South . . . to lift the morals of their men without lifting at the same time the morals of the women of the black race." And this could only be done "by making the black women their equals before the law, and at the bar of an enlightened public sentiment." If this was not done, Grimké predicted, southern white men would "drag downward slowly but surely with them toward the level of . . . black women the moral ideals if not the moral life of the white women of the South."[54]

Theophilus G. Steward's paper, "The Message of San Domingo to the African Race," was a loosely constructed and defensive examination of several themes which he believed had shaped Haitian history and made that country a significant symbol for African and African-derived peoples throughout the world. One was the deep commitment of the Haitians to their own freedom and that of other oppressed peoples. In support of this view he pointed to the concern for freedom and equality which appeared in the statements of Haiti's revolutionary leaders, Petion and Touissant L'Ouverture; the eight hundred freedmen of San Domingo, "black and mulatto," who, as part of the French army, helped the American colonists defeat the British at

54. Archibald H. Grimké, "The Sex Question and Race Segregation," ANA Occasional Papers, nos. 18–19 (1916?), 4, 5, 9, 12–16, 19–20, 22. All of Grimké's writings tended to be passionate in tone, as well as carefully reasoned. However, he displayed a special emotional intensity in this paper. This was almost certainly related to his strong feelings about his mother's early life as a white man's "mistress," and the difficulties he experienced because of his marriage to Sarah E. Stanley of Boston, a white woman.

Savannah in 1779; the Haitian government's secret support of Simon Bolivar in his fight to liberate Venezuela from Spain; and the "interest and sympathy" manifested by Haitians "during Cuba's recent struggles." Steward was also convinced that when Haiti became an independent nation in 1804 its government had to be a "military oligarchy" run without regard to individual rights. The country's backwardness, its sharp divisions along ethnic and complexional lines, and the fact that Haitians were not a "people," in the political sense, left its leaders no choice. He was not disturbed by the fact that in 1915, 111 years later, Haitians had not yet solved "the problem of reconciling government with liberty," for, he observed, "even our own country which in this respect is in advance of all others is at this moment . . . stumbling in this process." Lastly, Steward drew on the writings of Haitian intellectuals to justify his certainty that Haiti, through its successful demonstration of the black's ability to move independently toward national character, civilization, and achievement, had been a force for the "rehabilitation of the whole race of men."[55]

"The Status of the Free Negro Prior to 1860" was a superficial historical survey of the political status of free blacks in the northern, southern, and western parts of the United States. The author, Lafayette M. Hershaw, included some material on free blacks in the colonial period and during the first decade of the Republic's existence, but the greater part of his article dealt with the years from 1830 to 1860. On the basis of scanty research, he concluded that the situation of free blacks in the North improved from the close of the Revolutionary War to 1860, while conditions for those in the South worsened. In the West, "where new states were forming," he noted the passage of antiblack laws in Ohio, Illinois, Indiana, Michigan, Kansas, and Oregon. But, in spite of these statutes, Hershaw argued that the western part of the United States exhibited a "most friendly sentiment toward the unfortunate colored man whether slave or free." This, he explained, was due to the fact that, in each of these states, "there was a small active and effective sentiment which practically nullified" the antiblack laws.[56]

Arthur A. Schomburg's paper, "The Economic Contribution by the Negro to America," was a discussion of "the service rendered by Negroes" in the development of South America, Central America, and the West Indies. It

55. Theophilus G. Steward, "The Message of San Domingo to the African Race," in ANA Occasional Papers, nos. 18–19, pp. 25–27, 29–31, 35–37.

56. Lafayette M. Hershaw, "The Status of the Free Negro Prior to 1860," in ANA Occasional Papers, nos. 18–19, pp. 46–47.

was also, because of Schomburg's rambling and disjointed essay, one of the least impressive papers published by the ANA. In spite of the title, the author did not limit himself to the economic sphere, but devoted an almost equal amount of space to recounting the military exploits and cultural contributions of black Latin Americans. Schomburg believed there was a distinct difference between the slave system erected by the French, Portuguese, and Spanish, as compared to that established by the British. In his judgment the latter had been "prejudiced and arrogant" slave masters, but in the colonies of the Latin countries "the rule was milder, in consequence of a system of judicial laws which predicated a better understanding as a solution of the complex relations between master and slave." As proof of these differences Schomburg pointed to "the more liberal manumission laws" enacted by the Spanish-speaking colonies "as well as the more rapid assimilation of the colored people into the economic and political life of those countries" which had once been colonies of Spain and Portugal.[57]

The subject of William Pickens' paper, "The Constitutional Status of the Negro from 1860 to 1870," was the hostility of white southerners toward blacks in the immediate post–Civil War period. The essay's superficiality and lack of focus suggested strongly that it was originally a hastily written speech and that the author submitted it for publication with little or no revision or editing. Pickens' most consistent theme was the tactics employed by the white South to ensure that there would be as little change as possible in the legal standing of the freedmen. "If," he observed, "the former slave states had accorded the exslaves even half justice, it is very likely that the Negro's friends in Congress would have quickly forgotten him," but the unbridled hostility of southern whites toward blacks caused the Congress to pass, and the states to ratify, the Fourteenth Amendment in 1868 and the Fifteenth Amendment in 1870. Though Pickens described the Fourteenth and Fifteenth Amendments as measures which "substituted *must* for persuasion and virtually penalized discrimination against any race in the matter of the suffrage," he acknowledged that they had failed to insure equality and justice for southern Negroes. Even after they became law blacks continued to be discriminated against and, after 1870, the forms of discrimination multiplied. Moving from the past to the present, Pickens called on whites, North and South, to improve their "practices respecting democratic

57. Arthur A. Schomburg, "The Economic Contribution by the Negro to America," in *ANA Occasional Papers*, nos. 18–19, pp. 53–54, 61–62.

liberties and human brotherhood." He urged blacks to continue their support of the struggle for equality and justice, encouraged by "late indications" that the race's fight for "full-fledged citizenship" was not hopeless.[58]

"American Negro Bibliography of the Year," the last paper in the pamphlet, resulted from the following resolution, which was passed by the ANA at its eighteenth annual meeting in December, 1914: "That the Academy publish a list of books, pamphlets, magazines and newspaper articles bearing on the Negro Question, with appropriate comment." John W. Cromwell took charge of the task and, following a method recommended to him by the chief bibliographer of the Library of Congress, produced a paper that was essentially a five-page list with brief comments. The paper was divided into four broad categories: general books on the Negro; books "of a sociological nature"; books which "discussed political conditions of the Negro Problem"; and articles. Among the black authors whose works Cromwell listed were Monroe N. Work, W. E. B. Du Bois, Carter G. Woodson, William H. Holtzclaw, Booker T. Washington, W. A. Crossland, Theophilus G. Steward, John R. Lynch, Kelly Miller, William M. Ashby, and John W. Cromwell. It is interesting to note that all of these men, with the exception of Holtzclaw, Lynch, and Ashby, were, at various times, associated with the academy. Over half of the books and articles on the list were written by whites.[59]

The decision to publish these six papers in one pamphlet was made sometime in January, 1916, and, by fall of that year, the academy had begun to distribute them. The executive committee believed that the quality of the papers, the prominence of the authors, and the timeliness of the topics would produce brisk sales. To insure that additional copies could be quickly printed at minimal cost to the society, the committee took the precaution of purchasing the printer's plates for them. "I entertain no doubt," Arthur A. Schomburg wrote to John W. Cromwell, "that every copy will be sold. Grimké's paper on segregation will go far in giving the whites a glimpse of conditions that are a disgrace to the Southland." In spite of the group's op-

---

58. William Pickens, "The Constitutional Status of the Negro from 1860 to 1870," in ANA Occasional Papers, nos. 18–19, pp. 64, 66, 70, 72.

59. Proceedings, 198; John W. Cromwell, "The American Negro Bibliography of the Year," in ANA Occasional Papers, nos. 18–19, pp. 73, 75. William H. Holtzclaw was principal of Utica Institute in Mississippi. John Roy Lynch was a former Mississippi politician and federal officeholder, who, in his years of retirement, produced two books and a number of essays which contained important information on southern Reconstruction. William M. Ashby, a novelist, was, in 1916, a recent graduate of Yale University.

timism, there is no evidence that sales of the occasional paper exceeded those of previous numbers or that the papers as a whole excited great notice. Of the six, Grimké's essay, "The Sex Question and Race Segregation," seems to have received the most attention when it first appeared and in later years.[60]

Shortly after the appearance of Occasional Paper nos. 18–19, Grimké received a letter from Robert E. Park, an eminent white sociologist who in 1914, after nine years of association with Tuskegee Institute, had joined the faculty of the University of Chicago. Park praised parts of Grimké's paper, disagreed with others, and expressed the hope that it might initiate a full and candid discussion of the topic. Some of the impact Grimké's paper had on those who read it is suggested by the fact that in 1925, ten years after its publication, Arthur B. Spingarn, a prominent, wealthy white liberal, made reference to it in a discussion with the white writer and literary critic, Carl Van Vechten. Because of Van Vechten's desire to see the paper, following their discussion, Spingarn wrote the following letter to Grimké:

Some years ago I remember reading a pamphlet of yours in which you made the point that much of the prejudice of the south was due to sex antagonism on the part of white women. It made a deep impression on me and I mentioned it the other night to Mr. Van Vechten and he expressed a desire to see it. Could you give me its title and tell me where I can get a couple of copies; mine, unfortunately, having disappeared.

There is no way of knowing whether or not a copy of the paper was sent to Van Vechten and if so what he thought of it.[61]

The executive committee believed that the occasional papers not only contained important information about their race but that their very existence constituted proof that blacks were not intellectually inferior to whites. They also considered many of them convincing arguments that blacks should be accorded complete equality with whites. Yet, in spite of the fact that the occasional papers were distributed to a wide circle of black and white educators, journalists, politicians, scholars, clergy, and philanthro-

60. Arthur A. Schomburg to John W. Cromwell, July 8, 1916, in JWCG/M; Schomburg to Cromwell, July 8, 1916, in SC/MSRC. Mignon Miller, author of a study of the American Negro Academy, described Grimké's paper, "The Sex Question and Race Segregation," as "one of the most controversial topics published by the Academy." Ms. Miller, however, provides no evidence for this judgment, either in the body of the study or in the citations. See Mignon Iris Miller, "The American Negro Academy: An Intellectual Movement during the Era of Disfranchisement, 1897–1924" (M.A. thesis, Howard University, 1966), 75.

61. The R. E. Park letter is mentioned in Mignon Miller's study, "The American Negro Academy," 75. See also Spingarn to Grimké, November 28, 1925, in A. H. Grimké Papers.

pists, as well as to educational institutions and libraries serving both racial communities, relatively speaking, only a handful of people took note of the papers, read them, and reacted to their content. While the quality of the papers varied, in a society where few blacks had either the capacity or the willingness to engage the white community intellectually on the meaning of the black American experience or to probe the ways in which their ethnic group's strengths and weaknesses were intertwined with those of other Americans, all of them deserved notice and some should have been scrutinized carefully.

As it was, neither racial community paid much attention to the occasional papers. To be sure, they were read by a small group of blacks and whites who were concerned about the many racist proscriptions that limited the hopes and aspirations of blacks. But most of these readers had neither the power to focus public attention on the papers and the issues they raised nor the means to provide the academy with the kind of financial resources that would have enabled it to distribute its papers more effectively. Those people of both races who read the occasional papers and who did have power and money, or access to them, did not view the society and its publications as significant enough to warrant any special exertions by them in their behalf.

VII Interactions, Struggles, and Doubts

From 1904 to 1919 the concerted forces of political, social, and intellectual racism continued to push blacks to the margin of American society, stimulating the formation of new organizations and institutions designed to improve some aspect of life in the American black community. The National Negro Suffrage League (1903), the Equal Opportunity League (1903), the Niagara Movement (1905), the Committee for Improving Industrial Conditions of Negroes in New York (1905), the National League for the Protection of Colored Women (1905), the Constitution League (1906), the Negro American Political League (1908), the National Association for the Advancement of Colored People (1909), the National Urban League (1911), and the Association for the Study of Negro Life and History (1915) were only a few of the new groups which appeared. Other developments that strengthened the institutional life of the urban black community were the expansion of the work of the YMCA among Negroes and the growth of settlement houses in predominantly black areas. This process of institution building was reflected in the life of the academy by its occasional interaction with leaders of other existing associations or with spokesmen for proposed ones.[1]

In 1905, Richard Robert Wright, Sr., head of the Georgia State Industrial College for Negroes, wrote to the executive committee requesting its members to consider the possibility of the academy's entering into a cooperative

---

1. John Hope Franklin, August Meier, and Allan Spear each discuss developments in urban black communities during these years and the institution building which resulted. See Franklin, *From Slavery to Freedom*, 317–22, 327–32; Meier, *Negro Thought*, 256–78; and Spear, "Origins of the Urban Ghetto," 153–66.

agreement with the research department of the National Association of Colored Agricultural and Mechanical Colleges. Wright, who was a leader in the association, had been a founding member of the ANA but, after 1902, had dropped out. He continued, however, to maintain friendships with several members of the academy, including John W. Cromwell. In his letter Wright depicted the college association as a successful organization that was growing in numbers and influence. His suggestion that the two groups cooperate with each other was based on a belief that the goals and concerns of the association's department of research and those of the ANA were similar.[2]

The executive committee's response was cool. It authorized the secretary "to make acknowledgement of the communication and to state that the matter would have due consideration." However, the proposal was never taken up again. It may have been that the executive committee found Wright's request inappropriate after his failure to support actively the ANA's efforts or that it believed the proper way for members of the college association to experience the benefits of the academy's work was to join the ANA. Quite possibly, the executive committee felt that to enter into such a relationship with another group would lead to exploitation of work done by members of the academy, with the publicity and benefits all accruing to the college association.[3]

The following year, the Negro Young People's Educational Congress attempted to persuade the ANA to enter into a cooperative relationship. This group, which was scheduled to meet in Washington in May, 1906, invited the academy to send a representative "to take part" in the sessions of its executive board, with the understanding that this would be the beginning of an ongoing relationship. As a condition of acceptance the Congress required an annual payment of $25. The executive committee declined the offer "for lack of funds."[4]

In June, 1908, the academy was confronted with a proposal from its former president, W. E. B. Du Bois, that it and two other black organizations merge with the Niagara Movement, the militant protest group which he led. The other two organizations, the Afro-American Council and the Negro American Political League, were both engaged in racial defense activities. Du Bois had been the major figure in the formation of the Niagara Move-

2. Wright to Cromwell, January 17, 1905, in JWCG/M.
3. Proceedings, 119–20.
4. *Ibid.*, 136.

ment, a group of young educated blacks who publicly rejected the "accommodationist" stance of Booker T. Washington and aggressively criticized the racist policies and attitudes of white Americans. When this protest group was formed in 1905, Du Bois attempted to draw into it Archibald H. Grimké and Kelly Miller, two of the most prominent men associated with the academy. Both refused to affiliate because they had not yet reached the point where they wished to oppose Washington in this way. In spite of the fact that most of the members of the movement were able men who were generous with their time and money, by 1908 the group was finding it difficult to stay alive. As a result some of its leaders decided that one way to prevent its collapse and expand its effectiveness would be to merge with certain other organizations. Shortly before or at the same time he made the proposal to the academy, Du Bois wrote an editorial for *Horizon*, indicating why he thought a unification of the four groups made sense.[5]

The editorial, entitled "Union," argued that though "each of the four organizations once had its raison d'etre," all of them now stood for the "same things." Du Bois also pointed to the fact that all four shared an urgent need for money. In his opinion their various annual dues, which, when combined, totaled $14, were "a prohibitive fee for the mass of colored men." In addition, he charged that the fees collected by each of the groups were wasted by "duplication of work," as was the members' commitment by "duplication of energy." Du Bois did acknowledge that the academy, with its commitment to "Science and Art," had a different focus from the other organizations but, determined to minimize differences, he brushed this aside as negligible because they "all want the same things." As a practical plan for effecting a union he suggested that the council, the league, and the academy assemble with the Niagara Movement at its annual meeting in August, 1908, and there create one organization out of the four. To give proof that this was a sincere and unselfish proposal, Du Bois pledged not to accept any "office in the gift of the united organization."[6]

Du Bois also discussed his proposal with Archibald H. Grimké, who, without relating it to either the executive committee or an annual meeting, rejected the idea on the grounds "that the Academy being non-political such cooperation as that intimated was impossible." When, in late June, Grimké

5. For a discussion of the Niagara Movement, see Elliott M. Rudwick, *W. E. B. Du Bois: Propagandist of the Negro Protest* (New York, 1972), 94–120; Du Bois to Grimké and Miller, Aptheker (ed.), *Correspondence of W. E. B. Du Bois*, I, 112–13.

6. *Horizon*, III (June, 1908), 2.

informed the executive committee of his conversation with Du Bois, his response was "unanimously approved."[7]

Although the academy was committed, among other things, to "the vindication of the Negro race from vicious assaults," because its officers and members perceived the association as a learned society, they found it impossible to give serious consideration to Du Bois's proposal. Grimké and the executive committee believed that the essential work of the ANA—"the promotion of Letters, Science, and Arts . . . the creation of a form of intellectual taste . . . the encouragement of youthful scholarship . . . and the publication of works of merit"—would be hindered by identifying the association with "political organizations."[8] They knew that a merger with activist political groups such as the Afro-American Council, the Niagara Movement, and the Negro American Political League would work a change in its identity and goals, and almost inevitably alienate a good portion of its membership. The men who ran the ANA saw the organization as a forum which provided educated blacks committed to different ideological and political beliefs an opportunity to present and disseminate the fruits of their intellectual labors. For these reasons they were unequivocally committed to the Academy's maintaining an independent stance.

Although the ANA was unable, because of the expense, to develop a cooperative relationship with the Negro Young People's Educational Congress and chose not to involve itself with the Association of Colored Agricultural and Mechanical Colleges and the Niagara Movement, it maintained a number of close, but informal ties with the Negro Society for Historical Research. This association, a learned society founded on April 18, 1911, in Yonkers, New York, was described by one of its original members as the "fair daughter" of the American Negro Academy. The person most responsible for its organization was the journalist John Edward Bruce. One of the academy's founders and a lifelong active member, Bruce drafted the NSHR's constitution, which was, in many ways, modeled on that of the ANA. The purpose of the society, as described in its constitution, was "to instruct the race and to inspire love and veneration for its men and women of mark." In order to do this the members of the group committed themselves to the "collecting of data, pamphlets, [and] books bearing upon the history and achievements of the Negro race; [and] to establish a circulating

---

7. Proceedings, 151, 152.
8. ANA Constitution (1897), Article 4, Section D, in JWCG/M.

library for its members, the special feature of which will be the published writings of the Negro and the Negroes' friends upon subjects that enlighten and encourage the race in its struggles upward."[9]

In spite of the fact that one of the goals of the ANA, as stated in Article 4 of its constitution, was "to gather into its archives valuable data, and the works of Negro authors," the NSHR was not perceived as a competitor to the academy. All of the NSHR's active members were from the New York City area and Bruce urged his friends in the ANA to become "corresponding members" of the new group. Two who did were John W. Cromwell and W. E. B. Du Bois. When Arthur A. Schomburg of New York, a founding member of the NSHR, was elected to membership in the ANA in 1914, he became the third person actively involved in both groups. Though there were never any formal ties between the two societies the close friendship through the years of Bruce, Cromwell, and Schomburg stimulated feelings of connectedness and mutual interest.[10]

The reaction of the academy was very different when, a few years later, Monroe N. Work, director of records and research at Tuskegee Institute and George E. Haynes, a professor of social science at Fisk University, attempted to organize a society of black researchers. In August, 1914, Work, Haynes, and three other social scientists met in Atlanta and decided to establish an "organization to stimulate research work relating to the Negro by Negroes." Four months later, Work outlined the purpose and goals of the proposed association in letters sent to black scholars he thought would be interested in the project as well as potential contributors to it. One of the persons to whom he wrote was Howard University's Kelly Miller, who was also first vice-president of the ANA. Miller was struck by what seemed to him the similarity of the goals of Work and Haynes with those of the academy, and shared the letter with the ANA executive committee.[11]

As a result, the committee voted "unanimously" to request Work, Haynes,

9. Schomburg to Cromwell, August 6, 1913, in SC/MSRC; Ferris, *The African Abroad*, II, 861–66; draft of the constitution of the NSHR, in Bruce Papers. There were many similarities between the constitution of the ANA and that adopted by the NSHR: both provided for an executive committee, annual meetings, occasional papers, and honorary membership for distinguished foreigners. Several of the foreign blacks elected honorary members by the NSHR were also elected as corresponding members by the ANA, among them Edward W. Blyden of Sierra Leone, Caseley Hayford of the Gold Coast, West Africa, and Duse Mohamed of London, England.

10. Ferris, *The African Abroad*, II, 865–66; Cromwell to Bruce, August 18, 1911, in Bruce Papers.

11. Work to Miller, December 5, 1914, in JWCG/M.

and their three associates in the project "to make application for admission to the Academy under the conditions . . . specified in our [the ANA's] plan of organization." The corresponding secretary was directed to communicate this offer to Work and to explain the process whereby the academy had become aware of his project. In the letter he sent, John W. Cromwell assured Work—though, he pointed out, "I am merely speaking for myself"—that once he, Haynes, and the others were admitted to the academy there should be no problem in getting the ANA to issue a call for a meeting of black researchers under its auspices. Cromwell received no response to his letter, and none of the men applied for membership (though Work would do so four years later).[12]

Work's failure to communicate his plan to the academy, and the absence of any reference to the ANA in his letter to Miller suggests that he and his associates did not view the society as either involved in or willing to support the kind of research they wished to stimulate. However, even more ominous for the future of the academy was the failure of Work and Haynes, both able and influential black scholars, to respond to the executive committee's communication.

Though wholly informal, relations between the ANA and the Association for the Study of Negro Life and History, a learned and educational society founded in 1915, were marked by strong feelings of respect and goodwill on both sides. The objects of the ASNLH were "the mutual improvement and the dissemination of information among students of Negro history by collecting and publishing sociological and historical data bearing on the Negro." Despite the fact that these goals were similar to some of the academy's, many members of the ANA, including Archibald and Francis Grimké, John E. Bruce, John W. Cromwell, George N. Grisham, Kelly Miller, Jesse E. Moorland, and Arthur A. Schomburg, were among the active supporters of the ASNLH from its inception. The main reasons for their involvement were an appreciation of the scholarly abilities and commitment of the association's founder, Carter G. Woodson, and of the important work the ASNLH set out to do. Another strong attraction was the association's organ, the *Journal of Negro History*, which Woodson, as its editor, quickly developed into a major scholarly publication in the black community. Many men who were and had been members of the ANA contributed articles to early issues of the journal. Feelings of competition between the ANA and the ASNLH were minimized by the fact that Woodson was also a

12. Proceedings, 156; Cromwell to Work, n.d., in JWCG/M.

member of the ANA, and by the belief among some members of the academy that his work was an extension of the academy's.[13]

After the failure in 1901 of the ANA's second fund-raising campaign to finance a magazine, the idea lay dormant and the society put all of its publishing efforts into turning out occasional papers. Even John W. Cromwell, a strong advocate of the magazine idea, put the notion aside for a time. However, by 1909, or possibly earlier, Cromwell had begun planning with his friend, James Robert Lincoln Diggs of Baltimore, for the establishment of the American Negro Monograph Company, through which the two hoped to publish documents by and about black Americans. In this way they planned to address some of the same concerns an academy magazine might have. On August 31, 1909, Cromwell recorded in his journal the kind of materials he and Diggs wished to distribute initially. "In the many talks," he noted, "between Dr. Diggs and myself the publication of a series of monographs on Reconstruction from the standpoint of the Negro was mooted. We planned the whole series, selected an editor-in-chief and assigned to each state a Negro to take charge of its interests. During the conversations Mississippi was named as best suitable for John R. Lynch, retired paymaster of the U.S.A. He was written to and when the reply came from him one month afterwards the fact was developed that Mississippi will be the first monograph ready and within six months of the time of this writing or in season for the spring publications of 1910. This will be a most timely auspices for the entire series." One of the strongest factors that led Cromwell and Diggs to believe there was a need for additional histories of Reconstruction was their distaste for what has been described as "the Bourbon historiography which, at Columbia University under the aegis of William A. Dunning, was producing monograph after monograph detailing the 'horrors' of Reconstruction and the grandeur with which rulers of the South had managed to restore 'civilization'." They hoped that through the

13. "Certificate of Incorporation of the ASNLH," recorded October 2, 1915, at 10:49 A.M. in *Liber* 31 at Folio 441 as Instrument #13939, Office of the Recorder of Deeds, District of Columbia; manuscript of Carter G. Woodson's introduction to volume I of *The Works of Francis J. Grimké*, in Francis J. Grimké Papers, Moorland-Spingarn Research Center, Howard University, Washington, D.C. In the *Journal of Negro History* see the following: for information on J. E. Bruce, IX (October, 1924), 578; J. W. Cromwell obituary sketch, XII (July, 1927), 563; for information on Grisham, XXXVII (January, 1951), 19, and XXXVIII (January, 1952), 29–30; Kelly Miller was one of the early contributors, I (April, 1916), 99–109, and II (October, 1917), 333; Jesse Edward Moorland's work as secretary-treasurer is mentioned in II (October, 1917), 442, and XXV (July, 1940), 401–403; for information on Schomburg in this regard, XXIII (July, 1938), 403–404; Archibald H. Grimké's involvement with the ASNLH is mentioned en passant in the obituary sketch, XXV (October, 1930), 267–68.

ANMC's monographs educated blacks and "fair-minded" whites would have access to materials with which they could challenge ignorance and refute distortions about the role and place of blacks in the American past.[14]

Cromwell and Diggs shared the idea of the monograph company and their plan for a series on Reconstruction with several blacks, among them John E. Bruce and W. E. B. Du Bois. Bruce was most affirmative, and assured Cromwell that "the scheme you have in mind . . . is a fine one and if they [the monographs] are placed on the market at popular prices will pay handsomely." Diggs, in a letter to Du Bois, whom he knew had expressed a desire to write a history of Reconstruction, asked him to accept the position of editor-in-chief of the series, adding, "If not, perhaps Cromwell might." As further encouragement, Diggs pointed out that monographs written by blacks who had been involved directly in the political life of the ex-Confederate states would provide "a splendid array of facts for the larger work you are planning."[15]

Du Bois's reply has not survived, but he did not accept the offer. Interestingly, in December of that year he delivered a paper, "Reconstruction and Its Benefits," before the annual meeting of the American Historical Association. His refusal was perhaps because he was already beginning his new work with the NAACP as editor of *Crisis*. Whatever the reason, the failure to secure Du Bois as editor-in-chief may have produced the decision not to inaugurate the American Negro Monograph Company with a series on Reconstruction, but with other material instead. Cromwell was chosen as editor-in-chief, and the first publication appeared in April, 1910. Though the purpose and activities of the company coincided with some espoused by the academy, and despite the fact that the two men had turned to several members of the society for advice and support, it was established as an entity quite independent of the ANA. There is no evidence that Cromwell and Diggs even attempted, at the time the company was organized, to get the ANA to sponsor or endorse it.[16]

In March, 1910, the brand new American Negro Monograph Company

14. Cromwell, Journal, 146, in JWCG/M; Aptheker (ed.), *Correspondence of W. E. B. Du Bois*, I, 150. Lynch's history was eventually published not by the American Negro Monograph Company, but by the Nealle Publishing Company of New York which in 1913 issued it under the title *The Facts of Reconstruction*.

15. Bruce to Cromwell, [1909?], in JWCG/M; Diggs to Du Bois, July 12, 1909, Aptheker (ed.), *Correspondence of W. E. B. Du Bois*, I, 150–51.

16. Du Bois's paper was later published by the AHA. See the *American Historical Review*, XV (July, 1910), 799. Although Du Bois had expressed a desire to do a history of Reconstruction, he would not turn to this subject until much later in his career.

sent out a letter announcing its formation and first publication. The following statement of purpose appeared in the letter: "There are many rare historical documents of especial interest to the American Negro that are not accessible outside of the great libraries or special collections. In this day of rapid movements and stirring events there are frequently facts of far-reaching import that deserve the widest circulation and which should be brought within the reach of educators, professional men and women, scholars and thinkers, in the smallest hamlet. Now and then a new voice is heard in our behalf, demolishing and removing the traditions of generations, inspiring hope, giving new life. The perusal and study of these documents, the circulation of these facts, the pondering of these words of counsel and hope might prove a most important factor in our social evolution." To become a subscriber a person sent the ANMC his or her name and address and received each monograph as it appeared. For each paper received, the subscriber was to send the company $.10. A guarantee was given that no more than ten numbers would be issued in one year. The announcement carried endorsements from four black leaders, the Rev. B. F. Watson, secretary of the Church Extension Board of the AME Church, the journalist John Edward Bruce, Jesse E. Moorland, international secretary of the YMCA, and W. L. Houston, grand master of the Grand United Order of Odd Fellows. Interestingly, besides those of Bruce and Moorland, there were no endorsements from other members of the academy who, after all, were either prominent intellectuals, educators, or powerful leaders in black religious and fraternal organizations. Most curious of all was the absence of an endorsement from W. E. B. Du Bois, whose support was solicited in 1909, or one from Archibald H. Grimké, president of the ANA.[17]

The monograph company lasted for eleven months, during which time it published four papers, two written by academy members and delivered at annual sessions of the ANA. Its initial publication was *The Confession, Trial and Execution of Nat Turner, the Negro* as recorded by Thomas R. Gray. Included with the Turner document was "a list of persons killed in the insurrection in Southampton County, Virginia, August 21st and 22nd, 1831." The second paper, which appeared in May, 1910, was an address delivered by the Rev. Thomas G. Harper, a corresponding member of the

17. "American Negro Monographs" (two-sided flyer), n.d. [1910], in JWCG/M. On the inside, under "endorsement," the flyer carried a reprint of W. L. Houston's letter praising the new company and its goals. The other endorsers were mentioned only by name. There is no way of knowing to what persons and institutions the flyer was sent.

academy, at the sixth annual meeting in December, 1902. Harper's paper, *The Contemporary Evolution of the Negro Race*, argued that the key to future development lay in blacks' continued growth in morality and not in a slavish imitation of the "Saxon race." John H. B. Latrobe's *Biography of Benjamin Banneker*, the ANMC's third monograph, was published sometime in late 1910 or early 1911. The fourth and last was *The Social Evolution of the Black South*, a paper W. E. B. Du Bois delivered at the thirteenth annual meeting in December, 1909. Du Bois's paper was published in May, 1911, and all four monographs were advertised in the April and June issues of *Crisis*. Despite the hard work of Cromwell and Diggs, the company went out of business in the fall of 1911. Because the monograph company received no mention in the black or white press, and very little in the extant correspondence of academy members, it is impossible to know the exact cause or causes of its collapse. Cromwell resisted the idea that the venture was a failure until the evidence was undeniable. One sign of this was his printed announcement on the back cover of paper no. 4 that the next monograph would be a statistical analysis of "Colored Religious Organizations" based on the most recent United States Census. He also made an unsuccessful attempt, at the fifteenth annual meeting in December, 1911, to persuade the academy to take over the monograph company as one of its activities. "After a brief discussion it was voted to refer the matter for further investigation and action to the executive committee." No more was heard of the proposal.[18]

The failure of the American Negro Monograph Company was especially disappointing to Cromwell, who had been working at least since 1897 to establish a black scholarly journal. For a time it caused him to take a deeply pessimistic view of his race's willingness to do those things essential to improving its lot in America. A year after the collapse of the ANMC, in a letter to John E. Bruce, Cromwell expressed some of the disappointment, depression, and fatigue brought on by this defeat. "Don't you know," he told Bruce, "the Negro is asleep? Or if awake does he deserve to be treated like a man? Think of the barred doors and the compelling power to open which our hundreds of thousands could organize and exert. We have not one edu-

18. American Negro Monographs, no. 1 (April, 1910); no. 2 (May, 1910); no. 3 (n.d.); no. 4 (March, 1911). (For complete citations, see bibliography.) For information on the presentation of the papers by Harper and Du Bois before the ANA, see Proceedings, 105, 172, 184. The content of Du Bois's paper is briefly described in Chapter VI. See also *Crisis*, I (April, 1911), 323–33 and I (June, 1911), 8.

cational magazine in the land that can reach our large body of teachers. If we only had the instrumentality our future would be brighter further on even though it be through dark shadows. If we can not solve our problems to the extent of getting before the American public and the world our case we are doomed and damned. God will not go out of the way to help a race that will not employ the agencies within their grasp." [19]

Though the American Negro Monograph Company was not, strictly speaking, an academy venture, the major figures involved in it were intimately connected with the ANA and launched it, in part, because of their frustration at the academy's inability to establish some sort of magazine that carried scholarly, literary, and historical writings on the experiences and concerns of black Americans. Therefore its demise can be seen as another blow to one of the major goals of the founders of the ANA.

The occasional papers were the only publications the ANA issued. Yet, in 1914, a book appeared which indicated on its title page that it had been published by the academy. The volume was John W. Cromwell's study, *The Negro in American History*. This work, the result of many years of research and writing on Cromwell's part, in addition to providing a narrative history of blacks in America from the colonial period to the early twentieth century, contained a large number of richly detailed biographical sketches of leading figures in the black American community. Not surprisingly, a sizable number of the persons whose lives he briefly described were members of the ANA. Though Cromwell paid the entire cost of printing his magnum opus, he listed the ANA as the publisher, a public tribute to the important role the academy had played in shaping and encouraging his intellectual growth, as well as an expression of great pride in what the society represented. And as if he could imagine no higher title for himself, placed after his name were the words, "Secretary of the American Negro Academy." [20]

When the academy was founded in 1897, one of its stated goals was "to gather into its Archives valuable data, and the works of Negro authors." Because the officers and most active members of the society realized that this was a task requiring money, a building, and staff—resources that the ANA did not have, and which, as the years went by, it became increasingly

19. Cromwell to Bruce, February 3, 1912, in Bruce Papers.

20. Cromwell, *The Negro in American History*; F. H. M. Murray to Cromwell, July 13 and 14, 1915, in JWCG/M; interview with J. W. Cromwell's granddaughter, Dr. Adelaide Cromwell Gulliver, professor of sociology and director of the Afro-American Studies Center, Boston University, November 8, 1973.

clear that it would have little or no success in acquiring—the academy's activities in this area had two major thrusts.[21]

Throughout its existence the association attempted in an unobtrusive and somewhat erratic way to gather historical and other kinds of materials on the black-American experience, while encouraging several of its members in their efforts to persuade Howard University to commit itself to this work. At the second annual meeting in December, 1899, the members voted to request the administration of Howard University to establish "a collection of data pertaining to the history of the Negro in America." When the ANA sent the request to J. B. Johnson, secretary and treasurer of Howard, Johnson acknowledged the letter and promised to place it before the university trustees at their next meeting. At a meeting on March 14, 1899, the executive committee of the board of trustees referred the petition to their library committee, where the matter rested.[22]

After the trustees of Howard University failed to take action, Kelly Miller, a prominent member of the university's faculty, took it upon himself to urge the institution to gather materials that would allow it to function as an African and black American research center. In 1901, Miller sought to obtain support from the trustees of Howard for a series of studies the ANA wished to conduct and publish in the journal it planned to establish. "He offered to solicit funds for securing data bearing upon the contact of the 'African and Aryan races' in connection with students of 'sociology.' The Board voted approval of this suggestion provided it could be carried out without expense to the University." With the failure of the ANA's campaign for funds to create a magazine, the project had to be abandoned. Following Walter B. Hayson's death in 1905, Miller and John W. Cromwell attempted to persuade Howard University to purchase his papers, but Wilbur Patterson Thirkield, the white president, refused to consider the suggestion, pleading that the institution was too poor. Parts of the Hayson collection were later bought by Wilberforce University and Arthur A. Schomburg.[23]

Beginning in 1906, a number of ANA members pressed the academy to take definite steps to establish an archives and seek materials for it. At the tenth annual meeting, in December of that year, "the selection of quarters

21. ANA Constitution (1897), 3.
22. Proceedings, 55–56; Johnson to "Dear Sir" [J. W. Cromwell], January 9, 1899, Safford to Cromwell, March 15, 1899, both in JWCG/M.
23. Cromwell to J. E. Bruce, February 3, 1912, in Bruce Papers; Cromwell, Journal, 162–63, in JWCG/M; Ferris, *The African Abroad,* II, 864; Logan, *Howard University,* 115–16.

as a home for the Academy and for Americana to be collected by it" was discussed extensively, and eventually "referred to the executive committee with power to act." Despite this clear directive, the committee failed to take action during the following year. The reason was its inability to obtain money for purchase or rental of physical space, or for the hiring of full or part-time staff for a library. Unwisely, the executive committee did not offer any explanation to the eleventh annual meeting for its inaction. This disturbed Charles C. Cook and Jesse E. Moorland, both of whom were deeply interested in the matter. Early in the meeting Cook initiated a discussion on what the academy could do to gather "data looking forward to the establishment of Archives." When the discussion failed to produce any specific proposals or recommendations, Moorland took the floor, and again "raised the question as to . . . the accumulation of the library." After further deliberation, the matter was referred to the executive committee for reconsideration.[24]

When the twelfth annual meeting convened in December, 1908, Charles C. Cook presented a motion "that the Academy establish a library for the reception of books and pamphlets and pictures bearing on the Negro problem, that a librarian be appointed and a place be selected for the purpose." Cook may have presented the motion as a representative of the executive committee of which he was a member. If so, for some reason the committee had ceased to feel that financing this program was a problem or he may have presented the motion because he thought the executive committee or some of its members were too timid and fearful. Kelly Miller, another strong supporter of the project, moved the following amendment to Cook's motion: "That the secretary be appointed a librarian and a space for the purpose be hired." The Proceedings do not make clear whether the "secretary" Miller was referring to was John W. Cromwell, the corresponding secretary, or George M. Lightfoot, the recording secretary. Since Cromwell was both a historian and a book collector, he was probably the one Miller had in mind. Cromwell must have refused to add this role to his many duties, for Miller withdrew his original motion, and substituted another: "that Mr. C. C. Cook be appointed librarian and be authorized in accordance with the motion to request a collection of works on the Negro problem." The original motion and this amendment were then passed by the annual meeting. The strong desire to see this project get underway was reflected in two

24. Proceedings, 139, 147–48.

other actions taken by the annual meeting. John W. Cromwell "gave notice" that he would submit the following amendment to Article 1 of the Constitution: "to include a librarian among the list of officers"; and Arthur U. Craig moved "that the action of the Academy in establishing a library be communicated to the members." Craig's motion was approved, but there was no vote on Cromwell's proposal since action could not be taken on a constitutional amendment until a year after it was proposed. The amendment, however, was not brought up for action the following year, and it was not until the twenty-fourth annual meeting in December, 1921 that it was voted on and approved.[25]

Although Charles C. Cook informed the members and friends of the ANA that the society was actively developing an archives, and solicited contributions to it, he was unsuccessful in obtaining permanent quarters for the books and other materials that came into his hands. His major obstacle was the academy's continuing inability to purchase or rent space. Three years after Cook became librarian, when Mrs. John A. Gray, a prominent member of black society in Washington, donated to the academy pictures of Toussaint L'Ouverture and Abraham Lincoln, "the matter of depository was referred to the executive committee." The records and correspondence of the ANA and its officers lead one to believe that most of the materials Cook received were kept in his home. After Cook's death in 1910, John W. Cromwell performed the function of librarian, and housed the archives in his home. Cromwell's labors in this capacity were acknowledged at the twenty-fourth annual meeting in December, 1921, when he was elected the academy's "librarian and historiographer." From 1921 to 1925 either Cromwell or Thomas Montgomery Gregory held this office. After 1925, the academy did not include the post or its occupant (if there was one) in its list of offices and officers. There is no evidence as to what happened to the ANA archives after the disappearance of the academy.

Even after Cook's appointment as ANA librarian in 1908, Kelly Miller continued his efforts to get Howard University to develop a special African and black American collection as a part of its library. In June, 1914, he sent a letter to President S. M. Newman, urging him to enlarge and strengthen the school's library. Miller recommended the hiring of a librarian with "special knowledge of and interest in the development of our library along the line of books, pamphlets and documents bearing upon the contact of the races throughout the world." He also told Newman that he had consulted

25. Proceedings, 157–78; Washington *Tribune*, December 29, 1921.

with Herbert Putnam, Librarian of Congress, regarding "the feasibility of developing a special library of this type at Howard University." Putnam, according to Miller, "expressed his interest in the proposition and his willingness to do all in his power to aid in its accomplishment. He felt that an appropriation of twenty-thousand dollars would be needed and might possible [*sic*] be secured for this purpose." Miller concluded by urging Newman to take the lead in making such a library possible.[26]

When Miller failed to get an answer or acknowledgment to his letter, he wrote to Newman again in November, 1914, pressing the same concerns. "Personally," he informed the president of Howard University, "I have been interested in this plan for a number of years and have secured from Mr. J. W. Cromwell a most valuable set of many volumes of newspaper and magazine clippings covering the reconstruction period. . . . I have also, put my self in communication with several persons who have made important collections of this description. I have in mind a gentleman who, for a number of years, has been accumulating books and documents bearing upon this question and who I think, with proper inducement, would put them at the disposal of the university." The "gentleman" Miller referred to was his fellow academy member, Jesse Edward Moorland.[27]

Perhaps because it cost the institution nothing, Newman and his administration cooperated by offering the potential donor "the proper inducement." As a result, on December 18, 1914, Moorland turned over his collection of books on "the 'Negro' and 'Slavery' with pictures statuary, etc." to Howard University, giving as a reason his belief that this institution was "the one place in America where the largest and best library on this subject should be constructively established." In a letter written to Miller on the same day, Moorland assured his friend that his "connection and interest in this phase of work in the University" played a large part in causing him to donate his collection to Howard.[28]

Although periodic meetings and occasional papers were the chief means through which the American Negro Academy presented itself and its work

26. Miller to Newman, June 15, 1914, in Kelly Miller Papers, Moorland-Spingarn Research Center, Howard University, Washington, D.C. Like his predecessor, W. P. Thirkield, Newman was also white.
27. Miller to Newman, November 4, 1914, in Miller Papers. There is no definite evidence to prove it, but many of the clipping books in the J. W. Cromwell Papers in the library of Howard University were probably given to the school by Kelly Miller.
28. Moorland to Newman, December 18, 1914, Moorland to Miller, December 18, 1914, both in Miller Papers.

to nonmembers, beginning in 1919 each academician was encouraged to purchase an impressive certificate of membership intended for display in his office or home. This certificate was designed to be a public symbol of the significance, dignity, and work of the ANA. As far back as 1904, William H. Crogman had suggested to John W. Cromwell that academy members should possess some visible sign with which to identify themselves as members of the society. He recommended "a delicate little pin or badge," as "desirable for Academicians to wear, especially while traveling, so that they might know one another." Crogman's specific suggestion was never acted on, but in December, 1909, the executive committee discussed "the necessity of preparing a certificate of membership original in design with an anguette of Rev. Alexander Crummell the founder[,] and a appropriate seal for the Academy." The suggestion sparked strong interest on the part of one member of the executive committee, who, in February, 1910, submitted to the body "a plan for [a] certificate of membership." "After considerable discussion," it was referred to Arthur U. Craig and John W. Cromwell "for criticism and comparison" with the membership certificates of other learned societies in the United States and Europe. Five years later, in December, 1915, Craig presented to the annual meeting a "design" for a "diploma." Though the Proceedings only note that "this led to a wide discussion," there must have been considerable opposition to his design, since it was not approved and the matter dropped.[29]

Two years later, possibly after Craig had gotten over any hurt feelings he might have had, the executive committee asked Arthur A. Schomburg to discuss the idea with an artist in New York City. Schomburg, who was very enthusiastic about the assignment, began conversations with Robert H. Lewis of Brooklyn, whom he described to the executive committee as "a very apt and promising artist" who was "a gold and silver medalist of the Adelphi Art School." He also discussed the matter with another artist in New York whose last name was Braxton.[30]

In April, 1918, Lewis was chosen to execute the design for the certificate.

29. Crogman to Cromwell, August 8, 1904, in JWCG/M; Proceedings, 168, 176, 182. Although the Proceedings do not mention the name of the executive committee member, who, in February, 1910, submitted "a plan for [a] certificate of membership," it was probably A. U. Craig, who was an electrical engineer and a teacher in Washington's Armstrong Industrial Training School. If so, this meant that Craig twice submitted a design for the membership certificate, which was rejected both times.

30. Schomburg to Cromwell, April 11, 1917, January 9, April 18, 1918, all in SC/MSRC. Both Lewis and Braxton were blacks.

To express his support of the project Schomburg paid Lewis' fee. Working with general suggestions from the executive committee, Lewis made several preliminary sketches which he submitted to Schomburg, who, after getting the reactions of John E. Bruce, Charles D. Martin, and Jesse E. Moorland, New Yorkers who were ANA members, sent the sketches on to Washington. The executive committee approved one of Lewis' preliminary sketches in May, 1918, and gave final approval to the print of the diploma in December of that year. The following January, the academy had one hundred copies of the certificate printed, and in June, 1919, they were distributed to its members, each of whom was expected to pay a $2 fee for it. Although the fee must have been necessitated by the organization's need to cover design and printing costs, it constituted another tax on the membership. For this reason, the certificate may have seemed to some members less a token of membership in a learned society than a thinly veiled excuse for fund-raising, especially since its cost equalled a year's dues.

Shortly before the certificate was completed, John E. Bruce wrote the following description of it in his newspaper column:

The head feature of this diploma, which is approximately 15 x 20 inches, is taken from a very ancient wood carving in West Africa, which stands for African womanhood, so notably portrayed by Rev. Alexander Crummell, the founder of the Academy, in his famous address on the "Black Woman of the South."
The border is from the same design as shown in Frobenius great work "The Voice of Africa" in two volumes, and the artist Lewis has amplified it with additional borders in such a way as to harmonize, particularly with the lattice work. In the corner of the borders in niches will be represented science, belles lettres, art and music. The lower corner will contain the mystical symbolical Egyptian Bee from the oldest granary in Egypt where it stood for progress and the symbol of regal splendor in which Napoleon selected the bee instead of the Fleur de Lis of the Bourbon dynasty to represent the highest efforts of his career. The originality and symbolic as well as artistic purposes of the Academy here find expression.[31]

Schomburg was thrilled over the successful completion of this project. "I believe," he wrote to Cromwell, "that with the receipt of this diploma we have put one step forward in giving to the Academy one of its necessary weapons to enhance its standing. I hope the Academy will accept it as a contribution from one of its members and that the day is not far distant when

31. Schomburg to Cromwell, April 11, 1917, April 25, May 13, October 24, December 11, and December 24, 1918, all in SC/MSRC. See also Robert H. Lewis to A. R. [*sic*] Schomburg, November 7, 1918, Oberly and Newell to "Mr. Lewis," November 2, 1918, Norris Peters Company to J. W. Cromwell, December 14, 1918, Webb and Borcorselski to J. W. Cromwell, December 30, 1918, all in JWCG/M; "Bruce Grit" [John E. Bruce], signed article with no date and no paper found in J. W. Cromwell's Book of Clippings, in JWCG/M, 40.

its rays of usefulness will be known and enjoyed in all parts of the world where men of the race are doing their part toward their contribution to human uplift." Schomburg's seemingly excessive excitement over a piece of paper was an expression of his personal liking for tangible symbols of status and respectability, his belief that the certificate actually had the power of enhancing the "standing" of the association, and his satisfaction because the academy had successfully completed a task it had set for itself. The ANA's records provide no information on the number of certificates purchased, nor do they give any indication whether individual members framed and displayed them, making it impossible to say how they were received.[32]

From the time the ANA was founded, the executive committee did almost all of the work that kept the organization alive between meetings. For this reason, it was fortunate that most of the persons elected to the committee were active supporters of the "Academy idea." By 1913, however, even these deeply committed men felt disappointed with how little the organization had achieved. A continual concern over issues such as poor member participation, the high rate of dues delinquency, and the lack of public interest in the association's yearly meetings was one expression of these feelings. At annual meetings, executive committee members joined with other stalwarts in the society to pass measures they hoped would solve such problems. The failure of these efforts increased the frustrations of committed members. In addition, there was the discouraging reality of how few of the academy's goals had been realized. The projected full membership of fifty had never been attained; hopes that the society would become a strong influence on educated blacks—especially those in education and politics—had not been realized; efforts by the ANA to combat racist ideas propagated by whites received little attention from either racial community; and, when the organization entered the twentieth year of its existence in 1917, it still lacked a journal. The irregular publication of occasional papers remained its only printed offering.

By late 1918, many members of the ANA had come to believe that Archibald Grimké's removal from the presidency would be one of the most important steps toward resolving the academy's difficulties. That John W. Cromwell was prominent among those holding this opinion indicated how

32. Schomburg to Cromwell, June 26, 1919, in SC/MSRC. Archibald H. Grimké's membership certificate can be found with his other papers in the Moorland-Spingarn Research Center, Howard University.

serious a judgement it was. For a variety of reasons—some of which are difficult to document—during the last two years of Grimké's tenure the frustrations and dissatisfactions of a number of members came to focus on the president. One reason for this was the almost inevitable tendency to brand the head of an organization as the "scapegoat" because things were not going well. And, indeed, the general mood of the academy at the time of Grimké's election had probably created expectations which no one could have fulfilled. After the disappointments of Du Bois's incumbency, it was thought that Grimké would get the organization moving again, establish a strong public reputation for it, and secure much-needed financial support. Grimké worked hard at these things but his success was very limited. Given factors such as the multiple organizational commitments of the small group that constituted the black elite, the relative poverty of the black American community which made it impossible to secure major financial support from that quarter, and the general disinterest of even those whites who considered themselves friends of black development, it is hard to believe that any president could have fulfilled the members' hopes.

In terms of personal literary activity, the years Grimké served as president of the ANA were busy and productive ones for him. A vast amount of his time and energy went into writing addresses and essays on the racial issue, a large number of which were published in a wide variety of black and white newspapers and literary magazines, or presented as speeches in various parts of the country. Since Grimké was expected to deliver, each year, a presidential paper, many of his essays were read at meetings of the academy. In spite of several unavoidable absences from annual meetings, he delivered sixteen papers before the organization, several of which were later published. Of the twenty essays published in the occasional papers issued by the ANA from 1903 to 1919, six were written by him. No other member would have as many of his papers published during the entire life of the society.[33] Those members of the academy who, unlike Grimké, found it difficult or impossible to get their work published, and who, in part, had joined the society because it offered a means of overcoming that problem, eventually came to resent the fact that the president's papers were chosen so frequently for publication as occasional papers. Grimké's comfort in this regard contrasted sharply with the behavior of the two previous presidents of the academy. Alexander Crummell and W. E. B. Du Bois, both of whom were

33. *DAB*, VII, 633.

prolific writers whose pieces were welcomed in a variety of publications, were sensitive to the fact that there were few places blacks who lacked a strong public reputation or powerful connections could go to have their writings published, and were careful to make sure that the papers of other, less well known members received as much consideration as theirs. Despite Crummell's stature as the leading black intellectual of his day, and the fact that he was the founder of the academy, nothing written by him was published by the society until over a year after it had been in existence. Two of his addresses appeared as Occasional Papers, no. 3, following the publication of papers by Kelly Miller and Du Bois. No paper written by Du Bois was published by the academy during the five years he served as president of the ANA. Grimké's behavior led some observers to believe that he essentially saw the association as a platform for his ideas and only exerted himself in connection with activities which helped maintain his public reputation.

Grimké was also a leading figure in a number of other important black organizations. Two years after becoming head of the ANA, he was elected president of the Frederick Douglass Memorial and Historical Association, a group dedicated to honoring the memory of Douglass and to raising funds to purchase and preserve his home in Washington. For several years he was treasurer of the "Committee of Twelve for Negro Advancement," a coterie of black leaders who, led by Booker T. Washington, attempted to function as a lobby for black rights. In order to influence public opinion the committee published pamphlets on issues affecting blacks, including one written by Grimké, *Why Disfranchisement Is Bad*. In 1914 Grimké was elected head of the newly formed Washington chapter of the NAACP, and in subsequent years held two national offices in that organization. These activities competed with Grimké's responsibilities to the ANA for his time and energies, thus laying him open to charges of overinvolvement in other areas.[34]

It did not help matters that the president of the ANA never attempted to implement some of the important decisions made by the academy in its annual meetings. In December, 1906, a motion offered by Jesse E. Moorland that the ANA hereafter copyright all of its published papers and incorporate the society in the District of Columbia passed by a substantial majority. Grimké did nothing to carry out this directive. Perhaps even more serious was his failure to put into operation the constitutional amendment passed

34. "A Frederick Douglass Memorial," *Colored American Magazine*, VI (March, 1907), 199–200; *DAB*, VII, 633; Angelina Grimké, "A Biographical Sketch of A. H. Grimké," 47.

in 1915, allowing the executive committee to hold meetings in places other than Washington. John W. Cromwell had proposed the amendment and fought for its passage in three successive annual meetings. He and its other supporters must have felt both disappointed and angry to see this measure, which they believed held the key to increased attendance and greater publicity for the ANA, going unused because of Grimké's failure to implement it.[35]

Once Cromwell decided Grimké was unsuited to his office, the possibility that there would be a new president of the ANA became quite serious. The corresponding secretary's close involvement with Alexander Crummell in the earliest efforts to establish the organization and his continuous and committed efforts to support and strengthen it, had made him one of the most powerful figures in the academy. Cromwell's reasons for concluding that the ANA needed a new president could have been all or some of those cited above. Though his open opposition to Grimké's continuing as president cannot be conclusively documented until 1919, the deteriorating state of the academy and other influences probably had moved him to this position even earlier.

The strong criticisms directed at the ANA and Archibald Grimké by Freeman H. M. Murray, a man Cromwell respected and considered his friend, could have been one such influence. As early as 1909, Cromwell had endeavored to draw Murray into the academy. For several years he hesitated, questioning whether the organization was really a scholarly investigative group. Blunt and free with his opinions, Murray also feared that he might not get along with the men who ran the association. In 1914, however, he submitted an application and was elected a member. His fears about not being a congenial member were justified, for a year later he was disgusted with the academy and its leaders.[36]

In letters to Cromwell he charged that "it is worse than ridiculous than we [the ANA], posing to be the cream of the intellectuals of the race in America can offer no better excuse for existence—and the assumption of so grandiloquent a title—than one cheap pamphlet every two or three years." The society, he urged, "ought to attempt something worthwhile or disband." When Cromwell, in a reply to this letter, defended the academy and

35. Proceedings, 139.
36. Cromwell, untitled six-page report, December 28, 1909, Murray to Cromwell, December 17, 1913, both in JWCG/M; Proceedings, 197. There is a brief biography of Freeman Henry Morris Murray in the catalogue of manuscript collections in the Moorland-Spingarn Research Center, Howard University.

its operations, Murray restated his opinion in even more forceful terms. "You might as well be candid about it—the Academy is a fizzle. Witness the attendance on the meetings. Not one-fourth of the supposed or nominal members right here in the city attend the public sessions—and the executive sessions are almost farcical. No wonder people do not care to pay $2.00 for the honor of membership in it. I know I shall not unless there are *good* indications that there is to be a new deal." The fundamental problem, Murray continued, "is that the Academy is run and has been run for many years by a combination of self-seekers and fakers—those who have (supposed) reputations to conserve." Becoming even more pointed, Murray asked Cromwell whether the ANA had any other purpose "except to keep the president and his easy-chair essays before the public." In addition, the angry printer charged favoritism in the executive committee's selection of speakers for annual meetings and in its choice of papers published as occasional papers.[37]

Despite the financial problems the ANA faced, Murray's questions about the quantity and quality of the occasional papers were certainly valid. Poor attendance and failure to pay dues were also real issues, even though the officers were aware of them and had attempted a number of times to deal with them. In addition, his charges against Grimké and other officials of the organization touched on problems and tensions which needed to be taken seriously. Although Murray's arguments were, in part, self-serving and probably, at points, filled with exaggeration, he was offering answers to questions that deeply concerned Cromwell and other committed members of the association. It is not inconceivable that some of the seeds he planted landed on fertile soil.[38]

Two years later Cromwell was again confronted with a negative assessment of the academy as a scholarly body. In July, 1917, the executive committee requested Joseph J. France, a member of the ANA, to study health conditions among black migrants in urban communities and to present his findings in a paper. The paper was one of several assigned for the annual meeting in December, 1917, which focused on the current migration of black workers from rural to industrial areas. France, a medical doctor in Portsmouth, Virginia, accepted the assignment. Three months later he wrote to Cromwell, explaining why he had decided not to complete the

37. Murray to Cromwell, July 8, July 13, and July 14, 1915, all in JWCG/M.
38. Murray to Cromwell, July 13, 1915, in JWCG/M. In this letter Murray admitted that some of his anger toward the ANA might not be disinterested.

study. France had made two trips to Philadelphia, a city he felt was "ideal" for this kind of investigation. However, he quickly discovered that the information he sought was not "tabulated," but would have to be researched out of records. Because the amount of time required to do this was more than he could give, France contacted Whittier H. Wright, a black physician practicing in Philadelphia, who was experienced in gathering medical statistics for research purposes, and outlined his problem. Wright agreed to gather the needed information for a seventy-dollar fee. At this point France decided to drop the project. As he wrote Cromwell: "I should by no means hesitate to incur the expense were I thoroly [*sic*] convinced of the serious aims and purposes of the Academy. But, somehow, I have received the impression that the Academy is more of a dilettante society, content with sciolistic [*sic*] treatment of subjects rather than insisting on research and investigation." Cromwell's reply has not survived, but no paper on this subject was presented at the annual meeting.[39]

Murray and France were not the only members of the academy to express concern about the ANA. In January, 1919, Jesse E. Moorland, director of the work of the YMCA among blacks, was disturbed over the fact that Robert A. Pelham, a federal employee, had been nominated for membership. Writing "in strict confidence," to Archibald and Francis Grimké, Moorland emphasized that he had "nothing against Mr. Pelham as a man," but he did not believe him suitable for admission to the ANA. Behind Moorland's objection was an even more fundamental question, that is, "whether or not our Academy will not degenerate and fail to serve the purpose it was designed to serve if we are not more careful than we have been in the election of members." After considering "all the difficulties of getting an attendance of men who are worthwhile and the apparent lack of interest of some outstanding men in the Academy" he was, he wrote the Grimkés, certain "we ought to elect men who are more than merely bright, . . . men who have accomplished something." Moorland believed that only men who possessed impressive reputations as creative public leaders, authors, or scholars

---

39. France to Cromwell, July 27, 1917, unsigned draft letter in Cromwell's handwriting concerning "The migration movement," France to Cromwell, October 6, 1917, Wright to France, October 27, 1917, all in JWCG/M. Whittier Wright was the son of R. R. Wright, Sr., a founder of the ANA, and a brother of R. R. Wright, Jr., also a member of the society. Whittier had assisted his brother in gathering statistics for a sociological study on *The Negro in Pennsylvania* (Philadelphia, n.d., [1909?]). This study was also R. R. Wright, Jr.'s dissertation for the Ph.D. degree he received from the University of Pennsylvania. See also Washington *Bee*, December 22, 1917, p. 7.

should be admitted to the organization. Despite Moorland's letter Pelham was elected to the academy later that year.[40]

These letters point to a rising sense of dissatisfaction among committed members of the academy concerning the drift of the organization. By 1919, for some, this dissatisfaction had taken the form of efforts to remove Grimké from office. On January 4, 1919, John W. Cromwell, who had served as corresponding secretary of the academy every year from its inception, resigned his office.[41] By that act, Cromwell disassociated himself from Grimké so that he could, in good conscience, promote a change in the society's leadership. His resignation may have been the first step in a premeditated plan to achieve this end or possibly Cromwell turned to the task of seeking a successor to Grimké only after he had resigned. By summer, however, he was in the thick of efforts to assure the election of a new president and other officers who would revitalize the ANA. Cromwell did the work of coalescing a number of members in Washington into a group who shared his concerns and persuading them to assist him. His good friend Arthur A. Schomburg aided him by drawing most of the members in New York into the movement.

From July to December, 1919, Cromwell and Schomburg were constantly in touch by mail developing strategies in connection with the coming election. In an early letter, Schomburg wrote that he and three other members of the ANA, John E. Bruce, James E. K. Aggrey, and Charles D. Martin, had resolved to be in Washington for the next annual meeting. Responding in late July to a letter from Cromwell, Schomburg sent assurances that Martin and Bruce would arrive in Washington early enough for a pre-election meeting on strategy and expressed pleasure that John R. Clifford of West Virginia was also an ally. In November, Schomburg was attempting to draw Arthur U. Craig, a former Washingtonian who had moved to New York, into the scheme. Writing later that same month to Cromwell, he assured his friend that the contingent in New York was "committed . . . on 'who is who.' When we are ready to speak for the presidency I think we will be heard." Cromwell and his associates in Washington had begun to select a slate of officers, for, in the same letter, Schomburg refused the post of corresponding secretary on the grounds that he was already overextended and

40. Moorland to A. H. Grimké, January 10, 1919, in A. H. Grimké Papers. For biographical information on Pelham see New York *Age*, January 19, 1929, p. 2. Pelham was elected corresponding secretary of the ANA at the twenty-third annual meeting in December, 1919. See Washington *Bee*, January 17, 1920, p. 6.

41. Cromwell to Grimké, January 4, 1919, in JWCG/M.

because, in his opinion, it was mandatory that "the President and the Secretary . . . be in hailing distance of Washington."[42]

Cromwell and his friends found it difficult to locate a willing presidential candidate who would be acceptable to them. Eventually, it was agreed that Cromwell was the best man for the spot, even though he was uncomfortable with the idea. The reason or reasons for his reluctance are not known. One may have been his age—he was seventy-three years of age; another the fear that as the leader of the anti-Grimké faction he would be charged with opportunism. Whatever the anxiety, Schomburg attempted to calm it in a letter written on December 4, in which he urged Cromwell not to "shirk the higher office. You have served faithfully and can give view [*sic*] to the broad-minded policy of our first president[.] to serve for at least one year, would be recompense for your services. You would then be in a position to train younger men to the onerous duties of Secretary. I will hold to my views unless you insist after reaching Washington, D.C. and going over the ground. These views are held by most of the New York men." Cromwell agreed to run for the office of president and it was in his home that the men committed to Grimké's removal caucused on December 29, shortly before the opening of the twenty-third annual meeting.[43]

The annual meeting in 1919 attracted more members of the academy than any previous gathering. In all twenty-two men attended, fourteen who were residents of Washington and eight from other places. Those present included the following Washingtonians: Walter H. Brooks, George William Cook, John W. Cromwell, T. Montgomery Gregory, Archibald H. Grimké, Francis J. Grimké, Lafayette M. Hershaw, Lorenzo Z. Johnson, F. H. M. Murray, Robert A. Pelham, Robert H. Terrell, Neval H. Thomas, Edward C. Williams and Carter G. Woodson. The other eight attendants were James E. K. Aggrey of Salisbury, North Carolina; Robert T. Browne and John E. Bruce of New York; John R. Clifford of Martinsburg, West Virginia; Wil-

42. Schomburg to Cromwell, July 20, July 28, November 26, 1919, all in SC/MSRC.
43. Schomburg to Cromwell, December 4, December 12, November 26, 1919, all in SC/MSRC. From the scant evidence available it is difficult to know all of those involved in efforts to produce a change in the leadership of the ANA. Unfortunately, only Schomburg's letters to Cromwell survive as evidence of these events. Names mentioned by Schomburg as definite allies were: John E. Bruce, James E. K. Aggrey, Charles D. Martin, William H. Ferris, and John R. Clifford. Since Cromwell and Schomburg gave much thought to the selection of other officers besides the president, most of the men elected in 1919 may have been a part of their cabal. In Schomburg's letters there were brief, but cryptic references which suggested that Arthur U. Craig, James Weldon Johnson, John Albert Johnson, and T. Montgomery Gregory might have also been involved. These references are in the Schomburg to Cromwell correspondence from July 20 to December 12, 1919.

OFFICERS OF THE ANA, 1918 AND 1919

Positions	1918	1919
President	Archibald H. Grimké	John W. Cromwell
First vice-president	Kelly Miller	Robert T. Browne
Second vice-president	J. Albert Johnson	James E. K. Aggrey
Third vice-president	Matthew Anderson	John Hurst
Fourth vice-president	Lorenzo Z. Johnson	Charles V. Roman
Corresponding secretary	John W. Cromwell	Robert A. Pelham
Recording secretary	Edward C. Williams	T. Montgomery Gregory
Treasurer	Francis J. Grimké	Lafayette M. Hershaw
Executive committee	Kelly Miller	Lafayette M. Hershaw
	Jesse E. Moorland	Kelly Miller
	Arthur U. Craig	George M. Lightfoot
	Francis J. Grimké	Freeman H. M. Murray
	Freeman H. M. Murray	William Pickens
	Lafayette M. Hershaw	John E. Bruce
	John W. Cromwell	

liam H. Ferris of Philadelphia; W. Ashbie Hawkins of Baltimore; John Hurst of Philadelphia; and Arthur A. Schomburg of New York. This sizable turnout was almost certainly related to an expectation that there would be a contest for the presidency.[44]

On December 30, 1919, the second day of the annual meeting, John W. Cromwell was elected fourth president of the American Negro Academy. With the exception of Kelly Miller, Lafayette M. Hershaw, and Freeman H. M. Murray, a completely new group of officers was chosen to work with him. Of the twelve men elected (excluding Cromwell), only Miller, Hershaw, Murray, and George M. Lightfoot had previously served as officers, and over half of them had been admitted to the society since 1914. In sharp contrast to previous years only three founding members, Cromwell, Miller, and John E. Bruce, held positions. It is interesting to compare the officers elected by the ANA in December, 1918, with those elected in December, 1919, as shown in Table 1. For better or worse, this was a significant change in leadership. In describing the shift the New York *Age* noted that "Archi-

44. Unidentified newspaper clipping dated January 24, 1920, in JWCG/M.

bald H. Grimké declined reelection as president, and John W. Cromwell was named to succeed him." Unfortunately, this brief quotation from the *Age* is the only specific information which has survived concerning the election of officers at the twenty-third annual meeting. As a result, it is impossible to know if Grimké and his supporters and friends resisted, in any way, those who opposed his reelection; whether or not there was any bitterness around the elections; or how the members voted in the elections.[45]

Cromwell was immensely gratified by the results. Despite its terseness, this was reflected in an entry he made in his diary on December 31, 1919: "The outcome of the session of the Academy and to me the most personal was my election as president of the Negro Academy, third in succession from Alexander Crummell, the order being Crummell, Du Bois, Grimké."[46]

45. Washington *Bee*, January 17, 1920, p. 6; New York *Age*, January 10, 1920, pp. 1, 2.
46. Cromwell's entry in his diary is quoted in a letter from Otelia Cromwell to W. E. B. Du Bois, February 24, 1941, in W. E. B. Du Bois Papers, University of Massachusetts, Amherst.

VIII *Withering of Hope*

From 1919 to 1926 the fortunes of the American Negro Academy continued to decline. During John W. Cromwell's brief tenure as president, he and a small corps of members who had supported his election sought to strengthen the association by attempting to enrich the programs of the annual meetings, expand the membership, and rewrite the constitution. Some of these efforts were more successful than others, but none succeeded in transforming the academy into a major intellectual force. Under the leadership of Arthur A. Schomburg, Cromwell's successor, the situation became even worse, for the organization lost even the small degree of momentum it had acquired during the long presidency of Archibald H. Grimké.

John W. Cromwell headed the American Negro Academy for only a year, but during that time he and his supporters made strenuous efforts to revitalize the association and to rekindle public interest in it. One of the first matters he turned his attention to was the incorporation of the society. In December, 1906, the tenth annual meeting had directed that this be done, but until Cromwell became president, no steps had been taken in this direction. On January 30, 1920, the new president and four other members went to the office of the District of Columbia's recorder of deeds and there filled out and signed the appropriate forms, which were approved. Cromwell was accompanied by Kelly Miller and George William Cook, both faculty members at Howard University, by his predecessor, Archibald H. Grimké, and by Grimké's brother Francis, the former treasurer of the ANA. The presence of the latter two seemed to indicate that the organization's shift to new leadership had not produced a legacy of bitterness and hostility. Early in January Cromwell also began to take steps that resulted in the first national ANA meeting to be held outside Washington. This was the twenty-third annual meeting which met during July, 1920, in New York City.[1]

Another important action taken during the early months of Cromwell's presidency was the appointment, by the executive committee, of a three-man subcommittee on constitutional revision. It was Cromwell's hope that the work of the subcommittee would lead to changes enabling the society to realize its goals more effectively. The men appointed to the subcommittee were Carter G. Woodson, dean of Howard University's School of Liberal Arts; Arthur U. Craig, an electrical engineer employed by the city of New York; and Robert T. Browne, a New Yorker who wrote on scientific subjects. Woodson, the founder of the Association for the Study of Negro Life and History, was the most capable of the three. A stern, committed scholar with an amazing ability to keep his projects alive financially, his successful establishment of the association and its scholarly publication, the *Journal of Negro History*, raised hopes that he could point the way to success for the academy. Woodson's independence and almost rigid commitment to his way of doing things made Cromwell somewhat anxious about having him on the subcommittee, but Schomburg assured the president there was nothing to fear. "The way," he felt certain, "is opened for good work. Browne, Craig, and Woodson can be depended in [sic] bringing in a constitutional report which will surprise you for its clearness and strength. . . . Stick to Woodson tho [sic] he may be a little queer." The work of the subcommittee, which went on for almost a year and a half, culminated in a report to the twenty-fifth annual meeting in December, 1921, a year after Cromwell had ceased to be president.[2]

During the time he headed the ANA, Cromwell frequently turned to his old friend Arthur A. Schomburg for advice and encouragement. For many years, the two men had freely shared their thoughts and feelings on a wide range of subjects. In the last year of Archibald H. Grimké's presidency, Schomburg had become one of Cromwell's most trusted confidants and advisors on matters relating to the academy. After Cromwell's election as pres-

1. "ANA Articles of Incorporation"; Schomburg to Cromwell, January 7 and January 8, 1920, in SC/MSRC.

2. Schomburg to Cromwell, January 7, 1920 in SC/MSRC. For a discussion of Woodson's work in founding the ASNLH see Wesley, "Racial Historical Societies," 29–30; Charles H. Wesley, "Carter G. Woodson—As a Scholar," *Journal of Negro History*, XXXVI (January, 1951), 12–24; and Rayford W. Logan, "Carter G. Woodson: Mirror and Molder of His Times, 1875–1950," *Journal of Negro History*, LVIII (January, 1973), 1–17.

ident of the ANA, this continued to be an important way in which their friendship operated. In his letters to Cromwell, Schomburg always included a word of encouragement for his friend's efforts to stimulate the work of the academy, and constantly threw out suggestions on administrative issues, many of which were accepted. At Schomburg's urging, Robert T. Browne was invited to deliver a paper on "Einstein's Theory of Relativity," at the twenty-fourth annual meeting in December, 1920. And it was his suggestion which led to the inclusion of the ANA's membership roster in occasional papers published after 1920. While Cromwell was president, Schomburg generously expended both time and money to support programs and projects sponsored by the academy. The New Yorker paid half the publication costs of Occasional Paper no. 20. He also conducted numerous business negotiations to relieve his friend of some of the demands of his office. Cromwell was neither controlled nor dominated by Schomburg, but he respected his opinions and was deeply grateful for the understanding and support he received.[3]

During the year Cromwell was president, the American Negro Academy published its twentieth occasional paper, *Alexander Crummell, an Apostle of Negro Culture*. Presented by William Henry Ferris two years earlier at the twenty-second annual meeting, this paper marked the observance of the one-hundredth anniversary of Crummell's birth. The paper was a discussion of Crummell's life, the work of the academy, and the situation of blacks in 1918. In it, the author noted that the public had forgotten the ANA soon after its founding because of Crummell's death and the "industrial fad" which "swept over the country." He praised John W. Cromwell, Francis J. Grimké, Kelly Miller, Charles C. Cook, and John L. Love for their refusal to let the organization die, and for doing the work that insured its survival and successes. In answer to his rhetorical question, "Were the soaring ideals that inspired Dr. Crummell's effort dreams of the imagination, or were they grounded in reality?" Ferris argued that through the activities of its members the academy had kept alive Crummell's conviction "that the Negro needed the same kind of education and training that the white man needed, or he would lag hopelessly behind in the race of life." He also commended the ANA members for remaining faithful to this idea during a twenty-one-year period filled with discouragements, not only for the educated black

3. Schomburg to Cromwell, January 7, January 8, September 15, November 18, 1920, all in SC/MSRC. William H. Ferris was the author of Occasional Papers, no. 20, *Alexander Crummell, an Apostle of Negro Culture*.

American, but for the entire race. Between 1898 and 1918, he reminded them, whites had barred the majority of educated blacks from the employments for which they were qualified; reduced the black churches to a "narcotic and opiate" for the masses; stripped blacks of the right to vote; and locked them in a segregated world. Crummell, Ferris declared, unlike other black leaders, "who were asleep at the switch twenty years ago," had seen that the argument against higher education for blacks was only the first step in a conspiracy to keep black Americans ignorant so that they would be unable to protect themselves when whites stripped them of social and civil rights.

Ferris pointed to America's entry into World War I as the definitive proof of Crummell's wisdom, and as the event that awakened other black leaders to their stupidity in accommodating to white racism. "It was," he exalted, "a rude awakening that they experienced in the summer of 1917, when the edict went forth that all American citizens, black as well as white men, were subject to the selective draft. It was a rude awakening that they experienced, when they discovered that their sons must cross the ocean and give their lives to bring a freedom to war-ridden Europe, which was denied their race in this country. It was a rude awakening that they experienced when they realized that they who only experienced partial citizenship in this country were called upon to make the same sacrifice in blood and treasure as their fairer-skinned brothers, who had experienced the full blessings of citizenship." Ferris also believed that the war had made clear how much black Americans needed "trained and well-equipped" leaders, for it was only under the leadership of such men and women that they could use the new political situation in Africa, Europe, and America to improve their status. "At a time," he pointed out, "when the humanitarian plums will be handed out at the peace table at Versailles, at a time when the small and weak nations of Europe will have their day in court, at a time when the oppressed and suppressed people of Europe, Palestine, and Armenia will have their innings, now is the time for the Negro to make his appeal, present his plea and submit his case."

Henceforth, Ferris asserted, the world's estimate of blacks would depend on what they thought of themselves. Thus, if the race and its leaders were aggressive in their demands for equal treatment, they would be respected; if not, whites would do with blacks as they wished. This meant there must be an immediate replacement of those black leaders "who have pursued the Fabian policy of watchful waiting, who have been the creatures of circumstance, who have been the sport of chance, who have been determined by their environment, and who have been dependent upon the turn or course that events would take."[4]

After the academy made the decision in December, 1918, to print Ferris' paper, a small crisis was precipitated by his inability to meet the organization's requirement that every author of an occasional paper had to pay one-half the cost of publishing the paper. Arthur A. Schomburg resolved the difficulties by contributing $7.50, on the condition that Ferris' manuscript be given to him soon after the paper was printed. Presumably, Schomburg wished to add it to his collection of books and pamphlets by or about black Americans. Public distribution and sale of Occasional Paper no. 20 was begun in June, 1920, and included with each occasional paper was a "fine portrait" of Crummell.[5]

By December, 1920, Cromwell had decided to give up the presidency. No direct evidence exists to explain this decision, making it necessary to surmise his reasons. One possible motive was that the role demanded a kind of physical energy the seventy-four-year-old man lacked. Also, many of the younger black intellectuals he wished to see become a part of the ANA—men such as Benjamin Brawley, author, scholar, and professor of English at Morehouse College; Charles S. Johnson, a sociologist who was editor of *Opportunity*, the journal of the National Urban League; and Walter White, assistant executive secretary of the National Association for the Advancement of Colored People—were persons with whom he had little or no personal acquaintance. Given his less active role in the black community outside Washington, there was little chance that he would come to know them intimately. Moreover, he may not have enjoyed being the academy's presiding officer and major spokesman on public issues. Though he was a journalist, a capable essayist, and the author of a history of blacks in the United States, Cromwell reveled in the management of details and persons, and in the ANA, largely because of his earlier efforts, these activities were concentrated in the office of corresponding secretary. In an earlier period, Crom-

4. Ferris, *Alexander Crummell, an Apostle of Negro Culture*, ANA Occasional Papers, no. 20 (1920), 9, 10, 11–14.

5. Schomburg to Crummell, January 8, 1920, in SC/MSRC, Washington *Bee*, June 26, 1920, p. 4; photograph card of Alexander Crummell with following inscription in left-hand corner: "Accompanying Occasional Paper No. 20 The American Negro Academy," in JWCG/M. The academy began sale and distribution of Occasional Paper no. 20 on the same date it announced its plans to hold a midsummer meeting in New York City in July, 1920 (Washington *Bee*, June 26, 1920, p. 4).

well may well have been interested in the presidency of the ANA; but after 1899, such longings, if they existed, seem to have passed. His decision to seek the position in 1919 was the result of concern over the academy's future and, as he perceived the situation, the lack of any other suitable candidate.

Cromwell's decision not to run for office again brought him face to face with an old problem and a new one. Who would be a suitable replacement for him; and what would be his future role in the organization? The first was resolved by Arthur A. Schomburg's election in December, 1920, as the fifth president of the ANA.[6] In part, this solved the second problem. Since he lived in New York, Schomburg's situation was similar to Du Bois's during the years he was president. Normally, Schomburg could not attend executive committee meetings, and he was unable to supervise directly the working officers of the organization. It was, therefore, extremely important that he have a dependable ally on the executive committee. From 1920 until his death in April, 1927, Cromwell served his friend in this capacity. However, despite their close relationship, Cromwell retained his independence. There were, in fact, instances in which he questioned the motives and actions of Schomburg.

In several important ways, Schomburg was different from the other men who had been presidents of the ANA. Born in the Spanish colony of Puerto Rico, he emigrated to the United States at the age of twenty-three (1897). All of his predecessors were Americans by birth, and, with the exception of Crummell, the major part of their lives had been spent in their native country. Though Schomburg attended St. Thomas College in the Danish West Indies and was a graduate of the Instituto de Instrucción in San Juan, Puerto Rico, he possessed less formal education than any other holder of the office. When he was a young man, Schomburg had studied law but, after arriving in New York, he worked at various odd jobs, including teaching Spanish. Finally, he secured a position as head of the mailing division of the Latin American department of the Bankers Trust Company.

Previous presidents of the ANA had earned their livelihood through the professions or in related fields such as newspaper work and writing. Schomburg had written articles on black literature and history, some of which had appeared in the *African Times and Orient Review* and in *Crisis* magazine. One of his pieces, *The Economic Contribution by the Negro to America,*

6. New York *Age,* January 8, 1921, p. 7.

was published by the academy in 1916 as an occasional paper. He was best known, however, as a collector of books and art relating to the black experience in Europe and America, and as a bibliographer. He did not have the impressive academic background of Crummell or Du Bois, nor was he considered an outstanding writer and thinker in the way Crummell, Du Bois, and Grimké were. His most immediate predecessor, John W. Cromwell, was known primarily in the black community, where he was respected as an outstanding journalist, a dedicated race leader, and a fine amateur historian. Schomburg's activities were best known to a small circle of his friends and associates.[7]

For the academy to have elected him its president when there were members such as Kelly Miller, a prominent sociologist and writer on racial issues; Edward Everett Just, a distinguished research biologist who had earned a Ph.D. at the University of Chicago; and Carter G. Woodson, an outstanding historian and educator with a Ph.D. from Harvard University, was an unmistakable sign of decline. Either these or other eminent members of the academy did not value the office enough to want it, or the members no longer desired a chief officer with the stature and prominence of their first three presidents. In any case, Schomburg's election was an ominous sign for an organization that needed strong, creative, visible leadership. Despite the fact that the society's membership included men of superior scholarly attainments, with more impressive public reputations, Schomburg retained the office of president from 1920 until the demise of the academy in 1929.[8]

Because he was an absentee president, Schomburg was not only unable to participate regularly in meetings of the executive committee, but it was also impossible for him to oversee directly the work of the corresponding secretary. This important office was held throughout Schomburg's tenure by Robert A. Pelham, a clerk in the United States Census Bureau. Pelham, who was sixty-two when elected to the post, had been born in Petersburg, Virginia. When he was still a child his family moved to Detroit, where he at-

---

7. For a full picture of the details of Schomburg's life it is necessary to consult several sources. The following are the most helpful: Boris (ed.), *Who's Who*, 237; *Journal of Negro History*, XXIII (July, 1938), 403–404; and L. D. Reddick, Introduction to *Calendar of the Manuscripts in the Schomburg Collection of Negro Literature* (New York, 1942), ii–iii.

8. These three did not exhaust the pool of members of the ANA who would have met the same criteria for election as did Crummell, Du Bois, and Grimké. During the 1920s, the following men, all impressive intellectuals, were also members of the academy: Alain Leroy Locke, W. E. B. Du Bois, James Weldon Johnson, Jesse Edward Moorland, William Pickens, Matthew Anderson, William H. Crogman, Monroe N. Work, and Charles V. Roman.

tended that city's public schools until his graduation from high school in 1877. At the age of ten he began working for the Detroit Post and Tribune Company, which published the *Post*, the leading Republican newspaper in Detroit. This job drew him into journalism and Republican politics. In 1883, along with his brother and two other men, Pelham established the *Plaindealer*, Detroit's first self-sustaining black newspaper, and became its business manager. He left the Post and Tribune Company in 1891 and for the next several years worked as business manager and columnist for the *Plaindealer*. His chief source of income, however, came from a succession of political patronage jobs obtained through his activities as an "all-weather Republican with apologies to no one." In 1900 Pelham moved to Washington in order to accept a position as a clerk in the United States Census Bureau. Once established in the capital, he began attending Howard University's School of Law, and in 1904 received the LL.B. degree. By 1919, he had become a supervising clerk in the Census Bureau and a fixture in Washington's black social and political circles. While at the Census Bureau, Pelham designed, built, and perfected several office machines which increased the efficiency of his agency. Because of this he also enjoyed a local reputation as an inventor.[9]

From the time of his arrival in Washington, Pelham was drawn into association with some of the most important members of the academy. John W. Cromwell and John E. Bruce, both of whom had long histories as newspapermen and Republican activists, had known and liked him for years. His studies at Howard University and later activity as a strong supporter of the institution's alumni association established ties with faculty and other alumni who were members of the ANA. His active involvement in the Republican party and membership in exclusive clubs such as the Pen and Pencil and Mu-So-Lit made him also the acquaintance and friend of even more men who were members of the society. In 1917 Pelham was nominated for membership in the academy, but despite the fact that his backers included Cromwell and Schomburg, he was turned down. Two years later, when his name was again placed before the membership, Jesse E. Moorland opposed

9. The various details of Pelham's life can not be found in any one source. The best are: I. Garland Penn, *The Afro-American Press and Its Editors* (Springfield, Mass., 1891), 162–63; Warren, *Michigan Manual of Freedmen's Progress*, 87–92; Simmons, *Men of Mark*, 1022–26; Washington *Colored American*, July 9, 1898, p. 8, February 22, 1902, p. 15, March 29, 1902, p. 12, March 21, 1903, p. 2; New York *Age*, January 19, 1929, p. 2; Washington *Tribune*, January 11, 1929, p. 2; and Arris A. Mallas, Jr., Rea McCain, Margaret K. Heddin, *Forty Years in Politics: The Story of Ben Pelham* (Detroit, 1957), 2, 3, 4, 7–12, 16, 17–31, 34, 36, 86.

his election on the grounds that he was "merely bright" and had done nothing to justify admission to the organization. This time, however, his backers were successful in "pulling him over."[10]

Cromwell was the major figure behind Pelham's two nominations and his eventual election, as well as the person whose approval made possible his election as corresponding secretary in 1919. He thought Pelham's education and his work in journalism, politics, and the civil service had given him an excellent background for functioning as chief administrator and staff person for the ANA. Why Cromwell felt this way, even though Pelham had done nothing that could be considered a serious contribution to art, literature, or science, is hard to understand. In part his opinion may have been related to the fact that Pelham was a charming man who knew how to ingratiate himself with important people; or that he and Cromwell had both been newspapermen, civil servants, and active Republicans. There is also a possibility that Cromwell, after twenty-two years as corresponding secretary, had come to feel that as long as the person holding this office understood what the academy's goals were, was committed to them, and was an efficient and intelligent administrator, he did not necessarily need to be a creative intellectual.[11]

During the early months of his first year in office, Schomburg attempted to keep abreast of what the academy's officers in Washington were doing, but, increasingly, his efforts to do this were thwarted by Pelham's inefficiency and growing lack of interest in the association. The corresponding secretary frequently failed to implement decisions of the executive committee and annual meetings, to answer letters, or take counsel with the president on difficult administrative or policy questions. As a result, Schomburg became dependent on his friend, John W. Cromwell, for regular information on the executive committee. Unable to establish a working relationship with the corresponding secretary, Schomburg communicated with the executive committee through Cromwell and, occasionally, employed his friend as a secret (and sometimes not so secret) strategist to push through measures he approved or block those he did not like. Not surprisingly, the entire

10. Washington *Colored American*, March 21, 1903, p. 3; Warren, *Michigan Manual of Freedmen's Progress*, 91; "Certificate of Incorporation of the Mu-So-Lit Club," recorded April 24, 1920, at 10:32 A.M. in *Liber* 36 of Folio 51 as Instrument #15689, Office of the Recorder of Deeds, District of Columbia.

11. Schomburg to Cromwell, October 4, 1917, November 26, December 4, 1919, in SC/MSRC.

situation promoted divisiveness, hostilities, and further organizational inefficiency.[12]

During his first two years as president, Schomburg involved himself in a wide range of academy business, including publicity, arrangement of meetings, occasional papers, and recruitment of members. In the course of his third term, however, he became less involved. Schomburg's initial enthusiasm for his office was dampened by several factors: his inability to establish a working relationship with Pelham; the strenuous efforts required to keep a weak organization such as the ANA alive and functioning; and the meager return for his efforts.

As involvement in the ANA became less gratifying, Schomburg found it difficult to maintain an active interest in the academy. A man of varied interests, he began to invest more of his time and energy in his book collecting, historical researches, and masonic activities. As a result, after 1923 his correspondence with Cromwell was his chief means of relating to the mounting problems of the ANA. When he did attempt to influence the executive committee, Pelham, or the general membership directly, it was usually done at Cromwell's request. If his predecessor had not urged him to take action, Schomburg would have done nothing to prevent the collapse of the annual meetings in 1923 and 1925.

Between 1920 and 1924 the academy issued no occasional papers, despite the fact that Arthur A. Schomburg urged the publication of certain papers. In May, 1921, Schomburg wrote to John W. Cromwell, asking the former president to join him in assisting the executive committee "to plan ways and means to print some of the papers that were read" at the twenty-fourth annual meeting in December, 1920. Schomburg did not mention which of the four papers presented at that meeting he had in mind. Whether or not Cromwell functioned as his ally is unknown (it is difficult to believe he did not), but nothing came of Schomburg's efforts in this regard.[13]

Although Schomburg flirted with the possibility of resigning as president or not standing for reelection in 1923, and again in 1924, he rejected the

12. Schomburg to Cromwell, May 17, May 30, August 4, October 27, November 12, 1921, in SC/MSRC.
13. Schomburg to Cromwell, "Decoration Day" [May 30], 1921, in JWCG/M. The four papers presented at the ANA meeting in December, 1920, were "The Challenge of the Disfranchised" by John W. Cromwell; "The Negro's Part in the Spread of Christianity" by Charles D. Martin; "The Three-fold View of Character" by Theophilus G. Steward; and "Some Phases of the Haitian Situation" by James Weldon Johnson.

idea both times. Partly out of loyalty to the "Academy idea," and partly out of a liking for the title of president, he retained the office nine years. The repeated reelection of so dispirited and ineffective an executive was an indication that a majority of the members no longer viewed the ANA as a significant or viable organization.[14]

Most of the ANA members were relatively complacent about Schomburg and Pelham, but there were a few who found their behavior so disturbing that they attempted to replace them. Even though he and Schomburg were friends, John W. Cromwell was a major figure in these efforts. Friendship did not stop Cromwell from working for Schomburg's removal once he decided it was necessary. Sometime in October, 1922, in a letter which has not survived, Cromwell expressed his negative feelings about Schomburg and Pelham to John E. Bruce. The letter was an attempt to gain an ally and may have been one of several sent to various members of the academy. Bruce's positive response indicated that the message had fallen on "receptive ears." "I have been thinking," he told Cromwell in his reply, "along the lines upon which your letter touches rather meaningfully and I have read between the lines of your most recent, and heed the call. The Academy does not prosper under its present management, and it should not be permitted to snuff out its existence by its inaction[,] lack of interest[,] and pride in the object which called it into being twenty-seven years ago. Our half-breed brethren have dual minds and they are not to be expected to think black as did Alexander Crummell. The head of the Academy should be a *seasoned* well equiped [*sic*] mentally black scholar soaked from his toes to the outer surfaces of his caput in the ideas and ideals which Dr. Crummell held when he evolved the thought out of which grew the American Negro Academy. If I can in any way bear a hand in helping to bring about this result—health permitting—I shall be only too glad to tender what service I can."[15]

Bruce meant what he wrote. In another letter written and mailed that

14. Schomburg to Cromwell, "Decoration Day" [May 30,] 1921, in JWCG/M; Schomburg to Cromwell, May 22, May 22, (second letter), June 1, July 7, September 1, October 18, October 24, October 28, November 30, 1923, January 27, February 25, March 5, "Columbus Day" [October 8], December 5, 1924, February 16, February 24, March 3, March 3, (second letter), December 1, 1925, April 6, June 1, 1926, all in SC/MSRC.

15. Bruce to Cromwell, October 14, 1922, in JWCG/M. From 1920 until his death in 1924, Bruce was an active and prominent member of Marcus Garvey's Universal Negro Improvement Association. His use of the terms "half-breed brethern" and "mentally black scholar" reflected the heavy stress on pride in physical blackness and the antiassimilationist attitude of Garveyites. These views, however, were similar to ones Bruce had held most of his adult life.

same day, he urged John R. Clifford, editor of the *Martinsburg* (West Virginia) *Pioneer Press* to join him in an effort to put the academy into the hands of responsible and effective leaders. Clifford's answer was an enthusiastic yes. "Everything you said," he replied, "wholeheartedly do I agree with . . . and my ambition is as high as yours that Dr. Crummell's plans and purposes, to his honor and sacred memory be carried out fully." Clifford promised to busy himself urging "all our friends" to attend the next annual meeting because, as he put it, "they will be active in the same lines." One of the goals of this activity was perfectly clear to the West Virginian: "Cromwell must be elected secretary." After stressing to Bruce the importance of having "all the New York members attend—even if some of us have to pay their expenses"—Clifford urged him to write Freeman H. M. Murray, Joseph J. France, "and others you can trust, and I shall do the same." Rather innocently, he suggested that Bruce "urge Cromwell to do the same." [16]

Despite these intense exchanges among three senior members of the academy, both Schomburg and Pelham were reelected to their respective offices in December, 1922. Cromwell, Bruce, and Clifford were unable to garner enough votes to make the changes they wanted. It is impossible to say with any certainty why Schomburg and Pelham had as much support as they did. Possibly, a movement to unseat the two seemed like an attempt by a group of aged, domineering old men to assert their will over the younger members. Or perhaps the members who attended the meeting believed the organization's problems were larger than questions of who held what office. If so, they might have refused to accept the notion that removal of Schomburg and Pelham would make any great difference. A third possibility is that even the active members had come to believe that the academy would never be anything more than a periodic gathering of a small group of friends who shared their ideas with each other and published, from time to time, a favorite address. If such a view prevailed, Schomburg's and Pelham's failings might have been seen as annoyances rather than major problems. [17]

Whatever the reason or reasons that Schomburg and Pelham were allowed to remain in office, in the eyes of their critics, they were responsible for the decline of the academy. Consequently, criticism of the two continued as well as efforts to remove them. In April, 1923, John R. Clifford was fuming because nothing had been done by the president or the executive com-

16. Clifford to Bruce, October 16, 1922, in Bruce Papers.
17. Washington *Evening Star*, December 29, 1922, p. 18.

mittee to implement a decision made in December, 1922, to hold a second mid-summer meeting. When his letters to Schomburg and Pelham went unanswered, he angrily told Cromwell, "Something is rotten in Demmark. Fumigation! Fumigation!! is the answer."[18]

At the twenty-seventh annual meeting in December, 1923, Lorenzo Z. Johnson, a fifty-three-year-old Presbyterian clergyman who was a professor of English at Howard University, ran against Schomburg for the office of president. A graduate of Lincoln University and the Lincoln University Theological Seminary (1901), Johnson also earned a second theological degree and a master of arts degree from Princeton Theological Seminary (1904). After completing his studies at Princeton, he became pastor of the Madison Street Presbyterian Church in Baltimore, a post he occupied until 1918 when he accepted a position on Howard University's faculty. In 1909, largely on the recommendation of Francis J. Grimké, Johnson was elected a member of the ANA "by a unanimous vote." Although he was an active supporter of the organization and a faithful attendant at its meetings, during his fourteen years of membership he had only presented one paper before the academy, an address entitled "Racial Demands of the Hour," which he delivered the year of his election. His friends and colleagues respected him as a dedicated and effective teacher and clergyman but he had no major writings to his credit and, in terms of public reputation, was a minor figure both in the Presbyterian Church and in the academic community of Howard University.[19]

Beginning in 1912 Johnson served seven terms as a vice-president of the ANA. However, in 1919, when John W. Cromwell replaced Archibald H. Grimké as president of the academy, he was not reelected. Whether this was because he was one of Grimké's supporters or unacceptable to Cromwell and his friends for other reasons is unknown. However, the following year Johnson returned to office as a vice-president and was reelected in 1921 and 1922. In December, 1923, when he ran against Schomburg, he was third vice-president of the academy.

It is unclear who Schomburg's and Johnson's respective supporters were, but Johnson was defeated. In a letter written to Cromwell after the election,

18. Clifford to Cromwell, April 23, March 26, 1923, both in JWCG/M; Schomburg to Cromwell, July 7, October 24, 1923, both in SC/MSRC.

19. Cromwell, corresponding secretary's report to the thirteenth annual meeting, December 28, 1909, in JWCG/M; *Proceedings*, 168. For biographical information on Johnson see *Hilltop*, January 26, 1949, p. 12; and Washington *Star*, January 16, 1949, p. 27.

Schomburg, who had come to the meeting toying with the idea of not standing for reelection, argued that he had no choice but to enter the contest
since "Johnson was so emphatic in his annoyance to supersede the president
in every way and his candidacy having been announced to several other
members."[20]

Schomburg may have described Johnson's behavior accurately. There are
no other versions of the meeting, so we cannot know for certain. But whatever the clergyman did, his behavior caused a man ostensibly on the verge
of yielding the presidency to pursue it actively. In spite of a desire on the
part of Cromwell and some others to replace Schomburg, it is hard to believe that they saw this relatively obscure minister-academic as a suitable
president for the ANA. The decisive factors in the election may have been
the absence of an acceptable alternative to Schomburg plus a felt need on
the part of some members to demonstrate their respect for the incumbent
president in the face of Johnson's behavior. However, Schomburg's letter of
explanation to Cromwell suggests that he felt a need to convince his friend
that he had done the correct thing. Even though he had been reelected,
Schomburg may have sensed, or possibly he knew, how much Cromwell and
some others wanted him to step down.

Perhaps this is why, a month later, Schomburg announced to Cromwell,
"We will need a new president," in effect, making it clear that he would not
seek reelection at the next annual meeting. This disclaimer meant that
Cromwell and his allies were assured of the "touchy" New Yorker's support
if they could find suitable candidates for the offices of president and corresponding secretary. Cromwell and John Clifford immediately began pres-
suring the executive committee to insure that an annual meeting would be
held in March, 1925, and accelerated their search for the right men to run
for office. In late December, after a secret strategy session in Washington,
Cromwell communicated their plans to Schomburg. "Yesterday," he informed the president of the academy, "friend Clifford true to promise came
to house and held quite a conference in which he confirmed what was promised [by the executive committee?] as to faith in a meeting round or about
inauguration time and the right we have to expect and command support
for the proper men for officers. After going over the entire field we settled
down on A. L. Locke as an outstanding choice for president, a man who
had a preeminence because of his appointment as a scholar to Oxford

20. Schomburg to Cromwell, January 27, 1924, in SC/MSRC.

twenty-five or more years ago." Although Cromwell and Clifford clearly decided on their own that Locke was the best man for the post, two weeks before they made their decision, Schomburg had urged Locke's election as his successor.[21]

There was much to recommend Alain Leroy Locke for the office of president. He was a young man (in 1925 Locke was thirty-nine), a former Rhodes Scholar, the holder of a Ph.D. from Harvard University, an outstanding figure at Howard University, where, since 1916, he had held an appointment as professor of philosophy, and the author of numerous articles and several books. In terms of his education, scholarly achievements, and public prominence, he would have been a worthy successor to Crummell and Du Bois. Locke also had connections with a number of important white intellectuals and literary figures who might have been induced to provide some support for the ANA. But there were also some potential drawbacks to the idea. He was not, by aptitude or inclination, an administrator; and he was a very busy man. His roles as a teacher, researcher, and interpretor/critic of black-American literature and art left him little time for additional activities.[22]

How Locke reacted to the proposal that he become a candidate for the presidency of the ANA is unknown. Despite Cromwell's and Clifford's efforts, plans for a meeting in March collapsed, and when the academy met in December, 1925, Schomburg and Pelham were reelected to fifth terms. Either Locke had rejected the idea, which left the way open for Schomburg to run again, or Schomburg broke his word. Since Schomburg, Locke, and Cromwell were friends in the years after 1925, the first possibility is probably the correct one. Thus, what was the last effort to strengthen the association by attempting to provide it with new leadership ended in failure.[23]

Problems with officers were only a small fraction of the many difficulties plaguing the academy from 1921 to 1928. Another was the failure of various efforts to revitalize the organization, the most important of which was the work of the committee on constitutional revision. In July, 1921, after approximately nineteen months of work, its members, Robert T. Browne,

21. Schomburg to Cromwell, February 25, 1924, in SC/MSRC; Cromwell to Schomburg, December 31, 1924, in JWCG/M; Schomburg to Locke, December 18, 1924, in Locke Papers.

22. For biographical information on Locke see the *Journal of Negro History*, XXXIX (October, 1954), 332–34.

23. Schomburg to Cromwell, February 16, February 24, March 3, March 3 (second letter), 1925, all in SC/MSRC; New York *Age*, January 16, 1926, p. 2.

Arthur U. Craig, and Carter G. Woodson, reported back to the executive committee. The result of their labors was a proposed constitution providing for major changes in the articles dealing with membership, publications, and fees.

The constitution under which the ANA was governed—little changed since its ratification in March, 1897—briefly dealt with membership in Articles 2 and 3. In the place of Articles 2 and 3 the committee offered three new articles entitled, "Membership," "Qualifications," and "Rights and Privileges." Essentially, they provided for three "classes" of participants in the society, "Fellows," "Members," and "Associates." The "Fellows," whose number was limited to fifty, were to be the organization's "governing body." If this change was approved, all current members "in good standing" automatically became "Fellows."[24]

The process for becoming a "Member" required several steps. First, submission to the executive committee of an application fee, and a "thesis" dealing with the applicant's intellectual specialty or area of interest. Approval of the thesis by the executive committee meant that its author was nominated for election as a Member. A majority vote of the Fellows was required for a successful election. Any vacancies among the Fellows of the academy were to be filled by electing replacements from the Members. "Whenever[,] in the judgment of the Academy," it was deemed desirable, "Sustaining, Honorary, and Corresponding Members" were to be elected. Sustaining members were those whose primary support of the organization was financial; Honorary members were distinguished figures the society wished to honor by this designation; and Corresponding members were foreigners or other persons, who, though separated from the association by great distance, submitted papers and publicized its work.[25]

The third class of participants, "Associates," were to be persons who had "attained a measure of distinction in any branch of human knowledge or human endeavor." Admission to this level of membership required payment

24. ANA Constitution (1897), 2, 4. The constitution under which the ANA operated from March, 1897, to December, 1921, can be found in two places: the J. W. Cromwell Papers in the possession of Dr. Adelaide Cromwell Gulliver and in the John W. Cromwell Papers in the Moorland-Spingarn Research Center, Howard University. The one in the Cromwell-Gulliver Papers was printed by Robert L. Pendleton of Washington, D.C., probably in early 1898. The Moorland-Spingarn copy has the following phrase on its cover, "Incorporated under the General Laws of the District of Columbia," and no date. It was printed sometime between January, 1920, and December, 1921. Copies of the proposed constitution produced by Browne, Craig, and Woodson can be found in the J. E. Bruce Papers and in the F. H. M. Murray Papers. See pages 1–2 of the proposed constitution in either the Bruce or Murray Papers.
25. Proposed ANA constitution, 1, 2, in Bruce Papers and in Murray Papers.

of an application fee and approval by a majority of the Fellows. Each year the executive committee was directed to "extend the privilege of Associate membership to graduates of colleges for acceptance during the first calendar year after graduation."

Unlike the Fellows, no limits were set on the number of Members and Associates. And all three classes were given the privilege of identifying themselves publicly as members of the academy: Fellows by affixing the initials FANA after their names; Members, with MANA; and Associates, with AANA.[26]

One of the major objectives of the committee was to eliminate the practice of according the same privilege to everyone associated with the organization, regardless of his degree of interest or intellectual ability. A small number of Fellows, whose achievements were indisputable, were to manage the society and the activities of the three classes of participants. Requiring a thesis from potential members was an attempt to exclude from consideration persons who were not serious, productive thinkers. Most of the men admitted to the ANA had demonstrated, at the very least, a commitment to ideas and the increase of knowledge. Some—W. E. B. Du Bois and Carter G. Woodson, for example—were exceptional scholars. Others could only be considered intellectual dilettantes. And there were a few whose main interest was to be associated with a group of prominent men.

The creation of the three classes acknowledged that men of varied levels of achievement and interest would be attracted to the organization. They were also an attempt to ensure that each person who entered the academy did so at a level appropriate to his achievement and interest. But at the same time, they were meant to operate as an apprentice system, allowing the movement of young intellectuals (both in terms of age and experience) from the level of Associate to Fellow, if their accomplishments warranted it. The articles on membership affirmed the ANA's need for clearly defined membership standards, as well as for a widely based support group.[27]

The committee on constitutional revision recommended substantial changes in the process whereby papers read before the academy, and those published by the organization, were approved. The major purpose of these recommendations was to amplify and make more specific Article 5 of the constitution and By-Law 3 (passed December, 1897).

In the constitution submitted by Browne, Craig, and Woodson, the exec-

---

26. *Ibid.*
27. *Ibid.*

utive committee was left the responsibility for approving papers to be read at annual meetings, but all business related to publications was removed from their domain. Provision was made for the establishment of a "Publication Board, to consist of three Fellows of the Academy, whose duty it shall be to make all necessary arrangements for the publication of papers, monographs, etc., including the Annual . . . and to edit and publish all documents submitted to it by the Executive Committee."

Papers read before the academy were to be automatically entitled to publication, but "in such manner as the Publication Board shall see fit." In addition, the proposed articles directed that the papers published by the association were to be copyrighted in its name. Only after the first edition was "exhausted" could the individual who had written the paper "contract for the release of the copyright." [28]

The proposed articles on publications also specified in exact terms how expenses would be divided when a member's paper was chosen for publication. Fellows whose papers were published had to contribute one-half of the cost; Members and Associates, two-thirds of the cost. In each case the academy paid the balance. Besides the gratification of seeing his work in print, an author was to receive 40 percent of the number of copies printed "free of additional expense." [29]

The committee's obvious intent was to create a new body exclusively concerned with publications, thus lifting this specialized activity from the shoulders of the overburdened executive committee. The expectation was that the association's publishing projects would then receive the constant attention they needed and be supervised by a staff with expertise in this area. Carter G. Woodson's influence was especially visible in this set of recommendations. His impressive and successful work as editor and publisher of the *Journal of Negro History* made him the strongest and most authoritative voice in devising the details regulating how papers would be approved and outlining the prerogatives of the Publication Board. [30]

28. ANA Constitution (1897), 3, 4, in JWCG/M, and in Cromwell Papers, Moorland-Spingarn Research Center. At the ANA's organizational meeting on March 5, 1897, the academy delegated to the executive committee responsibility for publications. From that time on the executive committee had functioned as the society's board of editors. See also proposed ANA constitution, 2–3, in Bruce Papers and in Murray Papers.

29. Proposed ANA constitution, 2–3, in Bruce Papers and in Murray Papers.

30. The "Publication Board" or board of editors recommended in the proposed constitution was similar to the structure that Woodson used in reviewing articles submitted to the *Journal of Negro History*. Interview with Dr. J. Picott, Executive Director, Association for the Study of Afro-American Life and History, May 27, 1976.

In 1921 the academy's fees were comparable to those charged by many other learned societies and professional organizations at the time. When it was founded twenty-four years earlier, Article 7 of its constitution required a five-dollar admission fee (which included the first year's dues) and two dollars annually as a membership fee. In 1893 the American Jewish Historical Society required five dollars for admission and, after the first year, five dollars per year. Twenty-seven years later its fees were still the same. In 1890 the dues of the American Historical Association were three dollars for admission and three dollars per year. They were the same in 1920. The National Education Association in 1896 charged two dollars for admission and two dollars annually as a membership fee. In 1919 it was still possible to pay two dollars per year and be a member of the NEA, but five dollars a year was required if a member wished to receive the association's special publications. Where these and similar groups differed from the ANA was in their membership sizes, in the generosity of many of their individual members, who often gave special gifts in cash or stock, and in the greater regularity with which their members fulfilled their financial obligations. In terms of regular membership only, in 1897, the ANA had 36 members; in 1893 the AJHS had 172; in 1890 the AHA had 670; and the NEA had 1,464 in 1896. In 1920, the ANA had 45 members; the AJHS had 334; the AHA 2,524; and the NEA (1919) 24,000.[31]

The failure of the academy to even attempt to increase its revenues by raising the amounts of membership fees seems to allow only one interpretation: from the earliest years there was a belief on the part of the active membership that voting an increase would not make any difference. With so many nominal members regularly defaulting on a two-dollar-per-year assessment, it was probably thought that a request for more money would only add to the list of delinquents.

Whatever the reason for earlier restraint in this area, the committee on constitutional revision recommended a change. Article 9 of the proposed constitution fixed the admission fee for Fellows at ten dollars, for Members at five dollars, and for Associates at one dollar. In all cases, the required amount was to be exclusive of the first year's dues. In Article 10, Fellows

31. *Publications of the American Jewish Historical Society*, I (1893), 137, and XXVIII (1920); *Papers of the American Historical Association*, IV (1890), 35; *Annual Report of the American Historical Society for 1920* (Washington, 1925), 1; *Journal of the National Education Association*, XXXIX (1896), 1, and LVII (1919), 5; ANA Constitution (1897), 3, in JWCG/M, and in Cromwell Papers, Moorland-Spingarn Research Center.

and Members were asked to pay two dollars annually, Associates one dollar. The different admission fees for each class correlated the cost of entry with the amount of power and privilege one would receive in the organization. Retention of a low annual assessment reflected a hope that the Member and Associate classes would eventually be quite large, thus creating a broader base for revenue.[32]

These were the major constitutional amendments recommended by the committee on constitutional revision. Their report included other suggested changes intended to improve or clarify the wording and form of the constitution and by-laws, but they were essentially minor.

The executive committee directed that two copies of the "revised constitution as reported by the Committee" be sent to every member of the ANA. On one, members were asked to indicate their reaction to "suggested changes" and return it for the use of the committee on constitutional revision. The executive committee felt that it would be good to poll the members in order to obtain an idea of their reaction to the proposed revisions, as well as to give them time to study the document carefully in preparation for voting on it at the twenty-fifth annual meeting in 1921. Unfortunately, no information on the members' responses has survived.[33]

Unlike most of the academy's previous annual meetings, the twenty-fifth, which met December 27 and 28, 1921, held business sessions on both days. Discussion and voting on the various proposed amendments made this necessary. The result was a complete rejection of the amendments regarding membership, and approval, with only minor changes, of those dealing with publications and fees. Why the academy rejected the three classes of membership is unclear. Some members may have felt threatened by the proposed admission requirements. No current members were affected since all, automatically, would have become Fellows, but, in an organization where none of the members had written a thesis for admission, this may have seemed too radical a change. Many members, viewing the academy as a forum for discussion and debate, may not have seen any value in what seemed a complicated membership structure regulated by rigid admission standards. To them, the new membership requirements might have appeared to be a device whereby an arrogant clique could pass judgment on others. The three-man publication board was approved and it was given the rights and

---

32. Proposed ANA constitution, 3–4, in Bruce Papers, SC/NYPL, and in Murray Papers.
33. Robert A. Pelham to "Dear Sir," August 15, 1921, in JWCG/M.

prerogatives suggested. Any member whose paper was approved for publication had to pay one-half the cost. The admission fee for new members was raised from five to ten dollars, and annual dues were increased from two to five dollars.[34]

The most important outcome of the twenty-fifth annual meeting was the academy's rejection of the proposals submitted by the committee on constitutional revision for upgrading standards of admission and creating a larger support base for the society—both essential reforms. At the same time it voted down the proposals on membership, the academy established a new structure, the publication board. It should have been obvious to the members that the potential of the publication board could only be exploited if the society secured additional manpower. An expanded membership was also the only realistic way of trying to secure more money through dues. But instead of attempting to strengthen themselves organizationally in this crucial area, the members only added to their responsibilities. They committed themselves to provide personnel for another board and to pay higher fees. The decline of the academy between 1903 and 1919 had demonstrated clearly that the organization lacked the requisite manpower and funds to translate effectively its goals into realities. Some members could not support the organization financially or by personal involvement; and there was a sizable number who would not. The academy, by its rejection of the recommendations on membership, and its failure to formulate an alternative, disregarded the evidence presented by twenty-four years of marginal existence, and, as a result, compounded its problems.

The society's failure to take any new initiatives in regard to recruitment was reflected in its slow rate of growth between 1920 and 1928. A total of ten people entered the ANA during those years. Excluding corresponding members, the total new members for 1897 to 1903 were thirteen, and for 1904 to 1919, forty new members. Despite the fact that the attrition rate was quite high for the two preceding periods, the 1920 to 1928 figure for new members was embarrassingly low. Three of the ten new members—Henry Proctor Slaughter, Thomas M. Dent, and Alain L. Locke—were elected to the society in 1921. Slaughter, who was a graduate of Howard University

---

34. Washington *Tribune*, December 31, 1921, pp. 1, 5; Constitution of the American Negro Academy, adopted December, 1921, pp. 3–4, in Cromwell Papers, Moorland-Spingarn Research Center.

(LL.B., 1879; LL.M., 1900), worked in the United States Government Printing Office. He also edited the *Odd Fellows Journal* and various church periodicals. Slaughter had an avid interest in collecting books and pamphlets that documented the history of black Americans. Over the years he had assembled a unique collection, which contained a number of rare items. On at least two occasions prior to his election as a member of the ANA, Slaughter made his collection available to the academy for exhibits. Dent was a statistical clerk employed in the Foreign and Domestic Bureau of the United States Department of Commerce.[35]

In 1922 Frank Rudolph Steward and Henry Albro Williamson were elected to the academy. Steward, the son of Theophilus G. Steward, a founding member, was proposed for membership by his father. The younger Steward, who practiced law in Pittsburgh, was a graduate of Phillips-Exeter Academy, Harvard College, and the Harvard Law School. Before settling in Pittsburgh, he had served in the United States Army, and attained the rank of captain. Williamson's name was suggested by Arthur A. Schomburg, his close friend and fellow Mason. Educated in public schools of San Francisco and New York, he was a chiropodist with a practice in Brooklyn. Williamson had been editor of two Masonic journals and was a member of four Masonic bodies in the United States and three in England. At the time of his election he was collaborating "with several white and colored masons in the preparation of an official history of Freemasonry among the American Negroes." He was also a book collector and possessed an extensive library of volumes dealing with this subject.[36]

A year later, Schomburg was responsible for drawing two other men into

35. For a list of members in 1920 see the "ANA Articles of Incorporation"; for a list of members in 1924, see J. W. Cromwell, *The Challenge of the Disfranchised*, ANA Occasional Papers, no. 22 (1924), back cover. These are the only two lists of members that have survived for the period 1920 to 1928. There are forty-two names on the list that appeared in 1920 and forty-eight names on the one that appeared in 1924. See also Robert A. Pelham to "Dear Sir," August 15, 1921, in JWCG/M. For biographical information on Slaughter see Ferris, *The African Abroad*, I, 262; Logan, *Howard University*, 134; and Washington *Afro-American*, March 2–6, 1976, sec. 3, p. 2. For Dent see Pelham to "Dear Sir," August 15, 1921, in JWCG/M.

36. For biographical information on Steward and Williamson, see Steward and Williamson ballots and biographical sketches, in Cromwell Papers, Moorland-Spingarn Research Center. Biographies of Steward can also be found in the first (n.d.), second (1901), fourth (1911), fifth (1916), twenty-fifth (1921), and fortieth (1936) reports of the secretary of the Class of 1896, Harvard College. Each report was published in book form and entitled *Harvard University, Class of 1896*. Williamson's collection of books on the history of Freemasonry among blacks now forms part of the New York Public Library's Schomburg Collection.

the academy, Wendell Phillips Dabney and Arnold Hamilton Maloney. Dabney was owner, editor, and publisher of the *Union*, a black newspaper in Cincinnati, but his chief income was from the office he held in Cincinnati's municipal government, head paymaster of the treasury department. As a young man, he attended Oberlin College but, after a year as a student, he dropped out. A man of varied intellectual interests, Dabney was compiling material for a history of blacks in Cincinnati. Maloney, who was born in the British West Indies, came to the United States in 1904. He earned degrees from Lincoln University in Pennsylvania (A.B.), Columbia University (A.M.), and the General Theological Seminary of the Episcopal Church (B.D.). In 1911, he was ordained into the Episcopal ministry and, for eleven years, headed black congregations in that denomination. Eventually, he became disgusted with the way blacks were treated in the Episcopal Church, and, as a result, he ceased to function as a minister in 1922. After that Maloney began a new career as a lecturer and writer on racial issues.[37]

Sometime between 1920 and 1924 Cameron Chesterfield Alleyne, John Russell Hawkins, and John Mitchell, Jr., entered the academy. Alleyne was born in Barbadoes (British West Indies), came to the United States in 1903, and attended Tuskegee Institute for a year. He entered the ministry of the AMEZ Church and, after serving parishes in the South, New England, and New York State, was elected editor of the *Quarterly Review*, a magazine published by his denomination. Hawkins was the financial secretary of the AME Church. A layman, his job, essentially, was that of business manager and accountant for this important black religious institution. He was also fiscal agent for two of the denomination's schools, Kittrell College in North Carolina and Wilberforce University in Ohio, and sat on their boards of trustees. Hawkins' commitment to higher education and his business skills resulted in his election to the board of trustees of Howard University, a nondenominational institution, supported in part by the United States government. Mitchell, a militant opponent of racial discrimination, had been editor of the Richmond *Planet* since 1884 and was an old friend of both John

37. Information relative to Dabney's and Maloney's candidacies for membership in the ANA is contained in Schomburg to Cromwell, May 22, May 23, October 18, October 24, October 28, November 30, 1923, all in JWCG/M. For biographical information on Dabney, see Yenser (ed.), *Who's Who*, 115; Joseph T. Beavers, Jr., *I Want You to Know Wendell Phillips Dabney* (Mexico, D.F., 1958); and "One Man Newspaper," *Ebony* (February, 1946), 46–47. In 1926 Dabney published a history of the black community in Cincinnati under the title, *Cincinnati's Colored Citizens*. For biographical material on Maloney see Boris (ed.), *Who's Who*, 136, and his autobiography, *Amber Gold: An Adventure in Autobiography* (Boston, 1946).

W. Cromwell and John E. Bruce. He also conducted a small printing business, to which the academy had turned at various times for the printing of occasional papers and stationery.[38]

The ten men who entered the academy between 1920 and 1921 were all persons of ability but, with the exception of Locke, none were primarily intellectuals nor were they involved directly in such important developments in the black community as the Garvey Movement or the Harlem Renaissance. Locke's position as a distinguished academic and as one of the major spokesmen and interpretors of the "New Negro's" artistic and cultural "awakening" made him unique in this group. This is especially curious, since a number of men who had been members of the ANA before 1919 were active Garveyites or prominent figures in the Renaissance. William H. Ferris served for a time as editor and columnist of the *Negro World*, the major publication of the Universal Negro Improvement Association, Marcus Garvey's organization; and John E. Bruce, who also contributed articles to the *Negro World*, held a succession of advisory and administrative posts in the organization. Garvey considered Bruce so valuable a lieutenant that at one time he offered him "the presidency of the American section of the Movement." W. E. B. Du Bois, William H. Ferris, James Weldon Johnson, and Arthur A. Schomburg were members of the academy whose writings and activities contributed significantly to the Harlem Renaissance and influenced the course of its development.[39]

From the time of its establishment, the academy had drawn into its ranks many men who combined some form of literary or scholarly activity with occupations in business, government service, journalism, law, or ministry, but never had a group of recruits, over a comparable period of time, included only one person whose major activity was related to education and scholarship. In spite of the fact that the 1920s formed a decade when the black American community contained a sizable number of creative individ-

38. For biographical information on Alleyne, see William J. Walls, *The African Methodist Episcopal Zion Church* (Charlotte, N.C., 1974), 600–601. For Hawkins see Yenser (ed.), *Who's Who*, 198–201. For Mitchell see Penn, *The Afro-American Press and Its Editors*, 183–187.

39. In 1926 Locke considered the following books his most important written works: *The Negro in New Jersey: State Semi-Centennial Report* (Trenton, N.J., 1913); *Race Contacts and Race Relations* (Washington, D.C., 1916); the "Harlem Number" of *Survey Graphic Magazine* (New York, 1925) of which he was editor; and *The New Negro* (New York, 1925). See also Cronon, *Black Moses*, 35, 46, 47, 48, 69; Reddick, Introduction to "The Bruce Collection," in *Calendar of Manuscripts in the Schomburg Collection*, 165–66; A. A. Schomburg to Locke, September 9, 1924, in Locke Papers.

uals who were qualified to be members of the ANA—men such as Benjamin Brawley, George Washington Carver, Countee Cullen, E. Franklin Frazier, George Edmund Haynes, Langston Hughes, Charles S. Johnson, Claude McKay, Paul Robeson, Alrutheus A. Taylor, Lorenzo Turner, and Walter White—none, except for Locke, was nominated for membership. Could this have been a sign of the refusal by men of this calibre to have anything to do with the ANA? Whatever its cause, it was an unmistakable sign of the organization's decline. Although membership in the ANA, as was true of learned societies such as the American Philosophical Society and the National Academy of Sciences, came by invitation only, before 1920 the organization had been successful in attracting many recruits who were either the possessors of unquestioned reputations as scholarly intellectuals or persons showing promise in that direction. During the years that Cromwell and Schomburg served as presidents of the academy its recruitment policy came to resemble that of a private club. Locke aside, those men who entered the association in the 1920s seem to have been drawn in primarily on the basis of friendship with the officers of the ANA.[40]

The absence of voting records for the membership elections makes it impossible to know how the academy expressed its mind about these men, leaving unanswered such questions as, how many affirmative votes did each receive; how many negative; and how many members failed to vote at all? Given the association's rule that unreturned ballots were to be counted as affirmative votes, lack of interest on the part of the majority of members almost insured a candidate's election.

The one shred of information on membership elections during these years is a letter written in 1922 by William H. Crogman, a founder of the ANA and the president of Clark University in Atlanta, to Francis J. Grimké. After mentioning to his old friend that he had recently received the ballots for Frank R. Steward and Henry A. Williamson, Crogman shared his dissatisfaction with an election process which made it impossible to vote against a man by not casting a ballot. This, the educator explained, made the acad-

---

40. Brawley was a professor of English at Howard University and Morehouse College; Carver, an agricultural scientist on the faculty of Tuskegee Institute; Cullen, a prize-winning poet; Haynes, a sociologist; Johnson, another sociologist, editor of *Opportunity*, the journal of the National Urban League; McKay, a poet, novelist, and magazine editor; Robeson, a lawyer, actor, and concert artist; Frazier, a sociologist, who laid the foundation for the school of social work at Atlanta University; Hughes, a writer and poet; Taylor, a historian who specialized in the history of the Civil War and Reconstruction; Turner, an expert in English literature and African civilization; White, on the staff of the NAACP, a novelist, and the author of articles on race relations and related subjects.

emy's procedure so problematic for him that he had "never been able to act without some mental reservation." When there were moral grounds for rejecting a candidate, he did not hesitate to vote no. The difficulty surfaced on those occasions when his objection related to "qualification or fitness." "If," he wrote, "I have to vote against a man, I would rather, in deference to his own feelings, and in defense of my own, vote against him less abruptly by not voting at all; but the ruling of the Academy does not allow it." This concern, however, was only a preface to sharing with Grimké his reasons for deciding to vote against Williamson. "I don't see," he stated, "how I can consistently vote for Mr. Williamson in keeping with my idea of what the Negro Academy should be and should stand for. I can't for my life see what relation such marvelous achievements in Freemasonry have to do with an organization whose professed aim is literature, art, science and all kindred subjects. If I am in error, please be frank to tell me so." After assuring Grimké that his "chief and only interest" was "that the ideal of the Academy shall not be lowered," Crogman concluded with the request that his letter be kept "strictly confidential."[41]

William H. Crogman was a man of exacting standards morally and intellectually. There were others like him in the academy, but it is doubtful that many scrutinized the candidates for membership with as much concern and care as he did. Francis J. Grimké, a man of equally high standards, was probably one who shared this distinction. For this reason alone, it is unfortunate that Grimké's response to Crogman's letter has not survived. We will never know whether the two men joined forces with other like-minded members to try and keep Williamson out. Or if they did, what the vote on his candidacy was. Whatever the answer to these questions, it is even more significant that Williamson was elected to the academy later that year.

Between 1920 and 1928, the academy experienced a steady loss of members. Three—Roscoe C. Bruce, Arthur U. Craig, and Neval H. Thomas—withdrew sometime between 1920 and 1924. Bruce, who was superintendent of Washington's black public schools for thirteen years, left the city after resigning his position in 1921. His final months in office were bitterly controversial, a circumstance which probably caused him to sever most ties with Washington after he left. Craig, an electrical engineer employed in New York City's architectural division, served along with Robert T. Browne and Carter G. Woodson on the committee to revise the society's constitu-

41. Crogman to Grimké, November 20, 1922, in Woodson, *Works of Francis J. Grimké*, IV, 356.

tion. With the rejection of his committee's proposals on membership he may have judged the academy as unable to take the necessary steps to insure a meaningful future for itself. Nevel H. Thomas, a teacher in Washington's black high school, was a militant foe of racial discrimination. After 1920, his teaching and the District of Columbia's chapter of the NAACP were his chief involvements.[42]

Six other academy members were removed by death. They included Theophilus G. Steward, a retired military chaplain who taught history at Wilberforce University (1924); the journalist John E. Bruce (1924); Robert H. Terrell, a judge of the municipal court in the District of Columbia (1925); James E. K. Aggrey, a former faculty member at Livingstone College in North Carolina, who, at the time of his death, was assistant vice-principal of Prince of Wales College, Achimota, the Gold Coast (1927); John W. Cromwell (1927); and Matthew Anderson, pastor of Berean Presbyterian Church in Philadelphia (1928). In spite of the fact that many of these men were aged and some, as a result, less active in the ANA than they previously had been, all were committed members of the academy who believed in its principles, and who supported it financially and by personal involvement. With the exception of Aggrey, all of them had been founding members and friends of Alexander Crummell. Steward, Bruce, Aggrey, Cromwell, and Anderson had repeatedly served the association as officers, speakers at its general meetings, through the recruitment of new members, and as promoters of its work. They were all prominent and, in several cases, distinguished members of their professions and communities. Their deaths—and this was especially true with regard to Cromwell—deprived the ANA of some of its most important and influential members.

Throughout the 1920s the academy was also losing members through a process of attrition. Although the organization listed forty-two members in 1920, and forty-eight in 1924, these rosters must have combined, in the most generous way, the names of active members with those who were purely nominal. Between 1920 and 1928 a sizable number of the persons on the two lists simply ceased to involve themselves with the ANA. Some—it is impossible to say how many—continued to pay their dues, but otherwise

42. Bruce's difficulties during his last two years in office can be traced in the Washington newspapers. See especially issues from April, 1919, to November, 1921. The *Bee*, one of Washington's black newspapers, provided the most detailed, if not the most unbiased, coverage.

Bruce, Craig, and Thomas were listed on the ANA's membership roster that is found in the organization's "Articles of Incorporation," but they are omitted from the roster that appears on the back cover of Occasional Paper no. 22, published in 1924.

ignored the existence of the group. Those members who reduced or elimi-nated their involvement with the society did so primarily because they had lost interest in what was increasingly a problem-plagued organization, which gave every sign of having no future.[43]

There were other influences which also worked to reduce or eliminate the members' interest in the academy. Increasingly, after 1920, many of them joined "mainstream" learned societies. This was especially true of those who were academics. Others, including some of the ANA's most active members, were deeply involved in the work of the NAACP and the National Urban League. At a time when so many members of the academy were being drawn into a wide circle of organizational affiliations, the society con-tinued to maintain its restrictive membership policies, without in any way attempting to find new ways of sustaining itself. This rigid and unexperi-mentative posture meant that people who were committed to the promotion of artistic, literary, and scholarly activity in the black community, but who were ineligible for membership in the ANA, had no way of associating themselves with the academy. In most cases, especially if they were not Washingtonians, they probably did not even know of the society's existence. It is likely that Carter G. Woodson's organization, the ASNLH, which had a more flexible and imaginative membership policy, was able to attract many of these people. Dominance by its members living in Washington and a pre-dominantly eastern membership also hampered the growth of the society. Although there was a certain logic to the argument that the major officers of the academy should be Washingtonians, this implicit policy must have quickly cooled the interest of many members who lived in other cities. And, since active members who lived outside Washington had to be able to travel there for annual meetings, centering the group's life in the national capital inevitably produced the predominantly eastern membership. The failure to significantly alter this pattern—one mid-summer meeting in New York was the only variation—kept the ANA from developing a truly national membership.

Though some members abandoned the society quietly, others were vocal about their disappointment with it. Among those in the latter category were Archibald H. Grimké, his brother Francis, and Carter G. Woodson. Of the three, Arthur A. Schomburg found Woodson the most troublesome. In a letter written in 1923, he shared this opinion with John W. Cromwell.

43. "ANA Articles of Incorporation"; A. H. Grimké, *The Shame of America*, ANA Occa-sional Papers, no. 21 (1924), back cover.

"Something," Schomburg insisted, "must be done to counteract the effects of Dr. Woodson who is striving to break down the A.[cademy]. He has alienated the G.'s [Grimkés] who always want to either rule or ruin."[44]

After Cromwell's successful campaign against Archibald H. Grimké's re-election as president in 1919, the two brothers had good reason for less interest in the academy. Both remained members of the organization, though neither ever again held an office or delivered a paper. They were critical observers of the unsuccessful efforts of Cromwell and Schomburg to strengthen the ANA, which, after 1923, entered into such a precipitous decline that the Grimké administration seemed by comparison a "golden age." During the year Cromwell headed the ANA, Archibald and Francis Grimké expressed much of their negativism about the society through attacks on its president. In 1924 Arthur A. Schomburg reminded Cromwell that "the Grimkés tried to pull your work down, but I would not stand by it." The two brothers were members of the Association for the Study of Negro Life and History and friends of its director, Carter G. Woodson, whom they respected and deeply admired for the commitment and scholarship he brought to his work as head of the association and as editor of the *Journal of Negro History*.[45]

There were probably several reasons for Woodson's enmity toward the academy. One might have been the society's refusal in 1921 to reform its membership structure. Woodson had been the most influential member of the three-man committee that worked for a year and a half to produce a new constitution for the ANA. The committee believed that, if implemented, their proposals would have enabled the organization to grow in size, increase its revenues, and improve the quality of its publications. In turning down the amendments on membership, the ANA rejected one of the most essential reforms recommended by Woodson's committee. As a result Woodson might well have concluded that the members of the academy had no serious interest in attempting to strengthen the society. As the ASNLH, which Woodson headed, became an increasingly potent force in the American intellectual community, he probably felt that the academy had outlived its usefulness. Whatever the reason for his negative feelings, according to

44. Schomburg to Cromwell, October 24, 1923, March 5, 1924, in SC/MSRC.

45. Schomburg to Cromwell, March 5, 1924, in SC/MSRC. Archibald H. Grimké's involvement with the ASNLH is mentioned en passant in the obituary sketch published by the *Journal of Negro History*, XV (October, 1930), 267–68. Similar information on Francis J. Grimké is contained in the Introduction to volume I of Woodson (ed.), *Works of Francis J. Grimké*, xx.

Schomburg, they took the form of actions and statements both hostile and harmful to the ANA. To people such as the Grimkés, who believed Woodson had made his association into one of the country's most effective sources of unbiased scholarship about blacks, his judgment of the academy was authoritative.[46]

Jesse E. Moorland's behavior was typical of those members whose withdrawals were quiet, but equally damaging to the society. As late as 1919, the year he protested the candidacy of Robert A. Pelham and the executive committee's invitation to A. Philip Randolph to deliver a paper, Moorland was an active member of the academy. Perhaps it was because his protests were futile or even because his two intimate friends, Archibald and Francis Grimké, ceased to be officers in 1919, but in any case Moorland was no longer an active member after that year. In February, 1924, when they encountered each other at a meeting, Schomburg told Moorland "that the Academy needed his presence[,] that it would be a shame to let Prof. Cromwell, and a few faithful carry the burden." The president of the ANA was certain his comments had affected Moorland and, in his next letter to Cromwell, Schomburg expressed his belief that "we will have him out [with?] us next year." Possibly they might have, but for the fact that when Moorland inquired in December "what the Academy had prepared for the year," Schomburg had to tell him that "he had no knowledge of what they were doing, except for Cromwell, there was silence." That same month, John R. Clifford of West Virginia wrote Cromwell asking, "Is it [the Academy] dead or dying?" Some members had already answered this question for themselves. "The members from New York think the Academy is dead," Schomburg told Cromwell in a letter dated "Columbus Day," 1924, implying that he had thought so too. The judgment was premature, but not by much. The ANA had a few years of enfeebled existence before it, but the end was drawing near.[47]

During the years Cromwell and Schomburg headed the academy, very lit-

46. Carter Goodwin Woodson was elected a member of the academy in late 1913 or early 1914 (see Woodson to ANA, December 18, 1913, in JWCG/M). Though he sat on the committee on constitutional revision, Woodson was never an officer of the organization. He delivered two papers before the academy, "Educating the Negro before 1860," in December, 1914 (Proceedings, 199) and "Anti-Slavery Agitation prior to the Advent of Douglass," in December, 1916 (Washington *Bee*, December 30, 1916, p. 1). For an excellent life sketch, which reflects the intensity of his commitment to scholarship, black American history, and the ASNLH see *Journal of Negro History*, XXXV (July, 1950), 334–48.

47. Schomburg to Cromwell, February 25, December 5, "Columbus Day" [October 8], 1924, all in SC/MSRC; Clifford to Cromwell, December 4, 1924, in JWCG/M.

tle was done to build ties with black intellectuals outside the United States, or to maintain those the academy had established earlier. This was all the more remarkable since the years 1920 to 1928 were filled with signs of growing unrest and rising racial consciousness among Africans, as well as among peoples of African descent in the Caribbean and Central America. The most basic cause was World War I, which had demonstrated the many vulnerabilities of the major colonial powers, thus encouraging the release of pent-up hostilities. Most often, the black colonials who gave expression to this new mood were members of the educated classes. They pressed whites for a larger role in their local governments, greater educational opportunities for their people, and increased respect for native cultures. The academy never attempted to connect itself with these developments by electing some of the "new black voices" corresponding members. No "distinguished foreigner's" name was even put in nomination.[48]

Both Cromwell and Schomburg were intellectually committed to expanding the society's contacts with foreign blacks, but neither man did much to encourage the society to take any new initiatives in this area. Schomburg, who was quickly frustrated by the demands the office of president placed upon him, rarely turned his attention to anything other than annual meetings or recruitment. During his one term as head of the academy, Cromwell was preoccupied with basic issues such as the revitalization of the annual meeting and constitutional reform. However, on one occasion, he did demonstrate how much he desired to link the ANA with the new forces that were stirring black Africa.

In February, 1920, James E. K. Aggrey was appointed to the Phelps-Stokes Fund's commission to investigate the work of mission and government schools serving nonwhite Africans. Aggrey, a native of West Africa's Gold Coast, had lived in the United States since he was twenty-three. He left Africa in 1898 to attend the AMEZ Church's Livingstone College in North Carolina, from which he received an A.B. degree in 1902. After his graduation, Aggrey joined the faculty of his alma mater and its sister institution, Hood Theological Seminary. For eighteen years he taught English, Latin,

---

48. Two foreign blacks, Duse Mohamed and Chief Amoah III, did address the academy during the years Schomburg headed the organization. Mohamed, a corresponding member and editor of the London-based *African Times and Orient Review*, visited the United States in 1921–1922. He presented a paper, "The Necessity of a Chair in Negro History in Our Colleges," at the twenty-fifth annual meeting in December, 1921. Seven years later, Chief Amoah III, a West African leader, was invited to address the thirty-second annual meeting in 1928. (Washington *Post*, December 28, December 29, 1921; Washington *Tribune*, December 28, 1928.)

and New Testament Greek in these two schools. In 1914 Aggrey began taking courses at Columbia University during his summer vacations. Two years
later, he registered as a candidate for a degree and began work which he
hoped would lead to a Ph.D. in sociology. According to his biographer, Aggrey's appointment to the commission was due to his "African origins, his
marked ability as an observer, his broad training in sociology and education, and his constructive attitudes towards the perplexing problems of race
relations." The various colonial governments in Africa promised to cooperate with the commission and its expenses were to be shared by the major
European and American missionary societies and the Phelps-Stokes Fund.
Cromwell was aware of the great influence the commission might have on
African education, and of the unique and crucial role Aggrey would play as
its only black member. He also saw it as an opportunity to forge new links
between the academy and African intellectuals.[49]

Shortly before the commission left for Africa, Cromwell sent a letter to
Aggrey designating him a representative and agent of the academy during
his travels. After pointing out to the African educator that it was the "ANA
. . . and the race" who were honored by his appointment, Cromwell issued
the following charge to Aggrey:

While you are making observations as to conditions . . . you are particularly com-
missioned to seek after and interest here and there, the brightest minds you will find
willing and eager to make contributions to our store of knowledge pertaining to
our racial potentialities, both here and throughout the world. In the discharge of
this duty I trust you will leave no stone unturned, for much will grow out what you
observe and report from time to time.

Owing to the urgency of this letter I cannot enter in details[.] I pray you therefore
be governed by the spirit that, I am sure, you will interpret from what you have
noted in our deliberations. Always you may count on the prayers of every member of
the Academy as you journey among the sources of civilization and culture.[50]

One result of Aggrey's work with the Phelps-Stokes commission was his
emergence as a major interpreter of black Africa to missionaries, educators,
and government officials, especially those who were British and American.
There is no evidence, however, that between 1920 and his death in 1927, he
did anything to build or strengthen the academy's connections with Africa.
Cromwell's letter, which had no practical result, was the association's last
attempt to involve itself, in more than a perfunctory way, with black intellectuals in another country.

49. Smith, *Aggrey of Africa*, 144.
50. Cromwell to Aggrey, July 27, 1920 [copy of draft], in JWCG/M.

IX *Men of the Academy*

The ninety-nine men who, at various times, were members of the American Negro Academy were a complex, diverse, exciting, and creative group. The details of their lives and careers illustrate the skill and perseverance with which many talented black Americans sought during the early part of the twentieth century to obtain an education, build careers, wield social power, and make a contribution to society. It is difficult to appreciate the significance of their efforts and achievements without recalling that they lived and worked in the midst of a people who denigrated their work, disregarded their achievements, and frequently denied that black intellectuals even existed.

Of the ninety members of the American Negro Academy whose birthplaces are known, fifty-seven were born in the South, nineteen in the North, and fourteen in foreign countries. Forty-one of those who were southerners by birth came from one of the south Atlantic states, while the other sixteen were natives of states in the deep south (two), the so-called border states (eight), the District of Columbia (four); and Texas (two). Eight of the nineteen northerners were born in Ohio; five in Pennsylvania; three in New Jersey; and one each in Connecticut, Massachusetts, and New York. The fourteen foreign-born members—all of whom became citizens of the United States—were from the British West Indies (six); Liberia (two); the Gold Coast of West Africa (one); British Guiana (one); Canada (one); the Danish West Indies (one); Haiti (one); and Puerto Rico (one).

At no point during its thirty-one years of existence was the academy composed exclusively of one age group. When the association was formed in 1897, six of its thirty-six members were fifty years of age or older, twenty were in their thirties and forties, and four were in their twenties. Sixteen years later, the age of its membership had shifted upward: seven of its thirty-six members were sixty or above, twenty were in their fifties and forties, four were in their thirties, and one was twenty-nine. The academy achieved its most balanced age spread between 1913 and 1920. In the latter year, its membership was divided in the following way: seven members were in their seventies, eight in their sixties, nine each in their fifties and forties, and six in their thirties. By 1924, the group's membership was split between those sixty years of age or older, and those fifty-nine years of age or younger. There were twenty-two men in the first category, most of whom were in their sixties, and twenty-one in the second, over four-fifths of whom were in their fifties and forties. The oldest was eighty-three, and the youngest thirty-six.

Only for a short period after 1897 did the academy have a sizable number of members in their twenties and thirties. In the year it was founded, men in these two age groups constituted a third of the membership, and during its first six years, several of them held important offices. However, from 1903 until the ANA disappeared in 1929, men in their forties, fifties, and sixties filled most of the society's offices and the majority of the positions on the executive committee. And by 1913 the largest group of members ranged in age from forty-one to seventy-two. The aging of the initial membership group, as well as the standards of admission for this society of "authors, scholars, artists, and those distinguished in other walks of life," made it inevitable that a significant proportion of members would be mature men. But the association's heavy attrition rate meant that there were always new places to be filled. In spite of this, the organization drew in relatively few men in their twenties and thirties. Since the period between 1897 and 1927 was a time when the number of black college and university graduates steadily increased, and when many younger black Americans were gaining reputations for excellence in several academic fields, the graphic arts, literature, and the theater, this was a sign of the organization's decline. The overall age pattern among members of the academy suggests an organization in some ways unable, and in some ways unwilling, to incorporate younger men who could have met its standards.[1]

Throughout the thirty-one years of the ANA's existence there were only small shifts in the size of its membership. The list of members published by

---

1. Franklin, *From Slavery to Freedom*, 372–82, 417.

the society in 1897 contained thirty-six names, but by 1898 the size of the roster had dropped to twenty-eight. Two years later, the number was back to thirty-six again. This figure must have remained constant several years, for in 1908 the *Handbook of Learned Societies* described the group as having "about 35 active members." A year later, the Washington *Evening Star* counted thirty-eight. The failure of the group to reach capacity was a great disappointment to its friends and supporters. No one was more disappointed than John W. Cromwell, who noted, in an article written in 1910 for *Horizon* magazine, that although "its [the academy's] membership is restricted to fifty, there have never been so many as forty members at one time." In 1913, the *African Times and Orient Review* printed a list of academicians that, for some reason, omitted the names of four persons—attributing only thirty-two members to the association—when it actually had thirty-six. By 1920, the year it was incorporated, the academy's membership had grown to forty-two. The last membership list published by the ANA, which appeared in 1924, contained forty-eight names—the organization's peak in terms of numbers. The association never attained its constitutional capacity of fifty, and, after 1924, experienced a steady loss of members. In all, ninety-nine men (excluding the twelve corresponding members) were associated at various times with the academy, a fact which speaks loudly about the ANA's inability to sustain the interest of almost half the men associated with it.[2]

Forty-seven of the ninety-nine members of the academy lived and worked in more than one part of the country as adults. This was especially true of the clergy, whatever their denomination, though similar patterns of mobility were part of the careers of a sizable number of educators. Altogether, only thirty-two members of the society spent all of the years between 1897 and 1929 in one place. At various times during the life of the society, thirty-six of its members lived in the District of Columbia; twenty-seven in the south Atlantic states; twenty-four in the mid-Atlantic states; twelve in the middle west (including Ohio); five in New England; four in the border states; and one in the far west. In terms of where its members lived and worked, the ANA was essentially an east coast organization.

The statistics on officeholding in the ANA make it indisputably clear that the association was dominated and run by members who lived in Wash-

2. Proceedings, 61, 79; Hillyer (ed.), *Union League Directory*, 148; *Handbook of Learned Societies and Institutions: America* (Washington, D.C., 1908), 30–31; Washington *Evening Star*, December 26, 1909, p. 2; *Horizon*, V (February, 1910), 11–12.

ington. During the twenty-one years from 1897 to 1918, nine of the twelve men elected to office five or more times were residents of the national capital, as were all of the members elected to the executive committee, with the sole exception of W. E. B. Du Bois. There was little change in this pattern after 1919. During the last years of the academy's existence, seven of the twelve members elected to office three or more times were from Washington. However, three of the eleven men who at various times served on the executive committee lived in other cities. Given the continued, and indeed heightened, crisis in membership interest and morale from 1922 on, it is probable that this reflected a dwindling of interest in the organization on the part of local members, rather than a movement to broaden geographical representation on this board. And, since only one of the three members of the executive committee from outside the District of Columbia, Joseph J. France of Portsmouth, Virginia, lived close enough to Washington to be able to attend meetings without incurring great personal expense and a loss of time from his work, from 1919 to 1928 the ANA was probably run by an even smaller group of Washingtonians.

The issues, which from time to time divided the membership of the ANA into opposing groups, were largely organizational, that is, they all turned around the question of why the society was not living up to the hopes and expectations of its founders and supporters. In a variety of forms, this basic concern recurred constantly. Yet, despite the frustrations and disappointments they experienced, the active membership continued, at least until 1929, to pursue the original three goals outlined in the academy's constitution—the publication of scholarly work, support of efforts to educate black youth, and the preservation of "valuable data and the works of Negro Authors."

The social origins of the ninety-nine men who held membership in the academy were diverse. Of the eighty-two for whom detailed biographical sketches exist, seventeen were born into slavery. This group included Walter Henderson Brooks, John Edward Bruce, George Wylie Clinton, George William Cook, Archibald H. Grimké, Francis J. Grimké, Lafayette Hershaw, Kelly Miller, John Mitchell, Jr., Inman Edward Page, Charles Henry Parrish, Daniel Jackson Sanders, William S. Scarborough, William A. Sinclair, Alexander Walters, Booker T. Washington, and Richard Robert Wright, Sr. However, only ten of the seventeen—W. H. Brooks, J. E. Bruce, G. W. Cook, A. H. Grimké, F. J. Grimké, I. E. Page, D. J. Sanders, W. S. Scarborough, B. T. Washington, and R. R. Wright, Sr.—were slaves for five or more years. Few members of the academy experienced slavery directly, but even for those who did, the acquaintance with the institution was relatively brief.

On the whole, the academy was made up of men from humble, impoverished beginnings, who, by a combination of ability, personal effort, and luck had moved into professions and roles where members of their race were few in number. Most were also new entrants into the small, but expanding black upper classes.

There were, however, several members of the ANA who came from a different background. James E. K. Aggrey's father, a man of secure but modest income, exercised great influence in the black West African community. By occupation, the elder Aggrey was only a clerk in the employ of one of the Gold Coast's leading merchants, but through his possession of the hereditary office of *Omankyiame*, that is, "Spokesman or Mouth-piece of the Chief," he was one of the most influential elders in the Council of Amonu IV, the Paramount Chief of Anambu. Solomon Carter Fuller was another foreign-born member from a prominent family. His father was a Liberian coffee planter and government official. Two of the black American community's most prominent families were represented in the ANA by Roscoe Conkling Bruce and Charles C. Cook. R. C. Bruce's father was Blanche Kelso Bruce, former United States senator from Mississippi, a federal government officeholder, and a lawyer in Washington. John F. Cook, the father of C. C. Cook, was described at various times as "the largest taxpayer of his race" in the country and as "the wealthiest Negro in the District of Columbia." In addition to carrying on his numerous business activities, J. F. Cook served terms as an alderman and tax collector in the District of Columbia. John Wesley Edward Bowen was the son of Edward Bowen, a prosperous free black contractor in New Orleans. The fathers of Peter H. Clark, James Weldon Johnson, and Charles Victor Roman had each built up modest but secure incomes from their respective activities as barber, hotel waiter, and freight hauler. Johnson's mother also added to the family income by teaching school. The occupation of William H. Ferris' parents is unknown, but the family was not poor. Perhaps this was due, in part, to his maternal grandfather, Enoch Jefferson, whom Ferris described as "a prosperous and highly respected farmer of Wilmington, Delaware." Arnold Hamilton Maloney's parents were both prominent, influential members of the black community in Trinidad, British West Indies, where his mother taught school and his father was a "successful merchant . . . builder[,] and contractor." Three other members of the academy, Thomas Montgomery Gregory, Frank Rudolph Steward, and Richard Robert Wright, Jr., were the sons of distinguished educators.[3]

The college and university backgrounds of the eighty-six members of the ANA for whom biographical data is available fall into three patterns: those who attended black institutions solely; those who attended black and white institutions; and those who attended white institutions solely. There were twenty men in the first category; thirty-three in the second; and thirty-three in the third. Eight of the men—namely, John Edward Bruce, Peter Humphries Clark, Paul Laurence Dunbar, John Mitchell, Jr., Robert A. Pelham, Alexander Walters, and Henry Albro Williamson—possessed only a secondary school education or were, as Bruce described himself, "self-educated."[4]

Fifty-three or 62 percent of the eighty-six with college or university training received all or parts of their higher education in institutions that to all intents and purposes only existed to serve blacks. Many of the members of the academy who graduated from these institutions were southerners for whom these schools were close, familiar, and not prohibitively expensive. This, however, was not true for W. E. B. Du Bois, a graduate of Fisk University who was born and reared in western Massachusetts; for Charles Victor Roman, a native of Pennsylvania who earned his medical degree at Meharry Medical College for Negroes; for Arnold Hamilton Maloney, a West Indian who graduated from Lincoln University in Pennsylvania; or numerous others. For most blacks, whether they were northern, southern, or foreign born, black schools were the only educational institutions consistently open to them. Only a small number of qualified blacks were able to gain entry to predominantly white institutions and, once admitted, they often lacked the financial resources to complete their degree programs. During the late nineteenth and early twentieth centuries, educated blacks were a relatively small

3. Smith, *Aggrey of Africa*, 20–26; records in Alumni Office, Boston University, Boston, Massachusetts; *DAB*, II, 180–81; G. Smith Wormley, "Educators of the First Half-Century of Public Schools of the District of Columbia," *Journal of Negro History*, XVII (April, 1932), 138–40; Green, *The Secret City*, 91, 133; Washington *Bee*, August 27, 1910, p. 4; Meier, *Negro Thought*, 211–12; Simmons, *Men of Mark*, 374; Eugene Levy, *James Weldon Johnson: Black Leader, Black Voice* (Chicago, 1973), 3–21; *Journal of Negro History*, XX (January, 1935), 116–17; Boris (ed.), *Who's Who*, 65, 81, 136, 231; Maloney, *Amber Gold*; F. R. Steward election ballot and biographical sketch, in Cromwell Papers, Moorland-Spingarn Research Center; R. R. Wright, Jr., *Eighty-Seven Years Behind the Black Curtain* (Philadelphia, 1965).

4. There are five members of the ANA for whom I have no educational information: Robert Wellington Bagnall, J. Max Barber, Thomas M. Dent, Joseph J. France, Freeman Henry Morris Murray.

minority within their racial community and the nation, but those who had received all of their higher education in white institutions were a minority within a minority.

Perhaps the only group of educated black Americans even more unique were those who had been able to include in their formative education a period of study abroad. At least ten members of the academy possessed this distinction. Three years after his graduation in 1862 from the Philadelphia Institute for Colored Youth, John Henry Smyth spent a difficult and disappointing year in London studying acting. In 1866 poverty and discouragement forced a return to America, where Smyth sought other lines of development. While still an adolescent, Owen Meredith Waller became a protégé of the Anglican monastic, Richard E. Benson. As a result, in 1880, when he was twelve, Waller's family consented to his removal to Oxford, England, where he attended St. John's Classical School of St. John's Hall. After seven years in this institution, Waller received, "by examination," the degree of Associate of Arts from Oxford University, and returned to the United States.[5]

The experience of studying abroad was more conventional for the other members. After his graduation from Cornell University in 1890, Charles C. Cook traveled in Europe and attended lectures in the Universities of Edinburgh, Oxford, and Heidelburg. In 1895, Arthur U. Craig graduated from the University of Kansas' School of Electrical Engineering and became the first black American degree holder in his field. That same year Craig began a period of European study under engineers in England and Sweden. One of Alexander Crummell's marks of distinction in the eyes of both his black and white associates was the A.B. he earned at Queen's College, Cambridge University, where he was a student from 1848 to 1853. A grant from the Slater Fund enabled W. E. B. Du Bois to attend the University of Berlin from 1892 to 1894. While there, he studied economics, history, and sociology under Adolf Wagner, Heinrich von Treitschke, Max Weber, Rudolph von Gneist, and Gustav Schmoller. Carter Godwin Woodson spent a semester studying history at the Sorbonne in Paris before going on to do graduate work at the University of Chicago and Harvard University. Solomon Carter Fuller, one of the first blacks to enter the field of psychiatry, continued his training in Germany after receiving a medical degree from Boston University in 1897. He was a student of Professors E. Kraeplin and A. Alpheimer at the Psychi-

5. Simmons, *Men of Mark*, 873–77; Washington *Colored American*, June 20, 1903, pp. 1, 5.

atric Clinic of the University of Munich, and of Professors Bellinger and Schmaus at the Pathological Institute of Munich.[6]

Other members of the academy who had the opportunity to study abroad worked equally hard to gain the most comprehensive training for work in their chosen fields. John Wesslay Hoffman, who graduated from Michigan Agricultural College in 1895, continued his studies at Canada's Ontario Agricultural College. From Canada he went to Denmark where he was a student observer at the government biological station in Copenhagen. Alain L. Locke's receipt of a Rhodes Scholarship in 1907 made it possible for the young graduate of Harvard University to study philosophy at Oxford University from 1907 to 1910, and, the following year, Locke continued his studies at the University of Berlin. Richard Robert Wright, Jr., after earning a graduate degree in theology from the University of Chicago, studied two years in Germany, attending lectures in 1903 at the University of Berlin and in 1904 at the University of Leipzig.[7]

The knowledge, experience, and insight these men gained from time spent outside the United States often added to their store of professional skills, but inevitably they forced a broadening of their frames of reference as individuals, and especially as black men seeking to secure a respected place for themselves and their people in a hostile, racist society. They could not help but become more conscious of such universal realities as cultural, ethnic, and class differences. And even the least intellectually curious was touched by the new currents of thought being expressed in the ideas of Marx, Freud, and the various forms of European radicalism. For many, time spent in England and continental universities also provided opportunities for meeting and exchanging ideas with their counterparts—in age and aspirations—from African, Asian, and Latin American countries. Such encounters constituted one part of the developing dialogue between intellectuals in those colonial areas which were growing increasingly restive under the political dominance and economic exploitation of the European powers. Study abroad deepened these young blacks' understanding of their native country, often brought them to a greater intellectual sophistication, and frequently

6. Washington *Bee*, August 27, 1910, p. 4; Nichols and Crogman (eds.), *Progress of a Race*, 354–55; Walter B. Hayson, "Alexander Crummell," *Southern Missioner*, X (January, 1899), 1; Broderick, *W. E. B. Du Bois*, 26–32; Aptheker (ed.), *Correspondence of W. E. B. Du Bois*, I, 10–29; *Journal of Negro History*, XXXV (July, 1950), 344; Boris (ed.), *Who's Who*, 70; and *Crisis*, IV (May, 1913), 18.

7. Washington *Colored American*, October 7, 1899, p. 1, and Mather (ed.), *Who's Who*, 138, 294; *Journal of Negro History*, XXXIX (October, 1954), 323–33.

provided opportunities for conceptualizing the positive and negative aspects of being men of African origins, who were, by culture and birth, minority members of white, culturally European societies. To the degree that their travels and studies added to their professional skills, as well as their insight and wisdom about the world, they were stronger leaders in the various organizations and movements with which they were connected.

The ninety-nine members of the academy were engaged in a variety of occupations. Almost all of them were professionals, and slightly over a quarter were active in more than one profession or work activity. The reason for this was usually either the need for additional income, or personal interest, or both. In terms of numbers, the fifty persons who had been or were directly engaged in educational work constituted the largest segment of the society's membership. This was, of course, only natural, since the goals of the ANA appealed most strongly to educated men with intellectual interests and a strong sense of racial pride. In the black community, such persons were usually teachers, essentially the only profession, other than the ministry, which promised blacks with a college or university background predictable job mobility and a reasonably secure income. Twenty-eight of the educators associated with the ANA were primarily involved in higher education; twenty did most of their work in secondary schools; and two were theological seminary professors.[8]

Thirty-one of the ninety-nine members were clergy and, as such, composed the second largest occupational group in the organization. Seventeen combined the role of clergyman with other work—in most cases, some form of educational activity. Sixteen of the clergy were associated with three all-black denominations—the African Methodist Episcopal Church, the African Methodist Episcopal Zion Church, and the Negro Baptist Churches. The ANA counted as members nine ministers of the first denomination; three of the second; and three of the third. With the exception of the Roman Catholic Church, all of the predominantly white denominations with a

8. The following quotation from August Meier's *Negro Thought in America, 1880–1915,* is particularly germane to the chapter's discussion of the occupations in which members of the academy were engaged: "Most Negro . . . college educated individuals [in] the late 19th and early 20th century [were to be] found in the ranks of the professions. . . . Actually the number of professional people was extremely small. In 1900 they numbered somewhat over 80,000, or about 1.2 per-cent of the gainfully employed population. As late as 1910, though their numbers more than doubled during the decade, only 2.5 per-cent of employed Southern Negroes and 3 per-cent among Northern Negroes were in the professions, and this number included many ministers and teachers who lacked a college or high school education" (p. 207).

sizable black constituency were represented in the society. Five of the fifteen other clergy were Episcopal; four were Congregational; four were Presbyterian; one was connected with the Methodist Episcopal Church, North; and one was a minister of the Church of the Moravian Brethren, a group which had only a tiny percentage of black members.

The AME, AMEZ, and Baptist clergy for whom the activities and goals of the academy had an appeal tended to be the better educated, more cosmopolitan ministers in their denominations. They were also religious leaders who felt comfortable operating outside ecclesiastical settings. A number had functioned either as editor of a church newspaper or as an educator in a denominationally run school. Such work brought them into contact with blacks engaged in similar endeavors outside the church. Typical examples were Levi Jenkins Coppin, Benjamin F. Lee, and Richard R. Wright, Jr., all of whom served at one time as editor of the *AME Church Review*. Churchmen-educators included Theophilus G. Steward, professor of history, logic, and French at Wilberforce University; Charles H. Parrish, founder and head of Eckstein Institute in Kentucky; and Albert W. Pegues, professor of theology at Shaw University. Several ministers in the black churches also had a history of leadership or active participation in broadly based secular organizations, which included large cross sections of the black community. When Alexander Walters was elected to membership in the academy, he was not only a bishop in the AMEZ Church, but president of the Afro-American Council, the leading black protest organization, and a major figure in black Republican politics. AME bishop John Hurst was a trustee of Howard University, a member of the NAACP's national board, and chairman of its Spingarn Award Committee.[9]

The ministers connected with the predominantly white churches were, on the whole, better educated than their AME, AMEZ, and Baptist counterparts. They also tended to be among the more race-conscious black clergy in their denominations. Many were pastors of elite congregations whose members occupied political, social, and economic leadership roles in their communities. Most of these ministers, along with their parishioners, had a

9. The biographical sections of the following books are the most helpful in terms of getting a picture of educational levels and career experiences among the clergy of the black denominations: Richard R. Wright, Jr., *Bishops of the AME Church* (Nashville, 1963); Wright (ed.), *Centennial Encyclopedia of the AME Church*; Bradley, *History of the A. M. E. Zion Church*; Walls, *The AMEZ Church*; Samuel William Bacote (ed.), *Who's Who among the Colored Baptists of the United States* (Kansas City, Mo., 1913).

strong commitment to respectable racial protest. Consequently, they gave their most enthusiastic support to organizations, such as the ANA, which affirmed the necessity of carefully reasoned attacks on racism. Alexander Crummell and Francis J. Grimké, two founders of the society, were classic examples of the type. All of the clergy, however, whether connected with black or predominantly white churches, possessed a strong, religiously grounded belief in the role of educated black leadership as the essential force in the struggle of black Americans for social justice.[10]

Fifteen members of the academy were journalists, but only three, J. Max Barber, John E. Bruce, and John Mitchell, Jr. ever made journalism their major work. In part, this was because several were editors of service publications, that is, newspapers or magazines that existed primarily to carry news and communications of interest to a specific organization and its supporters. These included: *Crisis*, a journal edited by W. E. B. Du Bois and sponsored by the NAACP; the *AME Recorder* and the Garveyite publication, *The Negro World*, both of which William H. Ferris served for brief periods as editor; and Carter G. Woodson's *Journal of Negro History*, the ASNLH's publication. However, men like John R. Clifford, editor of the Martinsburg *Pioneer Press*; John W. Cromwell, sometime editor of the Washington *Record*; and Wendell P. Dabney, editor of the Cincinnati *Union*, had a different reason for being part-time journalists. These newspapermen loved their work, but knew they stood little chance of surviving economically unless they supplemented their income by holding other jobs.[11]

A similar situation existed for the academy's nine members who were lawyers. Only four of them were full-time legal practitioners. It was certainly not a coincidence that three of the four—Frank R. Steward of Pittsburg, Samuel L. Williams of Chicago, and Butler R. Wilson of Boston—were northerners. The fourth, William A. Hawkins, lived and worked in

10. Otey Scruggs's discussion of Alexander Crummell in his essay, *We the Children of Africa in This Land*, affirms my description of this Episcopal minister. C. G. Woodson's introductions to vols. I, II, and IV of the *Papers of Francis J. Grimké*, which he edited, do the same in regard to this Presbyterian clergyman.

11. Bruce and Mitchell were full-time journalists for most of their adult lives. Barber was a full-time journalist from 1904 to 1907, when he was editor of *Voice of the Negro*, and from 1907 to 1908 when he edited the Chicago *Conservator*.

Other men who edited service publications were Hightower T. Kealing (*AME Church Review*), Levi Jenkins Coppin (*AME Church Review*), Daniel Jackson Sanders (*Africo-American Presbyterian*), Henry P. Slaughter (*Odd-Fellows Journal*), and Richard R. Wright, Jr. (*AME Church Review*).

Maryland's Baltimore County, the most urbanized and most liberal section of a border state.

There were eleven medical practitioners in the academy: six physicians, two dentists, one neurologist-psychiatrist, and a chiropodist. Two of the physicians, Charles V. Roman and Herbert C. Scurlock, as well as the neurologist-psychiatrist Solomon C. Fuller, were also educators. Roman taught in the Meharry Medical College for Negroes, Scurlock in the Howard University Medical School, and Fuller at Boston University. William A. Sinclair, also a physician, was a unique member of this group in that he did little medical work. Sinclair preferred to spend most of his time in organizational activities for black protest groups such as the Constitution League and the NAACP. The other seven men practiced full time.[12]

A number of other occupations were represented in the organization. There were nine government employees (seven employed on the federal level and two by municipalities); four executives of the NAACP; two librarians; a publisher; an engineer; a businessman; a lay church administrator; a military chaplain; the director of a juvenile reformatory; a judge; an executive of the YMCA; and four members who regularly functioned as paid lecturers. Many of these men combined these employments with work in education, ministry, law, or some other field.

No less than forty-four of the ninety-nine men in the association wrote and published extensively. Some, including W. E. B. Du Bois, Solomon C. Fuller, Edward E. Just, Kelly Miller, Charles V. Roman, William S. Scarborough, Theophilus G. Steward, Marcus F. Wheatland, Edward C. Williams, and Carter G. Woodson, continuously produced scholarly work in their areas of specialization and related fields.

Several of these same men, along with other members of the academy, were widely recognized as knowledgeable and skilled popular essayists. The pieces they wrote were eagerly read by educated blacks and frequently printed in white publications. The best-known and most widely read essayists were Archibald H. Grimké, Kelly Miller, John E. Bruce, William H. Ferris, W. E. B. Du Bois, James Weldon Johnson, and William Pickens. These men produced a steady stream of articles analyzing and criticizing various aspects of race relations in America. Three clerics who also wrote exten-

---

12. See Otto H. Olsen's Introduction to Sinclair, *Aftermath of Slavery*, v–x. Arnold Hamilton Maloney also became a physician, but he did not receive the M.D. degree from the Indiana University School of Medicine until 1929.

sively on the same subject were Alexander Crummell, Francis J. Grimké, and Benjamin T. Tanner. Each constructed an incisive theological critique of Americans and American Christianity.

Other members of the academy made significant contributions in the areas of literature and art. The poet Paul Laurence Dunbar, on the basis of his remarkable talent and productivity, emerged as a major American literary figure during his lifetime. W. E. B. Du Bois, in addition to his writing in other areas as well as his extensive organizational work, produced poems, short stories, and a novel. And James Weldon Johnson, in many ways Du Bois's equal as regards multiple involvements, composed numerous poems, compiled two books of his poetry, and wrote several pieces of literary criticism. One of the early historians of black art was Freeman H. M. Murray, who authored a book on the subject. However, the preeminent figure in the area of literary and artistic commentary on works by and about blacks was another member of the academy, Alain L. Locke.[13]

By avocation, nine members of the ANA were outstanding collectors of books, arts, and other memorabilia connected with the history of black Americans. Four, Arthur A. Schomburg, John E. Bruce, Charles D. Martin, and Henry A. Williamson were New Yorkers, friends, and, quite possibly, collaborators. Schomburg was probably the most determined and dedicated of the entire group. Over a period of approximately twenty-five years, he collected "between five and six thousand volumes, 3,000 manuscripts, 2,000 etchings and portraits and several thousand pamphlets." In 1926, his collection was purchased by the Carnegie Foundation for ten thousand dollars, and given to the New York Public Library for housing in its Harlem Branch on 135th Street.[14]

On a smaller scale, the efforts of Bruce and Martin paralleled those of Schomburg. After Bruce died in 1925, much (perhaps all) of his collection was acquired by Schomburg and integrated into the latter's more massive holdings. The final disposition of all of Martin's acquisitions is unknown, but he had begun making "important gifts and loans" to the 135th Street Harlem Branch well before the New York Public Library received Schom-

13. The publications of the forty-four men mentioned in this chapter are too extensive to note individually. The reader is referred to the biographical sources given for these men in earlier chapters and the catalogs of major research libraries, especially in the Moorland-Spingarn Research Center, Howard University, and the Schomburg Collection of the New York Public Library.

14. L. D. Reddick, Introduction, in *Calendar of Manuscripts in the Schomburg Collection of Negro Literature*, 1–6.

burg's collection. Williamson, an important local and national leader in Masonic organizations, brought together a large and impressive collection of books on the history of black Masons. These also eventually became part of the library on 135th Street.[15]

Five other men, Jesse E. Moorland, Walter B. Hayson, John W. Cromwell, Freeman H. M. Murray, and Henry P. Slaughter, all of whom either lived in or had strong ties with Washington, were also active in the assemblage and preservation of historical materials. In 1914, Moorland, who had gathered a large collection of works bearing on blacks, gave his holdings to Howard University. Moorland's friend, Kelly Miller, was instrumental in encouraging and facilitating this decision. The gift consisted of "over 3,000 items": books, engravings, portraits, manuscripts, curios, pictures, and clippings.[16]

Hayson, following the death of his close friend, Alexander Crummell, came into possession of a sizable portion of the clergyman's correspondence and many of his manuscript sermons. To this body of material, Hayson added, at great personal expense, English, French, German, and Russian playbills issued in connection with appearances by the black Shakespearean actor, Ira Aldridge, as well as two hundred rare books by black authors. When Hayson died in 1905, the books were purchased by Wilberforce University, and his widow donated Crummell's letters and papers to the Negro Society for Historical Research in Yonkers, New York.[17]

The exact content of Cromwell's holdings is unknown, but there is no doubt that they were extensive. The items he had accumulated included books, but also things of the sort he made available for the historical exhibit sponsored by the ANA in December, 1920, such as, "lithographs . . . valuable letters and manuscripts." An inveterate collector, this activity was a direct support to his research and writing, for he drew on primary sources in his possession to write his book, *The Negro in American History*, which appeared in 1914. Seven years later, in a letter to John E. Bruce, he mentioned that Lafayette M. Hershaw and Theophilus G. Steward had urged him to write a second book "dealing with my impressions of men and events since my stay in Washington." Cromwell went on to discuss the numerous primary resources he had for such a project, but expressed a desire

15. *Ibid.*
16. Dyson, *Howard University*, 287, 288; Logan, *Howard University*, 171; Kelly Miller to S. M. Newman, June 15, November 4, 1914, Moorland to Miller, December 18, 1914, all in Miller Papers.
17. Cromwell, Journal, 162–63 in JWCG/M; Ferris, *The African Abroad*, II, 864.

to see it written by his children. Several years later (probably in 1926), Cromwell asked Carter G. Woodson, in a note, "Are you seriously in earnest about considering a bid for the purchase of my 'race' books?" He offered, if Woodson's answer was yes, to have them cataloged and appraised. Toward the end of the note, Cromwell assured the head of the ASNLH that "the ordinary books which one has and can find in the second hand libraries are not in the category I had in mind in speaking of valuations." [18]

No complete listing of Freeman H. M. Murray's collection has survived but, given his special interest in the image of blacks as reflected in American art, it is reasonable to assume that much of it dealt with this subject. Murray's contribution to the ANA's exhibit in December, 1920, consisted of "more than one hundred reproductions in photogravure of famous sculptures in the United States." [19]

Henry P. Slaughter came close to rivaling Schomburg in terms of the size of his collection, which contained many items on the antislavery struggle and the black experience during the colonial and early republican years. Eventually, Slaughter assembled more than "7,000 volumes, 200 portraits, 200 letters, 225 pieces of sheet music, and 200 autographs." The bulk of the collection was purchased from Slaughter by Atlanta University in 1946. However, in 1974, "13 cubic feet" of additional material, which had been part of Slaughter's original holdings, was discovered. These pieces—put in storage after Slaughter's death—were given to the United States National Archives. [20]

The average member of the ANA usually belonged to at least three other organizations besides the academy, and often many more. For men such as Solomon C. Fuller, John W. Hoffman, Edward E. Just, William S. Scarborough, Marcus F. Wheatland, and Monroe N. Work, whose lives were dedicated to their fields of expertise, these affiliations were almost exclusively learned and professional. This was not true for most of the other men, who claimed membership in an eclectic mix of business, civic, educational, fraternal, learned, political, professional, religious, and social organizations. Like their fellow countrymen during the late nineteenth and early twentieth centuries, the men in the ANA were avid joiners, constantly link-

18. New York *Age*, January 8, 1921, p. 7; Cromwell to Bruce, January 21, 1921, in J. E. Bruce Papers; Cromwell to Woodson, n.d., in Woodson Papers. (I have found no evidence that Woodson ever purchased any of Cromwell's possessions.)

19. New York *Age*, January 8, 1921, p. 7.

20. Logan, *Howard University*, 134; New York *Age*, January 8, 1921, p. 7; Washington *Afro-American*, March 2–8, 1976, sec. 3, p. 2.

ing themselves with others in associations that affirmed some important aspect of whom they were or were striving to be.[21]

Because most of the men in the academy lived in segregated communities and worked in segregated institutions, membership in a learned society was an important means by which they maintained contact with their professions and specialties, as well as with their white colleagues, who dominated and controlled these organizations. The social realities that required that black educational institutions engage primarily in basic elementary, secondary, and undergraduate education often meant that such men as William S. Scarborough, a classicist with broad scholarly interests, or Edward E. Just, an experimental biologist, were deprived of a community of colleagues capable of stimulating, supporting, or evaluating the advanced work they did in their fields. For those who mixed scholarship with other activities, and even for those who were not scholars, membership in predominantly white learned and professional societies affirmed their interest in and identification with fields of knowledge and forms of expertise important to them as individuals. Consequently, members of the academy were affiliated with a wide range of such organizations, including the American Academy of Political and Social Science, the American Association for the Advancement of Science, the American Classical League, the American Economic Association, the American Folk-lore Association, the American Historical Association, the American Institute of Sacred Literature, the American Medical Association, and the Archaeological Institute of America.[22]

21. The organizational affiliations attributed to ANA members in the above three tables are taken primarily from their biographical sketches in the various volumes of Boris (ed.), *Who's Who*; Gibson and Crogman (eds.), *Progress of a Race*; Kletzing and Crogman (eds.), *Progress of a Race*; Mather (ed.), *Who's Who*; Nichols and Crogman (eds.), *Progress of a Race*; Richardson (ed.), *National Cyclopedia of the Colored Race*; and Yenser (ed.), *Who's Who*. Other sources include biographical and obituary sketches from the *Journal of Negro History*, *Crisis*, the Washington *Colored American*, the New York *Age*, the Washington *Bee*, and numerous other primary and secondary sources. The reader is referred to biographical citations in earlier chapters, which follow the introduction of each academy member.

Undoubtedly, the members of the ANA belonged to many more organizations that those which appeared in their biographical sketches. Many were selective in the ones they listed, and frequently, the names and number of those attributed to them varied from publication to publication. For a few, this kind of information was unavailable. The discussion of their organizational affiliations is based solely on information found in the sources listed above.

22. John Hope Franklin has described the isolation and some of the special pressures to which scholarly blacks in a racist society were and are subject in his essay, "The Dilemma of the American Negro Scholar," in Herbert Hill (ed.), *Black Voices* (London, 1964), 62–76.

Aside from the isolation most black professionals experienced because of the terms on which they were forced to earn a living, their presence in learned and professional societies (black and white) was part of a widespread movement toward professionalization among educated, middle-class Americans. See Wiebe, *The Search for Order*, 111–32.

The memberships many members of the academy held in black professional organizations were a direct result of the intellectual and professional ghettoes in which most were forced to work. Often discouraged by white professional groups from applying for admission, or if admitted, finding themselves and their concerns ignored, black Americans formed and supported societies such as the National Medical Association, the National Association for Teachers in Colored Schools, the District of Columbia Union of Colored Ministers, and the Episcopal Conference of Church Workers among Negroes. Like the ANA, many of these groups were crippled by lack of money and a small active membership, but, in almost every case, they were able to initiate dialogue between blacks in a particular specialty and articulate their concerns and needs.

Some members of the academy were active in the numerous black literary and historical societies that flourished during these years. Most of these organizations were self-improvement groups which met weekly or monthly to hear lectures, public debates, musical presentations, and literary entertainments. The Bethel Literary and Historical Association in Washington, the Boston Literary and Historical Society, the Virginia Literary and Historical Association, and the Prudence Crandall Literary Club in Chicago all presented programs of this sort. Other groups such as the American Negro Historical Society of Philadelphia, the Negro Society for Historical Research, the Association for the Study of Negro Life and History, and the Alexander Crummell Historical Club of Albany, New York, had more focused goals. Though their stresses varied, all of the latter worked to promote scholarly interest in the history of black Americans, to develop race pride by making blacks more conscious of their past, and to collect and preserve historical materials. Not only were members of the ANA active in these and similar groups, but frequently they had been instrumental in their establishment.

For some members of the ANA, participation in the academy was only one of several ways in which they sought to protect black Americans from what the society's constitution called "vicious assaults." William A. Sinclair helped found the biracial Constitution League, which worked to promote equal rights through legal action. Charles E. Bentley played the same role in the organization of a group with similar objectives, the Equal Opportunity League. Charles E. Bentley, W. E. B. Du Bois, Archibald H. Grimké, and Kelly Miller all served, for a time, on the "Committee of Twelve to Advance the Interests of the Negro Race," a body which lobbied against the movements to segregate and disfranchise blacks. And, in 1905, when W. E. B. Du

Bois met with twenty-eight black professionals to launch the "Niagara Movement," J. Max Barber, J. R. L. Diggs, Lafayette M. Hershaw, Charles E. Bentley, and Freeman H. M. Murray were among those present. A short time later William A. Sinclair joined the movement. These six men were active coworkers with Du Bois in the losing battle he waged to keep the Niagara Movement and its publications alive. Most of the six joined Du Bois and others in helping to form the National Association for the Advancement of Colored People in 1910, and all of them were early members of the newly established organization. They, and numerous other members of the academy played indispensable roles in helping the NAACP become the most important lobby for black Americans during the first half of the twentieth century.

The Protestant churches were also organizations in which many members of the academy played important roles. Sixty of the ninety-nine men in the society were active members of a particular denomination, thirty-one as clergy and twenty-nine in a lay capacity. In local, regional, and national meetings of their churches, members of the ANA who belonged to the AME, AMEZ, and Baptist communions were leaders in efforts—many of them successful—to increase financial support for church-run schools, upgrade educational and performance standards for clergy, and increase the involvement of their denominations in the struggle to gain equal rights for blacks. Academicians who were clerical and lay members of predominantly white churches articulated similar concerns, but, in most cases, they were either ignored or their issues dealt with in ways that suited their white coreligionists. As powerless members of their denominations, excluded from church hierarchies and governance structures, they had little alternative except to "watch and pray." Consequently, the heaviest investment of black Congregationalists, Episcopalians, Methodist Episcopalians, Presbyterians, Moravians, and Unitarians was in their local congregations, where they worked to support educational and protest movements.[23]

Like the majority of adult black males who lived during the sixty-five years following the Civil War, most of the men in the ANA were Re-

23. The activities of ANA members who were members of black denominations can be traced in Wright (ed.), *Centennial Encyclopedia of the AME Church*; Wright, *Bishops of the AME Church*; Bradley, *History of the AME Zion Church*; Walls, *The AMEZ Church*; and Bacote (ed.), *Who's Who Among Colored Baptists*. Two detailed discussions of the difficulties under which blacks in predominantly white churches labored can be found in Bragg, *History of the Afro-American Group of the Episcopal Church*, and in Carter G. Woodson's biographical sketches of Francis J. Grimké, which form the introductions to vols. I, II, and IV of *The Works of Francis J. Grimké*, which he edited.

publicans. Because the Republican party assumed the allegiance of black Americans, without making any significant commitments to them, these men did not always support their party enthusiastically. But the dominant role which southern white supremacists played in setting the racial policies of the Democratic party left them with no political alternative. Despite this, W. E. B. Du Bois (who was a declared socialist) and Alexander Walters joined a small group of black leaders in supporting the election of Woodrow Wilson, the Democratic candidate for president of the United States in 1912. However, when newly elected President Wilson permitted segregation by race in the United States Civil Service and accepted the orthodox southern position on racial relations, he drove them back into the Republican party. All of the other thirty-two declared Republicans in the society were lifelong party regulars and several received appointments or other rewards from Republican administrations for their faithfulness.[24]

A sizable number of academy members were also active in black fraternal organizations and benefit associations. Some of the former, groups such as the Masons, the Knights of Pythias, the Odd Fellows, the Shriners, and the Elks, were large, multi-class social clubs, which attracted industrious blacks. Through their activities, they provided a meeting ground for blacks of different classes and occupations. The same was true of the Mosaic Templars, the Knights of Wise Men, the Court of Calanthe, the Royal Neighbors, the Good Samaritans, the Order of St. Luke, the Galilean Fishermen, and other benefit associations. However, in addition to their social activities, these organizations also offered insurance against sickness and death and aided the survivors of deceased members. Both kinds of groups were found throughout the black community, and some members of the ANA had entered them as young men. Aside from the practical and social benefits derived from membership, most academy members saw such involvements as one of the responsibilities imposed on them by their role as race leaders. Arthur A. Schomburg, John R. Clifford, John E. Bruce, Wendall P. Dabney, John R. Hawkins, Henry P. Slaughter, and others viewed their membership in these groups as an opportunity to teach other blacks, directly and indirectly, who their political friends and enemies were, as well as the importance of race pride, orderly habits, decorum, and business-like behavior. In addition, such connections often provided professionals tangible returns in the form of new clients for lawyers, new patients for physi-

24. Rudwick, *W. E. B. Du Bois*, 158–61; Meier, *Negro Thought*, 186–88.

cians, new parishioners for ministers, and new readers for newspapermen. Because of their education, high standing in the community, relatively secure incomes, and, in some cases, political influence, the kind of men who belonged to the academy were prized members of these organizations.

The criteria for admission to Sigma Pi Phi, Alpha Phi Alpha, Kappa Alpha Psi, Phi Beta Sigma, Pi Gamma Mu, Delta Sigma Rho, Omega Psi Phi, and other Greek letter organizations were different from that of the fraternal and benefit associations. These organizations were open only to men who had graduated from or attended a college or university. Along with the even more exclusive local clubs such as the Mu-So-Lit, the Pen and Pencil, and the Oracle in Washington, the Agora Assembly in Nashville, and the Crescent in Cincinnati, these were the preserves of the black upper class. Most of their activities were social, but it is impossible to underestimate their importance as settings in which some academy members, along with other prominent black Americans, exchanged ideas, sometimes formulated policy in regard to political, racial, professional, and community issues, and felt free to relax from the pressures of status and race.

X *Final Years*

During the last nine years of its existence, the ANA held ten national meetings. Nine were regular annual meetings and convened in Washington during the last week of December. The one exception was a midsummer meeting held July 3 to 5, 1920, in New York City. Six of the gatherings in Washington took place on the grounds of educational institutions located in the black community. In 1920, Dunbar High School was the meeting place. The following year it was Howard University's Rankin Memorial Chapel. In 1922, 1923, and 1925 the annual meetings took place in the Cleveland Community Center, a public hall in the Grover Cleveland elementary school. Beginning in 1921, the academy held its business meetings in a private club, the Mu-So-Lit; and, in 1927 and 1928, the annual meetings were also held there.[1]

The Mu-So-Lit Club, which was founded in 1905, included in its membership many of the more successful black businessmen, government servants, politicians, and professionals in Washington. Its name was a compound of the first two letters in the words, "music," "social," and "literary." The original members chose this name because they considered themselves outstanding figures in either the musical, social, or literary circles of Washington's black community. In its early years membership in the club was restricted to sixty, and weekly meetings were held in the Conservatory of Mu-

---

1. Announcement card for "Mid-Summer Session of the American Negro Academy" (July 3–5, 1920), announcement card for twenty-fourth annual meeting (December 28–29, 1920), Pelham to "Dear Sir," December 26, 1926, all in JWCG/M; Washington *Evening Star*, December 27, 1921, p. 26, December 28, 1921, p. 2, December 27, 1922, p. 3. Washington *Tribune*, December 15, 1923, p. 3, New York *Age*, December 26, 1925, p. 8; Washington *Tribune*, December 16, 1927, p. 1.

sic at 902 T Street, N.W. The focus of the meetings was often a lecture followed by a discussion. In 1908 a "Mr. Arthur Brown of Ohio" presented a review of Charles Dickens' *David Copperfield*, after which there was a general discussion of the book. On other occasions there were musical presentations. Because many members were actively involved in Republican politics, the Mu-So-Lit hosted a "smoker" for "distinguished out of town" party members in 1909 when William Howard Taft was inaugurated as twenty-seventh president of the United States. On this occasion Louis G. Gregory, a lawyer who was a member, offered a humorous, but accurate description of the group. "The Mu-So-Lit," he bantered, "is essentially an organization of quip and jest, of light and laughter; of song and story; of wit and eloquence; of whist and tobacco smoke. No intoxicating liquors stimulate our brains and darken our councils. Our meetings are sober, yet not grave; enjoyable, but not boisterous." [2]

During the next few years the Mu-So-Lit continued to grow in size. By 1912 the group had seventy-five members and was meeting in the "parlors over Martin's Cafe," one of Washington's better black restaurants. Nine years later there were two hundred names on the membership list. At least seven members of the academy, and possibly more, were members of the Mu-So-Lit. Those known to have been affiliated with both organizations were Roscoe C. Bruce, Wendell P. Dabney, Robert A. Pelham, Henry P. Slaughter, Robert H. Terrell, Neval H. Thomas, and Carter G. Woodson. In 1921 the Mu-So-Lit incorporated itself—the sum of incorporation was $15,000.00—and purchased a clubhouse. Its new home was "a 3-story and basement, hot-water heated, press brick front building, having a south exposure, and set on a lot 25 x 90 feet." It was here that the academy held its business meetings after 1921, as well as the thirty-first (1927) and thirty-second (1928) annual meetings. One or more of the men who were members of the two organizations made it possible for the ANA to use the facilities of the club. [3]

The idea of holding a national meeting of the ANA in New York City originated with several members of the society who had participated in the successful effort to remove Archibald H. Grimké as head of the academy in 1919. Along with new officers and constitutional reform they believed this

2. Washington *Bee*, December 21, 1907, p. 5, February 1, 1908, p. 5, May 9, 1908, p. 5, March 6, 1909, p. 5.
3. *Ibid.*, January 6, 1912, p. 5; "Certificate of Incorporation of the Mu-So-Lit Club"; unidentified clipping entitled "Club Decides to Aid Colored Race Uplift," in Mu-So-Lit Club Papers, Moorland-Spingarn Research Center, Howard University, Washington, D.C.

change would help revitalize the organization. Almost immediately after Cromwell's election as president a number of his supporters began to press for a midsummer meeting outside Washington. Beginning with the initial meeting in March, 1897, most of the association's annual conclaves had been held in December, and all of them had taken place in the nation's capital. Even after December, 1915, when a constitutional amendment was approved allowing for meetings at other times and places, this continued to be the pattern. Arthur A. Schomburg, in two communications to Cromwell, urged that a midsummer meeting be held in Atlantic City, New Jersey. Schomburg thought that the proposal for such a meeting should come from the president and be submitted to the membership as a referendum. He may have been referring to postelection tensions when he told Cromwell, in a letter dated January 7, 1920, that a poll of the members on the question of scheduling such a meeting would put him in "good graces." In a letter written the next day, Schomburg assured his friend, "If you can pull off the semi-annual meeting at Atlantic City or elsewhere . . . it would be a great thing to clear the ground for next winter."[4]

The procedure Schomburg suggested to Cromwell—polling the members in regard to a proposed summer meeting—was not in accord with the constitutional amendment passed in 1915, which allowed the executive committee, "on application of one-third of the enrolled membership," to hold meetings of the academy in places other than Washington. There was already a lengthy precedent for holding meetings at other times than the last week of December. The academy had met several times in March to coincide with the inauguration of Republican presidents and on the birth dates of several important political and racial figures to commemorate their lives and deeds. Perhaps Schomburg was ignorant of the exact wording of the amendment. In the end, he and four other members residing in New York submitted a proposal to the executive committee recommending that a midsummer session be held in their city, July 2 to 5, 1920. The request was approved, and the five New Yorkers were appointed a committee on program for the meeting. Why this process was used for getting a midsummer meeting approved and not the one described in the constitution is unclear.[5]

4. Schomburg to Cromwell, January 7, January 8, 1920, both in SC/MSRC.
5. Although the records of the ANA do not name them, the four New York members who joined Schomburg in proposing a meeting in their home city and who were appointed to the program committee for the meeting were almost certainly Robert T. Browne, John E. Bruce, William H. Ferris, and Charles D. Martin. All five were friends and shared an interest in the

The meeting took place in Harlem's Beth-Tphillah Moravian Church, where Charles D. Martin, a member of the academy, was pastor. John W. Cromwell and his supporters had a tremendous investment in the success of this gathering. Not only was it the new president's first general meeting, but it was to be a test of his argument that holding some meetings outside Washington would generate additional publicity and new members for the society.[6]

The main reason Cromwell and the committee wanted to hold the meeting in New York was the opportunity it provided for presenting the academy to Harlem, the large and dynamic black community in that city. Harlem was also a ghetto—few black New Yorkers could live anywhere else—but, despite its high crime rate and large numbers of poor, it contained a sizable minority of well-educated and relatively prosperous blacks. Moreover, Harlem was one of the most exciting centers of the Negro Renaissance, an outburst of literary and artistic creativity that occurred during the 1920s. Another factor in the choice of New York as a meeting place was the climate of race relations there. Compared to Washington, where segregation of blacks was enforced by law, New York, whose municipal code did not contain such provisions, seemed a much more liberal place.

In addition, the city contained an impressive number of groups and individuals concerned with the problems and aspirations of black Americans. The National Association for the Advancement of Colored People and the National Urban League, two organizations committed to improving the social and economic condition of blacks, were headquartered there. Both were interracially staffed and supported. W. E. B. Du Bois, who was editor of *Crisis*, the NAACP's magazine, lived in New York. As a former president of the ANA and one of its most distinguished members, he was expected to participate in the meeting, thus raising hopes that *Crisis* would give the gathering extensive coverage. New York was also the home of the country's two best known and most articulate black socialists, A. Philip Randolph and Chandler Owen, coeditors of the radical labor journal, *The Messenger*. It was also the location of the national headquarters of the Universal Negro Improvement Association, an organization committed to African repatriation and black political, economic, and religious separatism. Under the

---

academy. See Robert T. Browne to "Sir" [form letter to the five members of the program committee] February 22, 1920, in JWCG/M.

6. Washington *Bee*, June 26, 1920, p. 4; announcement card for "Mid-Summer Session of the American Negro Academy," in JWCG/M.

leadership of the dynamic and eloquent Marcus Garvey, it was rapidly growing in numbers and influence. The officers of the ANA believed that a meeting held in such a lively setting could not fail to produce positive results for their association.[7]

Details and arrangements for the meetings were handled by the committee of five members who lived in New York: Arthur A. Schomburg, Robert T. Browne, John E. Bruce, Arthur U. Craig, and Charles D. Martin. These men made a strenuous effort to structure a pleasant social occasion as well as an impressive assembly. Out of town members were guests in the homes of the local membership; there was a tour of "various points of interest in the city"; and, as the schedule rather artfully put it, there was "conversation to the members of the Academy by the women of New York." The usual program of papers and discussion was supplemented by two special events. As honored guests, members of the academy attended the Sunday morning service at Beth-Tphillah Moravian Church, where they heard the pastor deliver a "Sermon to Academicians." And the society sponsored a public exhibit of rare books written by important black American historical figures. The exhibit, which was assembled by Schomburg, consisted of selected items from his collection and those of Martin, Bruce, and the Negro Society for Historical Research.[8]

Charles D. Martin, one of the men who planned and attended the midsummer meeting, described it afterwards as a "splendid" gathering where "we were able to accomplish . . . much," and as an occasion when the "Academy . . . put on new strength." However, despite its location and the special events which were a part of it, the meeting was a disappointment in terms of publicity and recruitment. None of the newspapers, white or black, in either New York or Washington, covered the event and no applications for membership resulted from it. Moreover, toward the end of the meeting, something occurred—possibly a clash or a sharp disagreement between some of the major participants—which left bitter memories. The fragments of information that survive give no clear indication of what happened. It was so serious, however, that following the meeting Martin wrote to Cromwell, attempting to soothe his feelings of anger or disappointment, quite possibly both. "We must forget," the minister told Cromwell, "the inhar-

7. For a discussion of New York and Harlem during the 1920s see Nathan I. Huggins, *Harlem Renaissance* (New York, 1971).

8. Robert T. Browne to "Sir," February 22, 1922, announcement card for "Mid-Summer Session of the American Negro Academy," both in JWCG/M; Washington *Bee*, June 26, 1920, p. 4.

monious note which jarred suddenly at nearly the close of . . . [the] meeting. I forget it: pray do the same. The future will not only make it more distant but the years of comradeship and united effort for a worthy cause will completely erase the record." The fact that the meeting took place was a personal triumph for Cromwell and his supporters, but its failure to produce more tangible results made the triumph hollow.[9]

When the academy met again in December, 1920, for its twenty-fourth annual meeting, it sponsored a second historical exhibit, this one larger and more extensive than the first. The exhibit lasted two days, the duration of the meeting. Unlike the New York display, it was not limited to books, but included oil paintings, prints, engravings, letters, photographs, and statuary. Schomburg and Martin again supplied items, but others were loaned by blacks who lived in Washington. John W. Cromwell, Henry P. Slaughter, and Freeman H. M. Murray all made available pieces from their collections. In addition, two Washingtonians who were not members of the academy, Drs. John E. Washington and A. M. Curtis, contributed items.[10]

The exhibit was probably the most successful feature of the annual meeting. It excited the interest of the city's "Negro educators" and produced, on the first day, "a steady stream of visitors." On the afternoon of the second day "a special audience," as the Washington *Evening Star* put it, was given to two prominent white librarians, Dr. George F. Bowerman of the Washington Public Library, and a Dr. Roberts, who was on the staff of the Library of Congress. When the exhibit closed, there were expressions of regret from "many who were unable to make an inspection because of . . . [its] short duration."[11]

The idea of holding exhibits under the auspices of the ANA may have originally gotten its stimulus from a small gathering of friends following the seventeenth annual meeting in December, 1916. Henry P. Slaughter, who was not at the time a member of the ANA (he was elected in 1921), had attended this meeting and afterwards invited Archibald H. Grimké, John W. Cromwell, Arthur A. Schomburg, and John E. Bruce, all members of the academy, to visit his home and inspect his library. He also extended invita-

9. Martin to Cromwell, July 13, 1920, in JWCG/M.

10. Announcement card for the twenty-fourth annual meeting, in JWCG/M; New York *Age*, January 8, 1921, p. 7. The exhibit, which the academy, on its announcement card, especially urged "Students of High Schools and Colleges" to attend, was held in the library of the Dunbar High School.

11. Washington *Evening Star*, December 28, 1920, p. 2, December 29, 1920, p. 2; New York *Age*, January 8, 1921, p. 7.

tions to three other men who, like himself, did not belong to the ANA: Robert A. Pelham (who joined in 1919), Daniel Murray, a member of the staff of the Library of Congress, and the journalist T. Thomas Fortune.[12]

Visitors to the exhibit in December, 1920, were especially impressed by the items on loan from Slaughter. Many of them were "books, documents, and autographed letters illustrative of the anti-slavery struggle." The following year, when the ANA met for its twenty-fifth annual meeting, Slaughter, as a courtesy, hosted a luncheon for members of the academy, after which they viewed his entire collection.[13]

In November, 1921, Leo Wiener, professor of Slavic language and literatures in Harvard University, accepted an invitation from the executive committee to present, at the annual meeting scheduled for December, a paper on his research in the fields of African archaeology and philology. The idea for the invitation came from Arthur A. Schomburg, who, in late spring or early summer of 1921, urged John E. Bruce to do an article on Wiener's work for the *Negro World*, a newspaper published by Marcus Garvey's UNIA. Bruce had joined the UNIA in 1920, and shortly after began writing a column for this journal. By November, Schomburg was convinced that Wiener must address the academy. He secured John W. Cromwell's cooperation, and the two were successful in persuading the executive committee to invite Wiener to speak at the twenty-fifth annual meeting.[14]

Most black intellectuals first became aware of Leo Wiener sometime between 1920 and 1922, the years during which his three-volume work, *Africa and the Discovery of America*, appeared. In this lengthy study, Weiner argued that Christopher Columbus was not only correct in his judgement that the Americas' original inhabitants had traded with Africans, but that a clear and unmistakable African influence had preceded the period of European encounter. The assertion, for which proofs were presented in the first two volumes, rested on Wiener's discovery of a large number of the same Arabic words in the Mandingo languages of Africa, and in the aboriginal languages of the Western world. In the third volume, the linguistics scholar presented proofs that the spiritual culture of the American Indians was, in

12. New York *Age*, January 4, 1917, p. 5.
13. Washington *Tribune*, December 31, 1921, pp. 1, 5.
14. Schomburg to Bruce, n.d., in Bruce Papers. The editor of the *Negro World* was William H. Ferris, a member of the ANA. For a discussion of Bruce's and Ferris' involvements in the Garvey Movement, see Cronon, *Black Moses*, 46, 47, 48, 69. For a short biographical sketch of Wiener, see R. B. Blake and E. K. Rand, "Minute on the Life and Services of Professor Leo Wiener," *Harvard University Gazette*, March 9, 1940, pp. 123–24.

large part, of Mandingo origin. This assertion was based on his belief that many Mandingo words had been taken over in toto by American Indians, and used to express ideas with similar meanings in both cultures. Despite his international reputation as a scholar, at the time they appeared Wiener's interpretations were accepted by few philologists, Africanists, or specialists in pre-Columbian American history, and essentially have been ignored since they first appeared in print. His address, "The Problems of African Civilization," was a discussion of the main ideas in his study.[15]

The academy had a second guest speaker that year, Duse Mohamed, a corresponding member and editor of the *African Times and Orient Review*. Mohamed, who visited the United States in 1921, toured the East coast, giving lectures in New York and Washington. Between tours, he stayed with John E. Bruce in Yonkers, New York. The two traveled to Washington in December, 1921, for the academy's annual meeting, where Mohamed delivered a paper on "The Necessity of a Chair in Negro History in Our Colleges."[16]

Bruce, the only member of the academy to record his reactions to the papers Wiener and Mohamed presented, was pleased with both of them. A month after the meeting, in a letter to Carter G. Woodson, he mentioned his positive feelings about them and his pessimism as to their effect. "The last Academy meeting," he told Woodson, "was a success from a literary point of view. Prof. Wiener's talk was in the nature of a revolution to many of those who heard it. The home guard as usual did nobly. My friend Mohamed Ali Effendi's address on the Necessity for a chair of Negro history in the universities of the world was a thoughtful effort and evoked favorable comment. But our folks soon forget these things."[17]

These two papers must have made strong impressions on other members of the society who heard them because the Washington *Tribune*, a black newspaper, informed its readers that the two would "probably be published by the Academy." No subsequent action was taken with regard to Mohamed's paper, but Wiener's was approved for publication by the executive committee early in 1922. However, for reasons that are not clear, Robert A.

15. Leo Wiener, *Africa and the Discovery of America*, (3 vols.; Philadelphia, 1920–22); Washington *Evening Star*, December 29, 1921, p. 17; Washington *Tribune*, December 31, 1921, pp. 1, 5; Washington *Post*, December 29, 1921, p. 9.

16. Mohamed's visit to the United States is mentioned by Khalil Mahmud in the Introduction to the second edition of Duse Mohamed's book, *In the Land of the Pharaohs*. See also Washington *Tribune*, December 31, 1921, pp. 1, 5.

17. Bruce to Woodson, January 25, 1922, in Woodson Papers.

Pelham, the corresponding secretary, refused to implement the decision. Even though the academy's preamble did not indicate that its efforts to promote "the publication of works of merit" were limited to "works" by black Americans, no paper written by a white had ever been issued as an occasional paper. It is possible that Wiener's race was a factor in Pelham's failure to do anything.[18]

Whatever its cause, Pelham's inaction confounded and eventually angered John W. Cromwell, Arthur A. Schomburg, John E. Bruce, and John R. Clifford, all of whom felt the paper was part of an important and revolutionary study. Although each of these men applied their own brand of persuasion and pressure to the corresponding secretary, hoping to move him to have the paper printed, nothing was effective. Because all of these men enjoyed considerable prestige and power as major figures in the academy, it is impossible not to believe that the executive committee and the general membership sustained Pelham in his refusal to issue the paper as an occasional paper.[19]

If things had turned out differently, the twenty-fifth annual meeting would have heard a third guest speaker—Marcus Garvey, head of the UNIA. In October, 1921, John E. Bruce urged Arthur A. Schomburg to secure an invitation for Garvey to address the academy. Since the executive committee had to approve all speakers, before submitting the request, Schomburg sought John W. Cromwell's opinion as to how the committee would react. Schomburg told his friend that he had "no objection whatever to hearing Garvey," but he was "reluctant to bring the matter before the Executive Committee *and be* turned down." However, the way in which he described the request to Cromwell suggested that he was not particularly impressed with Garvey or the "Garvey Movement." "I have just returned," Schomburg wrote, "from all over the state [New York] to find Bruce's letter pleading for the opportunity to hear Garvey express his 'ideas.'" Toward the end of the same letter, he mentioned to Cromwell that Bruce had "given up a safe job for [one as] Priv. Secretary to . . . Garvey." He also warned Cromwell that Bruce had discussed a possible invitation to Garvey with Alain L. Locke. Since Locke and Cromwell had been good friends for many years, Schomburg may have feared and Bruce may have hoped that Locke

18. Washington *Tribune*, December 31, 1921, pp. 1, 5.
19. Clifford to Bruce, October 16, 1922, Schomburg to "Bruce Grit" [J. E. Bruce], n.d., both in Bruce Papers; Clifford to Cromwell, February 8, 1923, in JWCG/M.

would encourage Cromwell to support Garvey's inclusion on the program. Cromwell's reply to Schomburg's request for advice has not survived. However, a month later Schomburg had moved from an ostensible position of neutrality to one committed to the idea of inviting Garvey to address the academy. Shortly before the executive committee met to make its final decision regarding speakers, he sent Cromwell a note asking him to "put the matter over with . . . Garvey." There is no evidence to explain this shift. Whether Cromwell or Locke supported the proposal is unknown, but the executive committee failed to issue an invitation to the head of the UNIA.[20]

The following year, Robert Thomas Kerlin, a white professor of English on the faculty of the State Normal School at West Chester, Pennsylvania, delivered a paper on "Race in Culture." Kerlin had been dismissed from the Virginia Military Institute in 1921 for writing an open letter to the Governor of Arkansas, protesting the hanging of the black survivors of a race riot in that state. Even before his dismissal, Kerlin, who was also a Methodist minister, had attempted to challenge the racist assumptions which determined the treatment of black Americans. In 1919, his book, *Voice of the Negro*, appeared. It was a survey of black opinion as expressed in black-American newspapers. Kerlin hoped that his compilation would demonstrate the legitimacy of black claims for justice and better treatment. His *Negro Poets and Their Poems*, which was published in 1923, attempted to do the same thing by using the works of black literary artists. Arthur A. Schomburg was especially impressed by the latter, which he described as "a work many of our own men ought to have done." It was Schomburg who was primarily responsible for Kerlin's appearance. In his address to the academy, the exiled white Southerner argued that "culture did not follow race lines, but was rather a product of opportunity and environment."[21]

The historical exhibits at the two meetings in 1920 and the special guest speakers in 1921 and 1922 represented an effort by the academy to increase public attendance at the sessions where papers were read and to gain greater

20. Schomburg to Cromwell, October 27, November 12, 1921, both in SC/MSRC. Alain L. Locke was elected a member of the ANA in 1921, but it is impossible to determine exactly when. Since the ballot containing his name was mailed to members of the academy on August 15, 1921, he was probably not a member in October, 1921, when Schomburg wrote to Cromwell.

21. For a biographical sketch of Kerlin, see the *Journal of Negro History*, XXXV (July, 1950), 344–48. See also Schomburg to Cromwell, "Decoration Day, 1921" [May 30], in SC/MSRC; announcement card for twenty-sixth annual meeting, in Bruce Papers; Washington *Tribune*, December 30, 1922, p. 1.

publicity for the organization and its work. Because of the sketchy press coverage these meetings received—in the case of the midsummer meeting in 1920 there was none—it is difficult to say for certain how successful these efforts were.

On the whole, the results seem to have been mixed. The only extant assessment of the meeting in July, 1920, is Charles D. Martin's letter of reassurance to John W. Cromwell, in itself an indication that this was a problematic gathering. The fact that the meeting was not mentioned in the black or white press of New York or Washington suggests that it was poorly attended. The exhibit held in conjunction with the meeting in December, 1920, was visited by large numbers of people and seems to have been an outstanding success. However, lack of evidence makes it impossible to know, or even conjecture, whether the two exhibits and the guest speakers in 1921 led to increased public attendance at sessions of those meetings where papers were read. The presence of Robert T. Kerlin may have done so in 1922 when, according to one newspaper, "the sessions were well attended." But the fact that there were three other speakers and two public sessions (Kerlin spoke only at one) makes it difficult to attribute the attendance to Kerlin alone.[22]

It is possible to speak with more certainty regarding the amount of publicity the exhibits and speakers produced. While neither the exhibit nor the meeting held in July, 1920, were noticed by the press, the exhibit held in conjunction with the meeting in December, 1920, received coverage in the Washington *Evening Star* and in the New York *Age*, a black newspaper. The *Evening Star* and the *Post*, Washington's most important major white dailies, as well as the *Tribune*, the city's most important black newspaper, carried summaries of the address given by Wiener in 1921. In all three Duse Mohamed's paper was mentioned only by title. When Kerlin appeared before the academy in 1922, the Washington *Tribune* was the only newspaper to report on the content of his paper. Almost without exception—and this was also true of the black press—those few newspapers that manifested an interest in the academy found the exhibits and the opinions of the white guest speakers far more interesting than the association itself or the opinions of its members. Nevertheless, the articles which appeared were more

22. Martin to Cromwell, July 15, 1920, in JWCG/M; New York *Age*, December 30, 1922, p. 3. The three other speakers in 1922 were Arthur A. Schomburg, president of the ANA; Thomas Montgomery Gregory, professor of public speaking and director of dramatic arts at Howard University; and Joseph J. France, a physician from Portsmouth, Virginia.

substantive than most of those written about the ANA meetings during the Grimké administration.[23]

Whatever modest gains these efforts may have produced, after 1922 the academy began to experience directly the effects of its two major officers' growing lack of interest. Schomburg, discouraged by the demands of the presidency, began to reduce his involvement. And Pelham's lazy and inefficient performance as corresponding secretary, in effect, left the organization without an administrator. Deprived of regular, sustained leadership, and lacking an effective means of implementing its decisions, the executive committee quickly became immobilized. This breakdown on the part of the organization's two most essential figures meant there was also little possibility that decisions and recommendations made by the annual meetings would be translated into policy and programs.

These developments impinged directly on the quality of the annual meetings and, on two occasions, threatened their continuity. Pelham and the executive committee did little or nothing to prepare for the annual meeting scheduled to be held in December, 1923. Consequently, speakers were not recruited and no plans were made to enrich the usual program in a way that would have broadened its appeal to the public. In May, 1923, the president of the ANA, in a letter to John W. Cromwell, asked whether "the Executive Committee [had] ceased to function?" In many ways the answer was yes. Four months later, Schomburg again was disturbed by indications that plans for the meeting were not moving ahead. Unable to trust Pelham, he again sought information from Cromwell, asking, in a letter, was there "anything new regarding the Academy's work for the winter?" Cromwell's answer was so discouraging that Schomburg decided not to go to Washington in December, thinking that the annual meeting could not possibly take place. Only after the strongest urging from Cromwell was Schomburg induced to take the matter into his own hands and begin recruiting speakers. In late October he persuaded Charles D. Martin to present a paper and, by December, Freeman H. M. Murray and Frank R. Steward had also agreed to participate. Schomburg also decided to read Alain L. Locke's description of the opening of Pharaoh "Tutankahmen's" tomb in Egypt as a fourth paper. Early in 1923, before Locke left the United States to observe this event, Schomburg asked him to put his impressions on paper and mail

23. Washington *Evening Star*, December 28, 1920, p. 2, December 29, 1920, p. 2, December 29, 1921, p. 17; New York *Age*, January 8, 1921, p. 7; Washington *Post*, December 29, 1921, p. 9; Washington *Tribune*, December 31, 1921, pp. 1, 5, December 30, 1922, p. 1.

them back immediately. As a result of the president's exertions the meeting took place, but it left him feeling even more burdened and exhausted by the association.[24]

The following year Occasional Papers nos. 21 and 22, the academy's last two publications, appeared. No. 21, *The Shame of America or the Negro's Case against the Republic*, was Archibald H. Grimké's presidential address at the twenty-third annual meeting in December, 1919, as well as the last paper he delivered before the society as either president or member. No. 22, *The Challenge of the Disfranchised: A Plea for the Enforcement of the 15th Amendment*, was the presidential address delivered by John W. Cromwell at the meeting in December, 1920, which ended his one term as president of the academy. Both Grimké and Cromwell were given the honorary title of "president emeritus" that year, and the simultaneous publication of these two papers was intended as another acknowledgment of their contributions to the ANA. The honorary titles and the publications may also have represented an attempt to erase any bitterness that remained between the two men and their supporters as a result of Grimké's retirement from and Cromwell's election to the ANA presidency in 1919.[25]

Grimké's theme in *The Shame of America*, one of his most direct, pessimistic, and accurate indictments of American racism, was the radical disjunction between the professed belief of white Americans in the principles of liberty, justice, and equality, and their day-to-day treatment of black Americans. To document his argument he offered examples of the many ways in which racial prejudice had thwarted the hopes and progress of his people from the time of the American Revolution to 1919. In Grimké's opinion, this depressing record of white hypocrisy and exploitation proved unmistakably the naiveté of blacks, who had believed that someday their white fellow citizens would reject racism and accord them equal rights. There was never, he declared, any essential difference in the attitude of the

24. Schomburg to Cromwell, May 22, September 1, October 18, 1923, all in SC/MSRC; Schomburg to Locke, January 25, December 11, 1923, both in Locke Papers; Washington *Tribune*, December 15, 1923, p. 3.

25. Washington *Tribune*, December 19, 1925, p. 2; *Crisis*, XVII (February, 1920), 123; announcement card for twenty-fourth annual meeting, in JWCG/M.

Following the thirty-first annual meeting in December, 1927, the Washington *Tribune* reported that "The New Negro," a paper delivered by Charles S. Johnson, editor of *Opportunity*, would be published "under the auspices of the ANA." (Washington *Tribune*, December 20, 1927, pp. 1, 6.) Not only did this fail to happen, but the academy had ceased to exist a year and a half later.

North or South toward blacks, or any essential difference between the Republican and Democratic parties in terms of their basic racial policies and attitudes. In speculating on the future, Grimké saw no improvements ahead, and urged blacks to face "the stern reality" of their situation. "We are," he told them,

in the midst of a bitter and hitherto invincible race-prejudice, which beats down into the dust all of our rights, all of our attainments, all of our aspirations after freedom and excellence. The North and the South are in substantial accord in respect to us and in respect to the position which we are to occupy in this land. We are to be forever exploited, forever treated as an alien race, allowed to live here in strict subordination and subjection to the white race. We are to hew for it wood, draw for it water, till for it earth, drive for it coaches, wait for it at tables, black for it boots, run for it errands, receive from it crumbs and kicks, to be for it, in short, social mudsills on which shall rest the foundations of the vast fabric of its industrial democracy and civilization.[26]

One of the recipients of Grimké's paper was William Ernest Hocking, a philosopher who taught at Harvard University from 1914 to 1943. Sometime in the spring of 1924, Hocking and Grimké spent an afternoon together at the home of mutual friends in Boston, discussing, among other things, race relations in the United States. Several weeks after this meeting Grimké sent Hocking a copy of *The Shame of America*. In response, the philosopher returned a lengthy letter reacting to the paper. Ironically, the letter was an example of one of the major points Grimké made in the essay, the ability of whites who considered themselves liberals on racial issues to reconcile their principles with racist practices.

As he thought about race relations in America, Hocking told Grimké, it was "the political phase of things" which worried him the most. However, before turning to this concern, he shared with his correspondent the following basic premises which informed his thinking in regard to race:

1. All men have the same concern in right and justice. They are therefore equal, not alone before God, but before the law. . . . That being the case, it is intolerable that . . . [any man] should not be in a position to give political protection to . . . his civil interests.
2. Political life is something more than the administration of justice. It is the entire policy of the state in building up a type of public life, of fostering education, art, all phases of culture.
3. Races are very much alike in their judgements of justice, as they are exactly alike in their interests in justice.

26. Archibald H. Grimké, *The Shame of America or the Negro's Case Against the Republic*, ANA Occasional Papers, no. 21 (1924), 9–17.

Shifting from principles to practices, Hocking noted that although "there would be very little difference in the way a negro and a white man would view a case at law, . . . the negro would be, perhaps more lenient and sympathetic, and less inclined to rate high the value of adhering to the law for law's sake." This judgement, he assured Grimké, did not reflect on the character of his race. However, continuing in this vein, he expressed the opinion that "the judgments of negro and white would differ and ought to differ on such questions as What subjects are to be taught in schools, how much attention to music, languages, etc., etc.; how far the state ought to make higher education public, and in what branches; what kind of public buildings to build; what regulations for heights of buildings, widths of streets; what subsidies for canals and harbors; what rules for common carriers; and so on through a thousand matters of public judgment which are not necessarily matters of right and wrong, at all, but matters of choice and expression."

It was, Hocking pointed out to Grimké, the inescapable reality of these differences, which reinforced his conviction that "no race ought to be ruled by any other race, even if that rule were absolutely just and merciful." Lest there be any doubt as to how this applied to the subject under discussion, he added, "Black ought not to be ruled by white. White ought not be ruled by black." But, he continued, qualifying his previous statement, "the essential evil of our political situation[,] especially in the South[,] is that one or other of these evils must exist, for many years to come."

Though it violated his principles, Hocking felt himself forced to accept either white or black supremacy because of "race difference," an aspect of reality which, he told Grimké, "cannot and ought not to be forgotten." This belief was reinforced by his certainty that it was impossible for the two races to coexist as equals. As a consequence, he found the idea of amalgamation unacceptable because a "mixed race would tend to cancel the salient qualities of each." However, he added, even "if the solution lay in that direction, it would still be long deferred." Hocking also rejected the idea of full political empowerment for blacks. This, he felt, would result in "either the white ruling the negro or the negro ruling the white"; and, he reminded Grimké, "each of these situations is wrong." But, he maintained, "Of the two, the rule of the black by the white seems the lesser evil for, let us say, the next hundred years. For a. it is important that the political policy of the nation should be as homogeneous as possible; and the policy is the policy of the white races, taking the nation as a whole; and b. bad as the white peoples are at governing themselves, and still worse at governing others, the negro peoples are still learning, taking them as a whole. They are not yet ready to assume control of a state."

Until "a sound modus vivendi" was reached, Hocking recommended that blacks accept the fact of white political domination in the South; and that southern whites guarantee the Negro voter "his control of justice . . a fair vote . . . and a full right to make nominations" for some of the region's elective and appointive offices. In conclusion, Hocking offered Grimké the following analysis of the cause and effects of prejudice: "Prejudice allies itself with all that is base and hateful in human nature. But the persistence of prejudice is due, not so much to these base and hateful elements, as to some unsolved problem which the opponents of prejudice pass over too lightly. Prejudice cannot disappear until the rankling kernel of difficulty is dragged into the light and met with all the courage than [*sic*] men can summon to the task, and all the patience, and all the faith."[27]

In his reply to this letter, Grimké expressed general agreement with Hocking's initial "propositions." However, he challenged strongly the philosopher's opinions on the cause of prejudice, the importance of racial differences, and the possibility of "negro domination" in the South. Grimké asserted that the "rankling kernel" of prejudice was embodied in Hocking's overemphasis on "differences of race and the importance of preserving those differences." It was, he argued, the constant repetition of such ideas which caused whites to think themselves superior to blacks, thus making a "caste system . . . along the color line" seem perfectly acceptable. This meant that racial prejudice would continue to exist as long as Americans believed in "white superiority" and "black inferiority." When translated into public policy, these ideas produced the "inequality, injustice and violence" which made the existence of black Americans so difficult. Grimké maintained that there were only two ways in which racial tensions could be resolved, "annihilation of the weaker race by the stronger, or by their amalgamation." In urging amalgamation as the best solution, he argued that the strongest proof of its effectiveness lay in the fact that despite laws forbidding sexual intimacy between blacks and whites, "nature goes on in her biological laboratory mixing the blood of the two races where the white man meets the black woman."

Grimké discussed completely the notion of "negro domination," ridicul-

27. Hocking to Grimké, June 18, 1924, in A. H. Grimké Papers.

ing it as the "manufactured bug-a-boo of the South." There was, he told Hocking, no danger of this happening, even in the region's "black belt," if southern whites were fair in their dealings with blacks. A liberalization of the racial laws and a guarantee of equal treatment for all men would not only rectify much of the current injustice but, eventually, make the "relations of the two races . . . a national asset." "Will you not help," Grimké concluded, "with your great abilities to bring about such a change?" There is no evidence of further correspondence between Grimké and Hocking.[28]

John W. Cromwell's paper, *The Challenge of the Disfranchised: A Plea for the Enforcement of the 15th Amendment*, was a brief history of the disfranchisement movement in the South and a strong protest against the political emasculation of blacks which had resulted from it. Cromwell traced this movement from the overthrow of Reconstruction in 1877 up to 1920 (the year the paper was written). In his estimation, disfranchisement had eliminated southern blacks as a political factor on the local and national level, and destroyed the two-party system in sixteen southern states. As a remedy, he called on the United States Congress and the federal courts to enforce rigorously those sections of the Fifteenth Amendment which punished discrimination against potential or registered voters by "fines and imprisonment." There were no comments on Cromwell's paper in the magazines or newspapers of the black or white community.[29]

Since the academy continued to experience administrative problems it was obvious, early in 1924, that the next annual meeting, scheduled for March, 1925, was in danger. When the executive committee failed to make any plans or preparations for the gathering, Schomburg neither challenged nor protested their inactivity. There was no change in his behavior until late October, when Cromwell sent him a letter, pressing him to act in order to insure that an annual meeting would be held. Chastened by the letter, Schomburg, in his reply, promised "to do the right thing" in spite of the fact that "the members from New York think the Academy is dead." However, he set a condition on his involvement. If the executive committee formulated a meeting plan, then he would "circularize the members," and come to Washington in December. In other words, before shouldering any of Pelham's re-

28. Grimké to Hocking, August 8, 1924 (copy), in A. H. Grimké Papers.
29. John W. Cromwell, *The Challenge of the Disfranchised: A Plea for the Enforcement of the 15th Amendment*, ANA Occasional Papers, no. 22 (1924), 4–9.

sponsibilities or committing himself to travel South, Schomburg demanded proof that the executive committee was willing to do its part.[30]

Late in December, the executive committee complied with Schomburg's request and he went to work recruiting speakers. By the end of February, 1925, he had secured guarantees from Alain L. Locke and Charles D. Martin that they would present papers. However, for reasons unknown, plans for the March meeting, which was scheduled to coincide with Calvin Coolidge's inauguration as thirtieth president of the United States, went awry at the last minute and the affair had to be cancelled.[31]

This was the first time in its history that the academy had been forced to cancel a publicly announced meeting. The specific reason that made this necessary, as well as the causes that lay behind it, shook even John W. Cromwell's belief that the organization had a future. His discouragement, which was evident in the letter he sent Schomburg explaining the reason for the cancellation, provoked a prompt response. "Upon reading your letter this morning," the president of the ANA replied, "I noticed your tone of resignation. By no means, hold fast. I know fully well about the whole Negro Academy idea. Stand Pat."[32]

Schomburg's letter must have been a stimulant to himself as well as Cromwell, for a few months later, the New Yorker joined his friend in an effort to insure that the academy would have an annual meeting that winter. By December, three speakers had been recruited—William P. Dabney, Alain L. Locke, and Charles D. Martin. Locke's paper, "The American Literary Tradition and the Negro," was scheduled for the first session, in the hope that his local and national prominence would produce a sizable crowd, which could be induced to return for the second session. This expectation was doomed to disappointment. Only twenty-four people turned out to hear Locke, and the other session drew an even smaller number.[33]

One of the people who attended the first session was J. A. Jackson, a col-

30. Schomburg to Cromwell, "Columbus Day" [October 8], 1924, in SC/MSRC.
31. Schomburg had not yet heard from the executive committee when he made the following comment in a letter to John W. Cromwell, dated December 5, 1924 and located in SC/MSRC: "I was asked by Dr. [Jesse E.] Moorland what the Academy had proposed for the year. I told him that I had no knowledge of what they were doing, [*sic*] except for Cromwell there was silence." See also Schomburg to Cromwell, February 16, February 24, March 3, 1925, all in SC/MSRC; Schomburg to Locke, February 16, February 21, 1925, both in Locke Papers.
32. Schomburg to Cromwell, March 3, 1925, in SC/MSRC.
33. Schomburg to Cromwell, December 1, 1925, in SC/MSRC; Washington *Tribune*, December 19, 1925, p. 2, December 26, 1925, p. 3, January 2, 1926, p. 4.

umnist for the Washington *Tribune*, one of the city's black newspapers. A week after the meeting ended, Jackson's reflections on it appeared in his column, "My People and Other Folks." He prefaced his remarks with a description of the black middle and upper classes in Washington. According to Jackson, these groups were exceptionally proud of their "culture-loving" tendencies, and frequently boasted that their city was "the cultural center of the Negro group," a black American Boston. Certainly, Jackson continued, the capital contained the types of blacks who ought to have been able to live up to such pretensions. Its black residents included persons holding "executive and civil service offices"; the faculty of Howard University; the well-educated corps of public school teachers; "scores of lawyers"; and numerous doctors. In Jackson's opinion, these blacks and their families made up "a host of learned people, people whom one would suppose would be deeply interested in the American Negro Academy, that acme of race heights in the realm of letters."

Then, shifting from the language of a columnist to that of a black woman gossiping to a friend, Jackson made it clear that the very opposite was true. "The Academy," he told his readers,

meets yearly in Washington where those "dicty" people would naturally be expected to provide a correct setting and a proper atmosphere for the august body.

But Agnes they are all wrong. The idea don't work out. Why, my dear girl, don't you know that even with Alain Leroy Locke (former Rhodes Scholar and Howard professor, of many academic distinctions, and with a history of heavy sacrifice for the alumni of dear ole Howard to say nothing of being author of the reigning recent race book) on the program, the opening session was a dud. Girlie, really, would you believe me? There were actually nineteen men, and five women sufficiently interested in the history of our literature to respond. Nine of the few were from distant cities, one coming all the way from Wilberforce just to listen. The Academy is held in greater esteem elsewhere than in the centre of culture.

Those who came were handicapped in reaching the Cleveland school where the meeting was held by the cars parked before the curb on T street—cars that belonged to the patrons who thronged the Howard theater more than a block away where Ethel Waters and her girls were giving a demonstration in art in—in—, well, in about as little as the law allows. Our folks just must have their culture.[34]

The meeting in 1925 was a crushing disappointment, even to those members of the academy who were stalwarts. Its most important result was to stimulate many of the society's officers and members to ask a question openly which had been on their minds for a long time: Was the American Negro Academy still a viable organization? During the winter of 1926 the

34. Washington *Tribune*, January 2, 1926, p. 4.

executive committee met to discuss this issue. Their deliberations resulted in an authorization for Robert A. Pelham to send the following letter to all members:

> The annual meeting of the American Negro Academy will be held at the Mu-So-Lit Club, Washington, D.C., Wednesday afternoon and evening, December 29, 1926, with sessions at two and eight P.M.
>
> The usual literary program will be dispensed with in order to permit a full discussion of the question whether the Academy shall be discontinued, as having no longer a mission to fulfil, or shall be reorganized, as having yet a mission to fulfill, but of a kind calling for a new type of organization and activity.
>
> Prof. Kelly Miller, a charter member of the Academy, will open the discussion on the general topic.
>
> Every member should, therefore, be present or in event of inability to attend should be represented by a letter stating his views on the subject.[35]

It is clear from the letter that the executive committee wanted the annual meeting to make a definitive decision as to the future of the ANA. In the event that the members chose to continue the organization, the committee made them responsible for reorganizing it. The language of the notice communicated in unmistakable terms the committee's belief that, as presently constituted, the society had no future. One can only speculate as to why Kelly Miller rather than one of the major officers of the academy was chosen "to open the discussion." He was a "charter member" and sat on the executive committee, but the same was true of John W. Cromwell. The reason may have been Miller's ability to reconcile conflicting viewpoints. The problem to be considered at the meeting was a difficult one, which many members undoubtedly approached with strong emotions. Perhaps it was thought that Miller could set a tone that would encourage a calm, rational deliberation.[36]

The members who attended the annual meeting in 1926 decided not to disband the ANA. They also reelected Schomburg as president and Pelham as corresponding secretary; and, with two exceptions, retained all of their fellow officers. The basis on which they made these decisions is unknown.[37] There are no newspaper articles, individual accounts, or organizational records which provide answers to questions about the meeting in 1926, such as how many members attended; what was the tone of the deliberations; were there sharp clashes or disagreements between members; was a decision

---

35. Pelham to "Dear Sir," December 6, 1926, in JWCG/M.
36. *Ibid.* August Meier discusses Kelly Miller's important role as a "pragmatic harmonizer" in his *Negro Thought*, 213–18.
37. Washington *Tribune*, December 16, 1927, p. 1.

made to reorganize the association; and what roles did Schomburg, Pelham, Cromwell, and other prominent figures play in the meeting? The failure of publications which normally reported on the academy's annual meetings to provide information on this one might have reflected their essential disinterest in the organization. Unable to describe this meeting in the usual way, that is, by printing a list of speakers, paper titles, and times when the sessions were held, they may have decided to omit any reference to it. Or the society might have kept its deliberations secret. It would not have been strange for any organization to keep the details of such a meeting private.[38]

A year later, on December 28, 1927, the academy held an annual meeting which, in several ways, was different from earlier gatherings. Most previous meetings had extended over two or three days, but this one lasted one day. Of the two speakers on the program, only one, Arthur A. Schomburg, was a member of the academy. Since it was the executive officer's responsibility, each year, to prepare a "presidential address," this may have meant that no other member could be induced to present a paper. The other speaker, Charles Spurgeon Johnson, a black sociologist who was best known for his able and authoritative research on blacks in Chicago, lectured on "The New Negro." Although the meeting was advertised in the Washington *Tribune*, its public session was held in the meeting rooms of the Mu-So-Lit Club.[39]

The last-known assembly of academy members was the thirty-second annual meeting on December 28, 1928. The sole speaker at the one-day meeting was Chief Amoah III, a West African leader visiting the United States. Amoah's invitation to address the group probably resulted from his friendship with James E. K. Aggrey, who had died in 1927. Unlike all previous meetings, no papers were delivered by members of the association. There was not even a "presidential address." Amoah's talk was the entire program for the meeting.[40]

The academy's meetings from 1919 to 1928 were in many ways a barometer of its health, with the reading moving steadily from fairly positive to

38. A notice that the ANA would hold its thirtieth annual meeting on December 29, 1926, was carried by the Washington *Tribune* on December 10, 1926, p. 1. The only summary or review of the meeting to appear in print was a sentence in the New York *Age* on January 8, 1927, p. 7: "The American Negro Academy held an interesting session." Surely, an understatement, to say the least.

39. Washington *Tribune*, December 16, 1927, p. 1, December 30, 1927, pp. 1, 6. For biographical information on Johnson, see Richard Robbins, "Charles S. Johnson," in James E. Blackwell and Morris Janowitz (eds.), *Black Sociologists* (Chicago, 1974), 56–84.

40. Washington *Tribune*, December 28, 1928, p. 4. For a brief description of Chief Amoah III's background and interests, see *Crisis*, XXXV (November, 1927), 307.

very negative. The meetings in 1920 and 1921 were creative affairs, which stimulated a certain amount of new publicity for the group. After 1922, the situation changed drastically. The executive committee ceased to function, and the meetings continued only because Cromwell and Schomburg did most of the work of planning and executing them. But even their efforts failed to prevent the cancellation of the meeting in March, 1925.

However, even if all the meetings had been exciting, well-attended affairs this alone could not have sustained the organization. Similar thoughts led the executive committee to call a special meeting in 1926 to discuss the future of the society. The executive committee's action reflected a massive breakdown in member support for all aspects of the organization's work. As noted, the meeting in 1926 chose to keep the society going and to continue the annual meetings. How, why, and by whom this decision was made is unknown. Surviving records also give no information as to whether the meeting resulted in any changes in the organization of the society. They do indicate, however, that the same group of men who ran the association before the meeting remained in charge after it.

The meetings Schomburg and his fellow officers held in 1927 and 1928 were truncated versions of earlier assemblies—short in duration and almost totally dependent on speakers who were not members of the ANA. These meetings were not forums in which the members of a learned society presented to each other and the general public the results of their research and reflection, but gatherings of men with intellectual interests who listened to guest speakers. Such an exercise was a subversion of the original purpose of the academy and certainly did not justify members' traveling to Washington from other parts of the country. Perhaps, after the meeting in 1928, this was obvious even to Schomburg and his fellow officers. If so, it would help explain why that was the academy's last annual meeting.

XI *Epilogue*

The history of the American Negro Academy makes it clear that in many ways the organization failed to achieve its goals. Efforts to "promote publication of scholarly work" had only minor success. During approximately thirty-one years of existence, the academy, through its twenty-two occasional papers, presented a total of thirty-one articles to the public, the longest of which was thirty-eight pages. And of the articles published, some cannot be called scholarly. Nothing was done to "aid youths of genius in the attainment of the higher culture at home or abroad," either directly or indirectly. Not only was the society never able to fund such a program, but it failed to promote the work of unknown "youths" of ability or to assist their entry into institutions of higher education. The work of establishing an archive was not begun until 1908, eleven years after the formal inauguration of the society. However, despite the enthusiastic interest of several members, the collection grew slowly, never had a permanent home, and lacked funds for maintenance. The demise of the academy also led to the disappearance of the archives, which may have been returned to donors, or kept by one of the members, or distributed among several members.

The organization fell short of achieving its goals in other areas. Every effort to secure funds to publish an annual containing essays, literature, reprints of historical documents, and general information and statistics on the black American community was unsuccessful. And despite the fact that its occasional papers were responses and challenges to racist views, they were ignored by most whites who were seriously interested in black Americans. This lack of interest, as well as the ANA's inability to either secure the funds to strengthen its publishing efforts or have its members' papers published by white journals, was a direct result of white America's conscious and unconscious rejections of the American Negro Academy's validity as a learned society and of its members' claims to be intellectuals.

At the same time the academy's occasional papers failed as an effective means of publicizing their authors' ideas within the black community. The chief reason was simple: the black masses neither purchased nor read these often thought-provoking and usually well-written articles produced by the elite and upper-class members of the ANA. But even if they had, to the vast majority of blacks, who were either laboring people or poor agriculturalists, many of the subjects and issues the occasional papers addressed would have seemed distant. For most ordinary blacks, seeking to eke out a living, preserve their families, and, as a means of pursuing both goals, to minimize violent contacts with whites, the analyses of their problems, as well as the solutions and responses offered in the occasional papers would have been difficult to understand, hazardous to apply, and, in some cases, irrelevant. This helps to explain the stronger appeal in this era of the conservative race-building and economic strategies propagated by Booker T. Washington and other prominent blacks.

On the other hand, for the minority of blacks in search of a more radical response to their race's plight, the papers of the academy had equally little to offer. To these men and women, the visionary ideologies and programs of figures such as Bishop Henry M. Turner, Chief Alfred C. Sam, and Marcus Garvey—all of whom found the possibility of equality for blacks in the United States fantastical at best—seemed to contain fresh insights and to offer imaginable and practical alternatives.[1] As a result the readership of the occasional papers never expanded beyond a small circle of highly educated black Americans consisting of ANA members and their black and white friends. It may very well be that the failure of the academy to secure any significant forms of legitimation from whites was also an important factor in its rejection by blacks. However, the alternate ways in which members of the black American community, of all classes, invested their time, money, and energies indicated what ideas and strategies they believed had the most potential for protecting them and improving their lot.

Despite the strong belief on the part of many ANA founders and members that the organization should have strong ties with distinguished blacks

---

1. Wilson J. Moses, *Golden Age of Black Nationalism, 1850–1925* (Hamden, Conn., 1978) discusses the nature of the appeal these figures had for black Americans.

in other parts of the world, besides the election of twelve corresponding members, little was done to make this a reality. In fact after 1912, by never again electing another corresponding member, the society demonstrated an inability to maintain the vitality of its symbolic commitment to this goal. From 1912 and 1928, it was the activities of individual members that kept the memory of this goal alive.

Although the failure of the academy to achieve certain of its goals and its limited success in regard to others kept the organization weak, leading ultimately to its decline and disappearance, the society did accomplish a number of things which are tributes to the tenacity and dedication of its committed members. An organization of black American "authors, scholars, artists, and those distinguished in other walks of life . . . for the promotion of Letters, Science, and Art" was constituted and maintained its existence for approximately thirty-two years. During that time the society published and distributed twenty-two occasional papers that contained ideas, opinions, statistics, and historical information directly contradicting the popular belief among whites that all blacks were incapable of benefitting from higher education and devoid of intellectual sophistication, had never played a significant or positive role in American history, and were reconciled to their position as economic, political, and social inferiors in the land of their birth. The positive reactions by a small circle of thoughtful blacks and whites to several of the ANA papers, coupled with requests for copies from some of the country's major libraries and institutions of learning, strengthened the society's belief in the educational possibilities of pieces written by blacks discussing ideas and issues of importance to them and their race. The publication of the occasional papers also encouraged other academy members whose papers were not published as well as blacks outside the organization to continue their efforts to have their research and opinions on a wide range of subjects published in the form of articles or books.

The various books and other materials given to the ANA and designated its archives were a tangible expression of the society's commitment to gather and preserve "valuable data and the works of Negro authors." Conscious, however, of its limited financial resources, the academy attempted in a variety of ways to impress on the black community and the larger society the importance of preserving all sources of information on the black American past and of making them accessible to scholars and other interested persons. Through its various exhibits of books, pictures, and other materials related to black American and African history, its public validation of the activities of collectors of these items by including portions of their collections in ANA exhibits, and its official and unofficial support of Kelly Miller's ultimately successful efforts to persuade Howard University to establish a special collection of materials on Africa and the black American community, the ANA played an important role in the growing movement to gather, preserve, and interpret the materials that documented the ways in which blacks had shaped and influenced American culture and history.

The failures and successes of the academy make clear the many obstacles which confronted members of the black intelligentsia who, during the late nineteenth and early twentieth centuries, sought to influence the world of ideas and the discussion of major social questions; to obtain legitimation from the black and white communities for their work as intellectuals; and to provide forms of institutional support for themselves. However, to fully appreciate the historical significance of the ANA, it is also necessary to evaluate it as an expression of a particular strategy for dealing with the problems of black Americans and to assess its relationship to those ideas and movements that made the greatest impact on the black community from 1897 to 1929.

Both Alexander Crummell and W. E. B. Du Bois, the two most important figures in shaping the rationale for the ANA, believed that if black Americans were to progress economically, morally, socially, and ultimately politically, the educated members of the race would have to take the lead in pointing the way. There were slight differences in the way each man expressed this belief, but they were agreed on the importance of the race following what they considered its most enlightened and moral elements.

Although Crummell had argued throughout his long career that the educated members of his race, because of their special training and unique experiences, had to play the major role in elevating the black masses, this was particularly a special concern of his during the years he was helping to establish the academy and serving as its first president. To him, it was the responsibility of the "scholarly and enlightened colored men and women" to step forward and take the lead in every endeavor designed to promote "civilization" among their people. In essence, he believed that only the most strenuous efforts on the part of a black elite that was both moral and educated could save his people from being crushed, on the one hand, by white racism, and on the other, by black primitiveness. In his inaugural address at the ANA's organizational meeting Crummell made it clear that the members of the academy had to be among the most active agents in this work, for as "scholars and thinkers" who understood the spiritual, theoretical, and practical realities of human existence it was their responsibility to shape and direct "the opinions and habits of the crude masses."[2]

At least ten years before the establishment of the academy, Du Bois was stressing the preeminent role of educated blacks in promoting the advancement of their people. This belief was a product of his own analysis of the racial situation and the influence of Crummell. During succeeding years Du Bois continued to refine his ideas in this regard, becoming even more convinced that the enforced segregation of the black American community made it a necessity for a larger number of blacks to have access to collegiate and university education. As the number of educated blacks grew, he believed, so also in direct proportion did his race's prospects for social and economic advancement. Eventually, Du Bois produced an essay that was not only his major statement on this subject, but the source of a new term for the group of blacks he was describing: "The Talented Tenth." In the paper delivered at the ANA's organizational meeting in 1897, Du Bois challenged the organization to become the "intellectual clearinghouse" and national strategy center for the race. It was one of his most direct applications of his theory of the "talented tenth."[3]

The founding members of the ANA endorsed strongly both Crummell's and Du Bois's ideas on the importance of the educated black elite and the role of the society as one of that elite's most important instrumentalities. During its thirty-one-odd years of existence, the academy's officers as well as the majority of its active members continued to believe in the validity of these ideas and saw their involvement in the organization as a way of implementing them. As Otey Scruggs has noted in an essay on Crummell, his concept of leadership (and by extension Du Bois's), rife with notions of "elitism and missionary paternalism . . . raises the question of whether in their expressed concern for the welfare of the masses the black elite and the middle class have not in fact been more concerned with their own interests."[4] The point has direct application to the academy, for it is clear that this society was formed to promote the status and influence of its elite members as much as to promote the "civilization" of the masses of American blacks.

2. Crummell, "Civilization, the Primal Need of the Negro Race," ANA Occasional Papers, no. 3 (1898), 3–7.

3. Meier, *Negro Thought*, 190–201; Du Bois, "The Talented Tenth" in Booker T. Washington, and others, *The Negro Problem* (New York, 1903), 31–75; and Du Bois, *The Conservation of Races*, ANA Occasional Papers, no. 2 (1897), 10–15.

4. Scruggs, *We the Child of Africa In This Land*, 17.

Thus, even though they did not appear in the academy's constitution, among the organization's most important goals were its commitments to increase the size of the black leadership cadre, improve its quality, and broaden its influence. As is clear, the ANA's direct impact in these areas was so minor that its efforts can only be described as failures.

The founders and active members of the ANA also hoped that the organization would strengthen the intellectual life of the black community. And certainly, in a limited but significant way, the programs and activities of the ANA, indeed its very existence, helped to do this. But many of the society's most committed members hoped and worked for something more than just a functioning learned society. Crummell, Du Bois, John W. Cromwell, the Grimkés, Carter G. Woodson, and others supported the ANA because they believed that once the organization's potential was realized, it would be a continuous source of new ideas, insights, and strategies for their race's colleges, universities, churches, racial protest organizations, fraternal and beneficent groups, press, and politicians. Or, to put it another way, many supporters of the ANA hoped that it would play a decisive and positive role in determining the ideologies, policies, and perhaps even the personnel of those institutions, organizations, movements, and groups that were the intellectual centers of the black community.

Since the society was never acknowledged in the black or white communities as either the most important center of black intellectual life or the major source of ideas and programs relevant to the black community, never became a dominant force in the institutional life of the black community, and never acquired financial resources that would have made possible pursuit of its goals through the judicious disbursement of scholarships, grants, and contributions, all hopes for any larger role in strengthening black intellectual life were never realized. In short the ANA always lacked sufficient prestige, political power, and economic resources to play this role.

Many of the ANA's problems and some of its failures were related to the unresolved conflict between two of its goals, that is, the commitment to honor and promote intellectual achievement and the commitment to honor and affirm men whose careers were deemed to be positive models of racial leadership. Because Crummell and the ANA's other founding members had combined both functions in their careers, they built this double commitment into the organization's criteria for membership. In his inaugural address Crummell spoke for most of the men present as well as the majority of those who would later become members of the academy when he stressed the inseparable link between scholarly work and public service, declaring that true scholars were also "reformers" and "philanthropists."

This understanding was one widely held in the black American community, where many educated blacks viewed themselves and were viewed by the majority of their race as under moral obligation not only to make a contribution in the fields for which they were trained, but to serve their race in the broadest way possible. The fact that many white Americans had a similar conception of the responsibilities of intellectuals served to reinforce black commitment to this understanding. However, at the very time the academy was launched, this understanding was being challenged in both the black and white communities by societal and attitudinal changes that were steadily producing more sharply delimited definitions of occupational roles, particularly in the professions. After 1897, these forces would become even stronger, eventually displacing older conceptions of the intellectual's role. This development, which strongly influenced the self-concept of many black intellectuals, especially those educated after the turn of the century, accentuated the problems created for the academy by its two essentially antagonistic goals.

The organization's failure to clarify the relationship beween these goals had major impact in the area of membership, both in regard to the kinds of men who were elected as well as to what they were able and willing to do to support the organization. As a result, from the time it was founded the academy had a built-in problem in regard to its criterion for membership, one that would be made all the more difficult because for a long time the nature of the problem would be unclear. This resulted from the fact that during the first eighteen to twenty years of the group's existence, no one analyzed the problem carefully enough to get at the heart of the difficulty.

Although on paper a society composed of scholars, the academy elected a large number of members who were only marginally intellectual, men who respected scholarship and the life of the mind, but whose work and interests were neither scholarly nor intellectual. At the same time the organization contained other members who were engaged personally in the production of ideas, analyses, and research either because they valued such activities per se or as a means of furthering the goals of the ANA. Many of the continuous disappointments the organization experienced as it sought unsuccessfully to secure regular payment of dues, to increase member attendance at the annual meetings, and to persuade certain members to prepare and deliver papers at the annual meetings were, not solely but certainly to a large extent, related to this unresolved conflict of goals which had led to the election of many persons unable, unwilling, and uninterested in being working members of a learned society.

Throughout its existence, to some of its members, the ANA was an honorary society rather than a working group. In other words, many of those associated with it treated their induction and that of others as similar to election to Phi Beta Kappa or the Royal Geographic Society, rather than as admission to a working group such as the American Academy of Political and Social Science or the Society of American Historians. Although this problem affected the academy negatively from its earliest days, the first potentially effective solution was not devised until Carter G. Woodson and the other members of the committee on constitutional revision produced their report on needed changes in the structure of the ANA in 1921. Among other things, the committee's report recommended that a distinction be made between working and honorary members, and that control of the society be placed in the hands of the former group.

This section of the report was rejected. Clearly, the Woodson committee had noted and attempted to resolve a conflict and confusion that made the society unattractive to productive intellectuals such as Woodson himself. The rejection of the committee's recommendation was a refusal by the society to resolve a conflict of goals that had direct bearing on its membership problems. As a result, intellectually productive members continued to become inactive and those who had already done so found their decision reinforced. To black intellectuals who were not members, especially younger men, the decision was seen as a clear indication that the majority of the society's members were unwilling to permit changes that would transform the ANA into an authentic scholarly organization.

The failure to resolve this problem had another result. With the entrance criterion unchanged, marginal intellectuals continued to be drawn into the ANA until a point was reached where they constituted the majority of active members. Consequently, after 1921, as older members who were productive intellectuals withdrew, died, or became more involved in other activities, marginal intellectuals were elected to such key positions as president and corresponding secretary. These officers, detached from the scholarly tradition embodied by the ANA's founders and earlier leaders and out of touch with many of the most creative black intellectuals and scholars of the 1920s, were influenced strongly, in their choice of programs and selection of new members, by the society's honorific tradition. However, because the ANA was essentially unknown in the larger black community, there was really no legitimate basis for considering membership in it an honor. The special meeting called in 1926 to decide whether or not the ANA should be disbanded was a recognition that the society was no longer functioning as either a scholarly or honorific organization. The decision to ignore these problems rather than attempt to resolve them meant that the organization's collapse was inevitable.

The 1920s, the decade of the "New Negro," was a time of crisis for the ANA, for it was during these years that the organization was forced, in the most direct way, to come to terms with the ineffectiveness of its efforts to function as the intellectual voice of the "Talented Tenth." As indicated, the most basic reasons for this ineffectiveness were the society's poverty, its lack of a broadly based and supportive audience in either the black or white communities, and a goal conflict that both undercut its efforts to be a learned society and confused its public image. These, however, were difficulties that had a history as long as the society. In the 1920s the ANA was confronted by a new problem that proved to be as insoluble and as destructive as any of the earlier ones—the tension between the new mood of blacks and the "civilizationist" goals espoused by the academy.

Following World War I, a new spirit swept the black American community as blacks, proud of their patriotic contributions to America's victory, found racial barriers growing even tighter. Enraged by the continuation of old attitudes and practices, the rejuvenation of the Ku Klux Klan, and the country's tolerance of a series of bloody race riots that were attacks on, and in some instances slaughters of, black men, women, and children, many black Americans met violence with violence, believing that if they did not defend themselves no one would. This response betokened a new mood of anger, cynicism, and defiance that set the tone for black life in the decade ahead. It was accompanied by a growing tendency in the black community to question and in some quarters reject outright long-held beliefs about the superiority of white culture. These various feelings and attitudes found expression in a variety of ways, some of the most powerful and influential taking shape in the impressive literary, artistic, and musical works produced by black creative artists during the 1920s. The rise of Marcus Garvey and his Universal Negro Improvement Association was an even more important expression of this mood, chiefly because Garvey's black separatist and nationalist ideas and programs captured the imagination and support of the black masses to a degree unparalleled by any black leader before or after the 1920s.

The mood of the decade was a direct challenge to one of the most basic beliefs of the academy's founders and members, namely, that blacks, in order to progress as a race, gain the respect of whites, and become a political, economic, and cultural force in the world had to attain a civilized state by appropriating for themselves the most positive aspects of the more advanced cultures of Europe and the United States. This was an attitude that Wilson J. Moses has aptly termed "civilizationist," pointing to Crummell as one of its most forceful and eloquent proponents.[5] Certainly, the academy, as organized and directed by Crummell and other leading ANA members, was one of the black community's major institutional embodiments of this belief. During the 1920s, however, both the intellectuals who were participants in the New Negro Movement and those in the Garvey Movement demanded and secured recognition and respect for the courage, wisdom, and beauty of the black masses, celebrating them as a "mighty repository of strength rather than as heathens to be uplifted."[6] Thus, by the 1920s, the philosophy of the academy, unashamedly elitist, savagely critical of many aspects of black culture and committed to civilizing the black race through selective imitation of white Western culture, contradicted directly many of the ideas and feelings that the decade's most influential black thinkers considered important. Consequently, as the power of the New Negro and the Garvey movements grew, the philosophy, programs, and strategies of the ANA appeared negative and irrelevant, even to some ANA members who had long been ardent supporters of the organization.

There was irony in this development, for the ANA's goals and programs, as well as the ideas that led to its establishment, had in the black community of the late nineteenth century, reflected new attitudes of pride and self-confidence, attitudes which helped to create the unique emotional and intellectual consciousness that flourished among black Americans during the 1920s. Even the phrase "New Negro" had been part of the vocabulary of late-nineteenth-century black intellectuals, employed to describe black Americans with "education, refinement and money;" and, in some cases blacks of this description who refused to be treated as second-class citizens. Certainly, the term "New Negro" had a broader and more dynamic mean-

5. Moses, *Golden Age*, 20–21, 59–61, 76–77.
6. *Ibid.*, 254.

ing in the 1920s, but the dominant intellectual concerns associated with it—"a rising interest in Negro history; a new interest in Negro folk culture and in Africa; and the striving for a race literature and cultural life"—had been of great importance to many of the men who founded and promoted the American Negro Academy. Indeed, several members, through papers or publications—some read before the academy or published as occasional papers—contributed to the basic literature on these subjects.[7]

To members of the academy who, prior to 1920, had promoted scholarship by and about black Americans, affirmed their people's African ties, and pointed to the unique cultural contributions of blacks to American life, the much publicized New Negro seemed not so much a sign of a new kind of black but of a new attitude toward black intellectuals in the white community. The constant celebration of the New Negro so irritated William H. Ferris, a founder of the ANA, that in a 1926 review of ANA member Alain L. Locke's book, *The New Negro*, he challenged the legitimacy of the term. In doing so Ferris voiced sentiments shared by many academy stalwarts.

The review, entitled "The Myth of the New Negro," reminded readers that when the early works of Paul Laurence Dunbar, Charles W. Chesnutt, W. E. B. Du Bois, and other black intellectuals appeared between 1895 and 1908, they were not showered with the "fulsom praise that the New Negro has received." At that time whites believed "industrial education was the panacea for all of the Negro's ills." Continuing, Ferris pointed out quite accurately that one of the new factors differentiating the 1920s from the preceding thirty years was the seriousness with which whites now regarded the black's "higher aspirations," a shift he regarded as a "hopeful sign of the change in the attitude of the American mind towards the Negro intellect." In response to his rhetorical question, "Is the Negro of 1926 different from the Negro of 1895, 1900 and 1905?" Ferris answered that if, in 1906, all the issues of J. Max Barber's monthly magazine, *The Voice of the Negro*, had been bound together, the resultant volume "would have been similar in plan and scope and equally as instructive and entertaining as . . . [Locke's] *New Negro*." And, he continued,

if the papers read before the American Negro Academy in March, 1897, when Dr. Alexander Crummell spoke on "Civilization the Primal Need of the New Negro" and "The Attitude of the American Mind towards the Negro Intellect," Dr. Du Bois on "The Conservation of Race Traits and Tendencies" and Prof. Kelly Miller on "Hoffman's Race Traits of the Negro," the papers read before the same organization

7. Meier, *Negro Thought*, 200, 257–58.

in December, 1897 on "The Race Problem in the light of the Evolution Hypothesis" and "The Race Problem in the light of Sociology," if the papers read around 1900 on Disfranchisement, the papers read in December, 1902 on "The Negro's Religion" and the papers read in December, 1906 on "Negro Labor and Foreign Emigrant Labor" could be published in a single volume, the scholarship, philosophical analysis, sociological insight displayed would have startled the world and made as strong an impression as the essays on the New Negro.[8]

In his effort to remind the world that the achievements of the 1920s rested on the thought and labors of the preceding generations, Ferris blurred important distinctions between works separated not only by time, but in some cases by different understandings of the situation of blacks and the character of racism. Nevertheless, there could be no challenge to his reminder that much of what was being said in the 1920s was not new. "The Black Man," he concluded, "has been revealing his mind for the past thirty years; but the country did not take the revelation seriously."[9] It was a statement with which most of his fellow academy members would have heartily agreed.

When the academy ceased to function after its annual meeting in December, 1928, there was no public outcry or mourning; in fact its demise did not even provoke comment in any black or white publication. Well before that time—perhaps as early as 1926—the organization's many difficulties had caused the bulk of its members to believe that for all intents and purposes it was dead, even if it still existed on paper. For this reason, following its collapse, many of the men who had been associated with it could not say with accuracy when the society disappeared. In 1941—thirteen years after the last meeting—W. E. B. Du Bois, a founder and the second president, wrote to John W. Cromwell's daughter, inquiring as to the date of the society's last meeting and requesting a complete list of the founders and members, copies of the programs for annual meetings, and a copy of the constitution. The reply to Du Bois's letter contained a constitution, program cards for fifteen meetings (there had been thirty-two), and a list of fourteen persons for which there was clear evidence of membership, essentially all of the information Cromwell's daughter could uncover. This response must have disappointed Du Bois who, once again teaching at Atlanta University, had hoped to reconstitute the ANA. Interestingly, about the same time, the his-

8. William H. Ferris, "The Myth of the New Negro," *The Spokesman*, II (July–August, 1926), 9–10. Although Ferris' recall of the titles of some of the papers he cited, the dates they were delivered, and the themes of various meetings was faulty, essentially his statement was correct.

9. *Ibid.*, 10.

torians Charles H. Wesley and Rayford W. Logan and former ANA member William P. Dabney of Cincinnati had expressed individually the same idea. There was, however, no communication in this regard between the four and when Du Bois, after receiving the reply to his inquiries, abandoned the idea, no more was heard of it.[10]

After 1941, except among historians, little reference was made to the ANA until March, 1969, when C. Eric Lincoln, professor of religion and sociology at New York City's Union Theological Seminary, took the lead in establishing the Black Academy of Arts and Letters. Although the BAAL's organizational meeting took place in Boston, its national headquarters were later located in New York City. Joining Lincoln in launching the society were forty-nine other blacks, all of them recognized figures in their specialities. Almost half of the founding members were either scholars or writers; the balance came from diverse fields and included actors, graphic artists, musicians, singers, poets, an archivist, a choreographer, a dancer, a playwright, and a sculptor. The year the BAAL was founded it received a grant from the Twentieth Century Fund. The fund committed itself to "underwrite the academy for three years at $50,000. a year." After that time the BAAL was expected to be self-sustaining financially.[11]

The major purpose of the organization was "to 'provide recognition, encouragement and incentive' for people contributing notably to the interpretation and projection of the black experience in America." To this end the BAAL established a Hall of Fame to honor distinguished deceased black Americans and honored annually living figures who had made "'notable and sustained contributions to the arts and letters.'" In 1970, W. E. B. Du Bois, Henry O. Tanner, and Carter G. Woodson were named to the Hall of Fame and special recognition was given to Lena Horne, C. L. R. James, Diana Sands, Immamu Amir Baraka, and Paul Robeson. The installations and the distribution of awards took place at a meeting of the academy members and their invited guests. Ceremonies, which included a formal dinner and an address by Mayor Richard Hatcher of Gary, Indiana, were held in a ballroom of the New York Hilton Hotel. Two years later, when the BAAL honored Ernest Gavin, Michael Hayes, Chancellor Williams, and the College

10. Otelia Cromwell to W. E. B. Du Bois, February 24, 1941, in W. E. B. Du Bois Papers, University of Massachusetts, Amherst; editorial comment, Aptheker (ed.), *Correspondence of W. E. B. Du Bois*, II, 280.

11. New York *Times*, July 14, 1970, p. 34, September 21, 1970, p. 54, and September 22, 1970, p. 37; *Negro History Bulletin*, XXXIII (November, 1970), 156–57.

Language Association Journal, each award carried a $100 honorarium. This, however, was the BAAL's last public function and its inactivity since 1972 suggests that the organization is now defunct.[12]

While the BAAL existed, comparisons were frequently made between it and the ANA. At the BAAL's second meeting in 1970, according to the New York *Times*, "academy members noted that the group was not the first of its type" when Adelaide C. Hill, professor of sociology at Boston University, told "a social sciences panel she was moderating that the American Negro Academy was founded (by her grandfather) in March, 1897 for 'men of African descent.'" Shortly after this meeting, the *Negro History Bulletin*, in an editorial discussion of the two groups, linked them together, suggesting that the BAAL sought to perpetuate the "scholarly ideals" enunciated by the ANA. The editorial did indicate differences between the two organizations, calling the younger "more than a mere reproduction of the historic American Negro Academy" and reporting that the BAAL "was moving forward along its own lines." However, the first statement was untrue and the others, along with the comment by Hill at the meeting in 1970, were confusing, for they implied that the BAAL was a new expression of the ANA. In actuality, the goals and the work of the two organizations were quite different. Dr. Lincoln, who was president of the BAAL's board of directors, attested to this, stating whenever questioned regarding links between the two groups, that although members of the BAAL felt a "reverence" for the ANA, there was "no direct connection" between them.[13] The bald truth is that since the ANA's collapse, there has been no serious attempt to reestablish it or to create a similar organization, facts its founders and supporters would have found even more dismal than the failure of their own heroic efforts.

The American Negro Academy, the first major black learned society, was a unique organization. Prior to its establishment the black American community had no institution comparable to it. The ANA's failures and its ultimate collapse say much about the historical forces, within both the black and white communities, that have frustrated the efforts of educated blacks

12. *Negro History Bulletin*, XXXIII (November, 1970), 156–57. Horne was a well-known singer and actress; Sands, an equally well-known actress; James, a historian and writer from Trinidad-Tobago; Baraka, a poet, playwright, and essayist; and Robeson, a well-known actor and singer. See also New York *Times*, October 18, 1972, p. 74. Gavin was a novelist; Hayes, a poet; and Williams, a historian.

13. New York *Times*, September 20, 1970, p. 84; *Negro History Bulletin*, XXXIII (November, 1970), 156–57; Interview with Adelaide Cromwell Gulliver, November 8, 1973.

to influence the American scholarly community and to translate their thought on major questions into political and social policy. Its few successes and the various scholarly achievements of its individual members are a testament to the sheer determination and ingenuity of educated blacks who, in the face of crushing discouragements, remained fascinated by ideas and their relevance to practical problems. Perhaps the real wonder in the history of the ANA is that the organization was able to exist as long as it did.

Complete Bibliography

ARTICLES IN PERIODICALS AND EDITED WORKS

Akpan, M. B. "Alexander Crummell and His African 'Race-Work': An Assessment of His Contributions in Liberia to Africa's 'Redemption,' 1853–1873." *Historical Magazine of the Protestant Episcopal Church*, XLVI (June, 1977), 177–99.

[Cromwell, John W.] "American Negro Academy." *African Times and Orient Review*, II (November–December, 1913), 243–44.

Bennett, Lerone, Jr. "What's in a Name?" In Peter Rose, ed. *Americans from Africa: Old Memories, New Moods*. New York: Atherton Press, 1970, pp. 373–84.

"Biography of James Carmichael Smith." *African Times and Orient Review*, III (July 21, 1914), 419–21.

Blake, R. B., and E. K. Rand. "Minute on the Life and Services of Professor Leo Wiener." *Harvard University Gazette*, March 9, 1940, pp. 123–24.

Broderick, Francis L. "W. E. B. Du Bois: History of an Intellectual." In James E. Blackwell and Morris Janowitz, eds. *Black Sociologists*. Chicago: University of Chicago Press, 1974, pp. 3–25.

Bruce, John E. "The American Negro Academy." Boston *Transcript*, December 12, 1899, p. 9.

Contee, Clarence G. "The Emergence of Du Bois as an African Nationalist." *Journal of Negro History*, LIV (January, 1969), 48–61.

Cooper, Anna J. "The American Negro Academy." *Southern Workman*, XXVII (February, 1898), 35–36.

Cromwell, John W. "The American Negro Academy." *Horizon*, V (February, 1910), 11–12.

Crummell, Alexander. "Civilization as a Collateral and Indispensable Instrumentality in Planting the Christian Church in Africa." In J. W. E. Bowen, ed. *Africa and the American Negro*. Atlanta: Gammon Theological Seminary, 1896, pp. 118–30.

———. "Hope for Africa." In Alexander Crummell. *The Future of Africa: Being Addresses, Sermons, etc. Delivered in the Republic of Liberia*. New York: Charles Scribner, 1862, pp. 285–323.

Douglass, Frederick. "The Negro Exodus from the Gulf States." *Journal of Social Science*, XI (May, 1880), 1–21.

Du Bois, W. E. B. "The Enforcement of the Slave Trade Laws." In *Annual Report of the American Historical Association for the Year 1891*. *Senate Miscellaneous Documents*, 52nd Congress, 1st Session, No. 173.

———. "Reconstruction and Its Benefits." *American Historical Review*, XV (July, 1910), 781–99.

———. "The Talented Tenth." In Booker T. Washington and others. *The Negro Problem*. New York: James Pott Company, 1903, pp. 31–75.

Eisenberg, Bernard. "Kelly Miller: Negro Leader." *Journal of Negro History*, XLV (July, 1960), 182–97.

Ferris, William H. "The Myth of the New Negro." *The Spokesman*, II (July–August, 1926), 9–10.

Fortune, T. Thomas. "The Latest Color Line." *Liberia*, Bulletin no. 11 (November, 1897), 60–65.

———. "The Latest Color Line." New York *Sun*, May 16, 1897, p. 3.

Franklin, John Hope. "The Dilemma of the American Negro Scholar." In Herbert Hill, ed. *Black Voices*. London: Elek Books, 1964, pp. 62–76.

Greener, Richard T. "The Emigration of Colored Citizens from the Southern States." *Journal of Social Science*, XI (May, 1880), 22–35.

Grimké, Angelina W. "A Biographical Sketch of Archibald H. Grimké." *Opportunity*, III (February, 1925), 44–47.

Guttman, Herbert. "The Negro and the United Mine Workers of America." In Julius Jacobson, ed. *The Negro and the American Labor Movement*. New York: Doubleday, 1968, pp. 49–127.

Guzman, Jessie P. "Monroe Nathan Work and His Contributions." *Journal of Negro History*, XXXIV (October, 1949), 428–61.

Hayden, J. Carleton. "Alexander Crummell, Black Pioneer Founded St. Luke's, Washington," Washington *Diocese*, XLV (January–February, 1976), 13.

Hayson, Walter B. "Alexander Crummell." *The Southern Missioner*, X (January, 1899), 1.

Higham, John. "Origins of Immigration Restriction, 1882–1897: A Social Analysis." *Mississippi Valley Historical Review*, XXXIX (June, 1962), 77–88.

Holmes, Eugene Clay. "Alain Leroy Locke: A Sketch." *Phylon*, XXI (Spring, 1959), 14–27.

Karson, Marc, and Ronald Radosh. "The American Federation of Labor and the Negro Worker, 1894–1949." In Julius Jacobson, ed. *The Negro and the American Labor Movement*. New York: Doubleday, 1968, pp. 155–60.

Lerner, Gerda. "The Grimké Sisters and the Struggle against Race Prejudice." *Journal of Negro History*, XLVIII (October, 1963), 277–91.

Logan, Rayford W. "Carter G. Woodson: Mirror and Molder of His Times, 1875–1950." *Journal of Negro History*, LVIII (January, 1973), 1–17.

Mandel, Bernard. "Samuel Gompers and the Negro Workers, 1886–1914." *Journal of Negro History*, LV (January, 1955), 34–60.

Marshall, Ray. "The Negro in Southern Unions." In Julius Jacobson, ed. *The Negro and the American Labor Movement*. New York: Doubleday, 1968, pp. 128–39.

Meier, August. "Booker T. Washington and the Negro Press." *Journal of Negro History*, XXXVIII (January, 1953), 65–82.

Meier, August, and Elliott Rudwick. "Attitudes of Negro Leaders toward the American Labor Movement from the Civil War to World War I." In Julius Jacobson, ed. *The Negro and the American Labor Movement.* New York: Doubleday, 1968, pp. 27–48.

Moses, Wilson J. "Civilizing Missionary: A Study of Alexander Crummell." *Journal of Negro History*, LX (April, 1975), 229–51.

Olsen, Otto H. Introduction to William A. Sinclair. *Aftermath of Slavery.* New York: Arno Press and the New York Times, 1969, v–x.

"One Man Newspaper." *Ebony* (February, 1946), 46–47.

Porter, Dorothy B. Introduction to *Dictionary Catalogue of the Jesse E. Moorland Collection of Negro Life and History, Howard University Library, Washington, D.C.* Vol. I. Boston: G. K. Hall & Co., 1970, i–xv.

————. "Phylon Profile XIV: Edward Christopher Williams." *Phylon*, VII (1947), 17–29.

Record, Wilson. "The Negro Intellectual and Negro Nationalism." *Social Forces*, XXXII (October, 1954), 10–18.

Reddick, L. D. "The Bruce Collection." *Calendar of the Manuscripts in the Schomburg Collection of Negro Literature.* New York: Historical Records Survey, Work Projects Administration, 1942, pp. 162–166.

————. Introduction to *Calendar of the Manuscripts in the Schomburg Collection of Negro Literature.* New York: Historical Records Survey, Work Projects Administration, 1942, i–vi.

"Remarks of Mr. B. T. Washington." *Journal of Social Science*, XXXIV (November, 1896), 86–88.

"Remarks of Mr. Hugh M. Browne, of Washington, D.C." *Journal of Social Science*, XXXIV (November, 1896), 89–97.

Rief, Philip. Introduction to Kelly Miller. *Radicals and Conservatives.* New York: Schocken Books, 1970, pp. 7–24.

Robbins, Richard. "Charles S. Johnson." In James E. Blackwell and Morris Janowitz, eds. *Black Sociologists.* Chicago: University of Chicago Press, 1974, pp. 56–84.

Rudwick, Elliott M. "W. E. B. Du Bois as Sociologist." In James E. Blackwell and Morris Janowitz, eds. *Black Sociologists.* Chicago: University of Chicago Press, 1974, pp. 25–55.

Spear, Allan H. "The Origins of the Urban Ghetto, 1870–1915." In Nathan I. Huggins, Martin Kilson, and Daniel M. Fox, eds. *Key Issues in the Afro-American Experience.* New York: Harcourt Brace Jovanovich, 1974, Vol. II, 151–163.

Trapido, Stanley. "African Divisional Politics in the Cape Colony, 1884–1910." *Journal of African History*, IX (1968), 79–98.

Wade, Richard C. "The Vesey Plot: A Reconsideration." *Journal of Southern History*, XXX (May, 1964), 143–61.

Wahle, Kathleen O. "Alexander Crummell: Black Evangelist and Pan-Negro Nationalist." *Phylon*, XXVIII (Winter, 1968), 388–95.

Walker, Francis A. "The Tide of Economic Thought." *Publications of the American Economic Association*, VI (January–March, 1891), 26–42.

Warner, Charles Dudley. "The Education of the Negro." *Journal of Social Science*, XXXVIII (June, 1900), 1–14.

Wayman, H. Harrison. "The American Negro Historical Society of Philadelphia, and Its Officers." *Colored American Magazine*, VI (February, 1903), 287–94.

Weisenberger, Francis P. "William Saunders Scarborough." *Ohio History*, LXXI (October, 1962), 2–27; and LXXII (January, 1963), 15–45.

Wesley, Charles H. "Carter G. Woodson—As a Scholar." *Journal of Negro History*, XXXVI (January, 1951), 12–24.

———. "Racial Historical Societies and the American Heritage." *Journal of Negro History*, XXXVII (January, 1952), 11–35.

Wormley, G. Smith. "Educators of the First Half-Century of Public Schools of the District of Columbia." *Journal of Negro History*, XVII (April, 1932), 124–40.

Worthman, Paul B. "Black Workers and the Labor Unions in Birmingham, Alabama." *Labor History*, IX (Summer, 1969), 390–425.

ANA OCCASIONAL PAPERS

No. 1

Kelly Miller, *A Review of Hoffman's Race Traits and Tendencies of the American Negro* (1897).

No. 2

W. E. B. Du Bois, *The Conservation of Races* (1897).

No. 3

Alexander Crummell, "Civilization, the Primal Need of the Race" (1898).

Alexander Crummell, "The Attitude of the American Mind toward the Negro Intellect" (1898).

No. 4

Charles C. Cook, *A Comparative Study of the Negro Problem* (1899).

No. 5

Theophilus G. Steward, *How the Black St. Domingo Legion Saved the Patriot Army in the Siege of Savannah, 1779* (1899).

No. 6

John L. Love, *The Disfranchisement of the Negro* (1899).

No. 7

Archibald H. Grimké, *Right on the Scaffold, or the Martyrs of 1822* (1901).

No. 8

William S. Scarborough, *The Educated Negro and His Mission* (1903).

No. 9

John W. Cromwell, *The Early Negro Convention Movement* (1904).

No. 10

Orishatukeh Faduma, *The Defects of the Negro Church* (1904).

No. 11

The Negro and the Elective Franchise.

Archibald H. Grimké, "The Meaning and Need of the Movement to Reduce Southern Representation" (1905).

Charles C. Cook, "The Penning of the Negro" (1905).

John Hope, "The Negro Vote in the States Whose Constitutions Have Not Been Specifically Revised" (1905).

John L. Love, "The Potentiality of the Negro Vote, North and West" (1905).

Kelly Miller, "Migration and Distribution of the Negro Population as Affecting the Elective Franchise" (1905).

Francis J. Grimké, "The Negro and His Citizenship" (1905).

No. 12

Archibald H. Grimké, *Modern Industrialism and the Negroes of the United States* (1908).

No. 13

Jesse E. Moorland, *The Demand and the Supply of Increased Efficiency in the Negro Ministry* (1909).

No. 14

Archibald H. Grimké, *Charles Sumner Centenary Historical Address* (1911).

No. 15

Lafayette M. Hershaw, *Peonage* (1915).

No. 16

Archibald H. Grimké, *The Ballotless Victims of One-Party Government* (1915).

No. 17

Archibald H. Grimké, *The Ultimate Criminal* (1915).

Nos. 18 and 19

Archibald H. Grimké, "The Sex Question and Race Segregation" [1916?].

Theophilus G. Steward, "Message of San Domingo to the African Race" [1916?].

Lafayette M. Hershaw, "Status of the Free Negro Prior to 1860" [1916?].

Arthur A. Schomburg, "Economic Contribution by the Negro to America" [1916?].

William Pickens, "The Status of the Free Negro from 1860 to 1870" [1916?].

John W. Cromwell, "American Negro Bibliography for the Year" [1916?]. (No publication date appears on Occasional Papers Nos. 18 and 19.)

No. 20

William H. Ferris, *Alexander Crummell, an Apostle of Negro Culture* (1920).

No. 21

Archibald H. Grimké, *The Shame of America or the Negro's Case Against the Republic* (1924).

No. 22

John W. Cromwell, *The Challenge of the Disfranchised: A Plea for the Enforcement of the 15th Amendment* (1924).

AMERICAN NEGRO MONOGRAPHS

No. 1

Confession, Trial and Execution of Nat Turner, the Negro Insurgent. Washington, D.C.: American Negro Monographs, 1910. (A reprint of Thomas R. Gray's account.)

No. 2

Thomas Greathead Harper. *Contemporary Evolution of the Negro Race.* Washington, D.C.: American Negro Monographs, [1910?].

No. 3

J. H. B. Latrobe. *The Biography of Benjamin Banneker.* Washington, D.C.: American Negro Monographs, [1910?].

No. 4

W. E. B. Du Bois. *The Social Evolution of the Black South*. Washington, D.C.: American Negro Monographs, 1911.

No. 5

"Colored Religious Organizations, a Summary of an Investigation Made Under the Auspices of the United States Census Bureau." (Announced, but never published.)

BOOKS AND PAMPHLETS

American Historical Association Handbook, 1896. Baltimore: Press of the Friedenwald Company, 1896.

Anderson, Jervis. *A. Philip Randolph: A Biographical Portrait*. New York: Harcourt Brace Jovanovich, 1972.

Aptheker, Herbert, ed. *The Correspondence of W. E. B. Du Bois*. 2 vols. Amherst: University of Massachusetts Press, 1973 and 1976.

Bacote, Samuel William, ed. *Who's Who among the Colored Baptists of the United States*. Kansas City, Mo.: Franklin Hudson Publishing, 1913.

Baker, Ray Stannard. *Following the Color Line*. New York: Doubleday, 1908.

Bardolph, Richard. *The Negro Vanguard*. New York: Vintage Books, 1959.

Beavers, Joseph T., Jr. *I Want You to Know Wendell Phillips Dabney*. Mexico, Distrito Federal, 1958.

Berwick-Sayers, W. C. *Samuel Coleridge-Taylor, Musician*. London: Cassell & Co., 1915.

Boris, Joseph J., ed. *Who's Who in Colored America: A Biographical Dictionary of Notable Living Persons of Negro Descent in America*. Vol. I. New York: Who's Who in Colored America Corporation, 1927.

Bradley, David Henry, Sr. *A History of the A.M.E. Zion Church*. 2 vols. Nashville: Parthenon Press, 1956 and 1970.

Bragg, George F. *History of the Afro-American Group of the Episcopal Church*. Baltimore: Church Advocate Press, 1922.

———. *Men of Maryland*. Baltimore: Church Advocate Press, 1925.

Brawley, Benjamin. *The Negro Genius*. New York: Dodd, Mead, 1937.

———. *Paul Laurence Dunbar: Poet of His People*. Chapel Hill: University of North Carolina Press, 1936.

Broderick, Francis L. *W. E. B. Du Bois: Negro Leader in a Time of Crisis*. Stanford: Stanford University Press, 1959.

Browne, Robert Tecumtha. *The Mystery of Space*. New York: E. P. Dutton, 1919.

Buckler, Helen. *Daniel Hale Williams, Negro Surgeon*. New York: Pittman Publishing, 1954.

Chalmers, David M. *Hooded Americanism: The First Century of the Ku Klux Klan*. Garden City: Doubleday, 1965.

Chesnutt, Helen M. *Charles Waddell Chesnutt: Pioneer of the Color Line*. Chapel Hill: University of North Carolina Press, 1952.

Crogman, William H. *Talks for the Times*. Connecticut: Jennings and Pye, 1896.

Cromwell, John Wesley. *History of the Bethel Literary and Historical Association: A Paper Read before the Association on Founders' Day, February 24, 1896*. Washington, D.C.: Press of R. L. Pendleton, 1896.

———. *The Negro in American History.* Washington, D.C.: The American Negro Academy, 1914.

Cronon, E. David. *Black Moses: The Story of Marcus Garvey and the Universal Negro Improvement Association.* Madison: University of Wisconsin Press, 1955.

Crummell, Alexander. *Africa and America.* Springfield, Mass.: Houghton Mifflin Co., 1914.

Dabney, Wendell P. *Cincinnati's Colored Citizens.* Cincinnati: Dabney Publishing, 1926.

Daniels, John. *In Freedom's Birthplace.* Boston: Houghton Mifflin, 1914.

Davis, George A., and O. Fred Donaldson. *Blacks in the United States: A Geographic Perspective.* Boston: Houghton Mifflin, 1975.

De Santis, Vincent P. *Republicans Face the Southern Question.* Baltimore: Johns Hopkins Press, 1959.

Du Bois, W. E. B. *The Philadelphia Negro.* Boston: Ginn and Co., 1899.

———. *Souls of Black Folk.* Chicago: A. G. McClurg, 1903.

———. *The Suppression of the African Slave Trade to the United States of America, 1638–1870.* New York: Longmans Green & Co., 1896.

Du Bois, W. E. B., ed. *Efforts for Social Betterment Among American Negroes.* Atlanta: Atlanta University Publications, no. 2, 1898.

———. *The Negro Artisan.* Atlanta: Atlanta University Publications, no. 6, 1902.

———. *The Negro Church.* Atlanta: Atlanta University Publications, no. 7, 1903.

Dyson, Walter. *Howard University: The Capstone of Negro Education, 1867–1940.* Washington, D.C.: Graduate School of Howard University, 1941.

Ferris, William Henry. *The African Abroad or His Evolution in Western Civilization, Tracing His Development Under Caucasian Milieu.* 2 vols. New Haven, Conn.: Tuttle, Morehouse & Taylor Press, 1913.

Fine, Stanley. *Laissez Faire and the General-Welfare State, A Study of Conflict in American Thought, 1865–1901.* Ann Arbor: University of Michigan Press, 1956.

Fox, Stephen R. *The Guardian of Boston, William Monroe Trotter.* New York: Atheneum, 1970.

Franklin, John Hope. *From Slavery to Freedom.* New York: Alfred A. Knopf, 1974.

Frederickson, George M. *The Black Image in the White Mind: The Debate on Afro-American Character and Destiny, 1817–1914.* New York: Harper & Row, 1971.

Furner, Mary O. *Advocacy and Objectivity: A Crisis in the Professionalization of American Social Science, 1865–1905.* Lexington: University of Kentucky Press for the Organization of American Historians, 1975.

Gibson, J. W., and W. H. Crogman, eds. *Progress of a Race; or, the Remarkable Advancement of the American Negro, etc.* Atlanta: J. L. Nichols, 1902.

Gilbert, Peter, ed. *The Selected Writings of John Edward Bruce: Militant Black Journalist.* New York: Arno Press and the New York Times, 1971.

Gossett, Thomas. *Race: The History of an Idea in America.* Dallas: Southern Methodist University Press, 1963.

Green, Constance M. *The Secret City: A History of Race Relations in the Nation's Capital.* Princeton: Princeton University Press, 1967.

Grimké, Archibald H. *Life of Charles Sumner, the Scholar in Politics.* New York: Funk and Wagnalls, 1892.

————. *Life of William Lloyd Garrison, the Abolitionist.* New York: Funk and Wagnalls, 1891.

Gross, Seymour L., and John Edward Hardy. *Images of the Negro in American Literature.* Chicago: University of Chicago Press, 1966.

Handbook of Learned Societies and Institutions: America. Washington, D.C.: Carnegie Institution of Washington, 1908.

Handbook of the American Academy of Political and Social Science: Supplement to the Annals of the American Academy of Political and Social Science, 1891. Philadelphia: The Academy, 1891.

Handbook of the American Academy of Political and Social Science: Supplement to the Annals of the American Academy of Political and Social Science, 1897. Philadelphia: The Academy, 1897.

Hargreaves, John Desmond. *A Life of Sir Samuel Lewis.* London: Oxford University Press, 1958.

Harlan, Louis R. *Booker T. Washington: The Making of a Black Leader, 1856–1901.* New York: Oxford University Press, 1972.

————. *Separate and Unequal.* Chapel Hill: University of North Carolina Press, 1958.

Harlan, Louis R., ed. *The Booker T. Washington Papers.* Vols. I–VII. Urbana: University of Illinois Press, 1972–1977.

Hayford, J. E. Caseley. *Africa and the Africans: Proceedings on the Occasion of a Banquet, Given at the Holborn Restaurant, August 15, 1903, to Edward W. Blyden, by West Africans in London.* London: C. M. Phillips, 1903.

————. *Ethiopia Unbound: Studies in Race Emancipation.* London: C. M. Phillips, 1903.

————. *Gold Coast Native Institutions.* London: Sweet and Maxwell, 1903.

Higham, John. *Strangers in the Land.* New York: Atheneum, 1963.

Hilyer, Andrew F., ed. *The Twentieth Century Union League Directory.* Washington, D.C.: Union League, 1901.

Hoover, Dorothy E. *A Layman Looks with Love at Her Church.* Philadelphia: Dorrance and Company, 1970.

Huggins, Nathan I. *Harlem Renaissance.* New York: Oxford University Press, 1971.

Janvier, Louis Joseph. *Constitutions of Hayti from 1801 to 1885.* Paris: C. Marpon and E. Flammarion, 1886.

Johnson, Edward Augustus. *School History of the Negro Race in America.* Chicago: W. B. Conkey, 1893.

Kellogg, Charles Flint. *NAACP: A History of the National Association for the Advancement of Colored People.* Baltimore: Johns Hopkins Press, 1967.

Kenney, John A. *The Negro in Medicine.* n.p., 1912; rpr., Ann Arbor, Mich.: University Microfilms, 1973.

Kerlin, Robert Thomas. *Contemporary Poetry of the Negro.* Hampton, Va.: Hampton Normal and Agricultural Institute, 1921.

————. *Negro Poets and Their Poems.* Washington, D.C.: Associated Publishers, 1923.

————. *The Voice of the Negro.* New York: E. P. Dutton and Co., 1920.

Kletzing, H. F., and W. H. Crogman, eds. *Progress of a Race.* Atlanta: J. L. Nichols & Co., 1897.

Langley, J. Ayodele. *Pan-Africanism and Nationalism in West Africa.* London: Oxford University Press, 1973.

Lerner, Gerda, ed. *Black Women in White America: A Documentary History.* New York: Vintage Books, 1971.

――――. *The Grimké Sisters from South Carolina: Pioneers for Women's Rights and Abolition.* New York: Schocken Books, 1971.

Levy, Eugene. *James Weldon Johnson: Black Leader, Black Voice.* Chicago: University of Chicago Press, 1973.

Litwack, Leon. *North of Slavery.* Chicago: University of Chicago Press, 1961.

Locke, Alain L. *The Negro in New Jersey: State Semi-Centennial Report.* Trenton: State of New Jersey, 1913.

――――. *Race Contacts and Race Relations.* Washington, D.C.: Pendleton, 1916.

Locke, Alain L., ed. *The New Negro.* New York: A. and C. Boni, 1925.

Logan, Rayford W. *The Betrayal of the Negro.* New York: Collier Books, 1965.

――――. *The Diplomatic Relations of the United States with Haiti, 1776–1891.* Chapel Hill: University of North Carolina Press, 1941.

――――. *Haiti and the Dominican Republic.* New York: Oxford University Press, 1968.

――――. *Howard University: The First Hundred Years, 1867–1967.* New York: New York University Press, 1969.

Lynch, Hollis R. *Edward Wilmot Blyden: Pan-Negro Patriot, 1832–1912.* London: Oxford University Press, 1967.

Lynch, John R. *The Facts of Reconstruction.* New York: Nealle Publishing, 1913.

McGinnis, Frederick A. *A History and an Interpretation of Wilberforce University.* Blanchester, Ohio: Brown Publishing, 1941.

Mallas, Arris A., Jr., Rea McCain, and Margaret K. Heddin. *Forty Years in Politics: The Story of Ben Pelham.* Detroit: Wayne State University Press, 1957.

Maloney, Arnold Hamilton. *Amber Gold: An Adventure in Autobiography.* Boston: Meador Publishing, 1946.

Marty, Martin E. *The Modern Schism: Three Paths to the Secular.* New York: Harper & Row, 1969.

――――. *Protestantism.* New York: Holt, Rinehart & Winston, 1972.

――――. *Righteous Empire: The Protestant Experience in America.* New York: Dial Press, 1970.

Mather, Frank Lincoln, ed. *Who's Who of the Colored Race: A General Biographical Dictionary of Men and Women of African Descent.* Chicago: Momento Edition Half-Century Anniversary of Negro Freedom in the United States, 1915.

Matthews, Marcia M. *Henry Ossawa Tanner.* Chicago: University of Chicago Press, 1969.

Meier, August. *Negro Thought in America, 1880–1915.* Ann Arbor: University of Michigan Press, 1968.

Mohamed, Duse. *In the Land of the Pharohs.* n.p., 1916; rpr. London: Frank Cass & Co., 1968.

Moses, Wilson J. *The Golden Age of Black Nationalism, 1850–1925.* Hamden, Conn.: Archon, 1978.

Mossell, Charles W. *Toussaint L'Ouverture; or, Hayti's Struggle.* Lockport, N.Y.: Ward and Cobb, 1896.

Mossell, N. F. *The Work of the Afro-American Woman.* n.p., 1894; rpr. Freeport, N.Y.: Books for Libraries Press, 1971.

Murray, Freeman H. M. *Emancipation and the Freed in American Sculpture.* n.p.: The Author, 1916.

Nelson, Martha Furber, ed. *Index by Authors, Titles, and Subjects to the Publications of the National Education Association for Its First Fifty Years, 1859–1906.* Winona, Minn.: The Association, 1907.

Newby, I. A. *Jim Crow's Defense.* Baton Rouge: Louisiana State University Press, 1965.

Nichols, J. L., and W. H. Crogman, eds. *Progress of a Race.* Naperville, Ill.: J. L. Nichols & Co., 1920.

Nolan, Claude H. *The Negro's Image in the South: The Anatomy of White Supremacy.* Lexington: University of Kentucky Press, 1967.

Olsen, Otto H., ed. *The Thin Disguise: Plessy vs. Fergusson, A Documentary Presentation.* New York: Humanities Press for AIMS, 1967.

Osofsky, Gilbert. *Harlem: The Making of a Ghetto.* New York: Harper & Row, 1963.

Ovington, Mary White. *Half a Man: The Status of the Negro in New York.* New York: Longmans, Green and Company, 1911.

Payne, Daniel A. *History of the African Methodist Episcopal Church.* Nashville: Publishing House of the A.M.E. Sunday School Union, 1891.

Pendleton, Leila Amos. *A Narrative of the Negro.* Washington, D.C.: Press of R. L. Pendleton, 1912.

Penn, I. Garland. *The Afro-American Press and Its Editors.* Springfield, Mass.: Willey & Co., 1891.

Penn, I. Garland, and J. W. E. Bowen, eds. *The United Negro: His Problem and His Progress.* Atlanta: D. E. Luther Publishing, 1902.

Phillips, Henry L. *In Memoriam of the Late Rev. Alexander Crummell, D.D. of Washington, D.C.: An Address Delivered Before the American Negro Historical Society of Philadelphia, November, 1898.* Philadelphia: Coleman Printery, 1899.

Pillsbury, Albert E. *Lincoln and Slavery.* Boston: Houghton Mifflin Company, 1913.

Proceedings of the National Convention of Colored People and Their Friends. Troy, N.Y.: n.p., 1847.

Quarles, Benjamin. *Frederick Douglass.* Washington, D.C.: Associated Publishers, 1948.

Reimers, David. *White Protestantism and the Negro.* New York: Oxford University Press, 1965.

Richardson, Clement, ed. *The National Cyclopedia of the Colored Race.* Vol. I. Montgomery, Ala.: National Publishing, 1919.

Rodman, Selden. *Quisqueya: A History of the Dominican Republic.* Seattle: University of Washington Press, 1964.

Rudwick, Elliott M. *W. E. B. Du Bois: Propagandist of the Negro Protest.* New York: Atheneum, 1972.

Sampson, Magnus J. *Gold Coast Men of Affairs.* London: Stockwell, 1937.

Scholes, Theophilus E. Samuel. *Glimpses of the Ages.* London: J. Long, 1905–1908.

Schomburg, Arthur A. *Racial Integrity: A Plea for the Establishment of a Chair of Negro History in Our Schools and Colleges, etc. (Read before the Teachers' Summer Class at Cheney Institute, July 1913).* Negro Society for Historical Research, Occasional Paper no. 3, n.d.

Scruggs, Otey M. *We the Children of Africa in This Land: Alexander Crummell.* Washington, D.C.: Department of History, Howard University, 1972.

Simmons, William J. *Men of Mark: Eminent, Progressive, and Rising.* Cleveland, Ohio: George M. Rewell & Co., 1887.

Sinclair, William A. *Aftermath of Slavery.* Boston: Small, Maynard and Company, 1905.

Smith, Edwin W. *Aggrey of Africa.* New York: Richard R. Smith, 1930.

Spear, Allan H. *Black Chicago: The Making of a Negro Ghetto, 1890–1920.* Chicago: University of Chicago Press, 1967.

Spero, Sterling D., and Abram L. Harris. *The Black Worker.* New York: Columbia University Press, 1931.

Stephenson, Gilbert T. *Race Distinctions in American Law.* New York: Columbia University Press, 1931.

Steward, Theophilus G. *The Colored Regulars in the United States Army.* Philadelphia: AME Church Book Concern, 1904.

Steward, W., and T. G. Steward. *Gouldtown.* Philadelphia: J. B. Lippincott, 1913.

Stocker, Harry Emilius. *A History of the Moravian Church in New York City.* New York: Special Publications Committee of the Moravian Church, 1922.

Straker, David Augustus. *The New South Investigated.* Detroit: Feruson Printing, 1888.

Thornbrough, Emma Lou. *T. Thomas Fortune, Militant Journalist.* Chicago: University of Chicago Press, 1972.

Thorpe, Earl E. *Black Historians: A Critique.* New York: William Morrow & Co., 1971.

Torrence, Ridgely. *The Story of John Hope.* New York: Macmillan, 1948.

Walls, William J. *The African Methodist Episcopal Zion Church.* Charlotte, N.C.: AMEZ Publishing House, 1974.

Warren, Francis H. *Michigan Manual of Freedman's Progress.* Detroit: Freedmen's Progress Commission, 1915.

Wiebe, Robert H. *The Search for Order: 1877–1920.* New York: Hill & Wang, 1967.

Wiener, Leo. *Africa and the Discovery of America.* 3 vols. Philadelphia: Innes and Sons, 1920–1922.

Wilson, Monica, and Leonard Thompson, eds. *Oxford History of South Africa.* 2 vols. New York: Oxford University Press, 1971.

Woodson, Carter G. *The Education of the Negro Prior to 1861.* New York: G. P. Putnam's Sons, 1915.

Woodson, Carter G., ed. *The Works of Francis J. Grimké.* 4 vols. Washington, D.C.: Associated Publishers, 1942.

Woodward, C. Vann. *Origins of the New South, 1877–1913.* Baton Rouge: Louisiana State University Press, 1951.

———. *The Strange Career of Jim Crow.* New York: Oxford University Press, 1966.

Work, Monroe N. *Negro Yearbook.* Tuskegee Institute, Ala.: Negro Yearbook, 1919.

Wright, Richard R., Jr. *Bishops of the AME Church.* Nashville: AME Sunday School Union, 1963.

———. *Eighty-Seven Years Behind the Black Curtain.* Philadelphia: Rare Book, 1965.

———. *The Negro in Pennsylvania.* Philadelphia: AME Book Concern, n.d.

Wright, Richard R., Jr., ed. *Centennial Encyclopedia of the African Methodist Episcopal Church.* Philadelphia: Book Concern of the AME Church, 1916.

————. *The Encyclopedia of the African Methodist Episcopal Church.* Philadelphia: n.p., 1947.
Yenser, Thomas, ed. *Who's Who in Colored America.* New York: The Author, 1933.

MANUSCRIPTS (LISTED BY REPOSITORY)

Dr. Adelaide Cromwell Gulliver, Director, Afro-American Studies Center, Boston University.
Cromwell, John Wesley. Papers (unprocessed).

Library of Congress, Washington, D.C.
Terrell, Robert Heberton. Papers.
Washington, Booker T. Papers.
Woodson, Carter Godwin. Papers.

The Moorland-Spingarn Research Center, Howard University, Washington, D.C.
Brawley, Benjamin. Papers.
Cook, George William. Papers.
Cromwell, John Wesley. Papers (unprocessed).
Gregory, Thomas Montgomery. Papers.
Grimké, Archibald H. Papers.
Grimké, Francis James. Papers.
Locke, Alain Leroy. Papers.
Miller, Kelly. Papers.
Murray, Freeman Henry Morris. Papers.
Mu-So-Lit Club. Papers.
Schomburg, Arthur Alfonso. Correspondence to John Wesley Cromwell, 1912–1927.

Office of the Recorder of Deeds, District of Columbia
"Articles of Incorporation of the American Negro Academy," January 30, 1920. Instrument #15583 in incorporation *Liber* 35 at Folio 443.
"Certificate of Incorporation of the Association for the Study of Negro Life and History," October 2, 1915. Instrument #13939 in incorporation *Liber* 31 at Folio 441.
"Certificate of Incorporation of the Mu-So-Lit Club," April 24, 1920. Instrument #15689 in incorporation *Liber* 36 at Folio 51.

The Schomburg Center for Research in Black Culture, New York Public Library.
Crummell, Alexander. Papers.
Bruce, John Edward. Papers.

University of Massachusetts, Amherst
Du Bois, W. E. B. Papers.

PERIODICALS AND SERIALS

Annual Report of the American Historical Society for 1920. Washington: Government Printing Office, 1925.
Boston *Evening Transcript,* November 5, 1897, December 12, 1899.
Boston *Herald,* June 2, 1915.
Colored American Magazine, 1900–1909.

Crisis, 1910–1928.
D. J. Sanders Memorial Edition of *Johnson C. Smith University Alumni Journal*, I (April, 1928).
Harlem Number of *Survey Graphic Magazine*, XIV (August, 1925).
Harvard University Class of 1896 (Reports of the Secretary of the Class of 1896, Harvard College), first (n.d.), second (1901), fourth (1911), fifth (1916), twenty-fifth (1921), and fortieth (1936).
Hilltop (Student Magazine of Howard University), January 26, 1949.
Horizon, 1907–1910.
Journal of Negro History, 1916–1977.
Journal of the American Irish Historical Society, I (December, 1898).
Journal of the National Education Association, XXXIX (1896), XL (1897), LVII (1919).
Lagos *Weekly Record*, July, 1897.
Messenger, 1917–1920.
Negro History Bulletin, XXXIII (November, 1970).
New York *Age*, 1916–1929.
New York *Globe*, June 16, 1883.
New York *Sun*, May 16 and 24, 1897.
New York *Times*, July 14, September 20, 21, and 22, 1970, October 18, 1972.
Papers of the American Historical Association, IV (1890).
Papers of the American Society of Church History, VI (1896), VII (1897).
Philadelphia *Times*, December 25, 1897.
Publications of the American Jewish Historical Society, I (1893), II (1894), XXVII (1920).
Southern Workman, 1896–1930.
Spokesman, 1925–1927.
Star of Zion, December 2 and 16, 1897.
Transactions of the American Philological Association, XV (1884)–XXVIII (1897).
Washington *Afro-American*, March 2–6, 1976.
Washington *Bee*, 1896–1921.
Washington *Colored American*, 1898–1904.
Washington *Evening Star*, 1897–1930.
Washington *Post*, 1896–1929.
Washington *Star*, January 16, 1949.
Washington *Times*, September 12, 1897.
Washington *Tribune*, 1921–1929.

THESES, DISSERTATIONS, AND UNPUBLISHED MANUSCRIPTS

Appel, John J. "Immigrant Historical Societies in the United States, 1885–1950." Ph.D. dissertation, University of Pennsylvania, 1964.
Cravens, Hamilton. "American Scientists and the Heredity-Environment Controversy, 1883–1940." Ph.D. dissertation, University of Iowa, 1969.
Ferry, Henry Justin. "Francis James Grimké: Portrait of a Black Puritan." Ph.D. dissertation, Yale University, 1970.
Fishel, Leslie H., Jr. "The North and the Negro, 1865–1900." Ph.D. dissertation, Harvard University, 1953.

Josey, E. J. "Edward Christopher Williams: A Librarian's Librarian." Paper presented at the ALA American Library History Round Table, 87th Annual Conference, Kansas City, Mo., June 24, 1968. (Mimeographed.)

Keller, Francis Richardson. "Toward Human Understanding: The Life and Times of Charles Waddell Chesnutt." Ph.D. dissertation, University of Chicago, 1973.

Miller, Mignon Iris. "The American Negro Academy: An Intellectual Movement during the Era of Disfranchisement, 1897–1924." M.A. thesis, Howard University, 1966.

Moynihan, Kenneth James. "History as a Weapon for Social Advancement: Group History as Told by Jewish, Irish, and Black Americans, 1892–1950." Ph.D. dissertation, Clark University, 1973.

Williamson, Simon. "History of the Life and Work of Arthur Alonzo [sic] Schomburg." Writers Program Biographical Sketches. Schomburg Collection. New York Public Library. (Typewritten.)

Index

Academy of Political Science, 14

Africa, 20, 25, 51, 54, 54*n*, 57, 131, 132, 160–61, 274

Africa and the Discovery of America, 274–76

African Academy. *See* American Negro Academy: name

African Association of London, 54, 54*n*

African Institute. *See* American Negro Academy: name

African Methodist Episcopal Church, 30, 256–57, 265

—Book Concern, 167–68

African Methodist Episcopal Church Review, 29, 64, 73, 101, 101*n*, 106–107, 110, 111, 167, 256–58 *passim*, 258*n*

African Methodist Episcopal Zion Church, 265

African Methodist Episcopal Zion Church Quarterly Review, 238

African Times and Orient Review, 128, 148, 275, 221, 246*n*, 250

Africo-American Presbyterian, 258*n*

Afro-American Council, 73, 91–92, 100, 126, 190–92, 257

Afro-American League, 21

Aggrey, James Emman Kwegyir, 118, 118*n*, 142, 212, 213, 213*n*, 242, 246–47, 252, 288

Agora Assembly, 267

Ahuma, Attoh, 131

Aldridge, Ira, 261

Alexander Crummell: An Apostle of Negro Culture, 218–20

Alexander Crummell Historical Club, 264

Alleyne, Cameron Chesterfield, 238

Alpha Phi Alpha, 267

American Academy of Political and Social Science, 14–16 *passim*, 47, 81, 263, 297

American Association for the Advancement of Science, 263

American Bar Association, 14

American Classical League, 263

American Colonization Society, 25, 55

American Economic Association, 13, 14, 263

American Folk-lore Association, 263

American Forestry Association, 14

American Historical Association, 14, 17, 47, 196, 234, 263

American Institute of Sacred Literature, 263

American Irish Historical Association, 13, 46

American Jewish Historical Society, 13, 46, 234

American Library Association, 14

American Medical Association, 263

American Negro Academy: annual meetings, 67, 70, 79, 82–89, 87*n*, 88*n*, 92, 93, 117, 133–47, 206–210 *passim*, 216, 224, 225, 243, 246, 270–72, 279, 288–89, 296; archives, 122, 199–203, 290, 292; attitudes toward women, 38, 41, 59, 78, 134; certificate of membership, 203–206; constitution and bylaws, 24–25, 25*n*, 26, 40, 41*n*, 43*n*, 69, 86–87, 104, 109, 112, 125, 136–37, 146, 193*n*, 202, 208–209, 216, 230–36, 241–42, 244, 250, 269–70, 297; corresponding members, 69, 79–82, 127–30, 292; executive committee, 44, 46, 58–64 *passim*, 67–69, 68*n*, 71, 79–87 *passim*, 87*n*, 96–106 *passim*, 109–121 *passim*, 124–30 *passim*, 132, 135–38 *passim*, 142, 144, 151, 152, 156–66 *passim*, 168–69, 171, 177–81 *passim*, 186–94 *passim*,